Child Play

Its Importance for Human Development

DATE		

BAKER & TAYLOR

Child Play
Its Importance for Human Development

Peter Slade

Jessica Kingsley Publishers
London and Bristol, Pennsylvania

First published in the United Kingdom in 1995 by
Jessica Kingsley Publishers Ltd
116 Pentonville Road
London N1 9JB, England
and
1900 Frost Road, Suite 101
Bristol, PA 19007, U S A

Copyright © 1995 Peter Slade

Library of Congress Cataloging in Publication Data
Slade, Peter.
Child play: its importance for human development / Peter Slade.
p.   cm.
Includes index.
ISBN 1-85302-246-2 (pbk.)
1. Play--Psychological aspects. 2. Child development. I. Title.
BF717.S535 1995
155.4'18--dc20   95-16042
                                                       CIP

British Library Cataloguing in Publication Data
A CIP catalogue record for this book is available from the British Library

ISBN 1-85302-246-2

Printed and Bound in Great Britain by
Cromwell Press, Melksham, Wiltshire

Contents

List of Figures

To all who have ever worked with me in theatre,
education and therapy, and to children everywhere.

Acknowledgments

My thanks go to Sylvia Demmery who helped in checking details of the script and in confirming some of the events described; also to my typists who finally managed to read my writing; to Victor Thompson and Caters News Agency for taking photographs.

Introduction

After being invited to write this book, rather as a bringing up to date of earlier work, I have included some detail from the past and, of course, the main philosophy. There is some repetition of exercises. This is intentional, so as to show how to use a similar thought in a slightly different way for different groups and for different ages. In approaching complications of the present day, I have written of what I think ought to happen and why, trusting that parents, teachers and therapists will do what they can (if they understand the importance of the whole person), and not what they can't.

The Nature of Play and Some of Its Signs

One of the great gifts of life is to know how to play. When we are young, most of us know how to do this. As we get older, something of the joy dies and so-called reality sets our course to things more grim. Yet a small fire may glow on, deep inside, and occasionally flicker up. In a moment we are young again, we laugh and the world looks brighter.

This book is about play and delves a little into its importance, how it can reveal our state of being and how it can heal. We are not here concerned just with fooling about and wasting time, for there is such a thing as Serious Play and this is an experience deeply felt. It is also a way through which humans and some animals develop.

Play may be calm or active, sometimes violently so. It is divided into two main parts, which I have called Projected Play and Personal Play. The distinction is of considerable importance and, once you really discern it, the number of examples build up in your mind. You perceive more about children and people; and sometimes you can help them by your ability to gauge their need as between the two forms of activity – perhaps even by smoothing from one to the other.

Projected Play

Here the body is mostly still; the person is either lying down, squatting, kneeling or sitting and the idea, or dream in their mind, is projected into, onto or around objects outside them. 'Life' is going on in the objects during this activity, and there may be strong emotion or love or importance associated with them. In this sense they become Beloved Objects. In the midst of absorption a bee comes by, a bell goes, or an adult calls. The spell is broken. Then the test of this form of activity is that the person gets up (or the tiny child is picked up) and moves away; and the things played with remain as a memorial, a monument of their doing. Quite often there is an interesting art shape in which these objects have been left, particularly by the young. Thus, play with dirt, sand, string, stones, toys, dolls; creation of pictures, cathedrals, written work, equations and sums all come under this heading. They are all the 'left' things, which stand there after we have gone, they are the memorials of our doing and thinking, probably infused with importance. It may be understood, therefore, that the three Rs belong under this heading – play of the intellect. For that is what this form of play grows into. The best of its kind is carried out with extreme absorption. As the process becomes conscious a slow dawning of that which is 'me' and 'that which is around me, but not of me', takes place. And that is how the ego is formed. However, this leads to considerable defence mechanisms as we shall see.

Personal Play

In this the whole person is used, in a wider sense. The person gets up and moves about and takes total physical, emotional, or spiritual responsibility for the action. No longer can the toy or doll live life for you, you are now up and doing it yourself. Thus running, dancing, acting, swimming, active sports of all kinds tend to come under this heading. But it is ephemeral. Unless a photo or film is made of it, once done, it is gone forever. But the experience remains. No one can take *that* from you, only the dimming of memory. No doubt, that is why we invented the prize (for honour and memory). In acting and child drama, the best of its kind is carried out with marked sincerity. Not only are both these forms of play (Personal and Projected) important to the individual, but if circumstances allow the right amount at the right time of each, when needed, it helps in balancing the personality. And in therapy, those who can perceive and then read each of them correctly, are likely to come to an accurate diagnosis. In playtherapy I always feel that I need to see the same evidence arising in *each* sphere before being in any way sure of being on the right track. For me, proof in both spheres is essential. In cases of investigation, therefore, of sexual abuse, slightly slanted questions leading to play with dolls or painting only, without moving about, might not bring accurate assessment.

Concerned with Projected Play

The tiny child, either very sensibly (or because it has to) indulges largely in Projected Play, because it can't walk, or walk well yet. So it is easier and more comfortable to press your sticky hands into objects and make them live, rather than getting up and falling on your nose. Besides, the tiny person has a lot to discover in the feel and touch and rub and bang of things. Whilst doing this he/she may become very absorbed. This is exactly the quality we are going to desire of them later on in their lessons and in listening. Only we call it concentration then. We must take care to nurture this quality and I will mention later the value of Near Finish, whereby we avoid insisting on too abrupt a finish to a period of play, thus causing perplexity and some emotional stress.

In this form of play there is often silence and calm, although where a toy takes on a character or role, singing, talking or shouting may be heard at times. But the body may remain fairly still. The infusion of emotion into Beloved Objects in this play may extend to a simple rag, but also explains why a somewhat hairless teddy, with one eye and stuffing coming out, continues to rejoice in (to many tidy adult minds) an unexplained popularity. Indeed, such love is important and I have often felt that when people lose a certain sense of loyalty in later life this can be traced back to a break in such a relationship; for instance, if a doll is taken away and replaced by something new and more 'respectable'. I knew a clever man once, who had a favourite mascot whipped up by a master and thrown in the fire whilst, as a boy, he was sitting an exam. He explained the terrible feeling of loss that it caused. 'But I passed the exam', he said. Then slowly, 'Come to think of it, though, I have never passed one since'. Probably coincidence, but who knows?

As life progresses, we find it less convenient to carry about too many beloved objects. Think what trouble 'Westerners' were always getting into, carrying bags of gold about the place. In our posh – and we think more civilised times – we prefer to use symbols that represent the bags of gold. We call them numbers and hope the Bank will keep them tidy. Yet there are bandits even now, who invade the computers. But we are urged to remember a pin number to get money out of a hole in a wall. This represents a key. If you forget your number you have lost your key. To peruse our account numbers, when counting (with hope!) we are generally quiet and still, often sitting; we dream of having more. This is really projected activity too. Your plus numbers are certainly invested with affection, your minus with sadness. You may get up and walk away, yet your Bank statement of these numbers remains on the desk. It is certainly a memorial of your accruing. This is how Projected Play turns eventually into the three Rs. The same amount of *absorption* is needed for both. People talk, too, of 'playing the market', don't they? For this they use organising ability and skill. Because of the importance invested in monuments, it is interesting that sometimes a child will destroy its own, but woe betide anyone else who tries to do so! And, who has not felt sad or angry if the tide washes away our sand castle, as we lingeringly leave the beach?

Concerned with Personal Play

Once you can move about without too much risk of getting hurt, there is a new joy of discovery and freedom. You can make a journey. Journey is very important in child play, although only small journeys in a comparatively small room are likely for many small adventurers these days. But a comparatively small space may have a sort of warm security feel.

First journeys will probably be by crawling, but it soon becomes surprising how fast some children can run on their knees. After the first diagonal triumphs, the next essays may be in circular form. The circle makes an oft repeating appearance in behaviour patterns, particularly in the creation of primitive art and child drama. Not only in first room 'knee-running', but in gang discussions later, and in groups of thirty 'giraffes on roller skates' pounding round a school hall.

Later come the wonders of more obvious drama and dance, which bring deeper chances of emotional involvement, as well as the phenomenon of Running Play, where both arms are stretched out like the wings of a bird or an aeroplane and run often includes a peak moment onto a higher level. (You never see this type of Running Play in an unhappy school; it is an expression of joy.) I first saw the delight over the higher level of the pavement (and occasionally of steps) in road play, when observing children at great length in the streets of London; which is why I recommended there should be rostrum blocks in every school in the land. In this I was not entirely unsuccessful. In schools and homes, natural play can be guided. Would that it could be more! For that which is outside can become the wild drama of the streets. Today it is a dangerous exercise and often unworthy of the best in every child. But if expressive drama is part of child nature, we should harness it and use it in a guided and civilised way. At more adult level comes dance still, but also sport and athletics and the grown-up pleasures of disciplined techniques. I have written elsewhere (Slade 1968) of the fascination I had myself, when young, in perfecting the change-over of the baton in relay racing. Relay races are wonderful, because, even if you are not very fast, you can run with international stars in a team and at least be sure that you provide a perfect baton change for them. For me it has been one of the most exciting play experiences of life.

As to theatre itself, once you have acted in space and had the fascination of journey, using all the child drama shapes on the floor, I don't know how one can ever really enjoy working in the proscenium form again.

Perhaps it would be right to suggest here the difference between memorials and monuments. All those objects left, after projected activity has taken place, may be considered as, collectively, a memorial of the doing.

A Monument

May be one, or more, of these objects, or itself the one thing left. Rather than merely existing in itself (as *a* doll; one brick etc.) it is something actually built, or created. Examples would be a building of bricks, or match boxes, cards, sandcastles, or indeed, later a house or cathedral. A child may suddenly feel it wants to overcome, take vengeance, be dissatisfied with the monument and will then knock it down. Sometimes the movement will be straight down, sometimes the sideways swipe, devastating in so many ways, which may need civilising eventually. (Or it may evolve into a magnificent backhand at tennis.) I have written elsewhere (Slade 1954, 1958) of the tiny child turning this into an experiment in the use of sound, as destruction turns into various types of banging, an elementary form of music leading eventually to discovery of time-beat, rhythm and climax.

I wonder whether there is some warped link here with racist violence – that a monument label is mentally built up against a supposed inferior person or interloper, and the best way of getting rid of them is to knock them down. I expect not. It is more likely to be part, or full (uncivilised) Personal Play, wherein one must *win*, must conquer, must overcome, must be King of the Castle. But it is not impossible that all these things and others come into motivation to violence. So the good qualities that arise out of these two forms of play are *absorption* and *sincerity*. Absorption in Projected Play should be fostered and encouraged, for it is going to be necessary for all future forms of learning and study.

The sincerity which grows through role play and good acting (the *best* child creation, not the early laughing self-conscious attempts) and through deeply expressive Natural Dance, turns slowly into a habit of the personality and leads to an honesty of behaviour towards others.

Some observers feel there might, perhaps, be a distinction between realistic play and imaginative play. But, in fact, play (certainly in the earlier stages) is so fluid, containing at any moment experiences of every day outward life and of the imaginative inner life, that the one cannot accurately be distinguished as a different activity from the other. Example from an infant patient: whilst being a hippopotamus at the sea-side, he telephoned his grandmother in play, really because he was actually too shy to do it in real life (as she was often impatient). It was one of my steps towards helping him bit by bit to have the courage to do it in reality. It was his idea (in play), which I was to take up and develop. In the book *Experience of Spontaneity* I included a splendid picture of a Man from Mars suddenly interrupting what had been a very serious and realistic discussion by twelve- to thirteen-year-olds. 'A Man from Mars puts atomic sparks on the Government' was the caption.

Again, after a very realistic 'party' (which parents might not have approved of) a nine-year-old 'Man' said, 'Can't get a taxi? Then ring for a magic carpet yer fool'. It is important, of course, that the difference between imagination, dream and reality be understood, but the distinction pertains more to intellect and perception than to play itself. The healthy child develops towards reality as it gains experience of life. This is a process rather than a distinction. The only true distinction in play is that of Projected Play and Personal Play. Once you truly recognise this – and their difference – it enriches your understanding of people and changes your view of life.

The child who has the right opportunities will try out in Personal and Projected play many fragments of thought and experience. These two forms of play add qualities to each other, and also to the person who plays. Throughout the whole of life we are happy or unhappy in so far as we discover for ourselves (or circumstances allow for ourselves) the right admixture of these distinct manners of using energy. Both the type of person and the life occupation are connected with the balance of them. Thus, these two early types of play have an important bearing on the building of Man, and Woman, their whole behaviour and sometimes even their ability to fit in with society. Play opportunity, therefore, means gain and development. Lack of play may mean a permanent lost part of ourselves. It is this unknown, uncreated part, this missing link, which may cause difficulty and uncertainty in later years. For this and other reasons, backward children often respond to further opportunities for play, by which they build or rebuild their inner self, doing at a later stage what should have been done before. Particularly valuable is the possibility for those who fail in the three Rs, (Projected activity) to have plenty of opportunity for Personal Play in improvised drama, in which they can overcome 'enemies', as well as express sadness and anger, or the enemy within themselves. Even in the case of an overworked office manager on the edge of breakdown, drowning in 'eternal' Projected activity stress, may receive the advice from his doctor, 'Drop it. Take a holiday. Go and play golf'. Thus can one hope to use that type of play to strengthen us enough to face return to a different type of activity, which had begun to be so total as (without better balance) to overwhelm.

Journey Shapes

Once active Personal Play has started, we see an interesting number of shapes, drawn, as it were, over the floor space by the direction the child walks, runs or dances. The first is the circle, or part of it. Either alone or in a group, it is nearly always described in an anti-clockwise direction. I used to be asked constantly whether it was the same in Australia and had it anything to do with bath water going down a plug? The answer is 'Yes' to the first question and to the second, 'No'. It hasn't anything to do with dirty water or being upside down the other side of the world. I don't think there is anything magic about it, it is probably just that most of us are right footed and press a little harder with the right foot, or step a little farther with it, which sends us round to the left. People who have represented me in Australia assure me it is the same down under. It is said that people walk in a circle, when lost in a fog. Going anti-clockwise?

If someone near, or at the front of a group, say, in a Junior school, goes the other way, they are either left-footed, highly intelligent or just anti-social. You soon find out which. But the result in a large group approaches temporary chaos. Fun to sort out.

Other shapes apart from ◯ are the diagonal ╱ which is half of the cross ╳ The S which is half of the 8 and occasionally the zig-zag ⟨ , which one sees sometimes in violent dance (executed more often by a boy). If you are going at a terrific pace, it is a useful shape to employ. 'Good for avoiding girls' I was told, by one hot-headed Junior, 'Ptickly if yor in a hurry'. Very occasionally I have seen the triangle, nearly always evolving out of a sad slow walk, or a calm sweet dance by girls – at least, whenever it has appeared for me.

It may be of interest to note here that the same basic shapes occur in children's art and most primitive art patterns. They seem to be basic to our collective unconscious and are thus shared by both the active and the passive form of play as here described. The only other shape, not yet mentioned, is, so to speak, the spiral ⦿ . That is, a spiral as if it were seen from above. It occurs, under certain circumstances, in Infant and Junior schools and will be mentioned in greater detail later. In an earlier book (Slade 1954) I showed pictures of the 'spiral' forming in classroom drama and also a piece of child art. But there, the spiral was the other way round. But it was painted by a left-handed child.

Perhaps one should mention here, so as to be sure of the circumstances, that all these things appear as natural phenomena, but only if the person (or persons) involved, is allowed enough freedom to create things in their own way. Obviously, if people are working in a confined space, all jammed up together, say, on a stage and all told to stand here or move there, the unconscious shapes are unlikely to be seen. Not that this is any criticism of formalisation under the right circumstances. It is just that nature itself needs freedom and space for its most interesting and wondrous signs to appear.

One more thing to note in our consideration and observations, in general, of that marvel in our midst called Play, is the child's love of sound. One is tempted to say that all children love sound when they go into school, but, despite much good music training in many places, they do not always love it when they come out. What have we done to them in the meantime?

Love of Sound

Children divide sound into three main parts. They are Time Beat, Rhythm and Climax. Oh dear, what is the good of *writing* about sound, you really have to hear it. Nevertheless I will try: Time Beat is a sort of dead bam-bam that your baby uses, often when banging the table with your best mug in a dangerous way (for the mug *and* the child). Or worse, up-ending a fork and bamming that on your best new table that you haven't finished paying for yet, leaving a hundred interesting holes that look as if a large woodworm and family has moved in. Rhythm is different. Some people use the word 'rhythmic' somewhat loosely. They do not distinguish the two sounds; and what they really mean is time-beat. But rhythm is based upon time beat, yet as interpretation and personal expression enter the creation, the sound escapes slightly from the imposed prison and the whole takes on a new pattern and a magic life of its own. In an orchestra even, one might consider that early in rehearsal it is concerned largely with time-beat. But by performance, it is hoped that under guidance of the conductor and the warmed hearts of enthusiastic players working together, a shared creation of totally different character emerges for the pleasure of Worldkind. It has interpretation and pattern. It has *Life*. It is the same with the production of a play.

At the moment of writing, a child next door is walking about in their garden singing gently, 'Pin-pin-pin-pin'. It is mostly time-beat, no real rhythm at all, but what is exciting is the immense variation being put into loudness and softness and somehow of speaking from the heart in this repetition of one word. By a simple artistry in sound, I am somehow listening to a whole vocabulary being imparted through the child's testing and joyful intense experimentation. Oh, isn't life sometimes wonderful!

At an earlier time, I was delighted to hear a remark by Arthur Rubinstein. Very gently he had been trying to imply that a young musician had been playing in rather a dull and lifeless way. It was, in fact, almost dead time beat. She said (a little perplexed), 'But that is the way the music *says* it should be played'. Rubinstein answered, 'Oh, forget about that, all those lines and black dots. They so often get in the way, just play from your heart'. When rhythm and feeling come together it brings rejoicing. The notes and first time-beat are only there for information, they are an indication of intent, the final glory comes with what we make of them. When we really PLAY.

The third division of sound is Climax. It is a slow building up in loudness to a magnificent peak of sound. It is what all children want to do much of the time and we spend all of our time stopping them. This is not a plea for chaos, it is a fact. However, grown-ups need peace. So do children at times. But after decades of watching, observing, listening and discussing with the young, I came to the conclusion that they have great difficulty in finding peace without our aid. I therefore invented something I call De-climax. It is something the adult has to add to the natural divisions of sound; an intentional bringing down from loud, to soft, to silence. It is useful for parents to know about and sometimes use; it is extremely valuable for teachers in developing discipline; and I would say usually essential for therapists. De-climax is the opposite of climax-building. You start at the top by making a loud noise, and slowly bring it down to a quietness and finally to silence. There may be quite a long silence, if you have timed it right. And in that moment we all find peace. It may be done by using voice only, but in schools, probably a loud instrument like a drum or smacking the seat of a plastic chair may be necessary. It is much better than shouting.

Youngsters are used to that, so a sudden loud voice sound is not always so effective. I am inclined to think that all active lessons and certainly drama lessons should end like this. Why? Because they have been experiencing possibly strong active expression and movement, encouraged to give their all, probably in journey (Personal Play) and now they are going back to a class room to do three R work, in sedentary circumstances perhaps, and need to be in a totally different mood, not all excited, but calm and quiet, accepting restriction, and ready, one hopes, to be absorbed in the subject (Projected Activity).

Two examples come to mind. One was where a very active lot in an Infant school had finished their 'do' and I brought the twitching and heavy breathing down to silence, then suggested that we could hear the school clock 'tick-snoring' and we must not wake him up. They happened to be mice at the time, so a fair-sized mob of mice carefully tip-toed back down a long corridor in complete silence to their classroom, ready for the next QUIET THING.

Some people are very keen on de-rolement. This may be necessary and absolutely correct in some cases of therapy. But in this case I would not mind if that group stayed being mice for the rest of the morning as long as they were quiet, for I was told later that no one else had ever made them so before. Actually, of course, if they became in any way absorbed in their lesson, as time went on they would have slowly forgotten they were mice. De-rolement would have naturally taken place. But one hopes that they would remember the former session with pleasure and perhaps the amazing fact that you don't *have* to punch each other all the time (boisterous lot this). It is perfectly possible and not too boring, just for once, to be nice mice! Less bruising anyway.

The second example was at Manchester University, some forty years ago. I had been using my Ideas Game, a way of asking for three or four ideas, then making a quick story out of them and then acting it at once, with improvised dialogue. On another track, I had talked about using sounds and noises in the Infant school and so I banged a metal tray and asked, 'What does this sound remind you of?' One young man, hoping to take the mickey out of me said lugubriously, 'Sounds like banging a tin tray, to me'. 'Yes', I said, 'absolutely right, what a good idea, we'll use that'. He subsided. Then asking for one or two more ideas (fortunately rather more imaginative) which became our story, I moved on to mention use of De-climax. 'Bet you can't get this lot quiet' imparted my Chairman in a hoarse whisper. 'You're on', I said, or words to that effect. It was near the time for ending the session, so I started on my De-climax. It was a long slow business, but my nerve held and we ended with complete silence from one hundred and eighty people in a large hall for several minutes and I was able to say in a quiet voice, 'Thank you very much. Time for lunch'.

'God', said the Chairman, 'that worked, didn't it!'

Generally, at courses, if I am explaining De-climax, I get the silence, hold it as long as I dare, then very quietly say, 'See what I mean?'.

The important thing to remember about De-climax (and why some people can't work it) is that you *must cap* whatever noise is going on before you try to bring it down. How else can you catch the group's attention? If you only make a half-hearted noise, about equal with theirs, they are not going to hear it, let alone obey it.

In-Flow and Out-Flow

These both have their place in the developing person. Both are necessary and each tends to get blocked. They balance each other when natural development is allowed. In creating, the child has natural Outflow, as also in speech (and permission for it), and begins to feel its way towards In-flow by using experiences of life in its creations. It thus begins to 'draw-in' and use things. This goes on, to some degree, steadily from babyhood up to six or seven years of age, but, at the Dawn of Seriousness, the process comes to something of a climax in the fuller, more conscious desire to draw in *knowledge*.

If the right knowledge is available at the right time, the child is satisfied to some extent, a digestion process takes place and, because of the actual strengthening by the nourishment of interest in life, confidence and desire for more (development of the inquiring mind), *it becomes necessary for immediate new creations.* Here the child's drama is essential, because it is the chief medium of Outflow and it provides for the child the actual proof-trials of what has been experienced. What is learned is tried out. As some of the 'right knowledge' may have come from school lessons and therefore more likely to be of Projected type, the child's own form of painting would be a valuable outlet as well.

It is not far from the truth to say that without frequent opportunities for creative play, what is learnt is never proved, since it is not (doubly) physically and emotionally *experienced.* For this reason much knowledge is either rejected or forgotten – or sort of waffled in the mind, because it makes only half an impression, not a whole one. Our education needs to be aware of this and should not, on the one hand be so lax that only Out-flow takes place, instead of correction, discipline and learning at the right time. On the other hand there is some danger of a pendulum swing too far the other way, so that too much In-flow without nearly enough Out-flow may be attempted. The old bashing-in again. 'Indigestion' and non-proving (through play) in the child's mind can put off the Dawn of Seriousness and forms of uncertainty can have a bad effect upon behaviour. Some teachers may feel that it is even hard to keep order these days, let alone teach. Too *much* Outflow they will think. Yes, but of the wrong kind; and not supported by In-flow, it can have a deleterious effect. If the Out-flow is mostly waffle, bad language and bad behaviour, it is not creative and in Secondary schools would be a sign of precarious infant state. Something seriously wrong. More of this, and Dawn of Seriousness later.

In this book I have tried to keep things as simple as possible. In all my work I have tried to express terms in ordinary English, indeed only to suggest names as definitions of things which were important and that other people may not have noticed. I have been distressed, for some time, that each new book that comes out about education and psychology seemed to become more and more complicated; the terms used are almost impossible to understand – unless you have read fifty new American books that one has not always got time for; or have generally kept up with the extraordinary self-conscious jargon of the subject. Do we, in these fields, now want to prove how clever we are, thus making harder and faster demarcations of time, age-limits, slots and groupings and inventing an entirely new language? I hope not. Particularly boring is it to see some new long and complicated name for something which has already been named and probably known about for many years. We are complicated and interesting enough as human-beings, but our needs and impulses are comparatively straightforward. They have ordinary names like love, hate, sadness, anger, loss, grief, fun, joy, power, envy, compassion, forgiveness, sex and fear. I do hope we can keep them so.

The best opposite example I 'enjoy' is

'And now for the psychodramaterl*argical re-versal of roles*',

which in Child Drama just means 'change round'.

Thus, with some apologies, I offer you some terms and definitions which have stood the test of more than forty years now, and are still used in some places. They are used in this book and I hope they are not too complicated. They are for the good of children.

List of Terms Used

Absorption – being completely wrapped up in what is being done or what one is doing, to the exclusion of all other thoughts, including the awareness of or desire for an audience. A strong form of concentration.

Sincerity – a complete form of honesty in portraying a part, bringing with it an intense feeling of reality and experience, generally brought about by the complete absence of stage tricks, or at least of discernible tricks, and only fully achieved in the process of acting with absorption.

Near finish – point at which absorbed play may be interrupted with less frustration.

Projected play – in which the person projects an idea in the mind into, onto or around objects outside themself, so that life, as it were, takes place in the objects. They act as memorials of creation, remaining after the person has moved away.

Personal play – where a person takes on full responsibility for action, in mind, body and spirit. No longer may toys or objects live life for them. They must do it themselves, as in acting, running and dance.

Hinterland activity – activity going on for love, in an absorbed fashion generally out of view even when some other players are purposely *in* view. A natural development which takes place from time to time amongst children.

In-flow – the taking-in of ideas and experiences, which becomes easier after a balance with out-flow has been achieved. At moments when the child is prepared for or in need of out-flow, or when this amounts to a general condition in the child, because of lack of opportunity, in-flow to a marked degree is virtually impossible to achieve.

Out-flow – the pouring out of creative forms of expression, a tendency which can be regulated and encouraged, and which by frequent opportunity becomes a habit promoting confidence.

Language flow – flow of words and imaginative ideas with pronounced philosophic or poetic quality, obtained by carefully providing opportunities for out-flow, through improvisation or creative drama.

Body speech – the use of the body rather than the tongue to express ideas, often employed by the young child before being able, by lack of vocabulary, to develop language flow.

Group intuition – perception through intuition of the needs or desires of the group, as opposed to oneself alone. Often present before awareness of group sensitivity, but able to be developed further through training in group sensitivity.

Group sensitivity – a knowledge of the needs or desires of the group as opposed to oneself alone, arrived at chiefly through the senses after the dawn of seriousness.

In-the-round – acting in a manner which relies on inner creative expression, leading to absorption, which in turn tends to a performance which can only be described as acting from self outwards in all directions and therefore all round the body. It is the quality of this playing which makes it satisfactory when seen from any or all sides, rather than just from the front. Sometimes loosely used as a description of the form in which a play is presented. In any case, acting-in-the-round would be necessary to presentation in a circular form. Acting in the round is necessary for any good presentation in the Arena Theatre

Form, and for adults needs a special training. The child acts naturally in the round.

Dawn of seriousness – frame of mind becoming apparent at about six years of age, and developing rapidly for the next four years or so, bringing with it ability to discern good and evil, awareness of society and joy in work.

Running play – discernible phenomenon of intense and sudden out-flow caused by joy, which finds expression in an abandonment of all else to a form of fleet running, generally with bent knees and arms outstretched. Is in part a measure of the success in achieving out-flow.

Happiness-development – a stage in creative expression aimed at by the teacher. First signs of joy dependent on out-flow.

Child–teacher relationship – that which is purposely built up by trust, through confidence, sympathy, common sense and affection. The only sure base for learning.

Mostly for Parents

Play is a form of expression that concerns the whole nature of man and woman. Children become happy, confident and obedient by using their own form of drama, particularly if it is guided wisely and well in schools. And wise adults, by watching it and 'reading' it correctly see how far a child has got in life. For it is life itself being investigated, re-stated and proved before our eyes; and through children's pictorial art we find their secrets displayed. Sometimes it is a sweet whisper of inner state. Sometimes a loud shout of bright red joy, or the dark satanic black and dirty green of deep despair. As mentioned earlier, by knowing about play our attitude to people, particularly little people, may change and our understanding deepen. It is therefore of great importance to all parents, as well as to teachers, social workers and therapists. So here are a few suggestions about parents and the needs of a baby.

General Attitude of Parents

The most important thing in a baby's life is, of course, love, but love can be elusive or of the wrong kind. A baby must be wanted before and after it is born. Nevertheless, a baby not really wanted *can* be wanted and even loved after birth. The non-want can be made up. Devastating to the mother, though, may be the state of post-natal depression. This can affect the child too; and much depends on the care and thoughtful nursing by others during this time. Another complete book could be written about the trauma of having a baby at all and the attitude over help, the despairing tiredness of young mothers, attitude of fathers, step-fathers and living conditions; lack of space, heat, food, work, money (in many situations) – all too common in modern times – and the lonely fears of being a single parent. But in this book, if only for space, mostly (in this chapter) more normal and happy conditions are considered as present. Not that we are insisting on ideal conditions everywhere. But here are simply some standards to aim for, not intended as interference, but perhaps by way of reminder. For in parenthood a lot of things are there, down in the mind somewhere, but it may be helpful to bring some of them to the surface and make them conscious. So, things done for a child should be done for its real need and not for the sentimental whim of the parents. It is necessary to find a balance of affection, so that the child is not overwhelmed by emotion one minute and actively disliked the next. Just as the teacher in a child's later life, the parent should not try to be a saint, but discover early how to form a pattern of personality-behaviour towards children, a mixture of patience and affection. Constant perplexing abrupt change is what children find hard to bear or understand. Don't be put off by 'psychologists' to the extent of being too afraid to thwart. Don't follow everything just because it is *new*.

There are occasions for not thwarting, but that does not mean that you need not obtain obedience. (Anger may be shown when really pushed, otherwise, children don't know how far they may go.) To allow misunderstanding over obedience in the early years is unkind. It does not help any child. A few inhibitions are even necessary for civilised life. Make few rules, but see they are obeyed, kindly but firmly. Let them become custom. For elementary custom grows into a firmer ethos. In a good school ethos plays a large part in obtaining and shaping good behaviour. In a family it is the same and is likely to establish confidence and courage against the rigours of the outside world.

Mother should do most of the guiding in early years. In general, Father should be the big gun, the final authority. About 'father', this would not necessarily be true, though, for a step-father or a step-mother. A step-father has to be particularly careful not to hurry things. He has to try and make peace amongst all the bruised feelings and grief, after death or divorce. He should let the real mother do most of the guiding, for any children will think 'Why should I obey you? You are not my father'. Resentment will follow. (He should probably only join in judgement if his support is needed in a crisis.) So, this man has to try and ease himself in slowly and try to be a lasting friend. Show gentle occasional affection if a child allows it – and then more. For a step-Mum too, the task is to be wary. Let the biological father do most of the guiding. And Father, try not to leave your new wife alone too often too long with the children (you may even have to change your life style a bit), where she may be under strain, holding back; or suddenly her patience may break. She must be helped to ease in slowly too and not 'take charge'. Of course, if the biological parent of either kind is disliked, the situation is even more complicated. But the step-parent might then, if tactful, come into their own. Knowing how to promote happy play may be an enormous help to either step-parent.

Some modern families are finding, or are out to find, new ways of sharing with 'new man' husbands being more equal in running the home. In many instances this may work, but in a crisis the deeper stronger voice is occasionally needed. (Perhaps it will be more often Mum's in future.) But the voice is of extreme importance in the 'music' that rules a good home and to lose the effectiveness of a last-stand big gun is to let slip a natural plan, a pattern of order. This may tend to destroy the confidence of younger ones in the family atmosphere. Women are demanding more independence in their need for fulfilment these days and some different sharing is, no doubt, necessary. The greatest mistake, however, in social change, finance, religion or government, is for that change to be too sudden, too swift. It brings other problems.

We can be too swift and sudden even in small things, such as if a baby handles something that might be dangerous. Unless it is going to blow up or cut someone in half, don't snatch it away. Hold it but try to divert attention onto something else before finally taking it. This way you avoid disturbance. Remember, language is an emotional thing for children. 'Yes' and 'No' are learnt not only for their meaning, but as emotional music.

Example: Mother is cooking or washing in the kitchen and a child says

	'May I go in the garden Mum?'
MUM:	'No',
	'Oh, go on, *can't* I go in the garden?'
	(Let's say there is a good reason for Mum's decision.)
MUM:	'No, you can't.'
CHILD:	'Oh, Mu-u-u-um'.
	Then with a half sly smile, when Mum isn't immediately looking, the child tip-toes into the garden.

Mum turns and notices and thinks (possibly in more violent terms than I write it) 'Oh, well, I can't be bothered to call him/her back, I've got all this washing to do'. A simple occurrence.

But what happens is that 'No' now has a sort of 'Yes-ishness' about it. The music is not true. There is a tiny little uncertainty about it. And if nothing is done the child has got away with it and will try it again. Again, if nothing is done, the power of the meaning and music of 'No' has been weakened and begins to mean 'perhaps'. Continuation of such and other happenings leads ultimately to permanent disobedience and clear disregard for authority. This may be in a perfectly happy family situation. But one day, because of indecision, the child will go too far, and poor tired Mum will have a minor explosion. She will lose her temper, say strong things she may regret afterwards, or possibly hit her offspring. The result for the child will be amazement, shock, puzzlement, followed by resentment. A sad little block in understanding has been formed. Only a careful and *successful* explanation of, 'Will you, please, understand that when I say 'No', I mean it', will heal the rift. We are left to see what happens later. I don't want to exaggerate, but a worm has been born; and in later years of therapy I have more than once traced back more serious out-of-hand behaviour to early uncertainty about obedience over quite simple things. There is something profoundly uncertain-making if those words mean and feel one thing one moment and another the next. That is the simple insecurity which is at the root of some troubles in later life. Don't be afraid: Yes means *yes* and no means *no*. See that your children understand. There should be an almost automatic response to the *sound*. Correction is better done by tone of voice than smacking. But don't roar all day, keep your trump cards for the needed moment.

Don't expect your children to be clean all the time. They must get dirty during some forms of play, as they will in some forms of work when grown up. Washing comes after. For everyone to be clean all the time may suit some keen housewife types but can be a tyranny for children. Learn to decide about appropriate occasions for cleanliness. This is, perhaps, becoming more important to say (in an opposite sort of way), because one knows of children these days who rush from the garden, in a dirty condition, into a room full of guests (perhaps there for a meal) interrupting everything, shouting all the time to one parent or the other. This should be discouraged and gradually, but firmly, 'learned-not-to'. Just as rude and disturbing for guests may be children who neither say 'Hello' (let alone 'How-d'you-do') when the visitor says it to them. Not even 'Hi'. By Junior age this is sad. Older, it is *bad*. Teach them that good manners are based on kindness to people other than ourselves. Good manners are not just an old-fashioned bore. They are basic to duty towards our neighbour.

In an earlier book (Slade 1958), I mentioned – don't over protect your children by being too nervous to let them out of your sight. This is still basically true, but life has changed these days and violent crime is so much more common that protection on the way to school or to friends has, in many places, become necessary. Every abuse of freedom by the evil, or the unwise, is a step towards bureaucratic tightening of the reins, is ultimately a step towards dictatorship. So now, for many parents, what might have been considered over-protection, has now become protection. It is often necessary. It is a sign of the times. But such need shows a sad deterioration of a civilised society.

Notice that your children are growing up. Don't continually do things for them. Say sometimes 'See if *you* can do it', for example, putting on a coat and doing up the buttons. Encourage, but don't leave a child stranded and hopeless. There is a balance for each small person. We are all different. There should be a sense of community in a good home, a sense of fun, the feeling that everyone has the chance to speak without fear and to try things out in their own way; and a sense of safety.

In all our dealings with children, we should continually say to ourselves: 'If I were *really* that little person in that position, what would I do, what would I think, what would I say?'. The greater your power of perception in this line of thought, the more understanding you will become. Children apply just this attitude to their play, but with them it is often more straightforward. They think 'If I were *really* that Spaceman, that flying dragon or that atomic sausage, I would do this and say that'. Sometimes they obviously have hardly time to *think* even that. They just 'be it'. And that is their Child Drama. Where and when possible we should observe it and encourage it, for there is an unfolding pattern of human behaviour by which Man and Woman discover themselves and learn to think of others.

Yet Personal Play is catered for less in the home and may even be discouraged, because this drama of life needs space, some rushing about maybe and generally includes loud declaration. In a word it is noisy and inconvenient. Nevertheless, children should be taught not to scream. That is not only bad for them but totally unnecessary. Unfortunately, some parents, apart from all this, fail to understand the importance of such play and one hears then the devastating remark: 'Stop it. Don't be silly'. Or adults laugh at the wrong time. Too often the destruction happens at the very moment when the child, or a group, is creating at depth. There is then an embarrassed breaking off of play and the young are influenced to feel that what they were doing was somehow not right and not important. In this dramatic play the overcoming, the heroic, death-but-resurrection, are of deeper importance than most people can imagine, for the building of confidence and making good relationships in early gang groupings. Through it the young learn more control of their body and mastery of the objects they play with, as well as elementary social discoveries. For children, their own dramatic *personal* play means not only the playing out of TV and film experience, but the whole of the doing of life. For mental health, there must be Out-flow as well as In-flow from films and the TV. It is their natural and best way of developing movement and speech. Through it they develop this quality of sincerity, a very important part of their growing personality.

By squashing, or ignoring, this form of dramatic play, so many of us, unknowingly, cause the precise problems in children that we later deprecate. For they will find other ways of expressing themselves, which may be less desirable, and often away from adult view or supervision. Sometimes the public form of this expression is a built-up negative attitude to life, or an inner revolt against authority, rather too common amongst young people at the moment. So instead of the opportunity being available for acting out their imaginative dramas, when away from home they smash and also grab, for real.

Allow Dance

The very young show signs of this in jigging up and down to sound – any sound. Babies sometimes do this with their legs, even before they can stand, only here it is like the extremely quick leg twitching of an india-rubber frog. No bones. Increasingly, younger Juniors nowadays ape their elder sisters and brothers by dancing on the spot, as in a crowded disco. This is a pity. Encourage them to move over space more – gently, and if you get the chance. For their jigging on one spot, at this age, is really only acting at dancing, because they are copying. They have not made it *theirs*. It is not the genuine, free-flow and wondrous beauty of real Child Dance. Flowing dance on a lawn on a Summer evening can be something that stays in the mind as an experience – just before going to bed. But don't forget to arrange for declimax, or the dancers will remain unsettled and it will be more difficult to get them to bed and to stay there.

I saw such a sad thing in Birmingham once on the steps outside the Central Library. A child of about seven or eight was evolving an interesting and fairly complicated little dance. The sound of footsteps and higher and lower levels was obviously being enjoyed and purpose-fully used. Then the small girl sang a little tune of her own, to add to the dance. I sank down, a little way off, sitting on my briefcase (trying to look like a bit of furniture) to share the thrill. Just then a distraught mother dashed down the steps and shouted 'What on earth do you think you are doing? Stop that at once. Don't be so *silly*'. In a second, something not at all out of hand, something gentle, very quiet really and beautiful had been killed by an angry, embarrassed roar. I rose slowly and continued my journey to the Centre of Bureaucracy with a churning stomach at memory of the child's face.

Parents are often embarrassed by their children, but so are they of us. This mother could have watched for a moment, then said gently that it was time to go now. I often think about the things we miss, often because of hurry, because of life's rush. With small people, it is so often the small happenings that are the jewel-events. Do we notice them? Do we destroy without notice or without meaning to? Childhood passes and is so suddenly gone. Where are our mental snapshots now? Imagination is something to be cherished and encouraged, it leads to creation. I was so delighted when directing one of my Summer Courses at Keele University. I had invited a Professor to speak. He finished his talk by stressing the importance of imagination. He mentioned 'the imaginative theoretical concept'. That is the moment arrived at, based upon considered data, when you have to have the courage and imagination to take the next step out into the unknown – to take a chance, for you might be right.

So even physics can be aided by imagination and I had been encouraging this in schools and homes for years. I thought, 'Yes, if you train a thousand children to be imaginative in junior years, perhaps *one* might be a great scientist'. That is the way we fly to the moon.

Banging (Unfortunately?) is Important
It is a discovery of and investigation into sound. Listen for the divisions of sound and see whether you can distinguish between them. You can have discussions, have 'question and answer' sometimes, and more interesting pat-

terns by joining *in* on occasions. Help them, too, to realise that one can have soft sounds as well as loud. For instance, grains of rice, or tiny pebbles in a tin, make a soft gentle sound (you will think of others). Soft sounds lead towards civilisation, at a time when the young are full of animal restlessness, knowing little of anything but outburst. Such experience will help and prepare them for drama lessons in school too.

You might also play at 'What does this sound remind you of?' If no good idea comes quickly, after a pause, make a suggestion yourself. But make it imaginative. In that way children are encouraged to see they won't be told not to be silly, if they make a genuine answer. Example: A regular brush brush noise on a gravel path might remind one of an elephant cleaning his teeth. In school the same ploy would help children to see 'how far they might go'. Teacher can help them to find this, with less unwanted children's 'try-out'.

Painting and Drawing

Many children are pressed to draw too early, that is, in a way the adult considers correct. But there is a whole world of Child Art that can be missed by this. Those with a gift will *find* drawing and use it in due time. It is better to let them start with water paints. Poster paint is more in fashion, though. And don't confine them to small pieces of paper. Have large pieces, say, at least two by two feet square if possible; and don't be surprised if the first attempts don't look anything like what you expect. It won't look very 'real'. It might even be just sloshes of colour; and when anything you *can* recognise is shown, the colour of things or people will be unusual. When they paint a picture of You, don't be offended at the colour of your hair or at their general attempt. It will not be photographic. That is what adults expect, too often. Learn slowly about mass, colour, space and line in the creation. Don't laugh at it. Don't say things like 'But you haven't put the lamp post in'. It is their picture, not yours. You don't always have to say it is good. We all tend to say that, when it isn't. Then children have no standard to aim at. You can say things like, 'oh yes' with interest, or 'I really like that'. But you must mean it. But avoid saying 'Oh, I don't like that'. Keep your feelings in check and think *why* you don't like it. The picture may be telling you something of importance. An Art teacher can tell you about paper and materials. I used to select ends of wallpaper, going cheap in shops, as almost discarded.

It is as well to have some good covering on the floor when painting starts (and on the people too!) for it can well be a messy business in the early stages. The same with modelling. Many parents buy those books which already have pictures drawn in them (and children may quite like them), but then the child only has to colour them. It impedes their free thought and creation and unconsciously makes them think they ought to, or have got to, draw and do banal pictures of that kind. I am tempted to say – below their standard, but above their age. Real children's painting may be an acquired taste, like coffee and Staffordshire Pottery. It has a primitive splendour all its own, once caught, never to be lost. It contains the innocent eye. Crayons are less messy and often useful. Poster paints are taking over more now, but they don't have that wide, generous sweep of opportunity that powder paints have. It's the slosh that counts!

Suggestions for Assisting Play at Home

Allow: Banging noises sometimes (from babyhood upwards). Interest yourself in the many different types. Only take away what is dangerous, or will be spoiled, by drawing the child's attention to something else. Don't snatch.

Reason: Children love sound. They divide it into time beat, rhythm and climax. They find out many things about speech, music and drama that you don't know about, by testing sounds in their own way.

What the adult can do: Give delight by joining in sometimes. Use other noises. Don't irritate the child by taking his toy and showing how it 'should' be played with. Lead slowly on to a distinction between loud and soft sounds, long sounds and percussive sounds.

Examples: Bits of metal on string; tapping bits of wood and cardboard; stretched elastic noise; rice in a tin.

Think in terms of question and answer. Answer the child's 'statement' in sound. Just do it. Don't talk about it. Enjoy it and you will find that children not only follow you towards civilisation but lead you into a world you didn't know about. As children get older, let them see that there are times when you want to be quiet. There must be compromise and thought for others, particularly in small homes. You can train children, but don't destroy them. You don't need to be a musician for all this. Just be human and have serious fun.

Allow: Jumping up and down and standing sometimes (from babyhood upwards). Allow running about. Don't stop all running because you are afraid your child will fall down; it will, but it has got to learn how not to. Comfort it if disaster occurs and help arrange soft falling places if you can, or stand by ready to catch. But don't always prevent. Don't force a baby to walk longer than it wants to or before it wants to. Encourage.

Reason: Jumping and stamping lead to an interest in athletics later and are the basis of Child Dance. They are the first steps towards personal style and discovery of personal bodily rhythm which helps to save energy throughout life and may affect ability in cricket, tennis, football, and so forth in years to come. Forcing brings distaste and occasionally does some physical harm.

The adult can: Take an interest in the kinds of jumping and stamping. Occasionally join in, in time, occasionally to a different time. Don't imply that the child is wrong. Think sometimes in terms of question or statement and answer. Stamp back. The child will generally stamp again (this is the parallel in personal play to noise-making with objects). Use objects sometimes yourself, and mix the two kinds of play. Inspire the child to further movement by the sounds you make. This is the C-A-T of messages in sound. It is more important than the piano to start with. Longer sentences of sound should come later.

Allow: The occasional shouting and spitting and blah-blah talk of babies and very young children. Not when older.

Reason: It is part of the discovery of lung power, feeling the palate and search for diction and 'placing forward' of speech.

The adult can: Answer sometimes in blah-blah talk. You can carry on emotional conversations of supreme gaiety or of purple-faced seriousness even with babies this way, and a strong bond of understanding is built for short moments. Occasionally put in a real word. Repeat it.

Later the child will use it and extend its tiny vocabulary. Base all speech and music and communication on a *deep love of sound*. This is what leads to a really intelligent taste in literature later. It is the true way to genuine appreciation of poetry. Too much jogging up and down and use of sentimental rhyming jingles leads to 'versification', which is different, and to some understanding of time beat. It does *not* lead to an appreciation of live rhythm and true poetic perception.

Allow: The making up of odd new words. Don't call them rubbish.

Reason: This creation starts because of interest in language. 'Real' words are equally loved later.

The adult should: Accept new words. Learn to recognise the good ones. Some are very descriptive. Keep a few as family words and use them. They form a bond of 'home' between the family members.

Allow: Games about cowboys and gangsters and some dressing-up (as the children grow out of the toddler stage). Do not scorn it at home or make fun of it before visitors.

Reason: This is the real stuff. This is the drama by which an extension of vocabulary for expressing ideas is developed, by which emotions are thrown out, and in which a child tries all sorts of personalities until he discovers his own. He tries out *life* and finds himself. He creates a great art form of acting, too, both amusing and beautiful.

The adult should: Understand that your child is not a potential delinquent because a lot of killing happens during play. He or she is overcoming the imagined adversary. You want your child to win battles in life, don't you? This is practice and preparation for it. Long may they overcome! Take it seriously. If a child speaks to you as if you were subject to its kingship, you are being offered a confidence. Answer as a courtier should and keep the sincerity there; the better you behave, the better will you teach how one *should* behave in appropriate moments in life, which is being practised very deeply at these moments.

If you have a record player, put on music with pronounced time beat or exciting passages in it, during the acting. The music will inspire. Don't be upset if children talk while it is on. They should talk in their drama. They only draw on the sound emotionally at first. Later suggest a march-tune for part of a march round, and so on. Better still, just put it on when they *are* marching, and be ready to take the sound off when they have finished. You will become more and more clever at this by practice and, as you get to know Child Drama better, you will learn to guess their needs in advance. It is useful to have these categories of music by you: cheerful, exciting, sad and calm.

Finish up with 'cheerful' if the children seem moderately exhausted, or if you can still carry on giving them of your time and self after the game. Otherwise use 'calm'. This will often quieten them and they will be more likely to run off and play amongst themselves quietly. You will be aiding the teacher at school, too. For a sensible teacher will always finish a session of Child Drama with a calm feeling so as to prepare children for *projected* activity in the form of three-R work. You will be preparing children for this experience or helping to establish the good habit.

Allow: Other children to join yours in Child Drama if they want to and if you think you can manage them.

Reason: Children learn tolerance by playing together. By proper use of Child Drama you will teach them to be obedient, too, by arranging for their emotional activity to take place in a legitimate way under sympathetic supervision rather than by trying to dominate them. So many children are longing for this, without quite knowing it. All children need it. Many have homes or parents that make the whole business difficult. Sometimes the whole atmosphere of a street or village can be changed by one kindly imaginative grown-up arranging times for drama of this kind. If you become interested in this kind of play, a golden rule is: if there is a need, *the grown-up may suggest what to do; but don't show how to do it.*

Don't interrupt play. Talk about an episode afterwards if the children wish.

Some 'Don'ts'

Don't give your children too many expensive toys. Give paints, paper and simple things. Give them happiness.

Don't encourage showing off. Share success. Don't watch it too much.

Don't encourage ideas of theatre in early years. Everybody works in Child Drama. There is normally no audience. An audience brings self-consciousness.

Don't force a child to take part. Encourage.

Don't clear up things too regularly without thought. Notice if things are arranged in a pattern. A child may want to come back to it.

Don't ridicule any dramatic oddity or attempt at dance.

Don't thoughtlessly discuss your children with other adults. They have ears. They can be hurt.

Don't use puppets too much. The child himself needs to act.

Don't think your child must automatically be sent to a theatre school, ballet mistress or tap-dance expert, because it indulges in dramatic play. Grace can be achieved by practice in the child's own form of imaginative dance. Those other things, as with all formal work, are not fundamentals but perfections. They do not suit everybody and may give some children the wrong idea.

Some 'Do's'

Be thoughtful over possible jealousy of a first born.

Do leave strange things stuck in odd places if you can without too much untidiness. Father will know how he feels when his study or workroom is tidied, and everything put neatly where he can't find it. What would you feel if you were a 'cowboy' and someone pinched the rope you had hung on the armchair or tree? The cows might escape. Then what? Make a mental note and see things are collected at the end of the day. Tidiness can be learned without sorrow.

Do provide a room for children to be apart from adults some of the time if you possibly can, where they can leave a few things 'to be continued' next day.

Over quarrels, make a judgment. You may not be Solomon, but unsettled situations fester.

Do allow young children a moment or two to finish what they are doing if they are deeply immersed in a task. You will learn to judge whether they are intentionally being disobedient or merely absorbed. The latter is no sin, it is a virtue. Later they can learn to snap out of it more easily.

Do let children take up their own grouping during play. It will be all about the room or garden and a circle will often be formed. Places of far distance may be quite close in this drama. Avoid saying things like 'Don't turn your backs', as if you were dealing with proscenium theatre.

Do encourage children to improvise their speech and stories.

Do be ready for a quick change of character. Avoid laughing if a five-year-old becomes five different people or things in a matter of seconds. If you are asked to be a sign-post or a nail – *be* it.

Do refrain from laughing at the wrong moment (if by any chance you are asked to attend a school play). You destroy sincerity of portrayal and absorption in the acting and the atmosphere of the play. It is hard enough for any children under eleven years of age to attain these things in formal work, anyway. Don't make it harder.

Do try to learn a little about ray-guns and outer-space language. Don't be disapproving. You will cut yourself off from their confidence if you are (it may all become true in their lifetime, anyway), but will surprise and please them as an unexpected companion if you learn it. You may become the good gang leader, the leader all juniors unconsciously need. It is not always their fault if they come under the sway of a bad one. It may be the only one they meet. You cannot and should not quite take the place of a young leader, but you can show an example of good pattern.

Do encourage your children to be interested in life and beauty.

Encourage them to be clean and polite on appropriate occasions and at the same time to be courageous and virile. These attitudes arise largely from parental influence and home background. Avoid saying things like: 'Oh, I shouldn't do that, dear'. Are you one of those? Think hard. Get into the habit of considering what is the reason for the child *not* to do that. Was it just that you would be disturbed? One can learn to be positive: 'All right, dear. Try'. Such is the home which produces the confident adult. In a somewhat decadent world, modern life is crying out for a generation which will do and dare and take responsibility. Let your children say: 'I'll try anything once'. Your job is to help them to see what is sensible, to try it and to succeed.

Games

With Babies

Peep Bo! But don't put your face too close to theirs suddenly. Don't remain hidden long.

Make funny people with your hands.

Toddlers and Older Children

Carry on a conversation in noises only.

Pull the ugliest face you can think of and act a story about it. (Or the nicest face.)

Don't stay ugly long.

Tell a story round a circle of people, each one carrying on quickly from the next. Act it afterwards if desired.

Describe things in the room, a sort of 'I Spy'. But when you come to it pull a face or make a noise instead of saying the thing. We must guess what it is. Elaborations can take place, too. Example: 'I spy with my little eye...' or 'Je perceive avec mon grand space lamp (a horrible face is here pulled) over a (slam noise)'. It will turn out that the object is a clock or picture over the door.

Dolls' tea-parties or royal feasts.

Puppet tea parties and/or Olympic Games (not in a theatre. All about the room).

Cut out simple paper-masks. Cut away nose, eyes and mouth. Put on masks. Dab paint on nose and mouth. Take off the masks. Act what the extraordinary resulting people with coloured faces remind you of. Of course, the masks might have started things off. But children generally discard the masks if they are full ones, because they are too hot and difficult to see through.

Beat a drum or a box and kill an enemy at each 'konk'. Kill them hard. Overcome the *whole world* and all your troubles.

Get children to give you ideas in one or two words. Make up a short story to act from the ideas. Put on a record or cassette and

    (1) let people be what they think;

(2) tell a story about what the music says;

(3) just dance the story in your own way.

Hold a Red Indians' feast. Dressed-up war dances after tea to drum-beats and music.

Hold a gymkhana in the garden, with pretend horses and real jumps (and sweets or dandelions for prizes, if you are doing the whole affair properly).

Hold a motor-race meeting to hot jazz and a megaphone (bicycles, scooters, soap-boxes, barrows, etc., for outside. Just yourselves for inside).

Hold a pirates' regatta.

Have a painting party.

Hold a policeman's sausage party. (It can give certain children quite a different and improved idea of the Law.)

Hold a tea-party to meet the first 'Spacemen'. (Atomic pop will be laid on. Please bring your space guns.)

Other parties: Paper cutting, mask making, clay modelling and plasticine party (bring your own blobs).

Act stories out of a newspaper, book or magazine.

Consider acting stories out of the Bible, or from other faiths.

As the drama improves, you will be able to pop in an extra idea from them or yourself every now and again to enrich the whole creation. With a little dressing-up, some music added, and as long as you have fostered the qualities of sincerity and absorption, you will begin to perceive a grave innocence of demeanour and a grace of movement, a consideration for others and a sense of constructive cooperation. In all these types of play, you are helping children to get away from over-indulgence in TV watching or eternal computer addiction.

It will be realised, of course, that there are many people these days who live in crowded homes and for whom many of the above ideas would not be possible, or suitable. So, as in all suggestions, one selects and chooses only what *is* suitable or appears possible and appropriate. And again, none of them may work! I can only say they worked for me. One of the main sad thoughts I would have is that, in crowded places, leaving the objects in position after *projected* play would be difficult. In such homes there might be a sort of eternal mess or a desperate strict tidying up. So, going back in order to play with the objects – 'to carry on' – is not easily possible. And of course there is no room for much personal play at all. So it is even more important that it all happens in school. In better-off homes, I have noticed – if father becomes interested in model railways, after buying a small set for a child at Christmas, he is not prepared to pull those wretched rails apart each night, put them back in a box, pat the engine goodbye, or goodnight, each time and 'learn to be tidy'. He probably goes in for a wider gauge, so the engines won't fall off the track, gets a separate room if possible, involves electricity; and nails down the rails. *He* is not going to have his *projected* play interfered with! He has projected too much excitement and enthusiasm into, onto and around his track. The memorial of his doing is jolly well going to stay there without interference, so he can return to it unhindered and renew his new heart-throb addictions in happy memory where he left off.

Perhaps one should not end this section without underlining two points; about blah-blah talk and about Near Finish.

Blah-Blah Talk

For the baby and very young child, recognition of communication comes in this manner. The baby says 'Blah, blah' You say 'Blah-blah'. The baby, encouraged, says 'Blah-blah spit' *You* say 'Blah-blah spit'. The child may then do the same more urgently, with a certain raising of the body, rather like one does on a horse, which is trotting. Best of all – you *may* be rewarded with a seraphic grin. It is like the sun bursting through early morning mist. Communication has begun.

To develop language, one puts in a real word, as in 'Blah-blah-de-dum'. You answer, adding a real word, say 'Blah-blah-de-dum-dog' and point, if there is one. Try then 'Blah-blah-dog'. Repeat once or twice, but don't become a bore. One day, one of your words will be copied and included in this strange early language. There will be obvious rejoicing on both sides. But most important of all there will have been *communication*. It may teach the adult something too.

How sad it is, when attitudes in a family stiffen. One too often hears the words 'Of course, I could never really talk to my father'. Could indulging in blah-blah talk help the grown one to unbend, as well as the small one to speak? In a shopping queue the other day, a young mother had a young boy in a wheeled contrivance just behind me. I was just paying my due when the boy said (in language developed almost to the point of speech) something like 'Per-domb-pot-per-dom-stot!' with some finality. I turned and said very solemnly 'Oh, do you really think so?' (Because, obviously, he *did*.) It just happened that he then nodded. For some reason the whole queue was convulsed with laughter. Interesting moment.

Near Finish

The point is to realise and to notice that the child is deeply absorbed in play (more likely *projected*) and it is unwise, possibly even no good, to say things like, 'Right, it's lunch now. Come along' (slight pause) 'I said come along' (child still absorbed). '*Did* you hear what I said? Get up at once when I tell you and stop messing about.' So, slightly bewildered, the child may then do somewhat what is expected. My point is, as has been said earlier, do consider the importance of, and how deep is, the absorption. One can say 'It is going to be lunch time soon' (pause for some continued play). 'I'm putting things on the table now, start to finish what you are doing.' Then finally – as you really notice whether the child is coming out of its dream at the *near finish* of what it is being (in *personal play*) or more likely doing (in *projected* play), 'Right, come on now' – and mean it. I cannot stress too much how important this absorption in play can be, for a future habit of study and learning, as well as what one learns during the pleasure of play itself.

Both the 'now' and the 'then' are important. Deep pleasure in the 'now' is a good mental aid to avoidance of depression. If we can develop as a habit the ability to forget for a while our worries, by enjoyment in the 'now', it strengthens us, after emerging from our play dream (unreality) to face the fears of the future 'then' (reality). Adults often read novels for this reason, 'takes your mind off'. Some children go quite deeply into their concentration, but not always. Others may *not* do it generally, but then suddenly they do. So it is really important just to be aware of all this, to notice, to think about what is happening, to be considerate and decide correctly when is the need to be patient, whilst avoiding disobedience; to employ *near finish*.

Some General Points

Babies need to be picked up when they cry and given love and help. But they can get into a habit of it. There will be some difficult decisions to be made about whether it needs changing, is in pain or just trying it on. Not to be picked up, when needed, brings a feeling of lack of love, which can continue into later years.

When playing peep-bo, don't put your face too close. It can either be a bit frightening or go out of focus. Hugging is different, you are not expecting eye attention to focus in the same way. It is no wonder that the first people children draw or paint, in their own way, are like large suns, with rather unimportant legs and arms. All they see of other humans in their first part of life is a huge face, which looms over them. In any sort of 'hullo games' of me 'in' your life or 'out' of your life (say, behind fingers), don't disappear too long. It may cause anxiety. But finish with a hug. It is over now, and more safe to leave the room. One awkward thing is that babies and toddlers sometimes play with their own excreta. Do be careful that your own horror, despair or anger does not take over. If you are not there and the child gets bored, it doesn't know what to do with it and doesn't really know why it's there or what it is. So it begins to play with the mess and scribble, so to speak, as if it were paint. In cases of unhappy families, broken homes; or basically nice but severely overstressed parents; step fathers who don't understand and so on; this can be the beginning of violence. If any one is tempted – SEEK HELP.

The same goes for bed-wetting. There is always a reason. It may be physical, but quite often it is due to anxiety of one kind or another (as is stealing). The last thing one should do, despite the enormous inconvenience, is to fly into a rage and, not only smack, but bring ridicule on the 'offender', or impose increasing penalties for repetition. Many are the reasons for the situation, but they can include unhappiness at school, unhappiness over a brother or sister's behaviour, loss of a parent (brother or sister, home), or just fear. Careful and kindly discussion is needed; and comfort. It is something children can grow out of. But, if prolonged, see a doctor.

In First Schooling

Do not be surprised if there are worries and tears. Don't be impatient, console but try to build up confidence and courage. However, from early days (and at home) train them not to be late. Being always late is bad-mannered and very inconvenient to other people – it might later mean losing a job. A little later, there are new problems in these modern times.

Junior children (seven to eleven) are becoming sophisticated much earlier; often too early, one might think. It may be partly that sex instruction is more widely given and partly that there is more copying of teenagers than ever before. At the moment, the figures for families with 'no man in the house' are unexpectedly high. One or other parent suddenly departs. Uncles come to live. Sometimes they are bad-tempered. There are fewer family role models therefore, so the fashion is to ape brothers and sisters, or older school fellows. Fashion is thus in the 'up-glance', sophistication oozes down.

Other worse things happen than the cost of special types of shoe. And, by the way, if *all* parents stuck out against them, this ridiculous rip-off over cost and style would vanish. So would the ridicule, unkind remarks or sheer bullying in, or out of, school, for those not 'in fashion' – clothes, hair, shoes or boots. It is an abuse of freedom. Stronger rules about uniforms may have to come in to help; as also to spot truancy. But, of course, determined absconders will tear off any uniform and steal alternative clothing.

One of these 'worse' things, of course, is drugs (watch out for violent changes of mood, over dreamy attitude, insistent staying in bed, stealing money and headaches). Also very early sex and porn. The danger of very young girls becoming more sophisticated is that they become more sexually attractive, either in clothes, movements or habits. Sores at mouth or nose may mean glue-sniffing.

Girls tend to smoke more than boys, too, and this is becoming a bravado-habit in younger and younger children. It is a dare, particularly if you know it is bad for you. 'Aren't I brave?' No. Unfortunately, the older films on TV nearly all show people smoking, particularly glamorous ladies. The violence affects boys more. In search of role models (possibly for reasons stated above) or in the difficult search we all have to find 'who I really am', they think it is macho to be uncivilised. Apart from magazines, it is becoming known that a generation that seems to know, almost by instinct, about computers can switch in to porn on apparently innocent cassettes. Very young children can run upstairs and see things that would widen our eyes. These programmes also rouse hidden instincts and deaden sympathy in the young. Watch out for this – it will have to be in your own way – but be firm; anyway, about how much TV is watched, quite apart from *what* is watched. But remember there is a lot of unthoughtful talk (almost wishful thinking), about violence *seen* not having any great influence. This is a disaster. Evil seeps in, drip by drip, until finally one feels it is the norm.

Although much information is taught these days about sex, it is often given in a sort of hard, matter-of-fact way – possibly to avoid embarrassment. It is not always associated with relationships. This somewhat encourages early experiments in sex, to the downfall of many young girls and the resentment, maybe, of unexpected fathers.

Care of Skin

This is extremely important for adolescents. No one can know (or perhaps remember) what agonies some young people go through over this and over spots. At the very time when people are being attracted by the opposite sex (or, these days, more openly with each other), they suffer the pain and what they fear is repulsiveness. In both sexes a lot of time can be spent in front of mirrors and surprising hair styles appear. Fortunately, there are many skin preparations now which offer aid over spots. I hope they work. Girls may even begin to suffer from agoraphobia because of spots and refuse to go out, refuse to go to social occasions. And boys, in despair, can go to macho extremes and pretend they don't care for girls or anyone else, because of this affliction. They become withdrawn, or drink beer instead and shave their heads. I have often wondered why it so often seems that the nicest boys have the most spots. Poor girls, a lot of nice husbands must be lost that way. All adolescents will become difficult and moody. But the time *does* pass. They are going through not only the almost intolerable mixture of physical changes, but the eternal vexed question of 'Who the hell *am* I?' In discovery of this, there may be a revolt against authority and against parents. But don't forget; the deeper the real love for parents (and parents for children), the bigger has to be the kick to get away from that love-knot. Those young people who come through this period fairly easily should consider themselves lucky. There are some. With all the openness of sex information in many schools, in *some* schools it does not take place, or does, but in a very dainty degree. So, parents, the task is even more difficult now to find out what your young know. For, believe it or not, there are still some girls who are terrified at the first sight of monthly blood and boys who want to commit suicide over the embarrassment of a wet dream.

Worse still, they may have dreamed about somebody in the night and, when the day dawns, behold, they are in love! It can be an extremely strong feeling. They don't know they are probably not in love really (they may be), but next time it will probably be with someone else. But the experience can lead to sex trials with unfortunate consequences, because there is still a widely held superstition (which needs squashing) that you don't get a baby 'the first time', nor if you do 'it' standing up. Reports about AIDS in some parts of the world recommend more sex education. I hope it respects relationships.

We are living in very changed and often difficult times. We can only try hard and do our best for our children. Sometimes the pace of change may appear so fast that you don't know what to do. But don't be overwhelmed by the idea that you must give them all the things you didn't have yourself. Simple things are often better for young children than expensive toys. A box is loved and useful, just for putting things in and can itself turn into many different things by the power of child magic.

Until lately, I had a little tin box in which (when I was young), a dilapidated sugar-mouse used to 'go to Africa' each morning for some years, before breakfast. It is lost now and I miss it. If children kick or are violent, *talk* to them and try to get them to help you. Parents should play with their children, from quiet play in babyhood to well known games later. When I was six, my father came back from Egypt at the end of the first World War and, as I explained elsewhere (Slade 1968) 'I played cricket with a moustache and braces in the garden'. That's all I knew or noticed about him on first acquaintance. But I enjoyed the cricket, and his presence. Summing up: because of the changes in the world and our own society, things are more difficult.

But deep down, children are the same. Their needs and norms remain as they used to be; and play in all its aspects is still important, perhaps even more strongly so, in order to counteract other influences. And talking of other influences. There may be bullying at school. There is a very nice idea of a Children's Court being set up *in* school. The judges are the children themselves, who sometimes have a greater ability to influence those who are stepping out of line than the adults in their midst. The danger is, of course, of some secret semi-lawful bullying. But reasonable communication with teachers should avoid this, though some autonomy must be allowed. The same idea was used by A.S. Neil from many years ago, also by Lyward in his Sussex Centre.

If you are the slightest bit worried over possible bullying, or suspect anything else might be going wrong at school, go and see the Head. Don't wait and think whether you want to avoid wasting his/her time. As one fine man said on TV lately, parents should not worry about being a bother, 'That's what I'm here for'. However, on the other hand, don't leave too much training to the school alone to do. But *be* interested. So, if you are still worried, even after seeing the Head, ask about organisations that exist to help, such as Kidscape and others. You are not alone.

Oh, by the way, if your child is unhappy at school (and even if they are not), they may invent an unseen friend and talk to them. It is unlikely that your child is mad; more probably they are lonely. (You can even be lonely in a large family if you don't get on with your siblings.) Don't ridicule this or forbid it. If they are sane, they will grow out of it. Our main problem, in a non sentimental way is to preserve innocence. As Libby Purves (that remarkable lady) said lately, 'Innocence needs to be fought for'.

Lastly, again one must say: Don't make too many rules. But the ones you do make *must* be kept. Society needs this elementary understanding of law and order. Again – don't admire all advice just because it is 'new'; the old is often best. We must not be afraid of being occasionally unpopular.

If it does not sound too pompous, I would repeat the last words of a talk I gave on 'Parent Attitude', at a course at Wentworth Castle in Yorkshire, also at St David's in Wales and in a number of London Clinics. 'You will do this because I love you and even if you hate me for making you do it, I will still love you'.

If you have a Faith, take your children into it. If you have not, do not ridicule God. At least teach them to do to others as they would wish to be done by.

And Now the Separation

There may be regrets on both sides. The final parting may be soft and kind, hard, or even angry. Don't forget the love kick, which may have to be hard in some cases. Have we tried blindly to make our children too much what we wanted them to be, a pale copy of ourselves; or our imagined hopes? Have we clung to them too much? If so, they may never have full confidence in themselves. Yet, have we been *there* for them when they needed us? Have we allowed them to grow up at their own pace and largely in their own way, but with some caring guidance, and in a secure background? If so, they have some chance of breaking naturally free and discovering in a balanced way who they really are, and how to cope with LIFE.

Out of School Play and Fulfilment

We have spoken of things 'outside of me' becoming invested with importance and even love. But they can be used also for working off hate.

Example: 'That brick is wicked, I'll have to smack him. And if he's not good then, I'll stand on 'im. He's very rude. Keep 'im in prison.' In this particular case, the child (girl, five years) kept the brick in prison for some days. It was kept for hating. Better that the brick be hated than a person. If the hated thing is taken away – out of adult concern – animosity may start *for* a person; or sulky behaviour may begin. Again, with a boy of six years, whose greatest friend was a rather battered toy monkey (Jacko), he was given a clean new monkey by a truly loving mother, because the old one was so 'untidy'. The new one was admired for a time, but slowly affection waned and resentment took its place. Finally the mother discovered the child had tied up the new monkey and was beating him with the 'help' of the old monkey. 'Well, he was horrid to Jacko', explained the child. The mother was horrified and feared that her son was going to be a dangerous delinquent. Not so, of course. It was natural that she should be sad and alarmed; and a bit hurt that her gift had become an object of hate. But, on the plus side, think how important it was that the child retained his loyalty to his old friend, and reacted strongly to anyone trying to demean him, or take his place. The boy grew up to be quite a normal, rather kind man. The child's drama offers many opportunities for blowing off steam. The whole play urge, containing love, hate and all experience, if not allowed and fully provided for, will have expressions in other ways. Even adults talk of 'Taking it out of so and so' and 'Don't take it out on me just because…'.

From earlier times we have another example of played out hate (though here it was consciously linked with an individual) in the realm of witchcraft when wax images were stuck with pins, with the intention that evil happenings should occur to the hated one.

The child is usually not so conscious as this. It is, however, aware of the pleasure of hating things, and realises that drama adds to the joys of persecution, without necessarily recognising any person or circumstance that may have been the original cause of displeasure. The child is a great artist in witchcraft turning anything or anybody, into anything or anybody at any time – although white wizardry is usually the power employed.

Sometimes a cause for displeasure is deeply hidden and the therapist has to delve gently until things come to the surface. Nor should the parent or teacher find themselves in shock, if some stark pictures of life-background appear in play. Are we, the intelligent adults, afraid to face what the child has to face? It should help us to know what is going on – for instance, play at home about what happens at school. And sometimes very important, play at school about what happens at home. Allow for some caricature, though. Don't leap to conclusions too fast. Play about classrooms nearly always includes a very strict teacher, who is rude, cruel, sarcastic, or violent. One tiny voice sometimes dares to ask a dangerous question. How did this 'ever-recurring' symbol in the unconscious ever come to be there? Perhaps it's just a natural anti-authority lark, eh? It is often balanced up by over-strict parents when home situations are played out at school. So we must not jump to conclusions there either. Only prolonged confirmation of recurring symbols (which are sometimes symbols of other symbols) should give us pause to wonder. To get nearer the truth, with children who use this form of play regularly one can sometimes say (parent, or teacher): 'Bit tough, wasn't he/she! What about letting us see what school is really like?' Or, 'Home isn't *really* like that, is it?' Generally, there is a happy giggling 'No-o-o-h'. Be it understood, the ordinary teacher has not induced this play. They are not trying to pry into private homes; parents need not fear. Children just play these themes rather often, though even these are giving way more and more often to violent out-pouring of TV themes. Better out than in, though. However, Superman and Superwoman, still sometimes hold sway. How would the world manage without them? I was transfixed lately when a gentleman, in red tights and blue cloak, flew on the back of a rocket and guided atomic missiles into the sun. So thoughtful. But I didn't know his telephone number, so I couldn't thank him as I wished. By that time he was on another Planet.

Single Child Play

Often, one child playing alone with an adult can be very over organising; there is a lot of ordering about and the adult is told to do this and do that. Often we are in the wrong place and the play is very outgoing and, no doubt, valuable, but almost entirely selfish. Here is part of a descriptive report about such a situation:

> '"Battle" was an intense, violent and prolonged private game. Nellie was there (the adult), she didn't take part, but she was "with" me in spirit all the time. (Young teachers of young children could have learnt a lot from

her.) I fought, I threw cushions, I shot enemies, thousands of them. I died and died with terrible wounds and grinding groans but always rose again.' (Note: Child Drama, as mentioned, is full of the symbol of resurrection. In groups it sometimes leads to arguments: 'Yor ded,' 'I'm not.') The report continues: 'Down the years, after tea-time, I fought my war, sometimes as a ghost after being blown to bits... All I can say is that the outbursts must have had a great cathartic effect, for I have less inclination for war now.' Later this changed to more peaceful play – 'Upon the kitchen table shooting the rabbits (rapids) of Canada. Later on, Nellie did join in and was often in the way, but sometimes took paddle too in rough water.' But all warriors beware; 'Gosh it's awful to have a woman in a boat, specially if it's a canoe, they're so stupid.'

The remark was not supposed to be just anti-feminist, I am sure; it is an example of the fact that in certain situations the adult can do nothing right! Later, we learn by experience a bit more about what to do. But sometimes it is just our presence that is needed. I suggest exercises sometimes, to music, for students and older people, to enable them to discover textures and colours about a room and to rediscover a few moments of pleasure in a very simple way, either for themselves or for understanding children better. Sometimes just for a chance to be selfish for a bit!

One of the lessons from the above report is that one should take the young child's dramatic play seriously and see that it can have a perfectly natural cathartic effect. The child's discovery of its own individuality is bound up with this too (even through what may seem to the adult almost intolerable selfish imagination-events), how one expresses at all, then *what* one expresses and finally discovering that other people express too. Discovering the private empire of other people is part of learning to live with others successfully, even though it is awful at first to discover that they *want* to express and to rule *their space*. We each need our kingdom, our throne.

Hate

Another example (of hate) is that of Geoffrey. He said he hated people, hated school, hated teachers. He hated the people in his road and often ran up and down the street 'shooting' and 'bombing'. He noticed that people looked out of their windows in a disapproving way to see what the noise was about and Geoffrey soon found it was more fun, instead of throwing pretend bombs to throw actual stones, because this shattered the windows like a real bomb and these people had real blood on their faces. This was joy–hate against windows as such and he formed almost a complex about them. We had just moved into the road. G's general *single* behaviour soon attracted an admiring one or two companions, which grew into a small gang. At this point a child I knew well got into this wild group. She was six and G (I am not sure) about 11, so she fell for him. She changed in a few weeks into a screaming monster. Activities of the gang included anything from throwing stones, or beating smaller children, to rank theft. They had already encroached upon the use of my garage: 'A (the girl) said it would be all right,' I was told. In the end the only way to save the child we knew, and incidentally avoid, we thought, for the gang leader the necessity of going to an approved school, was to close the garage and open the house.

There was no Play Centre for them to be in, and apparently no adult interested enough to stop them getting into trouble.

So, for one long somewhat terrible summer holidays we felt obliged to turn our house into the gang headquarters. This was a bold and uncomfortable experiment – looking back now, I wonder how we dared do it. But we learned a lot from it.

Briefly, we (my wife and I) started a small private Child Drama Centre and ran it as a place for children to play in. By degrees we got the children off the street and interested them in sounds and movement and speech. I let G dash up and down the garden to loud drum beats, until he was tired (a dodge that came in extremely useful in later years when dealing with delinquent children at the Rea Street Centre). The neighbours were awfully good. They said they would put up with the noise and preferred someone to be doing something about it rather than having the gang in the street. As has been said, it is the wild, unguided street play that can become so dangerous. We need many places, where we can get youngsters 'in'; and then use their natural outpourings to constructive effect. By 'in', I mean a *somewhat* confined place. It is easier then to gain control. We had a house and garden walls, for instance. Outside, it would have been almost impossible to do what we hoped and intended. I instigated Red Indian attacks in the garden to 'hot swing' background music, arranging for the Indians to win. Behaviour began to get better. An old set of notes says that 'within three weeks honesty was noticeably improving' (though we lost things one way and another).

A great deal of overcoming was allowed and very energetic dance, sometimes highly imaginative. G often became peculiar animals (not too difficult, perhaps). He would hop a lot like a toad, he would jump fast like a kangaroo, he would box enemies, slay by the sword, but often be an animal unknown. *Sometimes* he would glide like a reasonable cloud, whilst other members of the gang danced as gentle dandelions and so on to Debussy. When 'War' was on, we shot a lot, and 'bombs' would sometimes be accompanied by a big bonk on the drum when the hot jazz on the record player 'told us to'.

Finally we had to give up, because the place became too popular. We could not deal with the constant stream of wistful little callers. But the little girl A was caught in the nick of time. She changed to another area after these drama experiences, and this move crowned a precarious success. I don't know what happened to Geoffrey, I can only say he improved out of all knowledge. He became calm and stopped hitting other children. He had fought so many imagined enemies that it wasn't necessary any more to hit real people. Oh, he started to attend 'a funny place' called school. More than that I don't know, because we moved too. The streets today, as I write, are too full of violent young people. We needed *numbers* of centres in past years, certainly in every big city, with staff trained in elementary dramatherapy. That we had not got them, through misunderstanding (?) or ignorance of Authorities, certainly ignorance of the skills, is the price we are paying today. Fortunately, there is more recognition now of the value of dramatherapy; but still not enough centres.[1] This is not to doubt the most valuable work done by individual therapists in this subject on individual children, often in lonely circumstances. But that is when the trouble is already *there* and may be deep-rooted. My plea is for prevention also, both in schools and in out-of-school centres. It seems ironical that Drama (not just theatre) which is concerned with the whole of the doing of life should still be taken unseriously, on the whole, by the Authorities. The value of Art and Music are increasingly, and in some places completely, recognised. But Drama is, I believe, still relegated to the somewhat inferior position of 'occupational' therapy, almost as if it is something in which you set some little task, then 'Let them get on with their imagined nonsense, I'll take notice later and see how they're getting on!' Nor is it considered the most important subject in schools. I know this is probably not true in many places, but no one who has not been in this fascinating world of drama – in theatre, education and therapy, can possibly be aware of the enormous weight you have to push uphill to get anything done, to establish the work, to get any money. Perhaps the worst obstacle is a sort of jocular prejudice that it is '*child's* play'. This is not the same – and doesn't sound the same when spoken – as 'child's *play*'. Unfortunately, of course, most of our education and therapy is in the *projected* realm and *personal play* is not so usual, nor accepted. It is a bit inconvenient, because it needs space – when other people need that space, particularly the school hall. What about empire now? But worst of all, dramatic play not only appears on occasion to be iconoclastic of dignity but, in it, it is hard to recognise *concepts*. That is its real unspoken naughtiness, so people can't judge its value. The *results* are what proves its value, in personal attitudes and behaviour. But for success in these, experience, skill and training are needed for those in charge. Also the ability to perceive distinctions. I think it was Beloc who said 'Only the finest men make the finest distinctions'. That goes for

---

1   There is an Institute of Dramatherapy

Women too, of course, who, on the whole, I often feel are better at it. But such training in depth is far to seek. Some people find it difficult to espy the elementary distinctions I make. And I *have* sometimes wondered how it was that I had to ooze myself into such a difficult profession, before its fuller recognition; in early days against, it seemed, almost impossible odds. Way back, when I started, it was a bit like trying to be a lonely (sometimes clumsy?) warrior marching very slowly forward, brandishing a flaming torch that nobody wanted to see. Indeed they might have been quite happy to see the flame put out. Fire is dangerous. And stirring of thought is uncomfortable for all of us, isn't it? So I mean this kindly.

Many years later, though, a University was trying to assess language in a Junior School. They kindly invited me to observe and possibly give an opinion. They got an elaborate marking scheme all worked out in the usual brainy pattern and then it started. But they felt it wasn't going quite right. When asked, I suggested that so far the whole test had been on written work and in an interview situation, one-to-one per child. What still had to be judged was active work in little groups of about six, the usual gang patterns of the seven- to nine-year-olds, in order to evaluate what I called Language Flow. They agreed and some Child Drama started. But suddenly they said they didn't know how to judge it. There were no formal criteria. So they suddenly gave it all to me to do. I therefore tested on vocabulary; ease of the flow of language; clarity, poetic or interesting remarks; relationships in the group; good story or interesting situation; loudness and softness, as against mere shouting by one boss. It was not all easy, because the school had been chosen because it was famous. But speech had never been practised much, as it had built up its name on dance. But one interesting thing became clear in the investigation, which one rather expected: those who did quite well in the interview and written situation were not (in any one case) those who became leaders and users of actual language in the practical sessions. Life is lived successfully very largely by good communication. And communication is the one thing given very little practice in our schools. I used to find this in Grammar schools and Private schools a lot. All those clever minds and nice young people, no doubt waiting to be our leaders in many spheres – ask them to talk about their work, give an address or make up a story and they were often at a loss. They had no Language Flow. Were they only encouraged to write and never to speak? 'Keep quiet, you, and pass your exams', I uncomfortably kept hearing in my mind – probably an echo from my own schooling. Of course, where opportunity *was*, and is now, given for clever people to practise speaking, the results were and are splendid.

As to the point I was making, particularly for teachers and therapists, about our judging the value of drama work by its results, I remember an occasion when I had managed to establish for a time the Child Drama Certificate course for teachers, nurses and social workers. As I have quoted elsewhere (Slade 1993), after the first course a Head said, 'I don't know what you will think of the drama, I hope you will think it is better. But what *have* you done to the teacher? She is keen now, seems to like children instead of being rude and impatient, stays on late and is constructive and helpful instead of arguing at meetings. She really seems to love her work. It's a miracle.'

Pete's Kitchen (forerunner of Rea Street Centre)

I was Pete. This was another small centre I started. It served for a time as a place of interest and wonder for a group of children (some very young, small) and for me. Pete's Kitchen was a large studio room, but a very special room. It was upstairs and fortunately had one sofa. This was for me. I collapsed on it when I got tired, because I could not go on acting, dancing or guiding as long as the other cooks. I mention it because I kept a list of the things used. These and what they could be used for show us the broad imaginative view and invention of the child. There was the ordinary cardboard box with smaller things in it: three pairs of brown shorts with animals' tails (I can't think where these came from); some coloured waist coats; some bright pieces of material; belts; paper hats; six wooden revolvers made from scraps of wood; some bits of tin for banging; some small bits of tin, not for banging, for wearing; some bits of wood for wands, swords and other things I had not yet learned about; a little box full of cardboard noses; a piece of a dragon; a pair of castanets; part of a mermaid's seaweed; some gold wrapping; a one-stringed fiddle; the bow of that fiddle (generally used separately) the horn from inside of an old speaker (for crashing noises, or a dragon's voice); a cymbal (for crashing noises, without a dragon's voice); other small things which varied, but bricks, stones, old bits of iron or wood would, sort of, turn up from time to time. One of *my* favourite things was a broken blind spring encased in a wide (sideways), long (up-ended) tin roller. You could rattle it or bounce it lengthwise, and it went on clanging and jumping in your hand long after you had stopped annoying it. 'It is a naughty snake really, who won't come out of the wizard's wand', I was told.

Now for what some of the other things were and what they could be used for:

Grandfather clock: Big Ben, Nelson's Column, the sun standing on a long leg, a lamp post, an oak tree, where the witch lives, the flying tadpole's house, pillar box, dungeon, grandfather clock.

Old boxes: For standing on, for eating off, making castles, throwing down to make a good noise, 'Tapping gently for being sad and when-your-friends-leave-you-or-you-leave-your-mother-or-when-a-puppy-is-hurt.'

Two small divans: For standing higher than other people, for jumping on. 'You can jump to the moon very high on these.' They made good mountains if piled on each other, and a slide at the fair. 'They are high walls to keep in naughty children.' And 'You shoot well from behind them against the enemy.' 'They are ships.'

A chair (its back twiddled): a factory, baby's cot, canteen, prison, throne, bit of a church, ogre's hat, chair.

Long green cupboard: A tree; (lying down with door open) a canoe, (with door shut) a coffin, a crocodile, a raft, a horse, a bridge, a rampart, (standing up) it was Lot's wife, turned to a pillar of salt; and 'The thin house, squashed by two trakershun engines for being wickitt'.

An old English square piano: Table, shop counter, operating-table, rabbits' house. Pandora's cigar box, organ, harp, piano.

Old gramaphone: Witch's spell machine, washing-machine, mincer, sausage machine; for playing records and learning to listen to sounds, for dancing, or 'For helping you to know what words to say'.

Baby's playpen: Tent (on side 'With things thrown over'), ladder, low wall, sheep pen, garden, part of a ship, pond, 'Me own own own room all to meself 'cos I've never 'ad it, see?' This 'room' had windows all round (looking through the bars) 'So you can see the sun whenever it smiles, see?'

Red tent: For wiping feet on, blood, disappearing cloak, parachute, and on very important occasions a red tent.

Old green curtains: Grass, blankets, tents, hammocks, table cloths, for tying up enemies, cloaks wrapping the dead, long hair, being married in, and when hung on special wooden beams, they were part of a tree.

Brown drainpipe: For looking through, speaking into, calling down with a funny voice, 'For being bigger than you are' (by shouting into), waste paper basket, clown's roller, 'Trakershun engine', cannon, trunk of a tree when the green curtains were hung on it as leaves.

Green oil-drum: Tea urn, high stool, table, ship's funnel, to roll about, to kick in time to music, cannon, lectern.

Fireguard: Breastplate, gunfire, thunder, gate.

Red candlestick: Drinking horn, headdress, candlestick.

Large black pot with tap in it: Tea urn, petrol pump, 'Place where the sea comes from', witch's cauldron, pirates' treasure casket, milk bar machine, lemonade holder, bath filler, air pressure pump for blowing up tyres, for blowing up babies ('Like a balloon, so they grow quicker'), babies' feeding machine. (It is still in my present garage today!).

Big red and black box: For standing on, sitting on, hiding in, drowning your enemy in, banging for guns, and eating off the red bit if you are happy and off the black bit if you are sad. 'It tells the weather too.' When the red side was showing it would be fine and when the black was showing, you must 'Quickly-very-fast-hurry-home 'cos of the big storm coming.' 'And it rained. But Noah was safe wasn't he, because of the Ark?'

The cardboard noses and half masks I made and adapted from basic designs of the Commedia dell'Arte. It seemed better for a number of reasons, chiefly because children can speak better with the mouth free, or nearly so. And these masks are less hot for vigorous adventures. Full masks were used too, to help them experience head angles and for improving speech by very reason of the difficulty (in a mask). But half-masks were used more in play for which they were to get well into the skin. The children seemed to get their best out of these. They gave the little actors character, but enough of themselves was still visible for them to have to act hard too. The half mask becomes more of *oneself* the *whole* mask changes one's whole personality. One extra thing was of benefit, I felt afterwards. As I am not very good at *projected* play, the results of my mask-making (particularly in trying to 'copy' the Commedia) were not very good. Almost a joke. They had a sort of primitive look. Almost a success for the wrong reason. But being somewhat naive, they evened out rather more appropriately with the little people and their creative needs. Rather than looking adult-clever, they matched childhood somehow.

It will be more easily understood, in these days, that there were no script plays in Pete's Kitchen. The spells were all brewed up in improvised play, it was genuine Child Drama. I joined in often, as this was a small group and more of a 'home place'. I was rather a surrogate father. Sometimes I only popped in a word to keep the action going. This might be the same in therapy too, at times. But in schools and in *large* out-of-school groups, I generally advise that the teacher, or the guider, keeps out of it and only occasionally instigates or provides sound (for atmosphere). Our main task here is to *observe*. If you don't watch, you can't *possibly* know what is going on in the group, how individuals are developing, what one ought to do next, what they *need* next, nor even what piece of music should be used in the evolving creation. You can't read, as it were, the *body speech* in dance. You can't see how beautiful it is either, if you are lumbering about in the middle of it all, trying to avoid knocking people over. Our footsteps are bigger than theirs. Unless we are more or less still, we create the wrong rhythm.

Although there were a lot of properties in Pete's Kitchen, they were not always used. The best work, as in school, was often done when the least dressing up took place. With a lot of dressing up, it sometimes becomes more of a mannequin parade and action is impeded by things too heavy, or too long, or fall-offish. These children had ample opportunities to use what they liked but did not always do so. They used the big furniture more, as the list implies. The great point was that they did not just pretend to be actors and play at acting, which often happens when children are put on a stage. When adults may have unintentionally influenced them too early. It is not possible to describe all that was done, but the imaginative use of furniture gives some idea. There was no stage, just space; no audience, no axe to grind, no money to be made, no grown-up to titter to disturb the acting, no showing off, no worries, no clapping, nothing done for propaganda. It was not a social event. It was all done for the right reason. We were absorbed in creating real Child Drama, because we loved it and because we felt (we actually *experienced*) that we were creating something wonderful and beautiful. We worked *very hard*, because we wanted to. It was the sort of acting you can't buy. Pete's Kitchen was a protection place, a warm nest. It was an Ark too, in the storm of life. 'But Noah was safe wasn't he, because of the Ark?' Yes, in that honoured club I felt safe too. It was all this, no doubt, which influenced my determination to have a bigger place and a training place too, the outcome of which was to be that historic marvel, the Rea St. Centre, in the Digbeth area of Birmingham. And talking of being appropriate, I didn't know till just lately that Digbeth meant 'the breath of a Dragon'!

Down the years I have often been asked 'how do you start one of these places?' (Mostly from Australia, Canada and Sweden in the past. Now occasionally, from Spain and Portugal – oh and once from China). I generally say, 'Don't worry if you can't get any backing at first. Talk to a few parents, gather a few children and *begin*. Don't think about it too long. Just start. If you are successful, people will notice and things develop.' I was often asked also, 'How did you and what made you begin?' More of that later. But most of it appeared in the book *Experience of Spontaneity* (Slade 1968).[2]

Thinking of it afterwards, the acting at Pete's Kitchen had about it a certain quality and at times 'a moment'. This moment I have experienced in adult theatre sometimes, in some awful Repertory, or a London theatre, or unexpected place. Suddenly, at about 10.30 or 11.00 in the morning, during a dreadful rehearsal, the miracle happens. It is almost a spiritual feeling and I have found myself saying to me: 'My God, that's it. My *God*, that's good; oh, God that's marvellous! It will never be the same again.' And it isn't. Note, at these times there was no audience. It was creation for creation's sake, an *Out-flow* of beauty.

---

2   Still to be found in the Durham University Drama in Education Library, in the Manchester University John Rylands Museum and Research Centre and, I am told, in the Victoria and Albert, National Theatre section.

When actors in some of my companies down the years have been despondent and said things like 'This is awful, I'm sorry, I can't really do it properly without an audience'. I have sometimes said 'Oh, come on. Try and make something true and wonderful *now* just for the joy of it, just for us in the group. The angels are watching anyway.'

Not only is it worth trying to make 'moments' but it is important to recognise them when they occur.

Figure 1 A wild mustang . The author's younger daughter Clare, at Whitmore House

Figure 2 'Land ahoy!' Reaside Drama
Playground, Birmingham

Figure 3 The Queen in her carriage.
Adventure Playground, Lambeth

School Years and Continued Growth

It is to be hoped that there will be a continuation of Nursery Schools and Playcentres. The first offer important opportunities for first steps away from family, for standing on your own feet, sharing and first group relationships, as well as many other things. Despite the very good and helpful work that belongs to them, I used to find over-dependence on the Wendy House and use of expensive toys instead of simple things being about the place. Going under a table creates a house in imagination, whereas the Wendy House is so often used merely for Hinterland play, where children merely go to be out of sight and obtain privacy from the crowd. That is, after they have had the first joy of 'real small house', which wears off after a time. But those in charge are often hindered by regulations. Sometimes children are not allowed to go under a table in case they get hurt (oh, dear, the flying antics of Pete's Kitchen). There is very seldom much *personal play* that I found. It was nearly all *projected* stuff, and mostly with expensive toys. Instead of having and/or encouraging simple things for discovery of sound, there was often a pile of tambourines and other expensive instruments. And when music started, someone might play on a piano and everyone would then beat something till they were blue in the face and grinning their heads off. They would then be encouraged to sing in that strange, sweet out-of-tune whine, which belongs only to places of that ilk. It was not music at all, really. It was a dead time-beat noise, largely to fill in time. I remember asking one youngish Guardian of the troops, 'What are you doing this for?' Her answer was 'Well…well, it is what everyone does. You've got to fill their time haven't you'. A statement that last bit, not a question. I am sure things are more purposeful now.

Occasionally I had the opportunity of trying to do something more constructive, but it took so long to clear away the expensive toys that there was hardly time for much *personal* play at *being* things, at the very time that they needed activity, when just at the age of learning how to use their legs without falling over and becoming less afraid of space. Many of the rooms I visited, up and down the country, were fairly small, which was good, because at that age there is a need for security and a large room can be alarming. But there would generally have been enough room for at least a little space exploration, through dancing and being things and the appropriate 'journeys' associated with them.

It might be better to have more out-flow. There is very 'comfy' (are you sitting comfortably?) reading *to* them (in-flow) but not very much simple short story-making by *them*. There could have been more conversation going on between the children and staff, particularly in play centres I don't mean interfering or obstructing play, but being positively interested. In one very small place there was really only room for climbing. It was rather like a green house with climbing 'plants' everywhere (highly coloured ladders and climbers of another nature). I went quietly up to one absorbed little lady (having noticed that the big lady in charge just sat, smiling and occasionally looking around). Getting very close and speaking in almost a whisper to avoid interference I said 'What's happening, would you tell me what you're doing?' No reply. 'Are you a balloon?' She was so obviously not, that I hoped to provoke an answer. I wanted her to be sure that I wouldn't think her silly too. It worked. There was a sort of snort and a half grin, but still in a quiet voice like mine she said, 'Na-ow, I'm a mun-ki'. 'Ah,' I said, 'do you live here?' 'No, see, I'm on 'ollidy'. There then followed quite a long description of her 'home' and her parents (monkeys still, but I wondered if they were symbols of reality). It was a lovely time and I remember it in some detail. In our whisper-talk, it was as if we were sharing the secrets of the whole world.

With shy children, or those in a situation where one does not wish to invade, I always begin by talking very quietly. One of the embarrassments of life is when other people *listen* and laugh in the wrong place. It makes you blush all over, either for the child, for yourself, or both. I had a young relation, who was very shy and I always spoke to her, at meals, like that. We sat next to each other and had long half-whispers. It helped us both, because I am very shy too and I know how she felt. To this day, it is easier for me to speak to three hundred people than go out to dinner with six. Committees are terrible. Not the people, the event. I don't mean to knock Nursery Schools, for they do a lot of very valuable work. But the assessment by a number of school Heads was that the most useful ones were those attached to an Infant School, so that (without destroying independence) they could be supervised as part of a whole. Smooth-over would be easier, children would know the Head before entry to the bigger place; and methods and attitude, with many things would be similar.

I would just like there to be more *personal* play, more constructive sound-making and more verbal communication. I am sure all these things are improving. One thing worried me quite a lot. When so many of the young come from poor homes in some areas, was it right that there should be so many rich toys at school? Would it not have been wiser, and anyway ultimately happier-making, to learn how to gain pleasure from simple things? Were we back to 'let them have all the things I couldn't have?' Would they miss them at home and be dissatisfied? Indeed there *were* troubles sometimes, when children wanted to take things home.

As to Play Centres, these are becoming more and more necessary with the growth of one parent families and mothers everywhere going out to work. Some of the ones I have seen could be compared with what has just been said and in most, but not all, the occupation is concerned with *projected* play. But there are new substances these days and ideas to charm the youthful mind. For instance, I did not have the pleasure of 'slime'.

The Developing Person in the Infant School

Do not allow yourself to be perplexed by the pendulum swing, which happens from time to time, in education. Keep your mind bravely on the conviction that Play is important and you will press for it and somehow find time for it. There is a feeling that things have become a little too free at the moment and it is true that the formal teaching of subjects has not always been as successful as it ought to have been. In the 1930s and earlier the problem was that balance of in-flow and out-flow was not considered 'really', perhaps not even *thought* of in that distinct way. It was not till 1954 that I was able to put it forward as an important factor and tried to make it conscious (Slade 1954). 1945 onwards was an exciting time in Education, but I did have reservations about so-called linguistics and its effect on good speech, almost belittling the standards of pronunciation, so that nothing mattered any more! Another pendulum pointer is, for example, choice between C.A.T. or 'look and say' method. I used to be naughty at times and mention 'look and see but-still-not-be-able-to-say method'. Of course, everyone is different and we probably need both. But the thing that really worried me was such a stress on projects and on creative writing. These tended to squeeze out more formal aspects altogether. People almost wore a badge and a football-type scarf. Either you were out of date and you believed in grammar, or you were a modern dashing chap, or chapess, who believed only in creative writing. Thank goodness for creative writing. But it is necessary to try and master the elements of grammar, spelling and punctuation too. English is a wonderful language. Anyone can just about speak it. It has no formal gender (only traditional ones like 'she' for ship), no fussy adjective endings that have to agree, and the verb comes quickly, so you know what you are talking about, unlike German where it comes at the end of the sentence. But to speak and write English *well* is not easy at all. I rather wish we guarded our language better, more like the French, but not quite so stuffily.

Children are not fools. It is perfectly possible to say something like, 'Now, you have been writing your own ideas for about three weeks; and I have not been looking too carefully at punctuation and spelling (because you, the teacher, wanted *ideas* to flow). But now, this time I am going to look for spelling and punctuation as well (not 'instead', or they will think you don't care about ideas suddenly).' They need help in both. And they need to know why.

Sometimes a teacher would say they hadn't got time for dramatic play. What they may really have meant, in some instances, is that they didn't know how to do it, to promote it, or they may have been a little bit afraid of things getting out of hand. When we looked at their time-table we nearly always found a time, even if it was only ten minutes in the lunch hour. (Time given to it is not so important as regularity.) The keen ones were prepared to use this and have a try, by their own volition – plus help.

It might be wondered why I stress the above points, when I have spent a lifetime encouraging the release of children's own speech. The first trials of this sometimes come as a shock, because, of course, they are in dialect, perhaps, or anyway in the child's natural speech. But just as in creative writing, we are trying for the free flow of *ideas* first, later, to practise communication in all sorts of situations ('If I were really...'), then to build a flow of speech containing a poetic use of words; and finally to improve grammar and clarity and pronunciation in so far as it is necessary, or thought appropriate.

But, as a basis for all good speaking is the love of sound. So for both music and speech we should decide at the very beginning of the Infant School to promote interest in it, taking note of the short sharp sounds, which are the equivalent of consonants and the long rich sounds which are the equivalent of vowels.

At one time (due partly to misunderstanding over a Ministry of Education document 'Story of a School') it was said to be better for Infants to 'do movement' rather than speech. It resulted too often in lovely grown-up people at a piano bashing away and reading music, so they had no idea what was going on behind them and many a 'giant', or 'ogre' was totally out of step with the music of the spheres – I should say 'of the wires'. No notice was being taken of the size of the step that tiny giants can take. This is not education for anything. It is much better to have a record player controlled by the teacher *seeing* the class, or using chosen noises. All teachers should rise up and demand record players; and demand that speed 45 and long players continue to be made.

Of course some teachers just turned on the radio for 'Music and Movement'. Very good it was. But not the same as you, the teacher, making your own immediate relationship in the same room. That was your big opportunity. But for today: if your own choice of sound is used, perhaps noises should be used first – as short statements. Later come sentences of sound, more easily then understood as TUNE.

The truth is, naturally, that speech should be encouraged from the beginning. But movement should be there as well, either separately, or together with speech. A simple example of the mixture is as follows. Teacher makes a statement. (Do not say 'I want you to'. They are not doing this for you, it is for themselves.)

TEACHER:	A frog was unhappy because he had lost his hat. You can all be the frog (*pause*) so off he went to look for it. He hopped along to the pond.
	(*everyone hops to the sound that teacher makes. Watch for keeping time. Wait for them to "look" a bit. Watch for absorption.*)
TEACHER:	But, no, it wasn't there. Off he goes again
	(*when everyone is ready, no hurry, the world will wait for you*)
TEACHER:	then he meets a happy snail. Ask the snail if he has seen your hat.
	(*they **speak** and ask*)
CHILDREN:	No?
	(*if someone says yes, you must be ready to be flexible and decide what to do*)
TEACHER:	Oh, suddenly Frog sees his hat under a tree. Run, Frog, and pick it up.
	(*they pick up an imaginary hat*)
TEACHER:	So he puts it on, says goodbye to the Snail and he is *so* happy that he dances all the way home.
	(*gentle drumming, two sticks or possibly cheerful jazz record*)

They will possibly dance a short cut 'home' to start with. Later they will use more of the hall and almost certainly go round anti-clockwise. This saga is quite long enough to start with.

After more practice in other short stories, you may want to come back to this one:

TEACHER:	Do you remember the Frog who lost his hat?
CHILDREN:	Ye-e-e-s. (*Whether they do or not, possibly a No.*)
TEACHER:	Well, he was so unhappy that he ate no breakfast and went out to look for it. He hopped along the road (*pause for hopping*) and where did he go? Where did he look for his hat first?
CHILDREN:	'Under a bush', 'Near the pond', 'By a gate'.
	(*You have stopped giving so much framework in order to release their ideas and get them to speak.*)

More talk would be encouraged for the meeting with the happy Snail. And when Frog has found his hat there should be a wow of rejoicing by now.

Jabber-Talk

One thing has become important in modern times. These days, there are more children in school who do not understand English very well. For this, though perhaps more in Junior Schools, I would use not blah-blah talk of the baby, but

Jabber-talk, which is an entirely made-up language, improvised on the spur of the moment. Sometimes, if you find a timid little group in a corner, it might be kind to pass by (as I have often done) and say very quietly 'Speak in your own language, if you want to; *or* do what the others do'. You then suggest the class meet a Spaceman, shall we say. And we have to speak *his* language. So Jabber-talk starts. If you quietly pass by the shy little group, you can probably tell whether they are speaking in their own language or not. Each child is now talking to an 'unseen' spaceman near him. And nobody knows we aren't all Jabber-talking.[1] My point is that *all* the children must be made to feel welcome and part of the group, part of the family, in any way one can. This suggestion may not work, but you will probably think out other ways that do.

The awful thing about being too shy to speak is that, once you begin to feel isolated, it gets worse; and then a sort of wall builds up inside you. You feel imprisoned and then you *can't* speak. I want to avoid this happening to anyone, for everyone. It is a particular danger for the children of new-comers to our Land and I would try to invent anything which avoids them feeling the least bit as outsiders, for this goes back home and may add to any separateness a *community* may feel. Of course I know some individuals, or little groups, will have to have separate teaching, but there should be times when everyone can come together. Drama is immensely helpful over this and so is dance, particularly if you dance a bit with a partner and then we change partners on purpose. Different little people eventually then *have* to meet each other and cooperate. It is a *beginning*.

Happy Entry

Perhaps this is the time to bring in an idea I had to promote and build up pleasure at being at school. When children have had some experience of active play lessons, taken at their own pace, allowing them to use imagination, to be lots of different people, to blow off steam and actually to run, the room where they do it should have some happy associations. So I thought it would perhaps be even nicer if the teacher in charge were in that room or hall and started a happy noise, or music, before the children came in. A sort of Pied Piper effect. It just takes a second or two of marshalling outside the open door by another teacher. It is not a waste of time. In any case, it is not long before the children know what is expected of them, before they enter, and line up by themselves. That on its own is good teaching for obeying simple rules by responsibility, rather than being continually shunted by an adult.

---

1   A recent report stated that as many as sixteen languages were discovered in one class.

When the happy sound starts, they run in fast and enjoy blowing off steam after a more concentrated lesson. A fascinating thing now happens. I always love to see it. As they dash in, the (usually) grinning crowd starts to form this spiral shape (as if seen from on top) and, naturally, go anti-clockwise nearly always. But they are so sensible, instead of running into each other, it is an occasion when even the youngest fold, so to speak, inside the first part-circle and again inside that. Ultimately it sort of fills in and goes on going round like a gramophone record with a hole in the middle. It goes on till the teacher stops the sound, by fading down to a de-climax. The wise teacher will then suggest they sit down, if they haven't already flopped, and after a breathy pause, starts to reveal what's next. I hope in her (occasionally his) mind is a clear idea of the purpose of the lesson. About: 'If they haven't already flopped'. They may not. It depends how out-going one or two are. For, truth to tell, most people of about five years old go about rather like little grinning letter boxes in these sessions, with somewhat extended tummies, often with dangling arms and palms to the front – the typical stance of 'me waiting for instructions'. Too much of this, particularly in slightly older children is not a good sign. They ought to be gaining the confidence to think for themselves.

Open plan

One thing that makes all this sort of work more difficult, indeed almost impossible to do well, is the idea of open plan buildings. You are always hearing other people's noise and they won't like it if *you* make too much noise. The other thing is that drama does need, and offers, noise-opportunity at times; but one of its great disciplines is in *quietness* – so often overlooked. Open plan offers the chance of children moving from one area to another but, unfortunately, this can be an interruption to any atmosphere the drama teacher is trying to build. It is agreed that teachers and children get used to the buzz of learning. But it is not certain that this is a good thing. When sound is so important at this age, other people's sound could affect concentration; and if it doesn't, then it might become such a habit that you can't concentrate without it (we already seem to have to have music in order to shop). Be this as it may, active *personal* play does better in a separate room, or preferably a hall. But the marvel about most teachers is that once keen on something they will do their best to use it and to make the best of what they have got.

Sharing

One of the most important things the child has been learning since Nursery or Playschool is sharing. At the age we are now, it should develop strongly, particularly through play with others. It strengthens the Me, in that you have to make relationships with others, but still learn to remain yourself (firm and resolute). If you are an only child or from a two-child family, this may be more difficult. But even those from a crowded home will not always find it easy. For, so far, the world has been largely Mine. Now it must be more and more shared. Is there room for so many other people in my life?

They fit:

(1) into my life by allowing others to share my emotions, property and rights.

(2) into the room I am in by sharing my table or floor space.

(3) into my play by sharing experiences and by participating in what I do.

Secrecy

Before considering further the use of space, we must take note of one extra thing. It is the point of shyness and a need for private thought. We have already mentioned shyness a bit, but now we have to consider it even more carefully. There are many children in our schools who don't understand English very well yet, and these may feel a bit lonely and 'apart' at times. It may even be necessary, or at least kind, to have an interpreter nearby (this *is* sometimes possible) occasionally to explain quietly what the drama guide has suggested. It won't hold things up too much. But they may not want to join in yet. Don't force them. There will be a lot of secret feelings and thoughts in all children at this age, but now in even more of them than ever, so, in case there is anything a child might want to say, but doesn't yet feel able to tell a friend, and certainly not a grown-up, I would sometimes say – in a very quiet voice 'If there is anything you are worried about, *anything* that makes you sad. If you have a secret you can't tell anyone – there is a hole near where you are sitting and a rabbit lives down there. Tell the rabbit your secret, don't be afraid, tell him *anything* you like'. There may follow quite a long whispering. Don't hurry it. I use this in therapy too sometimes, and in teacher and/or nurse, or other training.

In therapy the patient obtains an added loosening effect of thought and feeling; they are also able to project any dislike or temporary annoyance with the therapist into what they say to the rabbit (in a group situation). If they are still too tight, in a one-to-one situation; or defending their adulthood so much that they are still afraid of the child within themselves (or if the child is lost) they may be slightly offended and think it is silly. It is worth trying, then: talking to themselves in a mirror, or to an unseen guardian friend, or somebody down an imagined telephone, because you 'can't be seen'. When taking training sessions and including this exercise, and if we have been getting on well together, I often add ' – and perhaps tell the rabbit all the funny things this strange man has been asking you to do (this may give a start *or* an addition to what is said)'.

It is interesting to note, though, that most adults, on courses, take a long time over this imparting of secrets. In my experience it has been Directors of Industry that take the longest. Perhaps they have the most worries.

Art

This is one of the best ways for shy little people to express themselves and these days we find a wonderful mixture of things, people, clothing, animals and pictorial scenes (particularly in our cities), because of the mixture of ethnic background. The only thing is that it is a very private mode, is likely to leave the child in a 'one' state and does not draw them out into co-operative action, as does drama and dance. However, a step may be made by encouraging occasional group paintings. I have seen feet long group paintings of great vitality made by five or six children that showed such group intuition and sensitivity from each person to another that you would think they had been painted by *one* person. This is a wonderful step forward, but it is only part of a child's development. We shall see a little later what a difference a balanced programme of the Arts (where it is possible) can make.

All children are to some extent creative artists. Do not think that because they copy some things from life that it argues against this; this is part of the bringing in of life experience for enrichment, testing and proving. But think hard before offering them powerful things, such as theatre to copy (or paint) too early in their lives. Paintings of the funny things that go on in drama lessons are a different matter. Those 'funny things' are part of the real child's world – part of the Land that children go to in their play – so making a picture of *them* might be an encouragement for those who have not yet felt too inclined to take part, to do so. Modelling also, is part of the business. And building Monuments from bits and pieces. Let us say that at five years of age, before which every attempt should have been made to avoid showing off, and to *share* the child's experience rather than too obviously look at them as if they were clever (they aren't always). With our help they are going to create more things, so we are going to proceed to stimulate further – improvised movement, situation and language.

Casting

Now some interesting things happen. It is important not to cast people as individuals too early, as in a play. To start with, as has been shown, everyone should be all things and each character in the story. So we would have thirty, perhaps twenty-five hero people, although in the story there would be one. I would strongly advocate this, because each one of us has an area round us to defend. It is like an unseen hoop; but is so obvious at certain times in the Infant School, particularly in dance, that you *can* almost see it. At first, whilst children in the grinning-letter-box stage are not very in control of their bodies, this does not seem to matter and they bump into each other, but fairly cheerfully bounce off again. They will then continue to be the hero person, or whatever else, in an area near and round their body, in the dream play of life, overcoming, failing or winning. Later, this will become even more important. Something else happens too.

Years ago at the Bonnington Conference (1948: Comprising those in Theatre, Education and Psychology) members of the Ministry of Education asked that I be allowed to speak on what I had called acting-in-the-round. I tried to do so in this way:

> 'It is a phenomenon in which the person is strongly concerned with self, almost like an exploding dot of energy in the middle of oneself. It is this energy which seems to go out from the centre and enables acting to take place all round the body. So if you are seen from any angle, even the back, you are giving a message which is interesting and will hold anyone watching. In proscenium theatre, one is more concerned with a half convex circle only, outwards from oneself· to the body of attenders-to, the audience. In theatre-in-the-round it would be helpful if all actors knew about acting-in-the-round and tried to develop it. For, at the moment, those who are attempting this form of theatre present it more like a square, with four proscenium arches outwards'. (I did not add that their back views were therefore very dull to watch, because they had forgotten to make them alive, and where people were static, they often screened each other.)

I may have mentioned the shapes that children use in their play (I don't remember), particularly the 'S' shape, in which, if you can imagine it, when used inside a circle, or any central theatre shape, it allows the actor to be seen more than once in face, profile and back, by an audience seated round. (The 'shapes' were hardly known then. But they are the ones I have mentioned here earlier on.) Some people did not like this very much. I finished by saying 'Children act in-the-round quite naturally and unconsciously and we should learn from them'. This really upset people, I am sorry to say. But one must remember that the atmosphere was very different then (my book *Child Drama* had not yet been published) and those of us who wanted to champion the child had another forty or more years to go before establishing some things.

However, it led to my becoming Director of the Educational Drama Association, and to the invaluable help of many wonderful people across the world, also from some wonderful other Associations, which had been Child Champions long before the Bonnington Conference.

Apart from this, there is evidence that children are not ready for full casting, because they have invented something for *themselves*. So it is good to notice that there are three forms of casting other than the individual one we are used to. When the whole class is doing something it is different, despite the fact that each child is a hero in its own empire round its body. It is experience of community. But the three forms of casting, other than one individual, might be called:

(1) Tribal

(2) Group

(3) Conglomerate

Tribal

Family of frogs

Individual character

●

Small group

Conglomerate

An aeroplane all hang on
to be bigger than oneself

Together – being
as one banana

●
Teacher

Diagram 1

By 'Tribal' is meant literally a family, a tribe – of frogs, horses, lions, or gnomes, etc... 'And they live over there.' There may be father and mother and special types of their 'children' later. But to start with, as a lump, the gnomes live 'Over there'.

Group casting is perhaps the most interesting. It is when a little group is made up of children who are not yet ready to be even in a family, let alone be a lone

individual character. A sort of unity takes place. The children do not hang on
to each other. They move as separate individuals, but there is a sort of
psychological unity, so that they feel it perfectly normal for five people (say) to
share the enormous responsibility of being one cigar, or as we shall see later,
one banana. Once you know about this you can use it, sometimes, for children's
benefit.[2]

Conglomerate is the easiest to understand. Children just conglomerate literally
and hang on to each other to make something bigger than themselves. It is so
sensible. There is one snag, though. If you happen to be a dragon going round
the room too fast the components have not yet learned that the end of a group
nearly always seems to have to go faster than the front. So there is a danger
that the tail of the dragon may fly off into space; and anyone jumping onto a
conglomerate aeroplane, too suddenly, may find the cockpit caves in. It is better
to give warnings about speed and advice about these things beforehand, so as
to avoid woe. But they probably will happen anyway in some degree during
the process of this form of education. That is how we learn about space and
what to avoid doing.

As children love sound, by using various interesting noises in the Infant
School, we can inspire them to create in their own manner. So it is in this way
that I shall use the things I am taking into the hall: drums, gongs, whistles, old
tins, sandpaper, two sticks, and so on. I may sometimes use a piano or a record
player, but rather in the later stages.

Example – I should start by making sounds in the hall before the children enter.
Reason: They enter then with curiosity and pleasure. Because children hear
sound emotionally they take joy in it, and joy is necessary for their best creation.
When they become used to the work the entrance shape will be in a spiral, all
running with their hearts towards the centre. The big circle follows, then the
filled-in one as all move round.

I stop making the sound. All movement stops. I now have full attention
without any comments. I shake some small bells.

SELF: What does this remind you of?

CHILD: Sleigh bells.

SELF: Yes, *look* at the snow. Your sleigh would pull nicely. Are you
             ready? Pull!

---

2   This was brought to my attention by Miss P Lutley, a distinguished Head, who said she
     had seen something she did not understand. After careful observation, I suggested this and
     the other terms.

Several children begin to pull, some perhaps to trot round. All are creating, not just the little show-offs picked out. I give no directions but just alter the speed of the bells, slowing down when I judge fit. The children obey the sound. They are learning about climax, and a little about mood, and a little about absorption, that is, concentration for study as well as good acting. I blow a whistle.

SELF: What was that?

CHILD: A train.

ANOTHER: Please, a hot kettle.

SELF: Quite right, a train with a kettle-hat on his funnel. (*Laughter*)

I whistle and chuff. Everyone begins to join in. We speed up; we find time-beat together, rhythm together, we are all engines together, though I personally do not move except in spirit. The children bang into each other a bit. I do not criticise *anything*. I suggest what to do but do not show how.

SELF: *(thinking of tidiness-training and watching carefully for signs*
               of tiredness. When their creation is dying a little – we must watch very
               carefully for this – I say):

               Into the station we go.

               (Noise ceases)

               I must rest a little for the passengers to get out. Then off I
               go tidily backwards to bed.

Noise starts. I suggest backwards because they are a little out of breath, and they have to go more slowly that way. I say 'I' because each child is absorbed now; each of us *is* 'I'. We must observe, and know how to watch for this moment. Knowing only comes by experience.

SELF: There I am. (*Noise ceases.*) I'm very tired. So what shall I do?

CHILD: Go ter sleep.

ANOTHER: Undress.

SELF: Yes, I take off my kettle-hat and put it away carefully...

A giggle or two perhaps, but most are now quiet and intent. I leave time for miming to go on. At this point a child *must not be hurried*. Creation is taking place. I would wait the whole of the rest of the period, if necessary, and suggest nothing except to say 'good' at the end of it. But today creation is beginning to fade. There is only one right moment, and I try to catch it.

SELF: ...And take my wheels off and put them ready for cleaning.

Mime starts up again. If the imaginative suggestion has not met with approval, as being too unreal, there may be hesitation. I notice who hesitates. Is this one mentally older or merely unimaginative? I shall learn *much* about him or her in time, and it will be the greatest aid to me in introducing *all other subjects at school*.

SELF: Undress – mustn't forget to wash – and clean my teeth (etc.). At
               last I'm ready for bed (*children may begin to lie down*) – I'm very
               tired. Oh dear, I think – I'm going to – sleep.

The children are now all relaxed; some yawn. The mood and atmosphere of voice are important. I judge that that is enough and go to the piano and strike up a march, or put on a record. All children get up eagerly.

SELF:	What's this? Is this nice?
SOME CHILDREN:	Yes.
SELF:	Who are you?
	(*'You' again, not 'I', because I notice absorption has gone. They are very young.*)
CHILD:	King.
ANOTHER:	Soldier.

I accept all suggestions, and make others. We are horses, animals, motors, everything. Immense experience is gained, many parts are tried. I never say 'do that' in a strong way. *Reason*: A child might not obey. If there are no orders, there can be no disobedience. I avoid a false position. It is always 'I am', 'you are', *fait accompli* – or 'shall we?' Yet there is complete control. They are controlled by friendship, not me, by trust. They in fact learn to discipline themselves.

Up to seven years old there is quite a need for suggestion in *what* to do, but never show them *how* to do it. That would destroy creation.

Note: Piano *accompanying* movement aids creation. The discipline of a gramophone record *followed* by the children aids control. Do not be discouraged if at first you do not know when to do all these things, but no doubt you will understand the main outline.

I would do similar things week after week, but, in order to cement the bond of friendship and to offer creative opportunity, I would slowly begin to build stories such as may arise from *their* suggestions.

Example – Five to Six Years
The teacher is beating a drum and the children run in. She brings the sound up to a climax when the children are all happily dashing round in a filled-in circle. One last bang and they all stop.

TEACHER:	Sit down quietly. Now listen.
	(*She pings a bit of metal on a string with a nail. It is a very quiet noise and they have to keep quiet to listen.*)
TEACHER:	What does it remind you of? Listen again – now!
A CHILD:	Mouse.
ANOTHER:	Little man.
	(*There is a box of noises in the corner.*)
TEACHER:	Go and get a noise you like, Jane. Peter, you get one.

They are sent separately and come back separately in case there is too long a discussion at the box. Each teacher must judge such moments. Jane now has a tambourine, Peter a sort of metal scraper.

TEACHER: Lovely. Now – a little man with big, big feet lived in a castle and he had a little tame mouse he loved very much. (*Both ideas from the first answer have been used, even though difficult to fit.*) But there was a big and naughty kangaroo who lived outside. You show us the noise the kangaroo makes, Jane. (*Jane bumps her tambourine.*) You show us the noise the little mouse makes, Peter. (*Peter makes scraping noises.*) There. Now, stand up everybody and join in the story if you want to. The little man with the big feet is walking about in his castle – (*By using a tiny sound for big feet the children are helped to find how to make big moves without too much noise. All the children are the little man.*) – and his little mouse scratches to get in. (*Peter makes scraping noises whilst everyone else is a mouse.*) The little man takes him by the hand and they go for a walk (*ping, ping, ping, goes the teacher*). Suddenly the big kangaroo comes along, bounding over the garden. (*Jane makes bounding noises whilst all the rest are kangaroos.*) But the little man and the mouse run off just in time (*teacher builds up climax on a tambour – all the children run round the room away from an imaginary kangaroo*). He closes the door with a bang. You make the bang. (*Some children call 'bang', some stamp their feet.*) Don't forget to wipe your feet on the mat. Then sit down quietly in front of your fire. Very quiet; that's right. Let's sit quite silent watching the flames for a bit.'

This story is quite long enough to begin with. If they have run and been absorbed, they have done a lot. Long stories break down concentration at this age, and are one cause of getting children into habits of not paying proper attention. Short stories are easier to live a little more deeply and, in using them, habits of concentration for other school subjects are more likely to become established.

Example – Six to Seven Years
After about six years of age children may have what I have called *the Dawn of Seriousness*. Those who have are ready to be cast in small parts. But there is an in-between stage, and we can fill this in by *group* casting. The following is an extract from a report:

Story: '...and the banana didn't want to be caught by the policeman at all, and he ran away. But a motor-car came bundling along towards him. He stopped for a moment, and then the policeman caught him. The policeman stopped the car, he and the banana got in, and the driver took them to the prison. The banana was put safely behind bars and carefully locked up, and couldn't be naughty again.'

In this case, one child, who was ready for casting, was the policeman, two children were the man who drove the car; the car was four children, but the banana was five children. They were not all linked together physically, making one big banana, but were five separate entities linked emotionally, and so giving each other the group courage to dare that colossal act – being a banana.

Example

SELF:	(*softly rubbing together two pieces of sandpaper*)
	What does this sound remind you of?
CHILD:	Cat scratching.
SELF:	(*tapping tambour with a stick*) And this one?
CHILD:	Man running.
SELF:	(*stamping on a rostrum block*): And this?
	No answer.
SELF:	Well, it reminds me of – say, a door banging?
CHILD:	Yes.
ANOTHER:	Or a tyre bursting.
SELF:	(*delighted*): Yes! Now let's make a story out of these ideas.

'A man was walking down a passage in a big, big house, when suddenly he heard a funny noise. He thought it might be burglars, and he started to run. But when he got to the end of the passage he found it was only his cat scratching the door of a room, because he was shut out. So the man opened the door, the cat rushed through it, dashed to a window and jumped out. The man ran after him to see what had happened, but just then there was big bang. The door of the room had slammed shut again in the wind. But something else had happened, too: The cat had jumped right on to the back of a motor-car standing outside the house, and do you know his claws were *so out* and *ready* to catch at something, that they'd gone right through the spare tyre at the back of the car when he landed there, and the tyre was as flat as a fish.'

The story would then be acted. 'Who would like to be?' and so on. I would accompany the acting with sounds, for example tambour for the man running. The car would be made of several people and would no doubt collapse if the cat jumped off a chair on to it. Some children would be wind, others furniture in the passage, two or three the door. There might be many cars, many men, but slowly such attempts become more like a cast play as children approach six and seven years.

Because the children are suggesting the ideas that lead to the story, they are already sharing in part of the creation.

Note. 'Now let's make a story...' We're all doing this together. It's not just me telling a story. Later, they will be able to share in the creation even more fully. For instance, one of the ideas may be left out, or you may suddenly stop and say something like: 'And what do you think happened then?' or 'Who do you think they saw rushing along the road?' Such opportunities to join in are readily accepted by the children after only a little experience of this work. Teachers who are worried by feelings that they are unable to make up stories easily should take confidence from this. Ultimately, the children will be able to make up some stories entirely on their own, but until then they will often help us if we run out of ideas.

The above are some suggestions for ways of beginning in the Infant School. Be content with small beginnings, for the small things are really great. If, by the time the children have reached six and a half years, they have discovered the full significance of time-beat and rhythm, and their difference; if the older children do not bump into each other, and equi-distance has begun to appear during play; if they have learned to love sound; if you occasionally get good contrasts and climaxes; if you have achieved 'pin-drop' control; and if absorption and sincerity have been developed; if language has begun to flow and they can read a little and count, you will have done a magnificent job.

Remember that you are part of a team in your school and that it is important to use many quiet moments in play of this kind which give children a deeper aesthetic experience and help them to understand discipline. Always finish such a period with some quiet suggestion. For example

TEACHER: (*tapping a tambour very quietly*) I want to hear the clock ticking, so go out very quietly to your next class.

This has been *personal* play; they must be prepared for the *projected* play of other studies, don't forget.

You will help the work and the children if, in the Infant School, you try to avoid all playing to parents, use of formal stage and script plays, and use only a little dressing-up. These things interfere with the absorption, and thus the sincerity, if they are experienced too soon. The only exception is the Nativity Play. But that is more of a religious pageant than a social function.

Language Flow

There may be some flow of spontaneous language by six years, and, though movement is an important form of language at this age, spontaneous speech cannot start too early. Children learn to use and love language, and the sounds bring recognition musically. Language contains vowels and consonants. Sounds are roughly divided into elongated sounds and short, sharp ones. Strings, bells and gongs offer us long sounds, unless specially arranged otherwise. Sharp sounds come from percussion instruments, tapping and banging things, though of course there are intermediate sounds, too. By carefully nurtured love, first of sound itself and then of special sounds – short and sharp, then of sounds containing mood – it is possible to associate sound of many kinds (starting with the vowels and consonants) with language in general. The child then transfers its love to speech. Parallel with this should come spontaneous play where speech enters. Practice in speaking creatively and learning the love of sound is the best approach to language.

Here are some actual examples of spontaneous speech stimulated by these methods – it nearly always has poetic or philosophic content for children over six, and often religious thought, too:

GIRL (6):   Look! There is my own dear friend the first evening star.

GIRL (6.5):   And the warm came, and the rain came, and the sad, sad clouds. Then I knew it was time for bed.

GIRL (7):   (*dancing all over the room*) I am joy, riding over the sun on a bright nail.

BOY (6.5):   And I got me gun and I lifted it, and the angel came out of the sun and I threw it away.

BOY (7):   (*as the good Samaritan, turning over the wounded man and saying **very** tenderly*): Oo done it?

As the children grow older and, having had plenty of opportunity for opening up and establishing their personalities more, through play, round about six or six and a half you may notice a certain dignity in some of them. They begin to be more sensible, they can be relied upon to take a message, they keep the rules, they tend to be neat in clothing, they are punctual, they bring coffee without spilling it, they are cheerful and polite to visitors. In drama their language flow is quite rich (in the right sense!) and in dance they are now fully conscious of the area to defend round their bodies and they no longer like being bumped into – it is irritating in many ways, but particularly because it upsets the absorption in the task of creating and the sincerity in the way it is done.

This feeling of the circle round us seems to be deep in the unconscious. Not only does one perceive something of it in the feeling of retention of power during King-of-the-Castle games, when the King or Queen on top glances round to see if anyone is attacking them from side or rear; we speak of our circle of friends; but Nations feel it too. In ascendancy we hear things like 'We must have more Lebensraum (room for living).' In other words we feel the need to expand our circle of empire and defence (psychological) and we will do it by expanding our boundaries (physical). At the other end of the scale, when a nation is being beleaguered we hear 'We need help. We are being encircled.'

I always feel it is the dance which gives us the first obvious indication of something wonderful happening. You notice the other things afterwards. And if more than one child is approaching this stage, equi-distance between the dancers becomes clearly marked. It is a sign of civilisation; and the special stage being reached I have called the Dawn of Seriousness. I cannot overestimate how important this is, for if these lovely little people are strong enough (and because of their common sense), they become the first gang leaders. For gangs start in the Infant School and if there is no Dawn of Seriousness yet developed, the first gang leaders will be the tough, rather nasty ones, who are a bit backward and only lead because they are bigger, because they bully and others are afraid of them. It is of the utmost importance that these people should *not* become the first gang leaders, this is where a deep part of delinquency starts. Treating people in their later life I have become fully aware of this importance as well as the dangers of this period between six years and seven. I would therefore urge as many teachers as possible to be aware of this, to learn to recognise the stage of development when it dawns, and to realise how valuable serious and constructive play can be in aiding us to develop wise and balanced little people in our midst, particularly in simple social drama about situations and how to behave to animals and other people. Our aim should be that everyone should have reached at least *some* Dawn of Seriousness by the age of seven.

Art and Drama

At one time there came the chance to evaluate the relationship between Art and Drama. It came as an additional proof of my feeling that *projected play* (art) and *personal play* (drama) were both necessary; and that as they merged in various ways and affected each other, a balance in the personality was obtained and development hastened, so apart from the Dawn of Seriousness mentioned above, here is the outcome of the observation. By 1958 I felt able to say:

> 'An interesting and important fact is that painting and drawing improve in proportion to the sense of space discovered in movement over the floor. A young child who may be seen to run in an S shape, a cross or a triangle shape, is also producing these shapes on paper, and, as bumping into companions in movement on the floor space ceases, so pictorial composition improves. This is because children are beginning to sort out the difference between mass and space by experiencing it three-dimensionally. They notice their own body and the span between themselves and each other person. With the practice that drama (and dance) brings, bumping ceases earlier, and this in turn brings about improvement of the art.'

Art therefore is, as it were, a thermometer chart of where the person has got to in development; the 'chart' can be read by the experienced eye, even if the drama and dance do not make it obvious. When children have discovered and sorted out space, in the physical sense, and at the same time are wanting to be more serious about their drama in the emotional and aesthetic sense, they then achieve equi-distance. This appears both in the use of floor space (*personal play*) and in art (*projected play*). It is a step in the direction of mental tidiness and growing-up. It is also an important social advancement as children begin to consider the needs of others. And, of course, our job is to help them to do this.

In Child Art, equi-distance is the forerunner of what is termed composition, where mass, colour and space are more purposefully and intellectually arranged. Composition is always better where the equi-distance stage has been passed through properly, because the full three-dimensional experience of Child Drama and dance makes a need in the child's mind for good composition. The parallel of composition in art is good grouping in drama.

As we consider the grouping, we might have, say, one child ready to be a character on its own, in a commanding situation over a *tribal* group, with a timid group of several people being another *one*-person. The strong single character acts almost like a flag pole to the moving *tribal*, flag-like group, whilst the *group casting* bunch sometimes flickers uncertainly about the place, like an undecided gentle wind. It is fascinating. In this moment we have a moving picture of weight, space, mass and line and if in simple costume, colour too. It is as if a child painting had come alive in 3D and is one of the Wonders of the World for those who have eyes to see.

In therapy equi-distance for me is an important sign of improvement (or state). For instance, pictures by those with fairly severe learning disability show little indication of perceiving it; and with more advanced cases none. A further assessment over a number of years produced the fact that those who received what was considered a proper education through *both* Child Art and Child Drama (including dance) achieved their Dawn of Seriousness as much as a year earlier than those who did not.

Working under Difficulties

If you have little space and only a classroom to work in, try to arrange to move the tables. If this in not possible, do what you can and *use* them. Turn them into mountains, ships, horses or cowsheds. A certain amount of movement can take place amongst them. Use noises here also. If only a few can act at a time, encourage audience participation. Fight against the shape of the rigid theatre with actor's end (teacher's end) and audience end (pupil's end). If actors turn their backs on the other actors who sit and participate at their tables, do not on any account correct this. The actors who have more movement than the others are merely forming part of the circle, normal at this age, which we would see in its entirety under better conditions. Remember in Child Drama there is no real audience, and take comfort from the fact that, by your kindly sympathy, children will get much more than you think out of the worst possible conditions, because of their wonderful imagination. They need opportunity, that is all.

Common both to the best conditions and the less good is the task of the teacher in acting as a kindly and gentle guide. Encouragement is needed at this age, and some stimulation. If speech or play fails at a certain moment, learn to be sensitive about when to make a suggestion and what suggestion, and when *not* to. This is the art of nurturing.

It should not be forgotten, though, that life is not *all* play. And time given to it should be adequate but not more than everything else. Regularity is almost more important than a major slice of time, but much general education can be added into the art and drama by thoughtful teachers. Before leaving the infant sphere, one hopes that, besides being a balanced and pleasant little person, children should be able to read (at least to some extent) and to count.

Junior School

Seven to Nine Years: Continuing our Talk of Schooling

The child who has not had its Dawn of Seriousness by seven years is a slow developer, or may have become so because of having lacked the right play experiences.

The period is one of increasing skill, and often of great enchantment, as well as greater difficulty over control at home. But the extra sensitivity now gained brings the child to the most wonderful years of its Art and Drama. We find exquisite moments in their dramatic play from now on, in which deep soul experiences and ice-cold logic walk hand in hand. And because of the experiences they should have had, as described in the Infant section, they will have been noticing a lot about space through drama and dance, in the not bumping and the looking round and the notice of others. They look across the hall sometimes, almost like a Chieftain on an important mountain. In silence they perceive the world. In their art they cannot quite *represent* space in the way that many adults do, by perspective and so on, but they are learning about what Oswold Spengler calls 'depth consciousness'. Sometimes you see important figures in their Art being bigger than the others, just as in medieval painting. And you do see *things*, countryside, or people sometimes smaller in the distance, or a bit less bright in colour. That certainly means they are getting clues. But you seldom see shadows, unless we have messed up their type of vision. But then there are famous painters who don't use space, depth, or shadow either. It entirely depends on what you are trying to do, what is the *purpose* of your creation. In perspective, you often have to tell a lie in order to be clever. She is an unreliable mistress and often goes dead on you. Anyway, you are sometimes expected to follow her up to some misbegotten dot in space beyond your paper, where she often abandons the finest minds (or they her). How can young children understand all this? They don't. They manage without.

Teachers of this age group have an awful lot of work to do. Not only may children coming from Infant departments need extra help with the three Rs, but more and more of them have, as yet, no firm grasp of English. In this mixture of ability, through no fault of their own, there is even more need for stress on guided and constructive play, for this (as has been shown) is what aids *us* in helping children to feel secure and self-confident, and to make good relationships.

It should be clear by now that the adult's part in the Drama of the Child is a very special though not a dominating one. The adult's attitude has a considerable influence at all ages, not least at this wonderful period starting from the age of seven. Our task now might almost be looked on as that of ensuring that the child is going to *trust* adults. With its new interest in serious things, it is through the adult that the child satisfies its desire for deeper knowledge and, from the frank and trusting confidences exchanged, there arises a tremendous bond of friendship. Civilised life needs this bridge between youth and age, and unless it is satisfactorily established the child tends to become suspicious and then rude and disobedient. This cuts the adult off from the latest news of the growing generation, and for the child it often means the loss of a treasure casket of intellectual, emotional and aesthetic joys.

From the child's point of view, this is a period of rapid further development from Self outwards, which takes the form of a further sharing of life-experiences with its companions. These experiences often become, and should remain, a realm of mystic secrecy, from which arise the wonderful creative forms of group decision which not only help the confident personal development of the child, but enrich with such splendour its genuine Art and Drama.

Any break of trust with adults now, or removal of a loved one, may drive the child into an unbalanced form of life in which the realm of mystic secrecy is over-enlarged. This may be a solitary affair, or there may be a feeling that there is only one camp, and a sort of sullen secret rebellion is started in the younger set against the older generation. Even one unhappy child can cause a good deal of trouble now, and it often needs great patience, understanding and courageous action to get things right again.

Just as unhappy can be the condition where too great a reliance is placed on the adult, bringing contempt of companions, and suspicion on their part. Companions are an important part of normal life now, which is why we see the gang stage developing more fully.

The gang develops round a leader with a strong Self, not yet quite ready to integrate too far with the group. This strong Self is an intermediate personality between child and adult for the other members of the gang. It thereby becomes a living symbol of the needs of that age and, embracing as it does something of the strength and decision to be found in the adult and also the vivacity and actual youngness of the child, it often wields tremendous power. For this reason the group dynamic of a gang can have tremendous energy for good or for ill. It is to be hoped that the leader has had the Dawn of Seriousness. In the Drama it emerges, partially, as Group Sensitivity.

Group Sensitivity

At a time when this group feeling is growing, we notice a great development in community efforts. There is the straightforward group creation, where stories and ideas are built up by several children and acted out, but there is also the new feeling, both conscious and unconscious, for the place of others. Where properties are used, a child who is not certain in choice will be aided by others; a friend will rush up and thrust forward the right thing. There is also a much clearer conscious attitude about the need of space for others, although this is not yet fully conscious. There is far less bumping than with infants. Equidistance between each person becomes more rigid, and one may frequently see a child automatically moving out of another's way if the balance of equidistance is upset by any sudden unexpected happening. This is the outward sign of social awareness. It is part of the integration of Self with society. We see, also, particular movements taken up by several or all members of a group at once. This is further evidence of the growing one-mind, the shared intent. Seeing, hearing, feeling, noticing, all come into this. It is a sensitive business, and it pertains not only to each little Self but to the group. It can only be called Group Sensitivity.

With these developing senses come other things; from seeing – greater powers of observation; from hearing – more pleasure in time beat, rhythm and climax; from feeling – more intense joys in materials, such as clothes, colours, wood and clay. One often sees children of this age fully appreciating the *particular qualities* of materials, in a quite different manner from the earlier sense and Play trials.

With all this developing interest comes ability to concentrate, which the adult can aid by recognising, and by allowing frequent periods of uninterrupted Play. We can destroy it by over-rigid timetable, or by the type of shyness and fear of things getting out of control, which causes us to impose an iron-like discipline.

The further powers of observation bring the full flood of questions which we *must* treat with patience and answer fully and seriously. This is where the adult may escape into lie-legends and do great harm, or answer impatiently and even angrily, thus blocking the in-flow of knowledge. Important for teachers, but parents also.

Any one-way feeding-pipe to a small person is a slender thing and easily gets choked. Then nothing happens – the child and teacher eye each other across a fixed chasm like Dives and Lazarus; but if the teacher be Dives, his wealth is squandered. Thus it is that, despite the fears of those who dare not try out these things, or will not persevere with them, or else stubbornly reject them, children who have frequent opportunities for drama and other creating of their own kind, not only equal the success of other children, but frequently surpass them – even in scholastic attainment. We know this now from *years* of careful and close observation. The reason is that these students are more balanced little people. And as to happiness, good manners and obedience, there can be no comparison.

Group Creations

With all these developments taking place in the children, it is not surprising that the outward form of their Drama is affected. Where floor space is properly used, we see a change in the appearance of the circle. What in the infant class tended to be a big circle, splitting occasionally into other shapes, develops into a more frequent appearance of small circles. These circles in the junior class are the outward sign of the gang stage. Anything from about three to seven members is common, although they are sometimes larger when special imaginative creations call for more Persons (e.g. human cars, trains or lakes). These circles, besides being an outward sign of an inner condition, often even comprise members of a gang, for, whenever play takes place, the gang members tend to join up, and confidences are exchanged which grow into group creations either of acted scenes or of dance.

These group Drama creations tend to be made up increasingly by the children themselves now, often without any help at all. Sometimes they are made up after swift or lengthy whispered conversations, sometimes prepared for several days. Occasionally all will be done in secret, and the teacher will be asked, as a surprise, if they may 'act it'. These are improvisations, and the flow of dialogue is often amazing for its wit, charm, and mixture of naivety and deep philosophical content.

At the best moments of playing they are still unconcerned with audience; they are far away in 'the Land'. But sometimes a petering out gives indication of the 'near finish', and we can clearly see or feel them coming back to earth. Nevertheless, if they are not entirely convinced that any adults present understand that play is temporarily finished (or if they have never met an adult who knows 'finish'), they will often turn and say 'that's all', just to make quite sure. Sometimes the end is so abrupt that it is very difficult to be sure of its arrival, particularly as under these conditions the players often stay absorbed in 'the Land' and remain coma-acting for a minute or two. Adults here often mistake the end of 'theatre' for the end of play, whereas the two may be quite separate. Signs of theatre may or may not be present, but, if there are children not actually in the creation they always know when it has finished; they move, and that generally breaks the spell. These improvisations, if loved, may be repeated, but details are generally different. A polished improvisation is often better understood by the adult, but it is not necessarily as important as the original creation.

Dance is also made up by the children, but they often wish to build together with the teacher, and this communal building brings its own rewards and promotes confidence between child and teacher. It also helps to break up the gang, for which these little groups are sometimes quite pleased, for, though they are bound by fierce and voluntary loyalties, there is a certain involuntary tyranny about them which each child both loves and fears. It appears to be a relief, therefore, to have the gang split up sometimes by an outside agency, although much play will take place in, with and through these gang groups.

Too much repetition of a particular dance or improvisation brings laziness; some repetition, combined with fresh creations, brings the happiest results. It is particularly important that the little groups on the floor space, whether manifestations of the gang state or actual gangs, should have opportunity for play in the presence of a sympathetic adult and in a *legal* surrounding. In this way the gang dynamic is influenced for good by frequent constructive group adventures, when just one word from the adult is often enough to tip the scale of behaviour in the young gang leader or potential leader, who is ever ready to become dare-devil and lead others the wrong way. This is what is meant by saying that drama of this kind can be a cultivated flower.

The flower of the street is still wild and often thorny. It is no good pretending that it doesn't exist, because it does and has great vitality; indeed, it has such beauties that it pays us to cultivate what nature provides.

That is the norm, but things change very rapidly these days and the drama of the streets is changing into reality instead of play and a reality of a dangerous and sometimes evil kind. It is largely as a result of copying the wrong role models and because they have had no training in how to blow off steam in a reasonable way; and no place, under trained guidance, to do it in. So they take to the streets.

First Year

Now, as to play in the world of *inside* – in the first year of Junior School, because of circumstances already mentioned, children may, in many places, not yet be in the condition one expects of a seven-year-old. The burden on the Infant School is great these days. Although Dawn of Seriousness comes earlier, when adequate play experience of both kinds is arranged – which is why I changed the age of likelihood from between six and a half and seven, to six onwards – there may be many children who have not reached this stage of maturity. So for the first year of Junior School one should be prepared to treat things much as in the Infant School. For this reason it becomes more important to make little tests to see where they have 'got to'. This is true of Art (they may not always have had big pieces of paper). It is particularly true of the Drama. The sort of thing I mean is as follows, although I might try it anyway in a Junior School to see how things are, if I had not met those children before. If they are not active, you know they have not had enough dance; if they tend to grin and pause a moment before making their attempt, you know they have not had enough of their own kind of drama; if they appear sincere and plunge into creation quickly, you know they have had something of the right experience. Later, what you saw revealed in this *personal play* is also emphatically revealed in the Art. If they have not had enough *personal play*, the Art will be squat, square, rigid. If they have had the right experience, their painting and drawing will be full of energy and what the Japanese term 'movement'. One can always tell. If I was not quite sure that children were getting enough Drama, despite the strong assurances of the teacher, I always asked to look at their Art. This confirms almost everything you want to know. Nobody can take you in, if you consider both *projected play* and *personal play*; as said in the first part of the book regarding therapy; although more careful over indications, you may be more likely to be nearer the truth, if you know what you are doing when examining both.

EXAMPLE

SELF: 'When I put the music on, I am going to suggest some funny things to you (*note, not "I want you to"*). I'm going to make quick changes, just to see how quick and clever you are at getting into things. Ready?'

I put music on (*not forgetting to have put volume control down – always – before starting it, so no unwanted scrape or odd sound destroys the atmosphere*). I bring up some cheerful quick jazz.

SELF: 'You are someone in a hurry to do shopping. Off you go'.

(*I often give a quick clap here so that people know **exactly** when to start. It avoids a vague or lazy beginning and keeps a good strong control from the start. I hate to see a class that is not in hand. It is bad for discipline. The clap, in starting improvisation under these circumstances, is almost the parallel of the rise of the curtain in adult theatre. Everyone knows: **Now we begin**. When there is no curtain, there has to be something else and, to obtain the best work, it must be precise.*)

SELF: (*seeing the hasty shoppers have started off well, no doubt moving round the space anti-clockwise*)

'You see an amazing hat in a window. The hat whizzes out of the door to meet you. Put it on and start to feel posh.'

(*Not too satisfied, I don't criticise by saying things like "Oh, come on, you are not looking posh at all. When we are being posh we spread ourselves out like this, don't we?" **Don't show**. Be patient and **watch**.*)

'Feel even posher...yes, posher still... Throw the hat(s) away; you are a jumping Kangaroo (*they jump for a short time*); you are an ogre with a bad leg; you are suddenly a nice person – but with an ugly face. Be as ugly as you can. Now be horrid and pull a face at people near you as you pass by.'

(The shape of the group of bodies will be like a filled in gramophone record now, some going a little faster and passing others, perhaps.)

'A Wizard put a spell on you and you are suddenly very beautiful. Yes, aren't you nice? Not too cissy, though. (*I had noticed one or two boys mincing on purpose.*) Better not get conceited, so you are now a Dinosaur (*this will probably begin to show some ingenuity among them*). Right, you are a Dinosaur still, but upright now and you are skating; suddenly you see that hat the posh person threw away, pop it on and be a posh Dino-skater...ah, but you didn't know it was a magic hat.'

(The record is nearing the end, let us say. I fade it down and begin to finish things very quietly.)

'It turns you into a very nice person. It's Christmas time, so you have a present to give (*record finishes, short silence*). Give something to the nearest person to you. Sit down for a bit. Explain to the person near what it is and receive their present to you.'

I always include somewhere and somehow, the symbols of niceness, thought for others and giving. I have a strong belief that, by using them in play, these symbols etch themselves in the unconscious and become part of the evolving personality. Amongst all the horrors and disappointments of our present world, it is worth trying.

It will be noticed that this elementary exercise is a community act. We are all doing it together, though each person is being each suggested character within the group. To this extent it is like the beginnings in the Infant Department. But soon we can emerge a little, with luck, into doing things with partners. So continuing our task:

SELF: 'Right, you have had a bit of a rest now. So, up we get again... Good; here is some more music coming (*slower this time*), you are in an aeroplane. Off you go...now (*precise again*).'

If you are lucky, you may well see some lovely examples of *running play*, arms are outstretched, faces joyful (*later on, ecstatic*), and some more interesting journeys starting to be made. It is a bit early to expect the 'S' shape or the '8' but that will come.

SELF: 'You touch down slowly...and...get out...and you find yourself in a wonderful Land...all golden sunshine...wonderful trees (*my voice getting quieter*)...beautiful flowers...and wonderful fruit. You sit down and eat some of it...and offer some to the next person. (*I fade the music right down and off.*) Now tell each other what you saw on the journey, what you saw in this Golden Land...which unknown fruit is nicest.'

(I said earlier, always find opportunities for them to speak.) So far I have been up one end, guiding and controlling the music, but now I wander amongst those at play and listen a bit to what is going on. I may say something like (*and **mean** it*),

'Oh, that's a nice looking fruit, what does it taste like?'

If the answer is only 'Nice', you know you have got a bit further to go. Then, trying to make the child think, I might say 'well, is it sweet? Is it crunchy? Is it soft and squishy? Does it make you feel warm?' (Child may answer.) I would then ask others about what they saw or ate, dotting about the room quickly, so as to seem reasonably fair to the various parts of the group. Perhaps I finish with 'Oh, lovely, what a gorgeous feast, thank you for telling me about it.'

SELF: (*after going back to 'control' end of room, or hall*)

'It might be kind to gather some of this beautiful fruit and take it back in the aeroplane. So pick up as much as you can and put it gently into sacks. Help each other and talk about it if you want to.'

(*You may now be surprised that quite a buzz may start. Don't be alarmed, they are not being naughty.*)

SELF: (*watching carefully and taking a judgement*)

'Right, that's fine, I think we have got enough in the sacks now (*Note: I am changing from the "I" feeling to "we"*). Put them carefully into the aeroplane...ready? Good, then off we go. *Now.* (Music fast up, exactly on the word 'now'). We are going home with the sacks...(longish fly home). Here we are, down we come, slowly (*fade music down as an intended accompaniment to the action*). Touch down...and *still* (*music out*). Now we unload the sacks...but just as we have got them all out of the aero, the Lord Mayor of the nearest City arrives. Tell him about the fruit...oh, let's decide to give him some of the sacks. (*They all talk to an unseen Lord Mayor.*) ...He is very pleased, because he knows a lot of people who would be very grateful for it, because they haven't got much money. (*I might put in a happiness dance here. Lord Mayor starts and all join in.*) Now the Lord Mayor has to go. Shall we say good-bye?'

CHILDREN: 'Bye; g'byee', ('ta-ra', 'chow?').

SELF: 'And we watch him as he goes.'

This gives me a chance to note whether any child is becoming absorbed and whether the sincerity brings me a feeling of belief in the way their eyes follow him. All is quiet. What the theatre calls repose.

SELF: 'Now we have one more job to do. We are going to form a big circle. Stay where you are for the moment; and then, coming quietly forward, gently place the sacks in the middle of the room. They are going to be used for people abroad who have nothing to eat. You see, fruit from the Golden Land doesn't go bad. Fine, now form your circle. (*I bring in a quiet, chosen part of slow music.*) Now carry your sacks gently to the centre, then return slowly to where you were...(*very quietly*): Lovely. Now we have one more job to do. If there is something you really like and you want to be really kind, shall we place it on the sacks? All these things could then be used for people abroad who have nothing, absolutely nothing. If you haven't anything to give – there's some buried treasure behind you. Dig it up quickly and then you might give that. (*Pause for diggers.*) Now we are ready...and if you still have nothing to give, give them a thought. Now we are ready. When the music comes, we go forward slowly and place all the gifts in the centre of the room.'

They do it, but one or two hurry back to their place after the giving, perhaps. And it is all a bit untidy. So I suggest one final bit to improve the atmosphere and indeed the neatness of the creation. This is where it is so much more helpful to have a record player and records, rather than tape, because you can go back at once to the same bit you chose, without any unwanted noise and with no pause, so the atmosphere you have built can be felt and kept and may well remain in children's minds as an aesthetic experience.

> SELF: 'I am going to ask you to be really clever, because you have shown me what good things you can do. It's just to make things more neat and even better than before. Just now, some people put their present on the pile in rather a hurry then they hurried back to their place. That's all right, because they had done their job, hadn't they? (*Note, I did **not** say "that was a silly thing to do wasn't it?"?*) But this time, let's come forward all together, keeping the circle really a ring shape. Don't squash in, all in the middle, or people will hardly be able to get through to put their presents on the pile. Remember, it's a big pile, so the circle doesn't have to be too small. See it in your mind. But this is the clever bit: When you all have put your present, or your thought, in the middle, try to go *backwards* away from the pile to form the bigger circle, but keep the neat, round shape all the time. Let's try. Listen to the *sound* of the person nearby, to help you (*group sensitivity*).'

So we do; and it may be better. It may not be. Then we have learned more about the group; they are not ready for it yet? Don't think you have failed, you have been *informed*. Don't over-press to get it neat, don't try more than twice altogether, at this stage, or it will go stale and the improvisation will lose its quality.

However, if this exercise goes well, you will feel a reward. If done later on, it will be more rewarding. And if you have given it at the right time for them, you will share an atmosphere of significance in which everyone is deeply moved. Don't do any more. End the lesson on complete quiet. Just say, 'Thank you'. Don't *talk*. Most teachers talk too much. Just let the experience sink in. Of course, a similar exercise could be used for Religious Assembly; and a Holy Person, Prophet or Angel suggest that we give away the presents. Anyway, it is a fact that should you ever be dealing with really difficult children or delinquents, the moment that they *think* of giving, rather than grabbing for themselves, is a sign of hope that they are going to change.

Do you think the above is sentimental and won't work? If so, you have lost the battle. We have got to *make* it work, for the good of the next generation, living in a contaminated world. We must not be afraid of Education of the Emotions, nor be afraid of beauty. I am always sorry for those who are. And when they are doubtful about creating such 'moments', I doubt whether they have ever had one, or the skill to create it.

I remember on one occasion, I had been taking the drama students of New York University in a somewhat similar exercise in London. It was done so well and the atmosphere was so terrific that several of them, coming to thank me afterwards, said they had never had such an experience in their life. One sad thing – a girl who had been particularly moved, rushed out to buy me a rose, but by the time she had returned, I had gone – whisked off to the next thing by my chauffeuse. I heard about it afterwards.

In a book of this kind, everything, of necessity, has to be foreshortened, so the above exercise might not be tried for some weeks, during which lots of opportunities might be given for being different people and things in quick succession so as to learn to jump into a part and bring it to life. *Then*, longer periods can be offered, of being someone, or something. General play-work can pass slowly on from general community experience to more work with partners, then slowly towards the gang, which is so important in the first part of Junior School. Oh, in any situation of 'giving a thought', don't be surprised if a child very seriously takes, as it were, a lump out of its head and opening a clutched hand, plants a fistful on another child's forehead. They are not attacking them. The opened palm shows you.

EXAMPLE OF PAIRS

SELF: 'Look down at the floor in front of you. Lying there is a musical instrument. We are going to pick it up and start playing – *now*.'

(*On that word start music for a march round. I let them go on for a bit, then fade the sound down and stop.*)

SELF: 'That was pretty good. What was your instrument? (*Child answers.*) And yours? And yours? Fine. Now swap instruments. Tell the nearest person to you what yours was and tell them how to play it'.

Depending on what is the *purpose* of the lesson, and of this part of it, this chatting may be long or short. If you want them to practise speech, don't hurry it. The speech noise will come to its own climax and then begin to die. Listen hard and you will know when to make the next suggestion.

SELF: 'Good, now play that one. (*Quick march round for a bit. Music out.*) Fine. Place your instruments carefully by the wall, then come back... This time you look on the floor and there is an instrument that nobody has ever seen before. Pick that up and start playing – *now*. (*March music again.*) This time you are very clever, because besides playing an instrument no-one has ever seen before, you can march in step too.'

(*I stop it again.*)

'Now, swap what you were playing and tell the person next to you how to play *your* instrument.'

(*If the pairs don't match up, make a three and let them choose the best two instruments.*)

This may take some time. Again, judge whether to allow for speech and imagination; or do you intend to get to something else important if possible, and get on with the lesson? Don't be a slave to your plan, though. So many inexperienced teachers are tempted to try and force through every note of every idea they have prepared, whether it be appropriate or not. Decision about a general need is different – that is, better movement needed, better speech, time for more ideas, time to get better pair work, more co-operation and so forth. Or are you going to try for more absorption today and use whatever exercises or suggestions seem to be needed? Maybe not all you have thought of beforehand.

Generally, the unknown instruments bring out wonderful blobs of imagination and I would go amongst the players and perhaps ask a few questions. I also listen in to one or two explanations so as to be genuinely instructed myself.

Although the exercise might have been mostly intended as a purposeful aid for pair work (in this case), the final march round of the unknown instruments is nearly always interesting and more often fascinating. I watch with astonished pleasure at the amazing mimed inventions that come to being. Down the years, perhaps some of the best, in this sort of a 'do', have been conceived by high grade athletes, in training to become PE teachers – the ones who perhaps might think this sort of thing was not quite their cup of tea. But it was nearly always the 'killer sessions' invented for them in dance, that brought them finally round. They couldn't think it wet after that.[1] With children, certainly enjoy what they have invented. Treat every invention seriously and be *really* instructed. Laugh with them, but never (as adults sometimes do) laugh at them.

Now moving slowly towards the gang and back to the norm.

EXAMPLE

SELF: 'Move into little groups of about six' (*If a small class, say 'About five'.*)
        'Good. Now I am going to come round and give you, very quickly, three ideas for each group and you are going to (*not "I want you to".*) make up a story from them'.

I go round. And there are five groups of six people in a class, say, of thirty. (Teachers would be forgiven if they have written down a prepared list, if they think that fifteen ideas on the spur of the moment would be too daunting. In time it gets easier!)

SELF: 'Fine. Move away a little more from each other, groups.'

        For this group (1) the ideas are: A naughty elephant, an ice cream and a chair.

---

1   'Killer sessions' was a name given by students to highly active and difficult sessions of dance – leaping, lifting weights, hurdling chairs and so on. Her own version evolved particularly well by Miss Sylvia Demmery (who had worked so closely with me), when a Tutor at Loughborough. It is a way of ensuring respect.

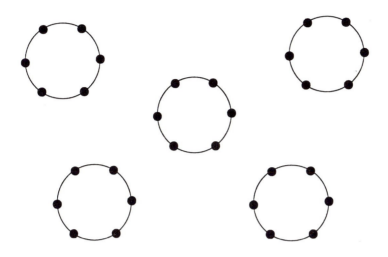

Diagram 2. Beginning the Gang groups. Typical circle shape

This group (2): A happy monkey, a red cloth and a tooth brush.

This group (3): A "bad" bucket, a blue hat and a kind cat.

This group (4): A piece of bubble gum, a table with a big tummy and a green parrot.'

This group (5): A pond, atomic roller skates, and a proud pony.'

At first there may be quite a lot of difficulty for them. If so, wander round and help them just a bit, not too much. It is their job. You will notice that the ideas given are fairly imaginative to help them to know 'how far they may go' and that I am not going to call them silly if they say anything imaginative or unusual. I included animals in each set, because the class has been reading about them and drawing them lately. The *kind* of help (which should be said *seriously*):

SELF TO GROUP 1: 'Stuck? Well, did Elephant want to sit down? Is the Chair strong enough for him? (*If more, or all, girls in the group, because they do go together very often to start with, I would, of course say "her".*) Does s/he sit on the Ice Cream?'

That might be enough. Don't be tempted to do it all, if you can *possibly* help it, like: 'The Elephant was greedy. He/she ate so many Ice Creams that she/he became too heavy for the Chair to hold up. So the Chair broke and Elephant fell down and had to be taken to hospital'. That would be long enough anyway for starting this. But if you wanted to make it evolve, after five (?) children had taken one (as Elephant) to hospital, they could all take flowers and bananas and magazines as a comfort when visiting. Of course, three children might try to take a conglomerate-elephant of three others to hospital. It would be unlikely to work. So if they want a big chap or chapess, suggest they try four taking a hanging-on lump of two, as a dilapidated elephantine patient. It might work better.

SELF TO GROUP 2: 'Why was the Monkey happy? Had he got shiny white teeth? Did he like wearing the Red Cloth? Did he use the Toothbrush for something else – like brushing his hair?'

SELF TO GROUP 3: 'Was the Bad Bucket *very* bad? Was he? Mm. Did Kind Cat wear the Hat and like it? What did Cat do with the Blue Hat?'

   (*Try not to suggest the Kind Cat gave the Blue Hat to the Bad Bucket and Bucket was so surprised and happy that it entirely changed Bucket, who was never bad or naughty again.*)

SELF TO GROUP 4: 'Why had Table got a big tummy? Did Table pinch other people's food from their plates, with one leg, when they weren't looking? Did Parrot try the Bubble Gum and did it work? Or did the Table use it? You think about those ideas and see if you can make a story now'.

SELF TO GROUP 5: 'Is it a big Pond? Is it deep? How many Atomic Skates are there? Enough for all Pony's legs? Do Atomic Skates go across water?'

(Don't say: 'Pony was so proud that he/she wanted to put on Atomic Roller Skates so as to be faster than anyone else. But it was too difficult to steer at that speed (I expect it was) and Pony and all the Skates hit some weed in the pond and got stuck. It was quite a time before help came'. It may be true, but that is their job, not ours.)

Next, we try to see what has been achieved. Although the preparation may have taken a long time; and sometimes one has to say 'Try to decide now. Don't discuss any more. If you haven't quite finished, be ready to show what you've got.' And, if time is running short for the lesson say, 'Just do the best bit(s) of your story', and let them know you are sorry we can't see it all.

Now comes an important part of the training. We are going to see their attempts, however elementary, but don't try and make it into an adult theatre show by saying such things as, 'Now, group one go up that end of the room and all the rest of us gather near as audience; and be ready to clap when they've done'. That breeds showing off and acting *at*, and for shy people it might make things difficult. Bring out the importance of *sharing*. Sharing *with* us, as a family of friends, what you have done. To help create this atmosphere, leave each little group, almost, or entirely, in its own place. They will act round and through any children near them. Sometimes they journey right across the hall. There should be *no clapping*. This is not theatre yet, it is Child Drama and is an inner experience that we are working for, not yet an outer event. The sharing attitude is a strong welding of the feeling of security, which in these days, alas, some children may find nowhere, unless you offer it to them in school.

After a time you will find that, with practice, they will get better and quicker at devising a story, and eventually by themselves without your help. As they get better at it one can sometimes say 'Think up your own ideas today for building your story'. But when you use this method, it is more satisfactory if each group acting out their story reminds us of what the ideas were, just before they begin. This informs those *sharing* the experience – and perhaps reminds us too of what we suggested! Before groups get really good at this (and sometimes even when they *are* good at it) it is often helpful to go round and just to save time, say 'Start trying it out now, don't discuss any more'. Thus all the groups (at the same time) may be having a little rehearsal after that. It seems to the unprepared eye a bit chaotic. But you only have to walk round to be made sure that they are pretty well involved. If one group seems ready before the others, get them to sit down. Choose the moment well and then invite the 'sharing' to start. Clap your hands or make a sudden noise, to make yourself heard. They must feel the security of your being in charge. Then suggest that the groups that were first to finish their rehearsal are first to start. Occasionally, when they are all about equal in the time they take in preparation, you might ask who would like to go first. Beware though, they might all want to, whether really ready or not. So be Solomon and judge wisely. When they finish their piece, don't automatically praise them, pick out something that might really have been good like: 'I thought the cat was so kind to Bad Bucket over the hat. I really enjoyed that'. When starting, train them to hold one or two seconds of silence before they start – always. This is not the moment when you are starting quick suggestions with a clap. *They* are in charge of the creation at this moment, and there must not be a messy beginning. The short silence brings much more atmosphere, the opening words, or movements, are not thrown away. There is a neat start. It is all part of discipline, in a strange way – and good form, and kind behaviour, thought for others, better-job-done.

As adults, we may not always quite understand every bit of what they create. Don't say things that are really critical like, 'John, whatever were you up to when so and so was happening? That bit was much too complicated, I hadn't the faintest idea what you were up to'. Don't blame them. I have occasionally heard this sort of mistake. It will not be an encouragement. I think one can be quite honest but also kind. If one expects good manners from the young, it is important to think carefully before appearing rude (perhaps without meaning to be) in what we say to them.

I sometimes have to say: 'You know that bit about so and so, I couldn't quite understand that. Could you tell me about it?' They are generally eager to do so. And in that moment you have established communication, a coming closer, every *second* of which is of extreme importance these days between the older and the young. Don't encourage the use of properties. The acting and the creation will be much better if they imagine everything at first. Later, they may wish to use a few things when they make up their own stories. But there can be an awful waste of time in sorting things out and then some groups may not have time to share their story with us.

One interesting thing happens. If there are rostrum blocks in the hall, for them quickly to set their scene (again watch for time), when it is done, one child may come up and move one block about an inch. Someone else will come and move it back again. With children with learning difficulties, this can go on quite a long time. With all groups, one would have to say quietly, 'I think the blocks are all right now.' Once or twice I just silently sat for a bit on the block that couldn't stay still. Then it did.

Let us say, they are now able to make up their own stories.

Cathartic Play

This is where one is moving towards, perhaps, the most important inner education of the Junior Child. It is where we offer them the opportunity of spitting out some of the evil we put into their minds through violent films, newspapers, magazines, television and pornographic video cassettes; also in adult conversation, which they ape. I have written and talked about this for years, discussed it with at least three Home Secretaries, have had a written question asked and have even spoken to a group of MPs at Westminster. It has been a constant anxiety for me that so often a group will be gathered together to 'investigate' this all over again. They come up with a verdict of 'no proof'. One could wish they would ask people who know something about it. But now, thank God, people are really beginning to think along these lines; and just lately a policeman in America has said there is definite proof that violence seen affects behaviour. And, of course, police everywhere have known about copy-catting for years, in various forms of crime.

When children make up their own plays, allow themes and characters of which you may disapprove. In this way family and personal worries are released and the unpleasantness of violence seen (or experienced) may be worked off. We should not forget that such moments may be sharing an important secret with us; they find relief in our friendship and understanding which allows them to play out illegal acts in a lawful manner. This form of play is partly unconscious, or comes from it (although intentional cartooning may be contained in it). It is a mistake to impose, too suddenly, conscious problems to enact. That is – guessing at a problem and structuring it too tightly for the child to create. Let them do it *their* way.

It used not to be difficult to start things off. In some areas of the country, now, children may start straight away, in others they may be numbed by experience and feel imprisoned over acting what they know. Others may be involved in crime already and aren't going to reveal any clues. My point is, though, that they *need* to act it out. Later in the book will come more detail.

Here we are only concerned with offering a simple opportunity. The acting out *can* be valuable at any age, but after more than 50 years of careful observation, investigation and experience, I would say that, in school, this age of seven to nine is the most important. They know quite well, by now, the difference between what is good and what is not; and if they do not get rid of at least *some* evil, by blowing off steam under lawful guidance, there is going to be trouble.

I sometimes start by saying something like, 'Well, we've been building up stories from ideas for quite a time, today you can make them up about anything you want to'. There may be some exaggerated stories about home or school, or a bit of violence may come into things. It is important to say here that there is often fighting and killing in Child Drama. Don't be alarmed. It is not necessarily a sign of delinquency. It is a symbol of overcoming. It is important that they should overcome and win through. It is an inner expressive practice, shown in outer form, for coping with competitive life 'as it am'. It is generally fairly easy to distinguish this Siegfried and St. George and the Dragon style of legendary action as against straightforward reality. Sometimes one may have to say, 'Did you see any films last night?' Or, 'Which ones do you like best?' Cops and robbers generally come higher on the list than cowboys and so forth, these days. So do spacemen, burglary, also cruelty to animals, sometimes computer fraud. In some tactful way, it is our job to let children understand that they are allowed to act whatever has impressed them in some way.

I know this may be a difficult point for some of those in charge. It used to be *much* more difficult years ago, when teachers were used to more formal styles of education and were only slowly enticed into freer types of constructive activity. Now things have swung too far in many places and the danger is that in stiffening everything '3 Rs' wise', the time *for*, and importance *of*, play may be squeezed out of mind and place.

I have given quite a long description of the possible changes and how to build up to this point, because it is so vitally important. Some time ago, it was (and could have been much more) important as a definite avoidance of delinquency, for children to act out violence they had experienced in any way. By 1958 I felt able to say, 'The playing out has a markedly improving effect upon behaviour, and can act as a simple form of prevention of neurosis. It is only a slight exaggeration to say that the child has to patch up by play methods what our education has failed to prevent'. Wouldn't it be more sensible to have this simpler form of prevention established on a much wider scale in education? Perhaps one day it will be.

Do not let anyone be disturbed by this reference to therapy. Much of it is a perfectly natural process, and, in any case, it is very important not to stifle any interest in adventure. This is a virile side of youth, a potential part of a virile nation; it only needs guiding aright.

In support of this, the late Dr William Kraemer (formerly Deputy Director of the Davidson Clinic, Edinburgh, and then of Harley Street) said: 'I find myself in complete agreement with Peter Slade's ideas on Drama. I have heard a good deal of his work and seen some, and I feel sure that drama as conceived by him will prove of great value to education and therapy, to society and the individual. Slade rightly emphasises the role drama should play in prevention of neurosis. There is hardly a patient who does not, in his artistic expression find a high road to health. It may be drawing or painting, music or poetry. It is all what Slade would call 'the drama of life'. It is always, as in Slade's definition, creative doing'.[2]

We did not expect to have to be sort of social doctors in schools. Except for schools of a special kind, therapy was not expected, only prevention through natural means, which happened to be therapeutic in themselves. But now we are up against it. We are all in a war against crime, some influenced by drugs. Parents, teachers, therapists, doctors, police, MPs, show-business, old people, churches – we must all be allies, not argue against each other, but see which part we can play as a *contribution* to the good of the whole. I am not pretending that just acting out violence and evil in a Junior School is going to prevent all crime. If it were ever true, that time has gone. Things have gone too far now. Society is ill. But the acting out *can* help. Whereas in earlier years it could have been considered as important and valuable, it is now vital. It can help in avoidance for some children, particularly those on the brink of being badly influenced. We must save whom and what we can.

In school, it is valuable sometimes to have discussion about doing good, or the opposite, after such acting. There is now a full place for Social Drama in Junior Schools. It is necessary in some Infant Schools already, as the virus of evil attracts the innocence of our younger and younger, beloved offspring. The sort of work and discussion I have talked about might be linked with the 'Primary Children Doing Philosophy', as outlined by Dr Victor Quinn, Karen Murris, Catharine McCall and others. Their work intends to call out the powers of *distinguishing*, of constructive critical judgement in children, which is their better part, waiting to be fanned into flame, before it is too late. Discussions in association with Drama can do the same. Watch out for *tyranny* of the gang, which is rife at this age. By subtle swapping round, leaders find themselves in another group and have less influence. Others suddenly *have* influence. Those 'put upon' before may be unexpectedly relieved when their leader (oppressor) is moved.

---

2 Statement made after one of the author's talks to the Guild of Pastoral Psychology. Reproduced in Slade 1954, p.120. Original words 1949.

Less Convenient Conditions

Although we have been concerned with the best, or better conditions for this work, that is, in a hall, it is perfectly possible to do much of it in a confined space, or in a classroom. Even if we are all to go back to formal desk placing, and black, or green board at one end, there is no reason why things should not be started by teacher suggestion. You can get someone, say, from desk, table, or chair, far right at back to ring up someone full left at the front about a crime that has happened. Criminals can call each other, so can police, even Interpol, dotted about between the desks or tables.

And many a good 'murder' have I seen beneath a desk. And, once, the end of *Macbeth*, with bodies on top of almost every desk in the room, though that was with young Seniors. But there is no reason why action cannot take place between desks. Indeed the avenues make good roads. If small circles begin to be made, out and away from desks at 'teacher's end' by children discussing, don't mix it up with theatre, as said before. Don't tell them not to turn their backs when acting begins. Remember, they are only trying to do their genuine Child Drama in less adequate conditions than might be. They may form circles. In this, they are often both actor and audience, creating from the centre of themselves all round their body, the more so, as they become the more involved in their task. At this time of deep involvement, they may be, and should be, totally unconcerned about those at the desks, who look like a planned audience – as they *are* for general school work. Of course, if, as a teacher, you wish to try this work, but are not quite confident about your ability to keep control in a large space, start it in a classroom by all means, but *do* it.

However, as a step towards it, as you, in yourself, build courage, why not clear the tables, or push the desks to one side if you want to? You know, in the theatre, it is possible to find some quite apparently simple looking people, who (you might not imagine it) can *suddenly* change a whole scene, partly in the dark in a few minutes flat. There is absolutely no reason why a group of healthy, normal children can't change a classroom in a few minutes too. It will be noisy at first. Get them to do it to help *you* and if it is so noisy, make them put it *all* back and jolly well do it again as quietly as possible. We must be concerned for other people, that is the class next door. Don't let them get lazy minded as 'Coo, move all that?' Expect more of your children and you will get it.

Getting Out of 'Violent Play'

Stress has been placed upon the importance of arriving at the time when children can play out evil. Once you feel it is time for them to do it, let it be regular and often. But although they may have discovered through your help, how to blow off violent steam in a creative way, they should not do it *all* the time, otherwise they will get stuck in a rut. There must be some way of getting

Teacher

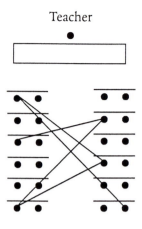

Diagram 3a. Telephoning, if in return to old classroom situation. Interpol can still exist

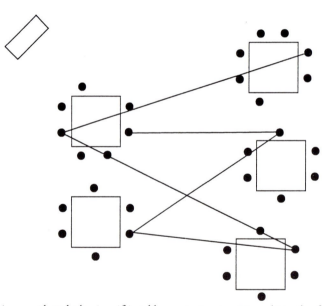

Diagram 3b. Telephoning, if in table group situation. Note: this makes for near family circles of
*   the gang*

them out of it, so that there is hope, at least in the unconscious, for something better. So, you might tease them gently and say something like, 'I bet you can't do a story today without guns'. By about nine years old, if the cathartic gang stage has gone well, they are beginning to need this change. Later, 'Bet you can't do a story without a mugging or a burglary'. Later, 'You have had your turn for three weeks, now it's my turn. So today we will have *no* killing at all'.

Later, work towards a general agreement about some story, which has no killing and no crime. It is important that it should be *agreed* about this. And once decided, it must be carried out. That is training in democracy. It is *our* story. We agreed.

Up until recent years, one might feel that children had grown out of the need for violent play and could now enter upon what used to be truly the glorious years of children's own Art Forms and creation. But now that is not always so. It may be in some areas, but in many there will be a continued need for some periods where violent blowing off of energy and sheer nastiness can regularly take place. Language may become uncouth. If you feel you should do something about it, don't interrupt play, but be firm about not having bad language in general conversation. Many fine teachers have tried to put this cathartic play into effect, but comparatively few have really known how to get children out of the rut. Hence the above suggestions. But my prediction is that, for a number of years to come, it will not be so clear cut as in the past, but we must also ease onwards to try and enter into acting stories, as it were, of cleaner content, so that young people can have experience of a different outlook at higher level. There may even be opportunity still for improvisations around the ancient myths and legends, and of stories that have stood the test of time.

In all this play about violence, it is best to have no props. All weapons should be of air, imagined. One can learn to use a three foot sword (gun or club) that isn't there, with tremendous energy and emotion and run through many a foe. Once learned, you can spit out the *feelings*; you do not have such urge to do it in the street for real.

FURTHER EXAMPLE OF GETTING OUT OF THE RUT

So, by careful judgement and a little tactful shepherding, it is possible for a gangster to end up as Christopher Columbus – which is wonderful, because Christopher Columbus is history and therefore respectable. It would happen through discussion:

> 'All right; well, we've had a lot of good gangster work. Now let's change the theme a little and have our gangsters in a boat. Anybody know anything about pirates? What do they wear? Who has to deal with smugglers? Anyone know?'

So we work towards considering coast guards; let them play a theme on that, and then follow with some such words:

> 'It must have been awful in the days when you couldn't put out to sea without being afraid of pirates. In some parts of the world it is becoming like that again today. Do you know the names of any people who might have found it difficult to put out to sea? Not necessarily anyone who was afraid, but someone who would have to think twice about pirates?

Anyone know the names of people in history who would have had to cope with this?'

If no one answers, supply a name. Have a voyage of discovery. Associate the rough behaviour of the original gangsters with a more constructive purpose; let them be explorers and savages with vigour, but, if you wish to ensure some moral instruction, see that at one time they understand that the good man can win. I always have one period dropping the hint that there can be such a thing as a good coast guard, and a good pirate, and that mercy rather than death, and justice rather than law, are important. It helps them to understand authority in school without resentment.

Rostrum Blocks

Still use only the floor space in the junior school. If a stage exists in the hall, use it only as a simple locale such as a palace. The world is the floor of the hall, where most of the action should take place in the development of genuine Child Drama.

However, do make use of rostrum blocks. They can be used in *projected* play, as a development of nursery bricks with which to build things, and in *personal* play as a means of developing a sense of music, rhythm and dramatic climax, and also for beginning to sense the effect of being raised up. I discovered this through studying the enormous empire of street play. There exists in street play a discovery of higher levels, because of the kerbstones and pavements contrasting with the road. Amongst many rhythmic adventures causing delight, I distinguished in running play the climax. This takes place when emotional music of the feet carries the child on to the pavement. The higher level in itself appears to be a stimulus and is clearly used with conscious satisfaction. I intend that as many children as possible shall have the opportunity of discovering this pleasure *in* school, where it can be even more constructive and is without danger to life.

Running play itself appears to be an expression of sheer joy accompanied generally by bent knees, arms wide and ecstatic expression. It only grows in a happy atmosphere, and I have never seen it in any junior school where a stage is extensively used and formal theatre with scripts takes place.

The use of the higher level provided by rostrum blocks is also a slow approach to the use of a stage. Any sudden use of a stage brings showing off, which can be injurious to the developing personality, as it is to the drama itself. This is part of keeping the child young. But sophistication today starts early, which tempts early 'adult-like' productions, good, indeed, though many of them are. The eternal 'Dreamcoat' is one of the most popular. I don't want to anger or offend any of those wonderful, enthusiastic teachers, who produce stage shows. I just put the point that if you want to preserve certain inner parts of Childhood (so increasingly necessary these days) there are other ways of developing the true drama of the child, which, if guided and slightly polished, can come to perfection at the age of eleven or twelve. Their true art still shows little perception of perspective. Proscenium theatre is *personal play* in perspective form. It is generally used a a social event. But we are concerned here with inner education.

Here is a further example of the 'Ideas' method of reaching a story, which I invented to help things along in the early 1930s and wrote about in *Child Drama* in 1954. It *might* help. I notice they are using something similar on television these days. This time without the use of sounds to stimulate the ideas. (This method would be of great value with junior children who have done none of this work in their Infant schools.)

EXAMPLE OF WORK TAKEN IN A SCHOOL, MOVING TOWARDS FAIRY STORY, A FURTHER STEP AWAY FROM VIOLENCE

SELF: 'Let's have some ideas.'

A CHILD: 'A river.'

ANOTHER: 'Little boy.'

ANOTHER: 'Willow tree.'

ANOTHER: 'Horrid mother.'

SELF: 'Right, here's our story, then:

'Once upon a time there was a *little boy* who had a *horrid mother*. She beat him, she starved him and made him work half the night. He never got any sweets, not even any bubble gum. And they lived by a thin silver *river*, the colour of the moon. One night, the little boy looked out of the window, and as he looked the moon was reflected in the river and he saw quite clearly the man in the moon. Whether it was the movement of the water or not the little boy didn't know, but all at once he saw the Moon-Man's mouth move and heard a voice saying: 'Don't stay, little boy, come out and live by the river.' Then a cloud came and the moon disappeared. The little boy threw on some clothes, took his favourite bit of string and a bright button from under his pillow, and crept downstairs and out of the house. Once outside, he ran as fast as he could until he dropped exhausted by the river bank and went to sleep. In his sleep he dreamt that a *willow tree* bent over him and hummed a leafy song. The tree sang: 'I will be your mother. If ever you want strength, suck the green twig I hold towards you and everything will be all right.'

'The little boy woke up and there, sure enough, was the willow tree, waving and waiting. He sucked one of the green fingers. A flood of happiness leapt up in him, and a taste of electric honey. He ran and ran, with the dew in his hair and an early sun shining through it. Suddenly he saw a farm, and the farmer gave him some wood to chop, and food for doing it. But the little boy never would stay with the farmer and his kind wife. He always went back to the willow, his new mother. Whenever he needed strength, he sucked the green twig. And he grew and grew and became the strongest wood-chopper in the whole district. But one day the river got angry and began to break its banks. He didn't know why, but the little boy, who was now quite a big boy, you remember, thought of his real mother. With a loud bang, part of the bank broke and the water began to pour through. The boy started to dash towards his old home and arrived just in time to save his mother. They made a raft of an old door and paddled towards the kind farmer. By the time they arrived safely at the high ground of the farm, the old mother had repented of her unkindness and the boy forgave her. They all lived at the farm, and the kind farmer's wife taught the mother how to stay kind all the time – a jolly difficult thing to do. But, do you know, when the river had gone back into the long bed of its banks, the willow tree had entirely disappeared. Wasn't that extraordinary? Sometimes the Moon-Man seemed to appear in the river and to wobble his mouth about, but for some reason that cannot be understood he never spoke again.'

A CHILD: 'Why did the river get angry?'

SELF: 'I don't know. What do you think?'

ANOTHER CHILD: 'E got angry wiv the mother 'cos she'd done somethink 'orrible.'

ANOTHER CHILD: 'The man in the moon said something 'e didn't like.'

SELF: 'Yes, there might have been all sorts of reasons. Now, when we come to that bit (all who would like to), think what would make *you* angry if you were the river. Then the river will get angry all right. The boy's house is over there. Let's have the river here. Make a nice pattern with it. Where will the tree be?'

(*They told me. I just wanted to give them enough of the geography for the essentials to be clear. They suggested the rest and chose the cast.*)

A CHILD:'Can we 'ave the table for the house?'

SELF: 'Yes, and the rest of it can be you three.'

(*I suggested this because three children obviously wanted to join the group but hadn't been invited yet. They made themselves into gables. But ten or fifteen children were still on one side of the room, and about eight on the other.*)

SELF: 'You ten be animals on the farm. The rest of you be the river.'

I didn't have to say any more. They organised all the rest. I just suggested when it should begin. Everyone joined in to make the special 'leafy humming' of the willow tree. Children who were being the river lay down in a curly line and got up in a swarm to overflow the banks. We used part of a record of the music of *Job* to accompany this. My task was to fade it in on the record player to provide an inspiring background. The story took twenty-four minutes to play through (see Diagram 4).

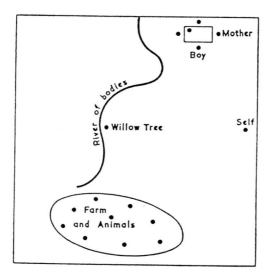

Diagram 4

Polishing Improvisations

Allow more repetition of the play themes and occasionally polish the improvised attempts by putting in suggestions. So that their enthusiasm is not
dampened, let them play through first and then discuss afterwards.

EXAMPLE

'Yes, I like the way you did that. Do you think we could make it (NOT – you'd
be better if) more interesting and exciting?'

Accept their answers. Use their suggestions, if any, and add something of
your own like: 'I thought it would be better if the messenger came in more
excited still, in more of a rush, then the people chasing him could rush in, too;
but instead of getting into a bundle near that part of the room they could use
the space in this part, fill it in and make a nice shape.' I don't tell them at this
age what shape to make, merely draw attention to some little piece of beauty
they may have missed. They do it – not me.

This one suggestion may be quite enough to give added life to the whole
theme. Few suggestions, but carefully chosen ones, are right. Too many
suggestions depress them. We must be very careful not to interfere or nag.

I hope this advice may aid those who are afraid direction will kill creation,
and, on the other hand, give encouragement to those who are convinced that
the sympathetic adult has an important contribution to make when present
during dramatic play in school. These moments are education as differentiated
from playing in the playground. Children do not come to school for nothing.

But it is wise to accept their way of going about things, and it is not dishonest to avail oneself of opportunities of building wisdom and finding achievement together.

Language Flow

Towards nine years, children should be well able to invent and act stories of their own, though dialogue becomes more earthy and wit is quicker. Here is an extract from the dialogue of one of these creations from way back, but I still enjoy it.

BOY: (*as factory owner, to spiv trying to get a job*)

'Owja get inter my faktry with them wide shoulders? The door's too narrah?'

SPIV: (*quick as lightning*)

'Ah, I coom in sidewiz.'

We get genuine dialect and a flow of language often coming straight out of home background at this age.

Outbursts of speech, creative or otherwise, are greatly to be encouraged. It is important that there should be practice. You need not fear that frank and open children will be impudent; on the whole they are not, and by winning their friendship and trust one is ultimately rewarded by their trying to be pleasant and helpful. But this entirely depends on whether the adult honestly treats the child as a decent human being or as something inferior.

Dialect is primarily a question of music, and the ear becoming used to certain sounds. Though we may love good speech, it is very important not to make children feel ashamed of the music of their home background. To force an artificial change of personal music may sever many ties and produce a fish out of water. Artificial, half-improved speech is a joy to no one. It is much better to let the dialect remain, but encourage some habits of clarity. At the same time it is perfectly possible to give the child the idea of turning on the tap of another kind of speech, which should not be presented as *better* but *different*. Most children are very adaptable in this way and can turn on the tap quite easily, and, if encouraged in the right manner, are quick to discover the occasions when the different types of language are appropriate. For instance, it is common for children to speak reasonably well and quietly in school and to be loud and unintelligible in the street. But it is interesting to note that where good opportunity for language-flow is given *in* school, rowdiness outside diminishes. This does not happen if formal training is the only training received, for one of the causes of stridency is lack of opportunity for outburst. There *will* be outbursts somewhere and somehow; we might just as well ensure that they are legitimate, intended, creative and beautiful.

We also get apparently incongruous and anachronistic pieces of life experience being brought in. For instance, a particularly holy band of monks I once met would burst out suddenly singing 'Roll out the barrel' at regular intervals. But, after all, there is a sort of logic about this.

Here is an example of inventive dialogue:

GIRL(8): 'I am the man with the electric nose. I speak and spark like the sun, and the wicked ones fear my sparking as I come. I fear it, too, but I don't tell anyone.'

If children try to tell you a story in school they may often start with 'There was this man, see...'. one should get them out of this gently. But if the type of play described has been taking place regularly, the flow of language becomes richer in content, often philosophic. And, if we have not messed up children's minds with rhyme, which they mistake for poetry, their words often flow with rhythm and a genuinely pure poetic quality.

Examples from children who have attained their Dawn of Seriousness:

ADULT: 'How's that porridge, is it nice?'

CHILD(7): 'It's full of smiles crushed up, thank you.'

CHILD(7.5): 'I don't think that workman is a funny man, he hasn't got wit in his face.'

CHILD(6.5): (*after having myths read by teacher in school*)

'Do you think their Gods would be pleased if I took my soldiers away? I could, you know. For I am the General of Generals, I am the strongest in the World.'

This last bit is rather like the Psalms isn't it?

Going back a bit in age I have just found an example of where a mother has practised *near finish* but the Child still has a *little* resistance.

ADULT: (*gently*) 'Come on, one minute's up.'

CHILD(5): 'Oh no, a minute isn't up till the apples are ripe on the tree.'

The following might also be put in the later chapter on therapy, but the language is so special that I put it here.

Conversation on a short walk after dramatic play.

CHILD(7): 'We are the posting men. We post the letters of the stay-at-home ones. I am the light-carrier. I shine my light up and out into the air...' (*The child had a torch.*)

SELF: (*rapidly interjecting*) 'But not at those who pass by, for they are the driving ones,who must have no dazzling...'

CHILD: 'Yes, they are the driving ones. For them I shine my light on the ground. That driving one has two large lights. One shines to heaven, the other...spits in a puddle. Oh, this is where we stop a moment.'

SELF: 'Looking right and looking left and looking right and looking left, and looking right... As we pass over to the far distant side.'

CHILD: 'Yes, we are the searchers, we are the posting men. We take the letters which will make happy readers over the sea. The sea is bright blue with white spots, for it is snowing. You can go in the shop now and buy a stamp. I stand here, for I am the guarding man. I guard the large mouth in the letter box. It is red.'

Note: By keeping more or less to the rhythm it was possible to give an urgent order without breaking the flow. The order about the light was infiltrated into the play and obeyed at once (by a quite difficult child), whereas a sudden stern command would, I judged, have caused a break, as well as resentment. The road safety instruction also considered the child's rhythm with sympathy. Looking at my own words, as they flowed then, they appear to be palely imitative of T. S. Eliot, whereas the child's are a reactive and unconscious approach to Arthur O'Shaughnessy's 'The Music Makers'.

CHILD(6):   'The rain is like dragonflies flying backwards down. Stripes of them.'

CHILD(7):   'I am a big boat, with a hundred funnels, dancing through the waves. Over the sea I go to the far far lands, and that little island is *England.*'

GIRL(9):   'Where is my bird, my dove? Where is my messenger? Call for him, call for him with a loud noise, use your highest voice and tell him the ON-DRAGON is coming.'

Overheard in a school corridor.

TWO BOYS: (*crouching down*) ''Ere she is, she's cummin, she is cummin. Crouch down 'ard. She mustn't see, or she'd slam the ear off yer 'ead.'

CHILD(6):   'Oh, look, there's the first dear star of evening, my friend. Look, shining there! If it comes over the roof, I'll climb out of the window and catch it in my hand.'

CHILD(6):   (*A child went behind an old radio and without turning it on (imagining that it was a TV?) started to announce*)

'Now we are going to the zoo.'

(*There followed a great variety of noises, including bow-wows, meows, cock-a-doodle-doos, sheep bleats and cow moos. These were very loud and rather trying, so an adult (not being able to stand it any more, but still remembering the child's play) stepped to the set and clicked an imaginary button*)

CHILD(6):   'I think we'll just see if there is anything on another programme'. (*A long pause, then child announcing*) 'All stations are zoo today, as it happens.' *The noises then redoubled. Clever indeed is the adult who can outwit the child in its own sphere of imagination.*

CHILD(6):   (*very declamatory style*) 'Come, we will down the passage go and fry the noses of those thieves. Do not be frightened 'cos I am the King's own royal royalist soldier and I have two guns, a sponge and a toothbrush with …mind the stairs which are there for falling down into hell.

Adam was a naughty man. (*Confidentially*) Do you think he tried not to sin?'

SELF: 'Oh yes, I think he tried hard, like we do.'

CHILD: 'Well, I'm not sure.'

This is an example expressing knowledge of right and wrong, which should be showing in their play at this age. If not, one should begin to wonder a bit and watch and listen carefully.

CHILD(6–7): 'Once upon a time there was a naughty little dog and he did such a naughty thing one day. And he did this. He told a little boy to not do what his mother said and to do what the devil said. And then he started to make the whole world to do what the devil said. And God was very sad and fighted very hard with the devil. And even *harder* than he used to do.'

BOY(8): 'Once upon a time there was a little boy and he did what his mother said. And he gave away all kinds of his food, and God sent an Angel to make him do some big fighting against the devil.'

CHILD(6): (*to mother*) 'When I saw that your breakfast was smaller than mine, I cried in my mind and tears fell on my heart.'

I am sure the reader will recognise the rhythmic value of the above; and the examples, with such unexpected ideas, offer us a sort of romantic enchantment. As for the boys in the corridor, I am tempted to say that there are some modern poets, who appear to win prizes for that sort of thing, though with these two it was quite unconscious. Whatever children say, we have a chance of discovery. We may miss some glorious words, if we don't listen. They may make up words too. I remember my joy when a child cried out 'Oh look at that *dilangwinary* cow.' What could better describe the dilatory, languid, heavy-hangingness, slow, and weary trudge home of that full lady?

Play and Other Subjects (Short Comments)

Before going on to consider the polishing process between nine years to eleven, perhaps we should note how drama-play can aid such things as foreign languages, history, geography, religious education, English, science, music and mathematics. This is particularly true of Junior education.

Foreign Languages

French first: here we are, of course, concerned with the actual learning of words. This is a slog and there is no way of getting out of it. Next comes some understanding, say, of French grammar. In times past, grammar was the most important thing, because that is what counted in exams. That and precision of all kinds. French is a very careful language. So much so that there are numbers of words and sayings that cannot be translated, so they have to use the actual English words and those of other languages, it appears.

One of the complications is gender. And I have been asked sometimes 'Why is such and such word feminine?' There is no proper answer to that. It just *is* so. And if you want further information you have to ask the French. But they shrug and look at you somewhat pityingly or show signs of thinking you are mad. I suppose, after a time, it becomes a matter of feeling, you just know *that* gender feels right and it becomes automatic. All this came to a climax for me when I suddenly realised that my parents were going to take me to France in the holidays and I would actually be expected to *speak* this stuff. I couldn't. After years of *in-flow* (i.e. bashing in of declensions, agreements, genders, pronunciation and ways of putting things), I had not had one single lesson all my school days in *out-flow* (i.e. how to speak the language). This goes back to what was said earlier about not having a wall growing up inside one, so that one feels imprisoned and then *unable* to speak. For this reason I have always felt it important for all little scholars to have the chance to speak and not be put off, when t is difficult. We should try. This means times for practice. But there is another thing I have tried with some success, that is our old friend Jabber-talk. I don't know whether it would work with you. But there are two ways of using it that seemed to be a help to some children. One is to let people jabber in their own made-up language and then stick in any French words they know – even if it's only one. It often brings a feeling of hope and encourage-ment, because 'I can speak French now, can't I? I just did.' Little sentences can follow in the real language.

There are numbers of records and tapes of foreign languages these days, for children to listen to. And this brings me to my second point. The English, in general, are notoriously bad at the actual pronunciation of other languages. As well as the meaning, the music of the words is so important. After having the chance of listening to an actual French (or other) voice on a record, or tape, I have had wonderful discussions in pure Jabber-talk, but using the actual music of a particular language. Some children are absolutely brilliant at this. And in French, I remember seeing beautiful gesticulations and shrugs to go with it. So – what is the purpose of the lesson today? To practise so as to loosen inner feeling and include more and more words? Or is this lesson to concentrate on sound alone? You must have a purpose, otherwise we can waste time.

I have spoken mostly about French because France is so close. Many people hop over there now to do their shopping and of course there should be practice by use of shopping scenes for children in school, as soon as they have enough command of the language they are studying. After this they could make up little plays. The best I have seen have been in Junior schools. It is the same for other languages too. Italian is a favourite one for Jabber-talk (oh, and also made-up improvised opera. This goes beautifully in Jabber-sing (together, I fear, with atrocious over-acting). Spanish and Greek are becoming useful to try. But I think I almost prefer German. 'Was it blenkinstein ferhatenburg *descreit sie* in heukenvil, behotten sich haber gevolting sein, ha?' and so on. Why should adventures into what people say outside our island not be fun as well as slog? To approach a task with pleasure is no bad thing.

History

In many Junior Schools the idea of acting stories of the past has been fairly established, but the world and ideas about history are changing now. Though there is still a place for heroes and wars, for it is no good pretending they didn't happen, the interest is moving rather more to how people lived, what they thought, what caused their behaviour to go one way or the other. The great families and 'great' men and women still exist, and great people crop up from fresh backgrounds every now and again. But their role is changing and history is becoming more concerned with the general public, their needs and with social events. History is not, perhaps, a young person's subject. They have not lived long enough to know what it means. But an enthusiastic teacher can work near miracles all the same. They can even raise some interest in heraldry. This can complicate the art, because heraldry needs precision and children's real art creation, at this age, is still fluid and often floppy at the edges. If however, you are not a stickler for detail, some wonderful unknown Arms, with rampant animals and oddments, gules, can be created. If *you* are a stickler, then we are probably back to the idea of the teacher doing the line drawing and children filling in the colour. But what is the purpose of the lesson? It may not be for Art, it may be for learning fairly accurately about the symbols used by our ancestors in the past (and by a minority of people, of course, today).

If the school does gardening, there is a wealth of connection with history from early agriculture to the formality of gardens – Henry VIII and Elizabeth and thence to Capability Brown. His change of landscape might lead to some wonderful child pictures, as would the formal gardens. Collecting herbs can be fun too. Making costumes, drawing and painting of events often come into this study, combined with 'brave' visits to museums and old houses. Short related bursts of period music should be included, perhaps with improvised dance (where possible), before any formal step training. A full community march round is valuable every now and again, as concentration may not last long at this age. But the drama, guided right, is what gets young people genuinely into the past. Until you have actually acted a character, really been *in* it, with all the sincerity that a child can muster, it may be hard for a young person to have deep interest. With many children in our midst of different ethnic backgrounds, it is important not to be too British all the time. We should learn about some of their history too; and how it came to be that so many of us are here *now* – to find a new peaceful brother and sisterhood in our classroom *together*.

Geography

Is a little bit the same. Like history, the details are changing, one used to learn the counties then their chief cities and what they made there, the rivers and why they were important. After that we learned which were the red bits on the world map. But today, rivers are different, some need cleansing, they are not (yet?) main transport throughfares. And in the cities they don't always manufacture what they used to. The populations have changed. So have even the counties. Geography now has to be seen much in conjunction with history. The world, 'getting smaller', brings us closer to many places we hardly know, or perhaps had never heard of. Even countries have changed. I remember directing a teachers course where we enacted a wonderful scene about life in an obscure part of Africa and ran a medical Mission. It went on for a whole morning. A remark I treasure from it was 'I never had the faintest idea how they lived and what they suffered and what their hopes were until this morning. I have really lived part of their lives.' Eskimos and Canadian Indians would be a good subject also, for a short project. In a world, which is suffering from global warming and holes in the ozone and forests being cut down and famine and drought, ecology comes into it all. Things are going wrong. Our children need to know something of this, without being too frightened. But they should see quite clearly, for their own future, that we are all in this together.

Religion

This, for some teachers, may be the most difficult subject of all. Not only may they not feel easy about teaching it, but there is a natural feeling of privacy about their own belief. As one teacher, who came to me in a very distressed state said, 'I don't feel happy about it. I know what *I* think, but I'm not sure I want to tell other people about it'. Well, of course one does not *need* to tell people what one feels oneself. There is so much to teach, other than that. Our task is to inform what we are told in Church, according to our own faith, and in scripture. But, of course it does help if our own beliefs are true and deep. And this can be associated with morals and attitudes. In a way we have been talking somewhat about religion already in parts of this book, because it has been about the psyche, the soul, the feelings and the inner part of the child, kindness and consideration. One visitor to the Rea Street Centre asked 'Why are you so successful with difficult children, do you think?' I believe I answered (as I would to any similar question) something like

'I don't know that I am. One can only tell some time afterwards. You just hope and go slowly on. First you have to find out "where they *are* in life"; and that comes by using the Arts, the Arts of the child's own kind (unsullied) shout it at you. We have to learn to read them correctly. Then, by their use, children in trouble, sad, lonely, bored, angry, backward, outlaws, find something inside themselves that they did not know was there. It is then that they begin to understand what you are talking about, if you bring up obeying a simple rule, or thought for others.'

It is immensely important that this guiding and investigation should be done in schools, not only in special centres. The two must go hand in hand. What you must *not* do, in school, is to burst into a room and state loudly, 'Right, sit down you lot, we're going to talk about God this morning – page FOUR!' I think we have to approach things carefully, for there are two parts to the matter. One is to impart creed and gospel, the other is to arrange experience, so that some deep inner chord is touched. The latter is the difficult part, but perhaps the most important, for without it, no religion is genuinely lived. Without it, we are left with mere religiosity; and it is this that can become either boring for the young, or dangerous (for the older also) when pressed to bigoted extremes.

I am speaking, first, rather from the viewpoint of Christianity, although fully aware that there are other religions in our midst these days. But the Church of England happens to be the state religion (Established church) of our country and, by historical descent from her forbears, the Queen is (at the moment) head of it. So, in a way, we are concerned with the law of the land and its tradition.

It is perfectly possible for an atheist, a freethinker, a humanist, an agnostic, or anyone else to teach the formal side of RE, if they are prepared to do so, without pushing their own views by adding propaganda like 'Of course, this is all rubbish really, you know'– or even giving the slightest inkling of such attitude. They are often kindly people, who could also impart a good message over behaviour and relationships. Children should not be brow-beaten into belief, but be given the facts, as we have been given them. These may be augmented by ammunition in their faith, such as prayers and stories from the Bible and some indication of the reasons for the forms of Services.

For teaching compassion, don't despise having discussions about the words of songs such as Simon and Garfunkel's 'Mrs.Robinson', or Matt Monro singing 'We're gonna change the world' (Matthews and Harris).

Although I have a great love for the old words and way of putting things (the old Book of Common Prayer is an English treasure), I realise that many young children do not always understand the simplest ones. An example is of the son of a famous doctor.

ADULT: 'What did you do at school today?'

CHILD: 'Ligion'

ADULT: 'Did you learn any prayers?'

CHILD: 'No.'

ADULT: 'What, not even the "Our Father"?'

CHILD: 'Oh yes, I know that one – Are Father, chart in Heaven, hullo what's your name?'

(My own first postcard home from school read 'We won genst Senter Gustins'.)

So one can't always be sure children understand, wherever they are. I don't suppose all children understood the Latin Mass in the Roman Catholic Faith. Some Latin is still used in the service of Benediction. It must have been a relief for many when the English version was established, although English words appeared on the opposite side of the page to the Latin in their Missal. As ever, pictures and acting and dance are valuable ways of imparting the message. I still remain deeply touched by a simple child picture of the crucifixion and under it the words, 'And there was Jesus hanging, hanging on the cross. And it was *raining*'. In the picture the rain fell as 'stripes coming sideways down'.

I am a great believer in community marching. This can be a great brotherly and sisterly act – literally marching round to music. I suppose that is at base the reason for protest marches by adults. It is best, in school, to have a reason for it too, in the plot of an improvisation – we go to wish the King 'Happy birthday', or we march to church to thank God for a fortunate escape from disaster. Otherwise we would be plonking round for no particular purpose except for 'teacher sez so'. Though that is not always a bad reason either!

In improvised dance, children sometimes become very graceful and very thoughtful. It is at these moments that we hope they may be touched by some inner feeling which they begin to discover in themselves. And, of course, if one becomes very happy during dance, this can be turned into prayer. Remember, King David danced before the Lord. Dance-Prayer, example also in 'I am the Lord of the dance, said He'. Swapping round partners is useful for helping different little people to meet each other, when otherwise they might have been hesitant. Please note that this is not just RE as a subject, but *experience* and education for life.

In future, sex education may take place as a subject in its own right. It should be concerned with relationships. Preparation for marriage is not far removed from teaching on religion. Nativity plays are not the usual social or money-making event, as is the school play; and parental audiences behave differently. Although there may be a slight titter if an angel wing falls off, a Wise Man trips, or a crown slips, the general feeling is of a warm hush at a sacred event. Our Lord said, 'Suffer little children to come unto me'. At certain moments, I believe we all become little children again during some of these plays. Innocence is in the air, particularly with Infant players, though with Juniors the acting can be superb. In Infant events we are full of forgiveness. Many of these enactments now take place on an open floor too, with audience in a circle outside the players (more like a family of *us*), so they do not over-sophisticate, as the stage might, but allow for Child Drama and its shapes to take place in a more natural way.

There can be mistakes though. I have to tell this story against myself. I had been working hard in my own area and in courses all over the Country to get more Junior and Infant Nativity Plays on the floor; and one school where the lady Head had tried to cooperate, had rigged up an extremely complicated system of ropes and pulleys, so that a nice fat cardboard star could guide all travellers (and there were many) and to really move! Unfortunately, at dress rehearsal, a rope had broken and someone just tied a knot in it and kindly put it together again. However, when the Kings were half way down the hall, there was a horrible jarring 'sputch'. The Star had struck the knot and stuck. A herd of bodies fell into each other and there was lengthy chaos. By that time I really *had* to go. 'I don't wonder', groaned the Head. To this day, I don't know if any of those travellers ever got safely to Bethlehem. When I left, the star was still shining over the wrong place. It is really better to avoid complicated props and so forth. Children *imagine* far better, and make us believe about things in the sky. It is also a fact that if children really look *up*, even your most difficult one can look quite holy.

One way of living our Faith is not to mock other peoples', nor to criticise in an unwise way. Some Roman Catholics may seem a bit haughty about the Church of England including in their creed... 'We believe in the holy Catholic Church and the communion of Saints...'. The Church of England explain 'We are Catholic but not Roman Catholic'. The Roman Catholics tend to ask 'What does that mean?' Then, some Church of Englands say 'Of course, you know, the Roman Catholics worship the Virgin Mary'. They don't, they venerate her. They only *worship* God the Father, God the Son and the Holy Spirit. They truly believe in the Communion of Saints and ask their help. They don't worship their statues, they honour them. They are like family 'photos.

A master at my last school would drawl out his annual joke: 'And now we come to the Holy Roman Empire, which was neither herly...Rerman...ner an Empah, hmm, hmm'. Friends used to ask whether he had got to that bit yet.

In so many ways, large or small, we may detract from each other and the Christians have not always behaved in any way well to people who believed something else. It is now important to recognise what is good in other people, not the opposite. There is so much we actually *share* between the Faiths. We all share a belief in prayer. The Jewish religion shares much with Christianity as a base, and with extremely wise words, advice and loyalty to their kind. (Since writing, the Vatican has signed an Accord with Israel.) The Quakers share holy silence with the Contemplatives. The Faiths of the East have often deeper spirituality than is general in the West. And African singing can put many of our congregations to shame. My own great sadness-full anxiety is that there might be a cataclysm between Islam and the West, ending in world tragedy. But apart from the militants, Christianity shares things in *their* basic faith too: the Angel Gabriel, apart from others. Let us truly come together.

Children, before they have been unduly influenced, often share treasures and actions and friendship in their innocent play. And often *together* they create beauty. I often think (and hope) that God feels thanked by us, without our knowing it, whenever we notice or really rejoice in beauty of whatever kind He has created.

In the formal part of training, the basic rules, regulations or history of Faiths have to be taught separately (perhaps partly in their places of worship) but there is no reason why groups should not come together sometimes and learn from each other.

As to general assembly, you may feel that an untidy mixture of thought and belief does not quite work. But again, we should try to discover what we share between Faiths and sometimes make a theme for the day.

Please help children to understand the dignity of SERVICE. This is often mistaken for 'being servile'. The two are not the same. Things that all humans have to consider are: kindness, thought for others, learning to forgive, not to envy, not telling lies, doing without things for a cause, not doing other people down, cheating, not giving way to violence; generosity, compassion. Any, or all of these could make a theme for the day, in readings, a short talk, perhaps a playlet, some music, singing – with a good finish. Be sure to start with silence if you possibly can. Are Allah and Jehova and God – or the First Cause – the same?

One thing is very practical; teach children not to drop litter. This is basic for many things. Help them to see how it spoils all our surroundings by its ugliness. It is a lazy, dirty habit and, sadly, adults are to blame too. But it is *not* kind to others to drop toffee papers and so on, particularly in their gardens. Tell children what to do instead. Repeat it – not all the time or they cease to listen – but from time to time, or (if it got better) it will start again.

Bullying may have to be brought out in the open in some places. Courtesy is important for all ages. The Archbishop of York has warned about a 'Culture of Contempt', filtering from the top down. This brings in the teacher, of course. Anyone who is going to take RE must be a good role model. We must ensure that we ourselves are firm, but polite and fair and not swift to anger. We can't all be saints, but we *can* act in a civilised way; and children, these days, need people they can look up to as never before. An older child on TV said last night (at time of writing), 'I think the most important thing in education is good relations. It is better if we can get on with teachers in a friendly way and they treat us like human beings. When you are happy you learn much quicker.' RE teachers should dilute any 'them and us' feeling, if it exists in their school.

Finally – two great commandments stand us in good stead. They supersede, perhaps, all formal prayers and all the modes of worship in our training; Christian or not, we are all brothers and sisters in an unstable world we share. But if we are Christian, we have been carefully instructed in the summary of the law, that we should love the Lord our God with all our heart, with all our soul, with all our mind and with all our strength and our neighbour as ourself.

Upon these two Commandments, we are told 'Hang all the law and the prophets'.

Since this was written, there have been suggestions that several Faiths should be taught to Junior children. This is very heavy, it is hard enough to really know *one*. Most Faiths have different ideas about what happens after death. Children of this age are likely to be confused by that alone. And, if overburdened with different views, will probably end up believing nothing. This would be a sad thing for them and for society. Should we not give them something definite of their own and just enough of others' to ensure understanding and respect?

English

Quite a lot has been written about this already, but to repeat in short: much depends on the purpose of the lesson.[3]

Creative writing is important at this age, which we should not mark or criticise over spelling, punctuation and so forth. But it is perfectly possible and sensible to warn that in this next lesson, you will not be looking so much just for ideas – though they are good – but at spelling and punctuation. It *should* have its place and it should be done *now* at this period in their schooling, or uncertainty will dog them all the days of their life. And that is not fair.

As to in-flow, it is important to read to them, prose and poetry, in short bursts because of concentration span. But don't put too much stress on rhyme. Read plenty of things without it. For it will be seen, by now, that their own outpourings can become a genuine language-flow and will include strange and wonderful ideas and use of words, often with philosophic or genuine poetic quality. We must learn to listen and hear it. Rhythm and ideas are more

---

3   So many changes in Education are happening almost daily. It is hard to know how to keep up with them. Just since this was written there has been an announcement of cuts in the numbers of those teaching English to ethnic minorities (Section II. Funding). But there is a serious need for all children living here to learn English in order to avoid misunderstandings, even teasing, but anyway to feel at home. Added to this there are young children, who have to do the shopping for parents, who cannot speak the language. If none of them can communicate, it is difficult to know how they will manage.

important than rhyme, if you wish to guard their true best. If you let children once get the idea that rhyme is what poetry is, they will begin to lose the quality of their own creation and try to use rhyme all the time. At first they won't even get it right and often use a non-rhyme, thinking it correct. This is a disease and a destructive one. Let them share with you some of the words, sayings or lines that *you* have enjoyed and point out how descriptive words are used to enhance (adjectives enriching a noun) meaning. Also encourage comparisons and similes. Example: 'Scuse me, Miss, but 'is 'ead was like an egg, see. He 'ad no 'air.' Robert Louis Stevenson was always quoted at us for his ability to use comparisons. There is no harm in helping children to find out what is a noun and what is a verb. It will enrich their understanding greatly; and please let us all tell them what is singular and plural. It does get us away from 'there was these men, see...'. Tense too; or is that asking too much? Or do we stay with the curiously endearing ''E done good?'. Two things I have to confess that rile me personally are not knowing the difference between criterion (singular) and criteria (plural). They are commonly used the wrong way round.

The other is 'was sat'. What could be more ugly? The first time I heard it was from a Liverpudlian comedian, who waited for a laugh, because he had said it wrong on purpose. Now it is common parlance, yet the only thing it *can* mean is that some one has bodily placed or forced you into a sitting position. Has no one heard of 'was sitting?' Quite a nice peaceful sound really. A nice comfortable music, which English can often be. 'Was sat' intimates force. Perhaps one more reflection of our more violent times.

A former well-known Member of Parliament always pronounced Apartheid as 'tite' at the end instead of 'tate'; and started the craze for form*i*dable. Can't anyone say formidable any more? It isn't very difficult. And the ugly word prim*a*rily is becoming established. It is a little more difficult to say pr*i*marily. But we might try. Other things of this kind I will leave till the Senior School. But if you want things to be more correct – and nearly all of us have our faults – it is worth starting early.

The reading of 'bits' to children can have a lasting effect. The odd line sticks. I still treasure and am moved by 'The ploughman homeward plods his weary way'. Later 'And leaves the world to darkness and to me'. First heard at the age of eight. Also 'There is a green hill far away, without a city wall.' I loved the sadness and the hymn tune long before understanding what it meant. Later in life I came across 'On stronds afar remote'. Oh, for them, when you are sad!

Some teachers do not like action in an English lesson. It is entirely up to them, but if judged useful, a period can sometimes be enlivened by action, either after story-reading from prose, by teacher; to, with, or because of a poem. By 'to' is meant miming, whilst each line is read, waiting slightly for action. 'With' = some action. 'Because' = after a poem is read, the 'story' is enacted separately.

Example of general idea:

> 'Old King Cole...he called for his pipe...*(actually call)*
> and he called for his bowl...*(call)*
> and he called for his fiddlers three...' *(call)*

This can either be partly cast, or everyone be everything, just for a break from sitting. The pause in the teacher's reading allows for the action. They can all go on 'fiddling' for a bit and make their own screeching noises.

It is quite difficult to find poems suitable for the young that don't automatically rhyme, but the action and pause dilutes rhyme quite a lot. (I am not entirely *against* rhyme, but other things are more important.)

Example:

> 'The North wind doth blow...*(they shudder etc.)*
> (*Up and fade a bit*) Music (*Ride to the Valkerie?*)
> And we shall have snow (*they could skate or be on sledges when it comes*)
> (*Up and fade*) Music
> and what will poor Robin do then, poor thing?'

> TEACHER: 'What do you think he will do? Can you help him?' *(discuss for a minute)* 'You think out what you might do to help him and we'll act that.'
>
> (*Slow music to back the action. Delius perhaps*)

Of course it can be done without music, but it helps to build atmosphere. Or to carry on the 'because', they could make up a little playlet because of the poem, including tea at home, digging a grave, and other things.

This one is generally popular:

> There was a man of Newington
> And he was wondrous wise
> *(all go about, probably like a professor)*
> He jumped into *(they jump)* a quick set hedge
> *(mild expletives)*
> And scratched out both his eyes;
>
> *(cries of hurt, they can wander about a bit. You may see them put arms out in front, like a cartoon sleep walker.)*
>
> But when he saw his eyes were out
> (*They could look in an imagined mirror to no avail*)
> With all his might and main *(muscles?)*
> He jumped *(they do)* into another hedge
> And scratched them in again.
> (*cries of joy*)

It might end up with a dance of rejoicing to jazz music. But bring them down to *de-climax* before the end of the lesson.

Before leaving Junior school, children should be able to read (many teachers take great trouble over this) at least to some degree. Do not entirely despise the best comics to help with this. The great thing in English is not to be imprisoned by the rules but to learn and abide by some of them and *enjoy* them. Not to be *too* posh about it, but to see what is sensible and what is ugly and what is not.

Above all, we should be joyous at the music of *words:* '…Sounds and sweet airs that delight the ear and hurt not. Sometimes a thousand twangling instruments will hum about mine ears…' Oh, let our children twangle a bit – then be calm after!

Science

Has made enormous strides in recent years and children often seem to have an extra sense about some parts of it and turn around and teach us. It used to be 'deadly' at one time, nearly all regulated to things in little bits of glass, boiling away over Bunson burners, filthy smells and stains everywhere. (An occasional 'break' but not much else.) It only became exciting when my brother blew up part of our yard, by mistake, in the holidays. 'That's gunpowder', he imparted.

In the Junior school, we are fortunately able to draw upon the *projected* play, which wise people have invented to show all sorts of imaginative experiments about balance and wind force, by use of balloons, and 'obstacle' journeys of objects (on the lines of Profesor Gregory's suggestions at Bristol. Also Dr. Ann Hubberd.) It is much better to stick to this, so as to really fire interest, than to try and push children too far at this age.

Opposite Example: A boy asked his Headmaster if he could stop learning science. 'Why?', asked the disappointed Head, 'Well sir, it's about light. It's all pins and string and we've been doing all pins and string for a whole term until we get it right and I always get my strings in a mess. It is so boring and I can't see what this has got to do with my future'. Quite a point. At least, in my school, we eventually got onto the sex life of a snail.

There could be interesting things in electricity and static. Making a cardboard village and lighting it up is generally absorbing. 'Attractions' can be fun too; also general magnetism. These are, of course, the wonders of our world and should be there *for* wonder, leading also to an inquiring mind.

To liven things up, near the November date, there could be some active drama about care and use of fireworks, ending up, perhaps, with Guy Fawkes trying to blow up Parliament. Blowing up is not a thing to encourage, but this is history-science. It is past, so because it's history, it's respectable. What we could discourage is the 'trick or treat' blackmail that goes on near this date (for moral training should be in all subjects). It may be fun to wear funny clothes and faces, but it is bare-faced begging really and often becomes an intrusion when so many groups, one after another, try it on. These days the 'trick' can be quite nasty if the demands are not satisfied. It is far removed from things like 'penny for the guy'. Also, these days, it is a ruse by which unpleasant intruders push their way into old people's homes, once the door has been opened. For Junior children, it is not very safe for them to be out at night either.

One of the new things is, of course, the computer. This is where the young seem to take to the future like ducks to water. There are children who literally teach their teachers at times. But there is the engrossing temptation of video games, which can be an anxiety for parents *and* teachers. The more violent of these may establish a need for the playing out of violence, as mentioned before.

COOKING

I wonder whether this is the right place to put in cooking. For cooking is certainly a form of chemistry. And if the Educational syllabus continues to revert somewhat strictly to basics, all subjects that really affect life, as actually lived, will have to seek a 'cloak' in order to be considered for inclusion. I am sure Science will be considered so, if what was called Social Science should fade. There is no reason why Junior children should not learn at least elements of cooking. It can be fun; and dangers can be pointed out and taught. There can be a strong link with Art too, for an important part of the process is, not just the reward of eating something nice, but the presentation. Praise may be given for shape, colour, neatness, imagination. Pictures may arise from such simple things as potato, carrot and lettuce. One teacher was advocating Funny Faced Pizzas. All dishes become more desirable if nicely served, and this is part of normal civilisation.

Healthy eating can be taught at the same time, with suggestions about relying less on take-away food. Both boys and girls should be allowed to have a go. Life in the home is changing. Husbands, boyfriends and single parents will all have to take their turn in future household chores. And children, whilst learning for the future, could help their parents too. No doubt, elementary physics can and will come into Junior education and we may find there is an inborn understanding of this also. (The indication that noise and anti-noise waves, where merged, cancel each other out, could form the basis for a good improvised play.)

With computers we are told that they can cope with regular shapes (in the harmony between maths and automatic reaction) but that they cannot cope with irregular shapes. Nor, so far, can they enter into feeling and intuition. We can. And that is called consciousness. The quantum state we are told, is computable. But there has been some proof that all things, that *might* happen, happen together.

So destruction and non-destruction can happen together. Example is of a laser beam that can travel through glass and burn up something behind it, but is deflected at the same time. Is that acceptance and rejection at the same time too? If things can happen and sort of not happen, my mind travels on to a moment when one day, perhaps, we arrive at a point where what is natural and what is not natural happen together. *Then* computers might feel. It is the sort of base for one of those complicated ballets that few but the dancers can understand. But it could also be the basis for a splendid piece of drama-play about a computer who/that feels. When it is happy, the air would be loud with clicks? When it was sad, tears might flood the office. I expect there have been films about this sort of thing already. But I doubt if they knew about 'all things that *might* happen, happen together'. But *we* all now know that is why it did happen.

Eight weeks after this was written came the announcement that experiments are being conducted on linking brain cells to computer action in a search for a computer that thinks. If it thinks, will it feel? The above suggestions are not so far fetched after all. The experiment even has a name. It is called Bioelectronics.

Music

One of the important things in this is to listen. Quite a lot has been said so far about joy in sound. It is not everyone who is going to be able to play an instrument – either well, or even for their own pleasure. But it is perfectly possible for children to learn to distinguish between types of sound and to judge their value. There are adults who affirm, almost with pride, that they are tone deaf. When and where does this start? It is sad for them, because they miss so much.

CHILD MUSIC

One thing which *may* help is for teachers to stir inquisitiveness over sound. Nearly everything around us has a sound and, of course, a 'feel'. Presuming that they are under control(!), children can tap gently and feel pipes, walls, curtains, doors – all things in the room or hall. Some will feel warmer or colder than others (i.e. stone as against wood; concrete as against curtain etc). The sounds they give, when tapped, will be different too. Curtains (although they can feel nice) are often disappointing for sound unless whacked, which may not be in order. But all this leads to an interest and an appreciation of materials (needed later for architects or mere civilised living) and may help in preserving the fabric of schools, rather than the aimless kicking and bashing that often goes on. Out of these sounds we can make elementary music. 'Tick-tack-scurr (pencil along a radiator) – plonk and so on. The teacher can select out of these. 'That's an interesting one. They are *all* interesting. But let's just try this…this…and that for a start'. Little changes may be added, or the sounds used constructively. So (with the above), we might create 'Tick-tick-tickety-tack-scurr-tack-plonk' and other such statements. Question and answer is fun too. 'Tack-tack-tick?' Answer a resounding 'scurr' or a decisive 'plonk' (No).

I have had some quite good short dances to 'room noises' and remember one fine circus band marching round with 'animals' (half class as circus, half making 'band'). Children, of course, of any age can create like this. It can start in Infant School therefore, or younger, according to teachers' decision. Naturally, if there are real instruments of a simple kind, children can progress to these and create their own music (composition is encouraged in the music syllabus). As earlier mentioned, mood is something they understand, in the same way as the adult can add atmosphere to drama and dance, by careful selection. For children – peaceful, happy, funny (with unexpected pauses and sudden plonks, angry and sad would be easily understood. Peaceful being very important at times. Probably needed more in future than we think, or guess. They will need some guiding to this, because 'happy' and 'angry' are the easier and more obvious to create. Both are fairly percussive. Funny comes next. Peace is flowing and rather more difficult.[4]

I mentioned children of any age can create like this. It is just interesting to note that not only young members of industry and retail trades (in Personality Training Courses) take to this well, but Directors of Industry do even better. My point here was – for alleviation of stress – to give them time to discover the detail of their surroundings (the feel and the sound and the appreciation), because, as they said, they had never given themselves time to do so, nor even to think of it.

Sometimes I would put on 'calm' or 'peaceful' Elgar, Delius or Debussy music whilst they did it. Often there was some difficulty in getting them to stop. They kept asking for more.

We should have short bursts of music of many kinds for children to listen to. And in dance, they should be aided to appreciate the difference between long sounds and staccato ones; and if a long sound ends a phrase or a piece, by this age we can encourage 'doing something more interesting' with a hand or leg to that long finish ('don't waste that nice sound') – and be dead on the beat with your foot sound, at short sharp noises. By *listening* we can help Junior Children not to sing flat. Don't be afraid to stop things occasionally and hammer a note for them to hear. For this singing flat is a disease in many schools. It is so awful, sometimes, that it almost becomes lovable. A noise never heard anywhere else, as when young Juniors are given a script play too early and you hear this extraordinary jerked out sound: 'Oh-dear,-I-am-so-angry-with-you-

---

4 Some time after writing, news came of the Northern Orchestra helping children to compose Mood Music.

do- please-go-a-way'. No one ever talks like that except in a Junior script play. It is fascinating, mais ce n'est pas theatre.

When children have been taught to hear, they can sing wonderfully. And, do teach them still to sing whilst some of their voices are still pure. Don't allow them to shout. This came in with the musical 'Oliver', it seems, where it might be said to have been appropriate, but it ought not to catch on so much.

As in many things these days, there are fewer good role models. The Pop scene is not always the best of its kind, though truly a world of glamour and high pay. But at its lowest it has bred things like 'I bet yew kant lerve me loik thut, bebey', which is a reasonable assumption in itself; but when it is sung about fifteen times on about three uninteresting notes, or a short phrase, it must be forgiven if some of us have got the message before the end of the piece. Sometimes these creations have no end and the same sort of things goes alarmingly on, until someone starts clapping. Then peace of a kind returns. I do not believe that this is really worthy of our young people. It verges on the moronic. Fortunately, we have the 'Proms' as an alternative. All those marvellous young people.

There used to be some good songs in Pop tunes and inflexions and some sweet people singing. The Beatles' 'Yesterday' is as fine an air as in many operas. Earlier on, the Jazz world had wonderful exponents: Jelly Roll Morton, Art Tatum, Earl Hines, Layton and Johnston, 'Hutch' (Leslie Hutchinson) with his throat-clutching voice and fascinating rich harmonies in his piano playing, never equalled for me. Billy Mayerl for his dexterity; Louis Armstrong, with his vibrant personality; Fats Waller and his rude cheerfulness; Flanagan and Allen singing (very quietly) 'Underneath the Arches' at the Palladium. Never to be forgotten Nat Gonella and his amazingly exciting *pace*, but also his outstanding trumpet playing. Some of the French men and women singers of the late 1930s. Then Bix, Ella Fitzgerald, Sidney Bechet. Sounds of Count Basie, Dave Brubeck, Glenn Miller, André Prévin.

Up to the advent and inclusion of Swing were great times. The accompaniements by orchestra of Frank Sinatra, at his height, will probably never be surpassed, nor his timing; but equally this can be said for Barbra Streisand, ABBA, and from over the sea the other way has come a stream of American musicals with the most wonderful songs. Other musical gifts to us were Errol Garner, the Beach Boys, the Nolan Sisters, Shirley Bassey (with her give-all), the Carpenters, Gilbert O'Sullivan.

This is only to pick out a few from the enormous world of High Class Jazz, all eminently musical. These days, it would seem that what is labelled Jazz has developed into an era of almost constant over-improvisation. It is extremely personal, rather like some abstract painting; probably great fun to play, including great cleverness and group sensitivity, but like some chamber music, not such fun to listen to. One begins to gasp for a tune, because it goes everywhere but doesn't seem to get anywhere.

Is it thought another example of to travel being better than to arrive? To improvise on a theme, or short tune, is another matter. Stating a tune first is like giving a concept. It is something one can hang on to. If good, it becomes a friend at once, and even during the wildest variations, one can sometimes still hear our friend, in welcome voice, repeating his point and trying to speak despite constant interruption. The recognition has its own pride in our hearing ability and its own intense excitement at the player('s) skill. They not only go all over the place but they get somewhere too. This is as true for Erroll Garner as it is for Beethoven.

I remember, in adult dance sessions, saying sometimes of Garner playing piano: 'Hang on, listen a mo, – don't go hell-for-leather yet – he will be making his point first. Dance carefully to this and see what he says – but now – off you go, he's AWAY!' (Great example is his triumphant rendering of 'I'll remember April' in Concert by the Sea.)

Something went wrong with the entry of Rock. For my own personal taste, the only decent rock tune was 'Rock around the clock', which is still an extremely jubilant 'classic' of its kind and a rousing exciting sound. It is explained sometimes that Rock has now a wider meaning to include good Rock musicals, but that Punk Rock is for the expression of Hate and for revolutionary outburst. A mirror of a violent world. Well this *is* a way of blowing off steam, no doubt. But to go on playing so loud all the time does not really assist in getting the message over. You have to cavort about the stage to try and help; and the facial contortions are very unattractive (which they are meant to be) for younger, or any, children to emulate. So many of these songs are so alike that one has to admire the fact that the singers and players can remember the words or the notes (I do not say tunes, as they are hard to discern), but I really do think this is very clever.

The combined loudness will affect hearing.

So much for taste in one section.

But, of course, children should hear classical music too, in short bursts. It can also accompany their drama and dance, creating mood and atmosphere. Marching, war, tempest, calm sailing, ghostly, sad and happy are the main categories needed.

There are essays now into joining the two worlds of Jazz and classical. We had Duke Ellington, of course, earlier, but now there is 'Crossover'. I hope there will be improvement on what we have heard so far, because it is often repetitious, like Pop.

But there should be some straight listening too. 'What does this remind you of?' can bring some interesting replies. Comparisons might also be useful. There are jazzed up versions of Bach these days, some of them very good. Then Bach can be played, in short pieces of the original. 'That's where it came from'. There are many classical tunes that have been pinched.

If children can learn to read music when young, this is a great advantage to them. But don't make it a burden.

Finally, of course, there is the learning of actual instruments. Children need not stay at tambours, milk bottles, flutes (self made) and recorders, good as these are. But that progression to other instruments is for the specialist teachers. And, with luck, may they get whoever is in authority to have those bizarre upright pianos tuned, which (however good the players) sometimes make our best hymns sound like a honky-tonk jam session.

All sound is interesting, but is richer as an experience, if used in a thoughtful and constructive way.

Mathematics

This gets called all sorts of funny things these days, but I am sure it will be understood here that we are concerned with being able to count and so on. Some Secondary schools have complained in the past that new arrivals from Junior schools have not this aptitude. It is partly a matter of perception, apart from memory. Memory is a gift, though it can be polished by use as well as by other methods. But perception can definitely be aided for many children. It is here that what was mentioned earlier as 'domino marching' comes in. It is important to remember that not all children take things in through *projected* activity and when they fail, or when they are discouraged, they need to experience *personal* play. I think I started to use it at my first Arts Centre in about 1937–8, when backward children were sent to me. Years later, round about 1947, I came across K. R. Scott of the famous Steward St. School in Birmingham. He had also had some ideas about 'floor visual aids'. We discussed a great deal and he saw what I meant by 'experiencing in three dimensions'. The outcome was that we used ladders painted on the floor. Children were encouraged to move forward as if climbing the ladder. This gives one a feeling of plus, by taking more steps and increasing 'height' and is therefore addition. Going backwards, 'down the ladder', loses what has been gained and loses 'height'. It is therefore subtraction. And children really *felt* this. Perception began to dawn. To this we added my domino marching.

DOMINO MARCHING

In this, as mentioned earlier, say five young people form into the domino shape of dots and count themselves. Four others start from another part of the room (or hall) after counting themselves and noticing their group shape. Music, or a simple drum beat, encourages them to march around in their dot-shaped groups, feeling the brotherhood of four and of five. Fading down the music, I would suggest – '…and now the two groups come together'. They march on. I am careful to cut the music, or drumming, before they bang into each other.

SELF: 'Have you kept your shapes? Well done. Now, count both groups together – all of you in a lump. What does that come to?' With luck it comes to nine!

SELF: 'Good. Now, see the shape of yourselves as nine and really feel it. Look carefully and try to remember it…When the music comes, march away from each other again in your two groups, as you were before. (*'Fade' up and stop music*). Feel as much as you can about becoming a smaller group again, after feeling yourselves as the big lump of nine. Count yourselves and remember the shape.'

I would then discuss a bit and help them to see what was meant by the coming together being addition, and splitting into the original groups again being subtraction. By such methods it was found that when they returned to the *projected* realm of symbols that we call number, these symbols began to mean something to them.

There are at least two good things about the domino shapes. First, the pattern of the dots is something children often remember and 'feel' more easily than the shape of figures, certainly backward children do. When I am tired, I still find myself falling into making dots over the top of numbers, if counting a long column. Pocket machines (calculators) can do it for you these days, but it is good to understand something of the process. (I can't understand why children shouldn't chant tables either. It is fun and I couldn't have done without mine!) The second good thing about the dots is that there is a decided equi-distance between them in their pattern. Equi-distance is a deep inner perception in the unconscious and is a stage of development we should all come to and pass through to more complicated awareness. I have not found out all its importance yet. But this I know, it is a stage, and a sign, of important elementary civilisation. Without some understanding of equi-distance and space, we cannot even live on this earth without hurting ourselves against objects (by 'between-under-standing') nor live peaceably with our neighbour, for by bumping, or invasion of territory, we invite their wrath. Despite all this, I have long doubted whether two and two really make four. The numbers we use are probably only toys to help us advance to an approximation of true fact – like time (as we use it), which is so inaccurate as to be almost a joke. We are always changing it to try and make it fit more important basic truths about space and our relationship to our sun. The only Time we come anywhere near able to control is the present.

As science progresses, we learn more of the amazing intricacies of smaller and smaller patterns in created things, which, with our eyes alone, we cannot see.

Shape, pattern and mathematics is going on in ourselves and the things around us all the time. But this, our world, is a very small part of an enormous process. Mathematics is an IS, going on outside ourselves. It probably exists as an apart, certainly independent of us, who have only mentally nibbled at its edge with our limited understanding. Is it perhaps a sort of vast memorial of the doing, in *projected play*, of what Cowper Powys termed the First Cause? (Also Thomas Aquinas, *Summa Theologica,* 1, q, 2, a, 3)

Years 9 – 11

Taking it that the normal progression has more or less taken place, children will be beginning to come out of the strongest period of spitting out. Under the best circumstances they should be entering upon the golden years that will never return again.

Improvised Dance

By eight years or nine we find tremendous advances in improvised dance. This can be done with or without music, or to noises. The sounds and the music have their own function. If the child needs aiding to freedom and personal expression, improvised music can be of value. This *accompanies* child creation. Music from a record player adds a certain discipline – it cannot alter, so the dancer conforms to it. This brings out obedience and a certain docility. It promotes confidence and stimulates dramatic mood. Also, 'It helps with ideas,' as a boy once put it. A further sign of group sensitivity, but of a higher kind, is that children at the far end of the room will catch time beat and mood from the group, when only a few at the near end can hear a soft record or weak record player, or poor tape.

This message is passed on through the various gang groups dotted about the hall. It helps the next stage of personal and group integration, which usually comes after ten years of age and any time up to twelve, though in first class conditions may appear earlier. It is the stage when not only the person integrates with the gang, but *gang integrates with gang.* Thus, slowly, we see the full group functioning as one, and, from the social point of view, this is a complete harmonious society. It is a vital experience and only takes place where children do this work; all others leave school without the experience, and society loses greatly thereby.

The experience begins as something unconscious through the dream state of the dance itself, but it is clear that children do in fact recognise the quality of it in time, and rejoice in the harmony and unity of it. From our adult dramatic point of view they are tasting something which only the greatest stage artists know – Group Intuition.

This Group Intuition is the furthest limit of *group sensitivity*, a sort of rhythm of wisdom shared by a group, the members of which know intuitively what is needed, what should be done and what others are going to do. It is one great perfection of the age we are discussing, arising out of the spiritual awareness after the *dawn of seriousness*. It is often lost in puberty when realism and competition threaten all.

The dance itself can be extremely well developed between seven and twelve years of age, where opportunity is given for it. By nine or ten we may expect to see intense imaginative work of either a flowing or a stylised kind. It can be ethereal or broadly comic, it can be of the gang (a few together), or of the whole community (all the class). Dances, dance dramas, as with plays, may be creations of the child, partly of the teacher; often children make the whole thing themselves. Great attention is paid to the sound of feet and to space relationships.

I remember when Martin Browne (former Director of the British Drama League) first saw some of this work, he said: 'I have only seen space used so perfectly before by first class ballerinas'. That, of course, was because these children had been allowed journey and floor space from an early age. They knew what to do with it. One thing always delights me. Sometimes young people of almost any age, say, eight to eighteen, indulge in a dance mime or dance drama about playing football. In this the intuition is marked. Nearly everybody knows where the ball is, they show it so clearly that I know where it is too – although it isn't there.

Group Intuition is no wild, unusual magic, but the adult reaches it, perhaps through discipline, the child through freedom and opportunity for creation. This is the measure of difference between youth and age, this is the chasm that has to be crossed. By facing the differences honestly and bravely, we may learn to understand each other better. Not only in dance but in life.

Play writing may begin now. But, although it should not be discouraged, it is often disappointing. Children of this age have no idea how many words have to be invented and written so as to last for a reasonable amount of time. So, when it is played, it is over almost at once and, in a way, not a lot has happened, one feels – even if all die. There has been no build up. So really, it is better to let them improvise. Sometimes this goes on almost too long and a wise teacher will say gently 'Bring it to an end now.' And behold, it suddenly is so. 'That's all Miss/Sir.' Teach them they do not *have* to say this. They should not be doing it just for you, we are supposed – all of us – to be sharing it. If they very much want to write, let them invent a story and after they have read it with a bit of rather sweet pride, they can act that.

Again – we must not forget that during the spitting out process children are sharing an important personal secret with us. The same may happen in acting their written story. They find relief in our friendship and our being interested, which allows them to play out illegal acts in a lawful manner. We should not shut them up, nor rebuff them.

I think, perhaps, it is this growing friendship that not only facilitates learning, but aids us now in helping *them* to escape a little from the tyranny of the gang. A gang, after all, is like a family and has its pleasures but its ties also. So, apart from what is acted *in* the gang, a small kick may be needed (not unlike the love kick in a real family) in order for a child to emancipate itself whilst still holding loyalty, into wider horizons. In a way, we have to provide the kick. Children cannot do it all by themselves. By a guiding process, the drama and its content should now become richer and thus to move gently away from violent themes towards legends, old stories from literature, even fairy tales (as in the story of the willow tree, earlier). You have to judge whether your pupils are up to this standard, or have not quite got there yet. (They should have met this in their reading, though.) If not, you may have to allow a bit of 'gangster' still, then begin the change, as when the gangster became Christopher Columbus.

Between the years of nine and eleven, when play has become established, the adult has the opportunity of adding further to their creations. It does not in any way destroy their best work to suggest themes coming from the myths and legends of the world. It helps us to introduce them to literature. They will have become familiar with some of these stories already in reading lessons, and by using them we give an opportunity for more complicated characterisations and situations, and the possibility of developing a deeper sense of plot and form. Some of these can be repeated and dressed, and, as long as freshness is carefully guarded, can give us remarkable glimpses of their art, Child Drama, now coming nearer to theatre.

Even in this type of creation we use the story only as a theme for spontaneous expression, and the movement may travel all over the room. But we polish.

EXAMPLE (SEE DIAGRAMS 5 AND 6)

This school was beginning an improvisation on the oft-used *Pied Piper of Hamelin*. It was going fairly well in places, but was rather unimaginative. The teacher intended polishing it a bit, but it wasn't improving.

TEACHER: (*To me*) 'What would you do to get it better?'

SELF: 'Well, first of all, try letting the whole thing open with the Pied Piper dancing alone – perhaps practising his special fairy piece. I always wonder where on earth he got that charm in his music from. You might discuss that one time. The children will probably give you good ideas for a whole new beginning to this story, which we grown-ups know so well! What we don't know is – was it the piper or the tune which put a spell on the rats and children? At least, I don't know. But, about what I've just seen: the town councillors are not alive yet. The mayor needs more character. Is he weak or a bully? The movement round, when they go after the piper, is dull. Let them use a big sweep all over the floor of the

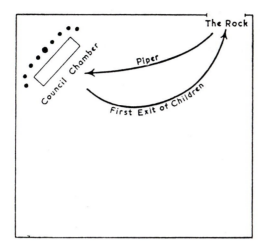

Diagram 5

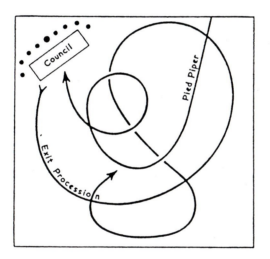

Diagram 6

hall. There might be slow drum-beats to accompany the slow steps when the piper approaches the guilty town council. Make it more at-mospheric. If no one can play a pipe, fade in some fairy music on the re-cord player for the march round, and be sure you lift the playing head straight off as the rock closes suddenly behind the children. In the quiet moment left by the sudden cutting-off of music we shall be touched the more deeply by the lonely rhythmic tap of the cripple's crutch.

Couldn't there be special rat music, too? Or discuss with the children what noises could be made by shaking things or making rattles for the scurrying noise. I think the mayor might have a proper feast, too. There ought to be crabs, candles, buns, ices, sea serpents, comics for napkins, mountains of pop bottles, noises of the popping of corks, crackers, and clinking noises for forks. It's a very dull meal yet. I can't believe the mayor ever got his 'corporation' on what you have allowed them to do so far.'

TEACHER: 'Oh dear, yes, I do see. I haven't got the imagination.'

SELF: 'Yes, you have. Deep down inside yourself it's waiting to come out. But don't try to create all by yourself. Discuss much more often with the children. They will give you ideas and help your mind to flow. Your task with this age is to add a little form to their work, like that very nice piece of music you are using to build up the finish of the play. They are all in time and there is a good strong exit. Really well done.'

TEACHER: 'Oh, I'm glad I've got something right.'

SELF: 'You've got a lot right. Courage. Go on. You are doing well. It is not easy to leap into a new world, but we can ooze ourselves in by finding more and more of what is in the child's mind. There is always something. We must find it.'

TEACHER: 'Would you take on for a bit?'

SELF: 'I'll just try to release them a little if you like.'

I then discussed with the children what would be the best feast in the world, hoping the teacher would take note. After having a good imaginary blow-out, they all became fat rats and danced to a rhumba record (appropriate somehow for heavy-tummied creatures). After talking about what real fairy music in this situation would be like, we finished up with a mighty procession of all the councillors, rats and children in the world being friendly together, marching as one in large figure-of-eight shapes about the whole floor, to the glowing strains of the ballet *Sylvia*. Speech had come much more freely, absorption had improved and the acting was much more virile and believable. Later, I heard that a witch finally told the piper what music to use, and a goblin riding on a camel took telegrams from the piper to the town council.

As might be in the entry dance of the Pied Piper, one of the important things about genuine Child Dance is that it helps develop an individual style of movement. A lot of movements are shared by everyone and you see them again and again (just the same with adults), but dancers begin to show individual invention as part of their personality. The individual style in dance is as important as style in handwriting. They are, again, the two sides of *personal* and *projected* play. The suggestion that there is an individual style, which evolves in such a rich way eventually through improvised movement, raises many questions about the desirability of imposing specialised movement too early. It is quite clear that individual style in dance is the parallel of character in handwriting.

By eleven years of age there should be extreme sincerity and absorption during play, much beautiful movement, and a healthy, easy flow of spontaneous speech which, compared with a learnt script, is as life against death. Do not write plays for them or use other scripted plays. Their own attempts at script plays are disappointing too. The junior child has not the facility for writing dialogue, though he is well able to speak it. The result, in comparison, is disappointing, and hours of their labour will produce a poor vehicle which is played through in a couple of minutes. It is much better to encourage them to write a story about what happens in their play. They will have success in this, and you will find occasionally that direct statements are included in the story. This is the beginning of dialogue.

Costume

Although children of this age take great delight in dressing-up, their grace and beauty of movement are still somewhat hindered by clothes. Where the work and conditions as described do not obtain, more use is made of clothes, but where the child's own drama is allowed and understood we find more pleasure in the actual drama itself, and children by their own wish may use only very little clothing, or discard it altogether. The adult should take care not to burden the child with dress, for this bewilders it. From the creative point of view pieces of attractive stuff are better than ready-made garments, as children can continue to create with these, building up a true character with costume to match. An over-elaborate costume often over-balances the creation, and true characterisation decreases because of interest in parading up and down. This, in turn, tends to mere showing off, and eventual deterioration in perhaps the whole period of work.

The creative use of bits and pieces also has valuable lessons in the sphere of choice and taste, with a whole range of most interesting creative needlework; bits of paper or objects may be sewn or stuck on to coloured stuffs. But the fuller version of this task is so absorbing that it is best done separately. Again, the final costume (which is better than that of ready-made garments) is often too greatly loved, admired and cared for to be a useful aid to good drama. It is used for a careful absorbed parading, which is rather more a personal fulfilment of the process of art creation, and is only drama of the less obvious kind. On the other hand, the quicker, simple creation is definitely intended as an aid to drama. The wearing of 'uncreated' garments is seldom art or drama; there is usually a motive behind it, often linked with the adult.

More Points About Working Under Difficulties

Don't forget, if you have to use classrooms, you can move the desks or tables. If there are sufficient reasons for not doing that, consider complete and permanent change of shape so as to allow more space in the centre. It will aid all teaching. The same number of desks may fit on three sides or in a semi-circle. Otherwise use the desks themselves, as you would for occasional finding of a higher level with rostrum blocks.

Do everything you can to avoid suggesting actor and audience as different. Do not encourage a narrator, who breaks up the scenes and talks to an audience. Encourage audience participation if some have to sit at desks or at tables. Do not stop actors turning their backs. We are not in the theatre. What is taking place is even more important. It is life in the making. There may be small circles in cramped space, or a half-circle against the back wall. Encourage play between the desks, also, if in rows with aisles as of old.

The existence of the gang makes splitting up into smaller playing groups a fairly natural process in the Junior school, but do not yet encourage actor and audience differences or you will get showing-off. The classroom is a perfectly reasonable place, though, for short playlets created by children and acted by groups in succession. Although space is lacking, much else is gained. Encourage language flow. If it has had a fair chance and a clear run from the infant school up, it will be good by now. Don't stop improvised speech because you can't put up with it, or don't see the point of it. You don't stop practice in writing because you are bored with children's essays. Do not stop practice in speech.

With juniors, as with infants, the teacher's main task is that of acting as a kindly, gentle guide. But in the Junior school more polish is needed occasionally when you do enter into things. However, responsibility for good creation should be handed more and more to the child, until with the older ones it is almost entirely handed over; together with this goes responsibility for good behaviour. This is the way to help parents and in part avoid delinquency. Successful Child Drama in the junior school is not only education at its highest, but prevention also. It provides a legitimate outlet for the atom-bomb energy of that social group we call the gang.

Our job at the top of the school is an approach to theatre, though using space. We can polish gently and their stories come to life. They can even stand an audience without being spoiled. The children are involved enough to take it. Think about the use of silence and of pause. Don't let them always hurry.

In polishing, I once remember saying 'Turn very slowly, *then* see your friend is dead.' I had said 'If your friend were really dead, do you think you would rush in looking quite so happy?' I have to say, against myself, that on this occasion, one boy answered, 'Well, you see, I didn't really *like* 'im, that's why I was grinning.' I have no doubt that I said something to the effect that, 'Oh, well that *is* a good reason. But, remember, we all agreed that you would come in looking *sad*, so that's the way it's got to be. That's democracy.'

I then continued, no doubt, on the lines of 'As I was saying, after a slower entry, turn slowly and *look* at your friend. Don't hurry. Wait. They go towards him, right across the hall, with *slow* footsteps. We'll practice that, first in time-beat to see if you can do it together. After that, don't think too hard about it, or it will look and sound unreal. After that I'll leave you to do it all by yourselves. By that time you will forget what I've said and have made it your own (the difference between rehearsal and production). I may give you a short piece of record music for the slow long walk, because you can now do these things so well – or we'll see just whether to use footsteps alone to break the silence. Decide what to do, when you are near your friend, then pick him up gently and make a slow exit to where we agreed. I will certainly give you music for that and fade the light as you go. Stay *completely* still and silent when you have gone, or you will ruin the end of the play. Right – ready? Make your own silence – then…begin!' I gently bring in the entry music.

By such methods we may blend what should be their creation, full of sincerity and absorption, with our knowledge of theatre. And in arena theatre, open space, or theatre-in-the-round, I always train future producers to think of, and treat, music as light and light as music. (We almost see music and hear light.) The fades go right then, and blend as they should. The result, combined with the best that those children can do, is like the end of an era. It is arresting, exciting, sad, utterly wonderful; it is first class theatre. With that group you will never see it again. It is the end of childhood. Its electric quality is not that of the Infant, it is more civilised.

If you have been successful, it will have a riveting effect; and its own high quality of innocence that may never be seen again. It is this that can astonish audiences and, one hopes, may affect the players. The world needs this innocence today, as perhaps never before. We are in some danger of losing Childhood altogether.

Figure 4 Story of a balloon: reception class infants

Figure 5 Junior school: the King and Queen dance

Figure 6 Junior boys: rescue from an igloo (teaching concern)

Figure 7 Gang boss (central figure) starting to organise group

Figure 8 Junior school: typical circle, caught in pause to a long musical note during improvised dance

Figure 9 Junior school: picture of shipwreck resulting from dramatic play

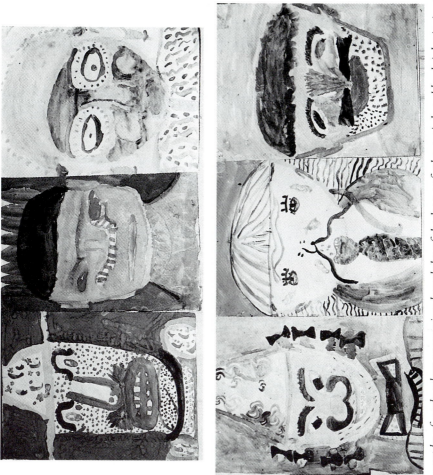

Figure 10 Junior school: examples of masks where unconscious knowledge of the drama of other periods and lands is beginning to show

Figure 12 Fishing (a study in absorbtion)

Figure 11 'If they paint your portrait it might not be quite what you expect.'

Figure 13 Robin Hood and his men attack from high ground. Note flow off stage. Old Secondary Modern School

Figure 14 Senior boys: good sword play using 'weapons of air'

Figure 15 Young seniors: this is a motor-coach. People are taught how to put luggage on the rack without knocking their neighbour. Eventually they will be taught not to stand on a seat (social drama)

Figure 16 Senior girls: dance drama (sincere feeling, good relationships)

Figure 17 Senior girls (good absorption and sincerity)

*Figure 18 Social drama: senior boys practising, through drama, how to behave at interviews.
The 'boss' is very absorbed in the imaginary credentials of the candidate*

Senior Schools

Now comes the great sea-change. For some young people it is a comparatively smooth passage, despite some fears mixed with eagerness, or excitement, on arriving at a new, probably bigger, school. For others, it is a considerable environmental shock, which we should not underestimate. For the gifted and for those with a good memory, the change should be fairly easy, once they have come to terms with the social atmosphere and rules of the new school, because they can immerse themselves into their lessons and begin to succeed almost at once – good teaching presumed.

Public Schools For those going from a Preparatory school to a Public, or Private school, the going may be tough. This would be particularly true, if the Prep school was a rather cosy one. (They are at least allowed contact with parents in many of them now.) They will have to undergo some unexpected experiences and behaviour from Seniors, which have been built up over the years and are part of the ethos and tradition of the place. There will be a number of new names to learn, of areas in the school and of masters and pupils. Woe betide anyone who does not learn quickly, or who forgets. Many of the new rules will appear ridiculous. Some of them are. But it is better to fall in with them, as a confined, somewhat monastic society is under a sort of soviet rule and has terrible ways of inducing you to conform. I do not mean physical cruelty (one certainly hopes not). But anxiety, stress and stern judgement combine in subtle ways to subdue. Some children in their Junior schools have come to senior position before leaving. They may have been prefects or the equivalent, or won first team colours, passed their exams and have even some friends on the staff. They have been given the chance to organise, have received trust and are respected. Not only are they delightful young people, but they have had a taste of being treated as grown-ups. For some of these, it may truly be said that (after getting over enforced separation from family), it was the happiest time of their life. Then comes a fierce change. You are suddenly at the bottom of the ladder again. It is a real test. The worst thing is that you may have no friend on the staff, at a time when you really need one; and you are not respected. Respect has to be won all over again.

It may not be a bad thing to be taken down a peg, to be humbled. A balanced little person may take the strain, survive and discover enjoyment once more and even have ambitions. Success at lessons ('work') is tremendously important, as you do not want to be in trouble with both teachers and older pupils at the same time. That may be too much to bear. One of the dreads may be 'prep' (home-work) at night, in the growing knowledge that teachers don't take kindly to 'I'm sorry, I didn't have time'. They tend to say 'I don't care what Mr/Miss asked you to do. I am only concerned with what you do for *me*'. Totally unjust, the child may feel. It generally is. But *one* of the important things these schools teach is that it is an unjust world; and the sooner you learn it the better. Cope! (You may, of course, be able to do something about injustice later in life.) However, there is a difference between being humbled and being humiliated. If things go in the latter vein too far, the young person will find it hard to bear. Let us hope that this does not happen very often. The majority of pupils come through quite well and enjoy themselves. These schools are much happier places than they used to be. For those few who are *not* happy, the one last straw is to hear constantly that 'This school, don't forget, is a microcosm of the world.' If that is so (for them) it is no longer worth living. They see no hope. They live in dark despair. Of those that I have known personally, more than one took their lives. Some, who are going to come through, think 'Oh, well, if they are going to treat me as an outlaw, I shall jolly well be one'. They get into trouble, but they survive. In later life I have been able to help a few young people in both categories (and even when young myself, one or two; more by luck than anything. But sympathy helped).

It should not be thought, by this, that there is any suggestion that Private Schools or Public schools, as we call them in the UK, are always, or generally, breeding grounds of unhappiness – children can be unhappy anywhere, for many reasons. They are usually fine places, giving excellent education. They just do not suit all people. I only state what *can* happen if thought, concern and understanding by both teachers and/or pupils is lacking. It is just as incumbent on pupils to learn concern for others early in life, as for anyone else. It is important for the leadership they are presumed to be going to take after leaving school, wherever they are, so as to influence (in ways large or small) the society in which they will live. Parents, be aware of these things, if any child has poor reports, or is distressed. They may not tell you about it.

Comprehensive Schools As part of history, it might be interesting to remember that Sir Edward Boyle was one Conservative Minister, who was in favour of this experiment. 'I think we should give them a chance', he used to say. My own view was for equal opportunity, but the size of the schools always worried me.

Sir Edward, as he was then, was unusually interested in play. But although his main interest was music, he attended and spoke at the first World Children's Theatre Conference in London (1964), when I was Chair of the Creative Drama Section. After this he became President of the Educational Drama Association, whilst I was Director. He then became Lord Boyle and I followed him as President after his retirement and sad death. He wielded a more important sword, at a crucial time, in the field of children's rights than most people knew about, or for which people gave him credit.

It is sometimes said that not all Comprehensives re-constructed their curriculum and sorted Secondary Modern thinking from Grammar in a constructive way, nor mixed it right. But many Comprehensives do a wonderful job under the most *difficult* circumstances.

For those who have been in state education and in a happy Junior school, the shock may be great on arriving at a Comprehensive school. The size is alarming to start with. You have perhaps lost your friends, and certainly the teacher you got on with. Here, the teachers may seem like creatures apart, anxious over many things (they can't help being so), with little time to answer questions and always in a hurry. You have to walk miles, once you have learned at all where to go. Perhaps you do not have a class teacher – no one to relate to. Perhaps you do not have a locker, nowhere strictly your own. It is also a fact that psychologically we can only relate to a certain number of people. Just when you think you can cope with about the first two hundred, you look out of a window, or pass a door and there are it seems about two hundred *more*. This alone can be an upsetting factor. In a 1500 or 2000 pupil school the shock seems endless.

So, for all these reasons, I always advocated (I do still), that at least the first year should be made, for newcomers, as near Junior school as possible. Here, of course, their lessons may be integrated with play and the play itself will show clearly where the children 'are' and how much they have been disturbed. The art may show dark colours and drama may be weak, with little *language flow*. I have known some children who were outstanding in their ability in Junior school, who suddenly became almost incomprehensible and incoherent in their new surroundings. In lessons these would go back also. It needs patience to bring them on a bit and in the arts, we may have to go right back to the gang stage. Indeed, in the new class, there may well be those who have had little or no such inner training. Therefore there will be mixed ability here too and, for a bit, quite low standard in the class as a group. I would beg teachers not to give up and think the improvised attempts are valueless; with practice they will improve.

Opt-Outs It is too early to know what the 'Opt-Out' schools will do about all this. We shall only know in a few years time. That is, if everything is not changed again. But in the meantime, it is likely that they will go chiefly for the three R's, and a few important things could be left out. I do hope not, for there are some wise and extremely fine Heads in these places, willing to take chances, and it would be the greatest pity if various pressures forced them to neglect the inner person for outer apparent success.

Middle Schools There do not seem to be so many of these now. Most of those I have seen appeared happy and efficient places. But for inner child-development, the general age-range is awkward. The arrangement seemed to settle down to a span of about eight years to twelve or more. This, of course, interrupts the main gang stage and cathartic years, which should start at seven. So if their school starts at eight, they may be better at three R's or, if the Infant school had difficulty with them, they will be backward. That can disrupt others ready to press forward. Anyway, they will have missed one important year of inner development, available in any Junior school that does anything like what has been suggested for play opportunity. At the top end, children may be more prepared in maturity to face life in a large Senior school, but if still at Middle School, they need expanding and stretching, not only in basic lessons, but also in the arts. A difficult period of evolving is arrived at in painting and drawing, as the children are becoming 'old' now. And in the drama, they really need a teacher who knows enough about theatre to blend their terrific potential in acting (nearing senior outlook) with the best of their own art form of Child Drama. Otherwise, their output is allowed to be either too child-like or too sophisticated and really misses the boat. This is asking an awful lot, so how one finds enough brilliant teachers, who know enough about Junior education to make up for the first lost year of gang stage and enough about the highest standard of polished improvised performance at the top end, I don't know. This must be true for other subjects too.

Secondary Modern Schools I must just put in a word about these. It was the inequality that people felt was wrong. But, for the most part I always found them happy places. Children may have been disappointed over the eleven-plus, but at least they were not pressurised. One received a terrific welcome from both staff and children. There seems to be some feeling that these little people were 'seconds', not quite up to standard. Perhaps Heads welcomed one, because they were not always quite sure what to do. So anyone who turned up and offered to do something different was almost an Angel in disguise. Happiness in these schools, it has been said, relied much on the inspiration of particular Heads or teachers. Perhaps, partly because the children were not over-pushed, they seemed eager and cheerful and the drama they did with me was, for me, some of the happiest ever. We did not consider ourselves second-class citizens and I was determined to give them confidence for life. In a few good Secondary Modern schools, Heads, who had reservations about the eleven-plus examination, were determined to push hard for better results. And, at least one that I knew, succeeded in seeing some of his pupils pass with high marks in tests they were not expected to take. They may have been late developers and the eleven-plus had come too early for them. (Recent reports suggest that one child in four was wrongly placed.) I added to this some fairly formal speech training, at the top end, in case it should help them to get a better job. They must be coherent at interview, I felt. It may be of interest to note that at the school that was most successful, the idea of making the first year like Junior school was fully implemented. Actually, my own feeling was that it was a little too 'youngish'. But the Head was convinced that it was this idea that gave his students the basic happiness and confidence to try really hard at their lessons further up the school. Time was still made for a lot of art, drama and dance. Changes in education may make this relevant all over again, even in different circumstances.

Grammar Schools We have lost a lot by getting rid of some of the finest schools in the country. It is quite understood that there may be reservations about their being elite. For this reason, some of them were manoeuvered into a half change. It was extremely difficult for them to retain their ethos, which had been built up, in some cases, after hundreds of years. For others, they died. So all those remarkable men and women, who appeared to be the backbone of institutions far and wide, will in future be lost, perhaps (though present government plans of 'back to basics', at time of writing, may mean re-instatement?). Whenever I really wanted something *done* in offices to which I was linked, I have to say, I always sorted out those who turned out to have been at Grammar Schools. The more posh (often University) types, the administrators (with a few outstanding exceptions), often gave the impression that they were only there to lose reports in, or under, the in-tray, or positively to obstruct development, which would aid schools. Once, after weeks of 'nothing done' it took me five hours to find the person who was actually responsible for an important but simple piece of *action*. This person had not yet heard of my suggestion. She turned out to be a bright, young, so-called secretary. Like Sergeants and Sergeant Majors in the Army, who really keep companies in order, she could read, write, count and organise. She really ran the department. I had been to her old Grammar school that morning, we discovered.

Now, the eleven-plus examination, here, worked the other way in Grammar schools from that described in Secondary Modern schools. Some children had been pressurised a bit, passed the examination, but were not truly up to standard and therefore could not keep up with the new regime. It was all much more formal, too, and life was often more strict. No doubt all children would suffer strangeness in their own degree at sudden change, as has been described. But, for the above reason, some pupils were cast into what was called the 'waste-paper basket' and I was called in to deal with them, because Heads said they did not quite know what to do. So, of course, I went in and asked to be allowed to do *personal play* with them. We did a lot of drama, a lot of blowing off steam, a lot of improvisations, which included their worries. This last bit sometimes led to discussions with teachers about handling, when lessons were started again. Most teachers, I am glad to say, seemed grateful and not offended. The process was generally successful, if (even under difficult circumstances) enough time and opportunity was given for the work. I was keen, in this, to build up confidence and supply hope. That was my main task. It was an elementary therapy here, which believed in relief from pressure and the right to happiness. One thing that gave great confidence was that on return to general schooling, their *language-flow* was better than that of their more clever companions. Why have I gone into all this? Because, at the time of writing, there are discussions and talks and rumours that we might be going back to some teaching on more traditional lines. If so, there will be more flexibility, I hope, for young people to go to a different place, or area, or kind of training, if at first assessed incorrectly. My hope is that there will be better vocational training, too; to *feel* useful brings one self-respect. There should also be a better mixture, of exams and long-term reports which are based on observation, by teacher, of behaviour and ability.

Mixed Ability These are extended classes of 'mixed', with the idea that some backward ones might perceive newer and grander objectives of what one *might* attain. But I hope careful consideration may be given to the idea of these classes of mixed ability. To master them is difficult. Every child is individually important. But this hardly justifies the resulting need for so many teachers of near genius able to give proper aid to the least able, yet still capable of stretching the most able at the same time. Pupils in the middle may get along with it, but those at both ends must often miss out. (Against this, though, one must consider the argument of wise teachers, who find that to put a few potential trouble makers into a well-behaved 'learning' class, gives a chance of teaching. If they allowed all the 'non-swots' to be together, they might be impossible to teach and probably out of control.)

We have considered the backward ones quite a lot so far, but let me say that I have known of obviously clever children who have neither been recognised as such, nor stretched, and have therefore become bored and then a nuisance. Sometimes this new found 'fun' (being a nuisance) grows into havoc, at growing contempt for what is seen as incompetent authority. This leads to 'Well, if they can't teach me anything sensible or they go on repeating this rubbish over and over again, I'd be better off outside in the streets, or doing video games'. If by any chance these young people have been wasted and go wrong, they may become leaders of an outside gang. This is dangerous, because they *are* clever. There is a notion that, in a mixed ability class, children will help each other. They do sometimes, but often under protest. The less able are shy to seek aid and the clever become irritated at interruption and do not 'get on with things'. My admiration goes to all teachers who have these classes. They may cope, but one never quite knows how successful one has been. At least we have come away from some attitudes. In stricter schools and older times, anyone who sought, or gave help to a class mate would have been punished or beaten for cheating. In written exams presumably the old rules still apply, but may be more difficult for students to accept or understand, if they have had other training.

General Outline for Senior Education

In the arts and particularly in drama, there needs to be proper outline of progression. In painting and drawing, there will probably be some approach to perspective and photographic representation; also technical drawing, which needs more concise detail. This all goes together with being more grown-up. But imagination should still be allowed a free rein, so that abstract work can be done, side-by-side with more formal work, and also to include architectural sculpture creations from old bits of metal and other materials. This could be linked with new suggestions for vocational training.

In the drama, there is great need for progression of the constructive kind, particularly because it is not, at the moment, in the General Curriculum for Education. It has often been looked upon as a frill and not very important, or as something those English chaps get up to when producing a play. It has never quite been seen or admitted, for what it is, in other words – when done properly – the whole of the doing of life. Has that been the Drama Specialists' fault? Have we not convinced authorities that everything we did was constructive and full of purpose? Of course, things are often stolen from the subject. Instead of 'drama', from across the water came 'role-play'. One term I heard lately is 'interactive theatre'. So we cannot even stick to one altered definition. It has to be altered all the time, then the work is often given to a separate specialist, who knows less about it than the drama specialist who has been doing it for years. 'Interactive theatre' is the least appropriate term so far, one might think, though the work may be valuable and good. It shows lack of perception and distinction between theatre and drama-the-doing-of-life. In education, the latter should be seen as the driving force for all we do and how the child 'finds' him or her self and becomes a balanced individual. Is not this the main preparation for adult life, which has to remain there after most of the lessons and subjects we have learned have been forgotten?

As in all things pertaining to human behaviour, boundary lines should not be thought of as rigid separate compartments. The boundary lines are fluid, but the needs of pupils, or the purpose in the lesson provides noticeable moments of clear distinction. I have not always found teachers seeing the need of pupils, nor having discernible purpose in the lesson. The drift towards 'games' – just because they are 'new' – does not always fulfil a need. (The only game recommended here is the 'Ideas Game' which is used for immediate purpose.) If not, it can sometimes do damage to the subject, as Heads, or others may see the result as mere messing about. All teachers have my deep sympathy over this. But one should be extremely careful not to let it happen, or the Heads could be right. Don't just fill time. Always ask yourself 'What am I doing this for?' and have a constructive answer in case someone *else* asks it.

If those guiding the work cannot see these things clearly, it is the fault of their training. Not of themselves. But real training at depth has not always been easy to find. Sometimes 'training' has been a pale imitation of University correct interest in theatre; and very little has really been done to make teachers fully aware of the detailed progression of drama, the doing of life. Sometimes they have been asked to write essays, or even theses, comparing one pundit with another, which may be good in theory, but it is a relief to hear that students are now going to spend more time actually in schools – where they may be surprised to find things called CHILDREN. For all these reasons I would suggest as a general line of progression that Senior education in drama be seen as in three divisions: Imaginative, Social and Theatre. They are not rigid boundary lines, but fluid as in need. They do progress in that order, partly regarding age, although they clearly relate to each other from time to time.

Imaginative

By this is meant the testing and playing out of numerous situations and of being people, particularly in the first year, even as in a Junior school to start with, so as to learn slowly, but more certainly, who you are *not* in order to perceive more clearly who you really are. This need not always be total fantasy play, but may be half fantasy. It concerns the need in adolescence to work out and off the half dreams of whom we would like to be, when we are not sure whether we are them or not! Greater certainty is closely associated with mental health and also good behaviour. The swift and more permissive changes in society have brought much uncertainty and it is essential to see that to play many imaginary characters in many different situations is not just messing about, but is of extreme value in seeing the eventual light at the end of the tunnel. It is also, as you get older, comforting to be occasionally able to portray people you have already *recognised* you are not, within a legitimate framework, so as not to have to be that person in real life. You should be able to go somewhere, to some special place and, without harm, '*be* them' and work that bit off.

Social Drama

This is primarily concerned with preparation for life situations before the actual event occurs, but eventually goes much deeper into relationships of every kind. It may start with telephone messages, telling people the way, dialling 999 and asking for all needed services, but continues through careful practice for interviews for a job, right up to important moments in life, which may cause real distress, such as attitudes of parents, with reversal of roles, so that sympathy can be obtained for another point of view; situations of hurt in relations with the opposite sex; what to do about serious on-rushes of jealousy, or isolation by shyness; care and consideration for others. Hygiene, beauty, care of hair and skin, care of clothes, choice of clothes, pleasant behaviour, compassion and patience may all come into this. But the inner person is what counts most. Sex questions may arise during Social Drama and rather than treat the subject in isolation, this is one chance to link it with personal relationships. We might include what is becoming necessary these days, discussions over what is sexual harassment during, or after leaving school. Getting boys to realise that no means no. (In America harassment is discussed at ten years of age. Should it be so here?) What is the purpose of and what is good about marriage? Being sure that when you say you will do something, you keep your promise and arrive at an appointed meeting on time. All this is not 'interactive theatre' (with many laughs), it is not mere role play, it is not put forward as psychosociomatic dramatalogical investigational interactionism either (although it may be). It is just plain common sense Social Drama. And drama teachers should do it. R.E. teachers might suggest subjects and situations for moral guidance (or sometimes share and join in the teaching, so also should Health Visitors).

Theatre

As said, distinction should be seen between drama, the doing of life and theatre. So far, we have been concerned with the use of drama in a specialised sense of inner growth and of training for life, arising out of the unconscious art form of Child Drama. But in the upper reaches of education, we should be moving towards the adult art of Theatre. This is like a beautiful bubble floating on the sea of civilisation; the unconscious part of drama is in the depths of the ocean underneath. It is the bigger part. Though the boundary line is fluid, and one merges into the other, the unconscious preparation (consciously guided by a good teacher) brings added superb qualities, when Theatre is arrived at, at last – with a sigh, often by teachers of English with a sincere love of literature.

For most people, being 'in a play' is an exciting experience. But to hurry others into theatre too early and without preparation can be a sadistic experience for those who have to do it, and certainly for those who have to watch it. At the top, and near top, of the Senior school theatre techniques should be taught in detail. Generally they are not. And if this is so, productions will be more dull than they need be. After all the wonderful goodwill and energy and hard work that has been put into them, this is a pity.

More About Imagination

It has been suggested that the first year, particularly in a Comprehensive school, should be akin to work in the Junior department. So, quick tests would be valuable, to see where they are in their creative ability.

> 'You are monkeys eating a banana'.

> 'You are parrots trying to get out of a cage. Can't get through the bars – can't – can't. The door bursts open suddenly and you *fly* about the room'.

> If in a class room they will not go far. If in a hall, or special drama room, they may run round it (probably anti-clockwise). If they do not run, their action is telling you they are not open or free yet. If they do, I would be ready to bring in music to enrich the situation, or some simple noise as background.

Finding out about experience is important now so:

SELF: 'How many of you have done anything like this before? Put your hands up, those who have.'

Let us say quite a number have. Those you could test out by letting them be separate and asking them to make up a little play of their own. Either help them by using the Ideas Game, as suggested before and building a story out of them, as in the gang groups and as described in Junior Department. Or, if they make up their own, they may be very elementary (this is what is meant by going backwards after change of school).

Example – In a Waiting room

DOCTOR: 'So, yer've got a bad finger 'ave yer?'

PATIENT: 'Yus.'

DOCTOR: 'Oh, look at that bird flying by.'

(*Patient looks up and out of window.*)

(*Gang of a few nurses (boys and girls), grinning and chanting together*),

'Chop.'

An axe came down and off came the finger. It fell in a waste paper bin and half the class rushed to find it. They tried to stick it on again, but the doctor said 'If it 'urts it's better orf'. That was the end of the matter. You know what doctors are like.

I had actually seen this idea in a Junior school too.

As this example was based on a place, one might ask, 'What other places can you think of to start a little scene'. Answers might be 'swimming bath; school; church; playing field; pub'.

Example – In a Swimming bath
Crowd jeering at boy on high diving board. (His father had lost a lot of money on racing we were told.)

CHILDREN: 'Goo on then.' 'Get on with it.' 'Chicken you!.'

Boy finally dived off chair in an ungainly splosh. Fortunately he met a dolphin in the swimming bath. Dolphin (a girl) swam up to him and whispered some hot tips in his ear, 'So his father was able to make a lot of money', I was told.

SELF: 'Bit short, isn't it? Let's try and make it longer. Very nice swimming, Dolphin (*gentle praise for one good thing*). But now let's have the next bit at home, where the boy tells his father what horses to back.'

Discussion started over whether the father would believe the dolphin. Finally it was agreed that he would (some of those who had not done drama joined well in discussion). But at first, there was a nice bit about when he was not sure (a bit of rich language that we had to discuss too): 'Why should I believe a **** fish?' But he did, and prospered.

After that I would try turning them all into dolphins, including the ones who had not done this sort of thing before (the ones who had joined full-bloodedly into the discussion), so as to avoid any feeling of 'them and us' growing up, but only US. Feeling 'in', in that first year, is largely what all this is about. Music would help the dolphins to swim and leap better. But if they did not leap well, it would be worth stopping everything and giving a bang on a table, chair, door (or drum, if you have one, or tambour), so as to make them *work* and run and leap as if they meant it, for a moment or two. Then go back to music and see the difference. At this age they should learn to put their all into it. Expect more and you will get it. The tightening of discipline will also help them to become accustomed to a possibly tighter regime in this big new school.

Example (eleven-year-olds): There had been some practice, in the above sort of opportunity, in this next school that I visited and the teacher had obtained the right sort of constructive freedom for the class to try things on their own. But he was a little scared, still, to show speech in front of visitors.

TEACHER: 'All right, just start things.'

> (*They started miming, quite happily. Going on what I suggested earlier about Play Groups and Nursery schools, also the importance of observing and being interested, I wandered amongst them. I wanted to hear talk too.*)

SELF: 'What are you shooting at?'

BOY: 'It's a fair.'

SELF: 'Coloured balls, or targets?'

BOY: 'Targets.'

SELF: 'Get any bulls?'

BOY: 'Yes, the last shot.'

SELF: *(to another):* 'What were *you* throwing?'

Boy: 'Balls at coconuts.'

SELF: 'Did you get any?'

BOY: *(absolutely decided)* 'Yes, four.'

ANOTHER CHILD: 'That's right, 'cos I picked up four, and I'm in charge of the stall.'

(Obviously this child would be ready for dialogue)

These remarks indicate that they were more or less fully involved. The last two really knew what they were up to. It is of course, fairly common for children to give what I call 'the constructive lie'. They say what they are doing (correct), but when asked 'balls, or targets?' they then make up 'targets', which they had not really thought of before; but you made them think it. New action may follow *from* that idea, in which the child is honestly involved. That is what one hoped would happen. But here it was also a hint to the teacher to encourage them to talk, not only mime, since their answers showed speak-ability.

TEACHER: 'Do you want to say anything to them?'

SELF: 'Oh, only that I enjoyed seeing you all doing things with so much energy. I was glad that the people I asked knew exactly what they *were* doing. That is the great thing, to really know what you are up to.'

> *Afterwards, I suggested that the teacher encourage them to speak.*

In this first period of Senior Education, circles will still be formed, but gradual changes in shape may begin to be seen during play from now on.

With those who have not had much experience, ideas need to be simple, as has been seen. But answers may sound a little 'older'.

Example – Someone has suggested a station:

TEACHER: 'What sort of people appear on a station?'

At Infant level, or even Junior, answers expected might be 'Train', 'Man with flag' etc.

Here, with young Seniors, could be 'A tired old lady'. 'An angry passenger in a hurry who has lost his ticket'; 'A frightened dog.'

We can aid them to more sense of character, situation and observation of the daily drama of life. The whole classroom or hall may be turned into a station. Later, when some practice at being these people has been experienced through simple creative play, a situation might be introduced.

Example: Someone snatching the lady's handbag; frightened dog barks at an old man; a passenger knocks someone down, thinking he is late for the train. Perhaps the angry man snatched someone else's ticket. 'About the ticket, do we ring the police? What would *you* do?'

If left alone, boys often play gangster or space themes. Girls have dress-shops – and even still get married! They often have long rows. Boys just hit, shoot, throttle or stab. Make sure they have 'weapons of air' and 'fingers of flannel'.

For children who have had experience of the arts and creative play, things will be easier.

Eleven to Thirteen Years Old (Experienced Children)

It is seldom necessary to give many suggestions at this age to children at all experienced in Child Drama. Ideas flow, though it is still necessary to watch carefully, and to encourage those that appear shy, for this is the age when self-consciousness may develop. We can prevent it from doing so.

Continue in the Senior school as in the Junior school. For at least the first year allow, encourage and expect play on the floor. Themes normally will be fuller and accomplishment more polished (though sometimes there is a trace of younger ideas because of emotional upset due to change of school), but outward shape of behaviour on the floorspace will often be the same, even though shape in painting may have begun to grope towards the future. For many children the peak period of acting in a manner which does not include the proscenium stage continues after eleven years old; also the consciousness and understanding of depth may not have any pronounced manifestations in outward forms of play until about thirteen years. Have in mind that here may be gradual advance over the floorspace towards the stage, or at least to play which takes place at one end of a room. With first-year children, keep the curtains of the stage shut (if you have any). This reduces the overwhelming influence of the stage upon their work. Any move towards using it is then likely to become a genuine inner urge towards new forms of expression and discovery.

At the age of thirteen or so, there is an accelerating need to show that you are grown-up. Boys may have to be more overtly masculine, girls begin to be more self-conscious, more interested in hair-style, make-up, earrings (or rings or jewels in noses etc). Their grown-upness may either take the form of too early an interest in what they think is theatre, before they have learned how to act properly. On the other hand girls may think (or give the impression) that 'All this art rubbish is too childish for me.' 'I really can't deal with this any more.' 'I had better pretend I am bored.' Both sexes, nonetheless, usually have an interest in *life* and situations that they have met, or ponder about, or are angry with. So this is where Social Drama in all aspects is profoundly useful. It is concerned with growing up and with attitude and behaviour at the very time when there is extra feeling of need for privacy in many new ways. The following example gives a picture of attempts at theatre, unguided, rather sweet, but not very constructive and attempted too early. Also there is a phenomenon arising out of inner need for privacy.

Twelve to Thirteen Years, Girls:
THE GYPSIES
Singing started, costume was used. Some girls used tambourines. Both stage and floor were used.

TEACHER: 'They asked to piece together bits of their school experience.'
One girl danced part of a dance which a group of fifty girls had danced on a former occasion. There were two rows of 'audience', not very interested.

Two big groups on a stage did not move for a long time. There was some singing, but the rest was very formal and theatrically dull – a bad copy of some second-rate adult show they had seen. Perfectly in order for them to try such a thing, but it was acting at what they *thought* was acting, not their own genuine creation (like the infants, mentioned earlier, dancing at dancing in attempted sophisticated movements, untrue of their own dance.) These girls had not been given enough opportunity to create in their own way.

Later I was invited to see work in classrooms. During my journey to one of these (off the hall), there were noises coming from the stage. The curtains were closed.

SELF: 'I wonder what's going on.' (*Hinterland activity, I guessed.*)
TEACHER: 'Oh, they use the stage like that quite often, inside closed curtains.'
SELF: 'Yes, I have often found that. They create in privacy, like in a private room.'
Hinterland Play: At this early adolescent age, it is natural that young people of both sexes should need privacy. So many things are happening to their body, chemistry and emotions. Why not in their creations also, as these are expressions, in part, of their inner state?

I have earlier described Hinterland Play as that which goes on upstream, as it were, in the hinterland, away from the main ocean of life and all that is going on there. It exhibits itself by use of the stage, not for showing off nor sharing a message and being seen, but simply as a place for shrouding oneself (or a group) in semi-darkness maybe, merely using the curtains as a 'warm' cloak, or private hidden cave. I have even come across groups inside the first front curtain, and if there was a half-way draw curtain up-stage, discovering another group behind *that*. Sometimes this would be going on at an older age too, just before opening up for rehearsal of a 'real play'.

After I had been speaking at London University on privacy, years ago, I remember writing to Sir Cyril Burt about the matter. He replied by saying: 'Now you have reminded me, I and my sisters (I think he said), used to make up plays, and we often played them inside curtains, so we could not be seen.' This shows the difference between the need for creation for oneself (and/or a small group) and that which is shared in a wider and more overt way, which we call theatre. If we can instil some of that fervent private creation into formal theatre, it imparts a special sort of electricity. Without it, much theatre is dull. Often, one has met with people who come up, after a course, and say – almost as a confession...'You know, I sometimes dance in my own room' or 'I declame to the mirror in my bedroom.' 'I prefer to do things like that in my own room, in case people think I'm a bit funny.'

Answer: 'Not funny at all. Very sensible. If there was not a need, you wouldn't do it.'

But, of course, if people can be brave enough to come out of the hinterland sometimes and share their creation, it brings release as well as a new exciting experience. But, in order to show understanding of this half-shy feeling, at Educational Drama Association Summer Courses we always started dance sessions in half-light, for beginners almost in darkness; and also for the late evening non-guided sessions – so that those attending could feel fully free to dance in any way they liked, inventing their own shapes and gestures. At my Rea St. Centre, all movement sessions and arena theatre had specially graded spotlighting. In therapy, one can raise the strength of light, over the weeks, in sympathy with how courage is beginning to grow and self-consciousness to wane.

Social Drama

We have talked about imagination most of the time so far. Now we are moving on more to reality themes (including 'Living Newspapers' i.e. acting excerpts) though unexpected imaginative people or happenings may flash in from time to time. There will be over-characterisation also, almost to cartooning. Bring this nearer to reality by questioning. 'Was it really like that?' 'Is it like that?' 'Yes...well, did you ever think what would happen if you behaved in a different way?' Then, 'Your father didn't actually beat you senseless or shoot you, did he? – Because you're here.' or 'What would *you* feel, if you were the teacher and this nasty thing happened to you?'

Out of such discussion, much attitude can be changed after drama about life situations.

The following may provide thought for teachers too.

Whether we like it or not, a group of very nice young people (selected from several schools) were asked by a TV person why did people scram off from school. How could this be improved? How could school be better?

Answers: 'More motivation should be given by teachers.'

'Tone of voice is important. Teachers are often so rude.'

'There should be less petty rules, particularly about uniform. We are quite prepared to obey sensible ones. If there were fewer rules, we would feel less in prison.'

'Teachers should be more friendly.'

'Why can't they smile sometimes and say "good morning?"'

'More colour about the place would make it more cheerful. It's so depressing, I just want to get out.'

'We would like chances to discuss our views. We don't want to mess things up. We just want someone to listen.'

'We want more communication from teachers. And we want more respect; to be treated like human beings.'

'If we are happy with our teachers, we learn more.'

That last sort of remark comes again and again. I am sure most teachers are aware of the need. The example following was almost unexpected and it smacks of work done with older people, that is, young adults after leaving school, when I was asked to take on 'Personality Training in Industry and the retail Trades.' Sounds pompous, doesn't it? But the description was accurate and of course, much of it was Social Drama. The shock was how little had been done in schooling or anywhere to guide these students' attitudes; to life, to work, to customers, to keeping your temper and loyalty to the firm that gave them work. Most of them could count, but they needed more than that.

Example – School Visit. Twelve- to thirteen-year-old girls
They had been improvising about a hat-shop scene for some time, on the floor of the hall in front of the stage. But their imagination started to fail a bit and the play petered out. I decided to take the opportunity, not just for drama improvement, but for social consideration.

SELF: 'Did you think the girls serving were very kind to the old gentleman buying his wife a hat?'

GIRLS: 'No.'

SELF: 'I know this was just your own acting, but should we try again
        now, and think carefully about how to serve well and consider the cus-
        tomer?'

We began again. The girls behind the counter talked. The customer waited.

SELF: 'It's better to pay attention to the customer straight away.
        Wouldn't it be kinder to offer the old people a chair, too?'

We began again. They were much more considerate.

SELF: 'Good. That's much better. I wouldn't mind going into that hat
        shop. Just one point, did you notice that the girl who went off to get a
        bonnet for the old lady pulled a face at the other girl? Now if you were
        really the old lady, what would you feel?'

ANSWERS: 'Be angry.' 'Be upset.' 'Walk out, I should.'

SELF: 'Yes, you might do any of those things. I don't think we realise often
        enough that when we deal in shops, banks, buses and offices, we really
        are serving the public. People have an absolute right to expect thought-
        fulness and good manners. It is much better for business, too. You sell
        more that way.'

We tried out several groups of buyers and sellers. Improvement came rapidly.

SELF: 'Now, before next time I want you to think very hard about this, and next
        week you can show your teacher the best run, most polite hat shop in
        the world. And I bet it will be good.' (See Diagram 7.)

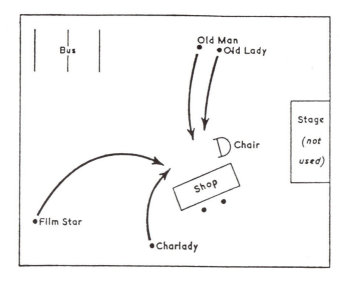

Diagram 7

With both sexes include discussions and improvisations on scenes from life to aid them in behaviour and being explicit.

Examples

> Welcoming a stranger to the school.
>
> Entering the head's room.
>
> Asking the boss for a rise.
>
> Being chairman of a meeting.
>
> Helping blind people across a road.
>
> Being courageous in an unpleasant moral situation.
>
> Telling people the way.
>
> Asking a girl for a dance.
>
> Being asked for a dance.
>
> Emergency calls for aid to firemen or police.

Also, we would discuss clothes of past periods and arrive at taste in present times, considering cleanliness and choice of colour – all of immense secret importance to the adolescent, giving rise sometimes to violent behaviour if not sympathetically dealt with.

Example

In a crowded classroom the master was taking some social drama – that is, drama concerned obviously with everyday life and how it affects us. He was helping them to think about what life would be like when they had left school.

> MASTER: 'I want you to imagine that you are going for your first job and you are being interviewed by the boss of a firm. It is very important for you to appear at your best.'

Some boys were sorted out and told to talk things over for a few minutes. They then used the master's end of the room as the office and he lent his desk for the boss to sit at. There followed the most incredible version of what an interview of this kind is like. The candidate for the job was brought in by, seemingly, two prison warders, and flung into the room. The boss slept with his feet on the table, and his foreman conducted the interview like a scene from the Inquisition. Ten applicants were tortured and no one got the job. Some of the remarks were:

> 'Ow much pay jer want?'
>
> 'Thousand dollars a week.'
>
> 'Kaw, you can't be any good; we only pay two thousand 'ere.'

Again –

    'Ow much jer want?'

    'Fifteen pound.'

    'A month?'

    'No, a week.'

    'Wot, a little tich like you? Take 'im away and screw 'is arm off.'

After a few such trials the master began to look at me with a strange countenance. His expression was a mixture of apology and despair, with a dash of apprehension in it – apprehension at what I might be thinking. All right, I thought, education is largely a matter of compassion. So I began to take over.

> SELF: 'Right. Now, let's talk about this. Remember, you are going for your first job. Would you want to be thrown into the room or not?'

A few answers of 'No.' They were weighing me up.

> SELF: 'Do you think you really would be?'
>
> ANSWERS: 'Dunno, sir.' 'No, sir.' 'Not if you was to be'ave, sir.'
>
> SELF: 'No, I think you can take it pretty well for certain that that won't happen to you. Now, what would happen?'

By now they were giving full attention, so I started to make the situation as personal as possible for each boy.

> SELF: 'It is really you, each one of you, going for your first job. How do you think you should look and behave?'

Answers came pouring forth: 'Look clean!' 'Tidy 'air, sir!' 'Stand well!' 'Be polite like!' 'Answer well!'

> SELF: 'Yes, that's great. That's more like it, isn't it? Now, the boss? Do you think he would really sleep like that? If the employee was going to take his money, wouldn't he try and see the person asking for the job and judge him carefully? I think, too, that he might want to ask some of the questions himself. In a very big firm the boss might not be there at all himself except when taking people into very high positions. His representative might do the job. But, anyway, I doubt if he would have a sort of foreman-executioner to do it.
>
> 'Now, let's try it again. Last time you were making a sort of cartoon of the situation, like something out of a comic. That's all right. It was fun and very believable in places. (*Notice how to keep their sympathy by not destroying faith in their first attempt. Always lead; don't crush.*) But let's make it more real now, more true to what is really going to happen to you in a year or so's time. This is quite serious grown-up stuff now.'

They did the same again, and there were several changes of cast. In one case I suggested a reversal of roles to let the boss feel how long he had left standing

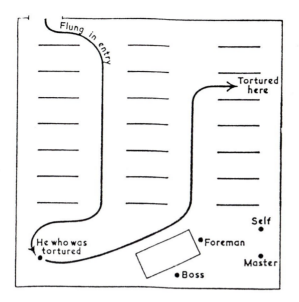

Flung in entry

Tortured here

He who was tortured

Foreman

•Self

•Master

•Boss

Diagram 8

a man seeking a senior post. We finally became deeply immersed in discussion about manners, cleanliness, thought for others, the boss's position and his care for the workers, and on their side what they owed the boss, or the firm, in hard work, loyalty and cooperation in return for a fair wage. No one had given these lads a firm picture of what the getting of a job really means or entails. It was a session of drama which somehow led us all nearer to manhood, and a finer maturity too.

It may be found that some form of social drama in this sense is the best way to start things off with older children who have already become self-conscious. They have a spurious contempt for art as such, but if neither the words *drama* nor *theatre* were stressed they might be very prepared to discuss and practise preparation for life, and particularly life after school. It makes them feel grown-up. Once having become released, they can be more easily introduced to other parts of drama as a whole.

Example (Girls fourteen years) – We had been talking about manners and boy friends and even about the value of Social Drama.

SELF: 'So, do you like your boys to be rough and manly, or not?'

GIRL: 'They *are* rough, anyway.'

SELF: 'So do you like that?'

GIRL: 'Not always.'

We then played a scene in which I suggested it was in a cafe and would they like to share with us all, of what was likely to happen. There followed a pretty rough 'do'. 'Boys' (tough girls) pushed their way in, shoved one girl off her chair and poured sugar down inside the front of another girl's dress.

SELF: *(after a bit, having listened to exactly when the noise was dying well down)*
'Is that what it's really like?'

GIRLS: 'Often.' 'Yeah.' 'Yeah, it is.'

SELF: 'Do you like that?'

GIRLS: 'Not really.' 'No.' 'What can you do?'

SELF: 'Do you know any of these boys personally?'

GIRL: 'Yes, I do, one of 'em. And he sometimes takes my money.'

SELF: 'Do you think he is really fond of you?'

GIRL: 'Yes, I think so.'

SELF: 'And do you like him?'

GIRL: 'Yes. *(a bit of laughter.)*

SELF: 'Are you afraid of him?'

GIRL: 'No.'

SELF: 'Well, there might be a chance of talking to him privately – when you are alone together, about what you feel. And if you are going to build to some sort of more permanent relationship you *must* make clear what sort of treatment you expect, he may be just showing off in front of his friends. And, if you get fed up with him taking your money, I think you might have to refuse to go out with him till he stops. Being pleased to lend him some is another matter. He should wait for you to offer it.'

GIRLS: 'I should dump 'im,' 'certainly refuse to go out with 'im.' 'I should 'it im.'

SELF: 'Who thinks you should hit him?'

(A number put up their hands)

'Well, it depends a bit what sort of young man he is, doesn't it? Hitting is probably not the best thing to do. He might hit you back. And this *could* lead to quite a nasty bashing. I think you would have to be pretty unafraid of him to start that! But, anyway, we are thinking of good manners. Do you think it's good manners to hit people?'

(Thoughtful silence)

ONE GIRL: 'Not really.'

SELF: 'As sensible women, I think you could work out more clever ways of changing men's behaviour. Of course, if it comes to it, you might feel this, or that type of person is not quite the right one for you. You could be brave and look for someone else. Or, a group of you could go to another cafe.'

(Pause, then quietly)

'Tell you a secret. We *want* to be liked by you; if some men don't always know quite what to do or how to start. Girls can have a civilising effect. Dare I say that that is one of your jobs in the world? You see, women mature earlier than men. So, you see, you are really dealing with lads who are rowdy children still – think about it.'

There was then some discussion about harassment during and after school. After this, I suggested making a scene about the nicest lad they could think of; how they would like to be treated; what sort of cafe would it be (all part of my Hope Process.) To give them an opportunity to think, I suggested it was time to dance (to 'Stranger on the Shore'. Acker Bilk.) There is sometimes a sort of occasion for dream-think, which helps one to perceive. Improvised dance helps here, and I judged this to be such a moment.

I finished with: 'Don't ever make the mistake that good manners are old fuddy-duddy stuff. Good manners are based on kindness; and if you want your men (or other women) to be kind to you, don't forget we can all try to be more polite. If affects everyone around us.'

It goes without saying that if you are successful in going, or daring enough to go this far, it would be said very quietly, bringing the session down to a complete De-climax, so that the 'closeness' of our shared admissions is *kept* and not destroyed.

Example Senior Girls – TV had heard about this work and I have written elsewhere in greater detail of a session when they came to a school where we were having a violent discussion (quite usual) about the front door key and being out late at night. So I suggested we have a scene about the most awful parents they could think of (in order to blow off steam). Then we merged into a real scene that had actually happened. It started off well and both 'parents' and 'daughter' built up a terrific climax. They were all truly upset. The daughter had come home at *midnight* and was very angry at any criticism.

Self: *(sensing that calming-down was needed)*

'Right, daughter, let's just change round now. Let's have the nicest family ever – or how you would like it to be. You be mother, someone else be father. Other family members could be there too, if you like. So, mother *(who used to be the real angry daughter)*, what time do you think your daughter should be home?'

MOTHER: *(without pause)*

'Oh, about half-past ten.'

Then the sweetest thing happened. Her eyes widened and she clapped her hand immediately over her mouth. There was a short pause, then we all burst out laughing. It must have been a moment of therapy for the girl, who joined in joyfully. The scene was then acted in a calm and sensible way. It enabled me to say: 'Well, that was a change, wasn't it? Let's consider this afterwards – did it ever occur to you that your parents don't mean to be annoying, but they want you to be home *safe* in reasonable time, because they love you?'

I am glad to say the absorption was terrific during the play-out and the TV chaps caught the lot. As said earlier, the boundaries are not rigid. So, included here is part of a short report I wrote some twenty-five years ago which is linked to the next stages forward.

Relating Life to Theatre

It might arise out of social drama or from scripted drama back to life. But in a period of social change and the Women's Movement, the role of the man in the home is likely to change. Boys and young men should have chances to look after a flat and learn to cook too, as has been said.

It might be fun to try how *not* to run a dinner party by reading, acting, or improvising on something like the one act play 'Lucretia Borgia's dinner Party,' then have a proper dinner party in modern setting. Guests need not be poisoned! In first deep relationships, a young man may want to take his girl out to tea or even dinner these days. Do we ever teach him a little about it, so as to prepare for a reasonably civilised life and possibly a happy marriage? Everything ought to be done to help young men mature more quickly, as girls sometimes suffer from 'not being looked after' and sometimes seek the attention of older men who are thereby pleased, but for the wrong reason, perhaps.

During Social Drama it is now necessary to have improvisations (role play) and discussions about drugs; what to avoid about being led into them; their harm; what to do to kick the habit.

As we shall be moving slowly out of Social Drama now (but never dropping opportunities for making a point), towards the adult concept of Theatre, here is an outline of a bit of both, mixed, as it usefully can be.

Grammar School

Sixth-form boys were rehearsing a play, but in even a small hall it was difficult to hear what they said, and the acting was not very vital.

TEACHER: 'Would you care to speak to them?'

SELF: 'Yes, if you wish.'

The rehearsal was stopped; I broke the whole group into pairs.

SELF: 'All the people on this side of the room, think of something rude to say to the person opposite you. Now let's hear you, one by one.'

They started along the row, but it was unconvincing.

SELF: 'If you were angry, would you speak like that?'

BOY: 'No, I'd be louder.'

SELF: 'Right. Be angry and *be* louder.'

Gradually all the voices got louder. They were beginning to attack their parts.

SELF: 'Now you are speaking loud enough. Don't drop below that when you are on the stage or you will not be heard. Remember, each one of you, the physical and mental experience of that loud talking. It must become a habit whilst acting.'

We then tried talking loud and *not* being rude, so as to keep the sound strong whilst portraying a calm mood.

There followed a discussion on the use of good manners.

Partners then tried both moods on the original speakers. Those who remained weak were put at opposite ends of the hall so that they could not hear each other until they spoke up. When all were fairly certain of speaking up, they were asked to improvise the scene they had been acting on the stage. This was done with tremendous life, all over the floor of the hall. Pace and climax improved tremendously.

SELF: 'Thank you. That's quite different, isn't it?'

A BOY: 'Yes, that felt real, somehow.'

SELF: 'Good. It sounded real, too. Now let's try it on the stage and use your scripts again.'

The acting was greatly improved, but was not as vital as the improvisation. The scene ended.

SELF: 'It has gone down a bit, hasn't it?'

NEARLY ALL: 'Yes.'

SELF: 'What will you have to do then?'

A BOY: 'Improvise more often.'

SELF: 'Yes, and what else?'

BOY: 'Learn the words better.'

SELF: 'Yes. The words are not known. Some of you are using books, some trying to do without them. You won't be expected to act so well whilst you have the books, but I understand you have been rehearsing for some weeks now. Compare these words with your improvisation. You can never gain the same life until you *know* what you are going to say. That means learn the words absolutely pat as soon as possible. It is better to know a great deal about the words before you start moving on the stage at all.'

A BOY: 'It's awfully hard learning the words.'

SELF: 'I know. Do you get a lot of prep?'

MOST BOYS: *(Laughter)*

'Yes.'

SELF: 'It makes a lot to learn, I know. But you do see now that it is a waste of time if you *don't* learn the words, don't you?'

ALL: 'Yes.'

A BOY: 'Couldn't we make up our own plays and do improvisation?'

SELF: 'Yes, of course you can, but don't neglect the wealth of English literature. At your stage you should do both. Create *and* learn.'

I then stimulated discussion on improvisation by telling them a little about the Italian theatre.

After that we went on to trying moves from the rehearsed play, on the floor of the hall. Everyone had practice in using the right amount of space and in asking an imaginary lady for a dance, also coming into a room politely and then rudely.

At the end of an hour we stopped.

A BOY: 'That is the most interesting hour I've ever had on drama. I never realized before what a wide subject it could be.'

SELF: 'If you relate it to life it stays alive. If not, it becomes dead literature, beautiful but dead.'

TEACHER: 'Thank you very much. What would you suggest we start with in doing more improvisation? I never saw the value of it before.'

SELF: 'I don't want to suggest too much. The ideas should come from them, but you might try with these lads the vast field of documentary plays, and feature programmes. Everyone can be included then, and you won't get those bored ones sitting about pretending to watch a dull play, as when I first came in. That's the way to hate drama. They're a grand lot, though; they responded very quickly and should do some excellent work.'

Before going further on elementary theatre and feature programmes, a word about other subjects which, if recent government plans come into being, will include more vocational training.

Other Subjects

These subjects become more formalised at this stage of education. But the general philosophy mentioned in the Junior section under this heading, will certainly apply. Only, the opportunities for lessons linked with play become less frequent. Students have got to get down to the serious *projected* activity of learning. Only the backward may prosper from any prolonged sessions of *personal play*, either to promote thought, improve behaviour, or aid understanding. Yet *some* opportunity for the arts would still be valuable for everyone, in whatever restricted bursts. It stops them from becoming narrow. Large amounts of time are less valuable than regularity.

LANGUAGES

More detail of grammar and correctness will be needed at this age But it is still important to have plenty of practice in speaking. This can be done by creating simple creative plays, after building up such ideas as ringing up for a doctor; hoping a friend is well; asking about trains; trying to find lodgings for the night; ordering a meal or drink. Then buying things in a shop; in a market place; not always accepting the first price. Probably the most important exercise is for shopping, as that is the most likely thing to have to do abroad. Concise written work is needed for letters and exams, but real practice in communication is what we are all going to need in the future, if we are not to remain imprisoned without *language flow* in our little Britain. Of course, English is widely used abroad and may be even more so. But those in foreign lands *do* appreciate it if we try to speak in their tongue. Remarks like 'good morning'; 'I'm sorry; 'good night'; 'thank you', win a lot of good feeling and are particularly helpful in business relationships. They promote good will at the start. Foreigners often love it if we stand up and make a bad speech. Perhaps we may look forward to the time when more of us become proficient enough to make a good one.

French, German, Spanish, Italian and Russian are likely to be the most useful in the near future. But if we are to become successful soon in selling, or trying to, abroad and apart from Europe, we shall face the deeper problems of Japanese and Chinese. Once the Chinese really get going, the rest of the world will wonder what has hit them. One enthusiastic teacher felt he must train background of a country as well as language.

HISTORY

Detail again. Some dates are important. More information might be given about *why* people go to war, how greed or national feeling can lead to violence. What movements in social change affect the balance of trade. We can also learn from the past, though we are not very good at it. But one thing is certain, you can't learn from the past, if you don't know it. The wax and wane of Trade Unions; poverty as a cause of crime; abuse of liberty being a step towards dictatorship – all those are of the utmost importance to discuss and understand about in the lives of our next generations. The expanding mind should be able to take these things in by now.

It may be better to link whatever is talked about in the past with what is happening today (as in Social Drama), otherwise interest can be difficult to engage. Here 'Living Newspaper' can be valuable, acting situations that threaten or enrich society.

Under likely curriculum planning in the near future, it is *un*likely that a three to four day project, where the whole school dresses up as if living in Elizabethan times takes place. I saw this in one school. Rushes on the floor of the hall, little families talking to each other (in circles!), a bit of Shakespeare going on, on a

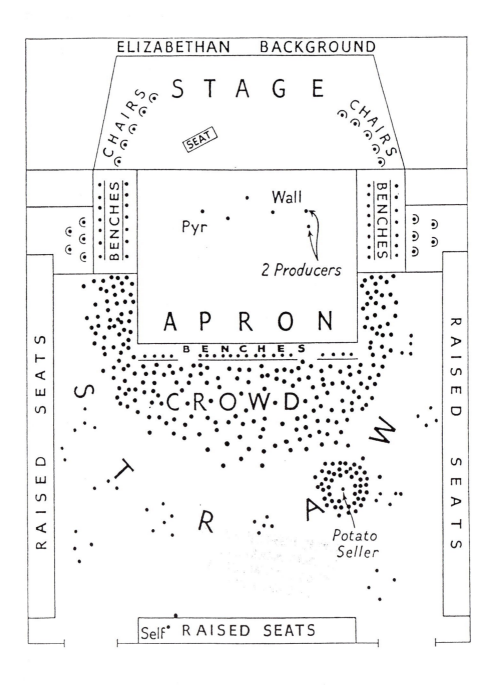

Diagram 9

projected stage. Good *language flow* and, all whom I spoke to, well in the part. One group wondered if I was a ghost of the Future, because of my funny dress with coat and tie [see diagram 9]. Although there is no time for such wonders now, it may be argued, it remains true that if you really want to feel strongly about and 'realise' a person or time, or situation, you have to act them and it. Then alone does feeling go deep.

GEOGRAPHY

Teachers of this subject will have quite a job keeping up with world changes. Almost every day we hear of a new war, a new catastrophe, an invasion, a boundary dispute. Oil, or mineral or metal finds affect nations these days and are the cause of suspicion or of strife. We might base some of the teaching still on what it is *really* like to live in such-and-such a part of the world, how climate affects them and their crops, what part do drugs play in trade, so as to build both understanding and compassion for those who live in very different situations from our own. This is going to be important in all the lives of our young. Terrible, wise decisions may have to be taken by them, for the world is still not a safe place. Again, true learning and understanding may go deeper by acting the part. We have got to understand other people and conditions better, because the world has grown 'smaller'. Geography, in a wide sense, under first-class teaching will have more importance than it has ever had before. Painting, photography, films and videos will, of course, be essential aids.

RELIGIOUS EDUCATION

This should be much on the lines as suggested for the Juniors in philosophy of integration, respect, learning about others and sharing like with like in separate religions. There is an added danger for mistrust now, which is girl friends. The sins of envy, malice and covetousness are very close to the surface over these too; perhaps even the passing thought of 'thou shalt not kill' appears (for swift moments) to say the least, inconvenient. There are ethnic boundaries too. Some religions prefer young people to marry someone of the same faith. There are also arranged marriages. Girls may know that they are supposed to marry someone their parents are planning for. Then they suddenly fall in love with someone else. This often provokes extremely unhappy situations for both sides – and for the parents. Being seen with someone of a different race can cause considerable anger. The RE instructor will have some very difficult times during discussion and attitude over all these things. It is best to try not to generalise, but to treat each case as separate and distinct. Our own prejudice, or strong views, can get in the way here and we must try to be objective. It is important to remain aware that there are still the two main tests – training in the details of a Faith and its beliefs; and helping the inner person in attitude and behaviour because of, or despite those beliefs.

Unfortunately, a lot of young people give up their religion at this time. Partly, this is because of adolescent revolt, partly as a love kick to get away and find oneself, but largely because of sex. What you want to do and what you are finding out about and what adults and religion *say* you should do, don't always fit together. The sort of question one often hears is 'Does God *really* mind if I do it?' Then often comes the thought 'Well, I'm going to anyway!' This is the way to get lost. It can refer to drinks and drugs as well. Dangerous myths have been mentioned earlier in the book, not getting a baby the first time, or you don't get one if you do it standing up. This *must* be mentioned and the idea strongly discredited. Occasionally it is true that nothing happens ('you don't'), but the safest answer is firmly 'You DO!' Some young ladies try to have a baby on purpose. They say it is like winning a competition, it creates envy and admiration. They do it to get the fuss and popularity of their friends. Even being pregnant at school seems like when a boy gets in the first team for football. There is no proper consideration of what it means to have a child, nor thought for the child's future. When it really becomes clear what a responsibility it is to *deal* with this creature, it comes as a considerable shock. Then, 'What am I going to do with it?' The thought should be – 'what is going to happen to it?' More very young (probably single) mothers should come into schools (under Health Authority, or any appropriate label and subject) to show exactly what coping with and bringing up a baby really entails. Training for marriage could well come in here.

Once young people have, even temporarily, lost their faith, they often become surly, bad tempered and cynical. They try out bad behaviour to see what you are going to do about it. Unfortunately, it can happen because those in charge of them have been too strict. Their pupils cannot understand how those who believe in a god can behave like that to them. Some boys, particularly, who have had much physical punishment in the past, or verbal abuse, suffer this attitude greatly. Girls suffer it from any teachers who show a sort of holy vindictiveness.

Grown women, who have been to Convent schools (either unhappy or very happy) admit to being left with a strong and irresistible desire to please. Their conscience has been enlarged – artificially or for their good. They often suffer from not being able to say what they really think or believe, either in case of hurting someone, or for fear that they will not be approved of, they say.

Many children, according to home training, know little or nothing about religion, or do not care. But if young people are in a desperate dilemma, in a large school, we might not know about it. But if we *do* come to know of it and they appear to be absent, before deciding they have played truant, it is worth taking a little walk down the corridor (or getting a member of staff of the appropriate sex to help) and paying a visit. Not for 'bawling someone out', but for condolence. For desperately unhappy children often talk to God in the lavatory. With luck, (during lessons) it is the only quiet private place to be. You may be able even to lock the door on the whole world.

About the detail of Religion, we have to bear in mind that Christian children are often puzzled by, yet take some note of, the New Testament, but are bored to death by the Old Testament. On the other hand, those of Jewish Faith would be far more interested in the Old Testament and might avoid, or be distressed by the New. They, and those of Islam, would regard Jesus as an unusual teacher, perhaps, but no more.

If occasions arise, when it is thought useful, or advisable, to do things or pray together, paying respect for each others' beliefs, themes might still be helpful. This was suggested for the Junior School, where it is essential that enmity and misunderstanding should not grow up in young minds. But here it might be the time to use what will later be described as Feature Programmes. In these, script, poetry, readings, improvisations, music and dance can be linked together in a theme. The theme can offer windows on human doing; and act, therefore, as a parable to correct behaviour. Again, the main teaching should not only be in learning prayers and scripture of whatever sort, but in kindness, honesty, reliability, courage, forgiveness, patience, gentleness, understanding and what to do about love – both for God and neighbour. Above all, there must be respect. It is essential that we strive all we can to inculcate the feeling of sisterhood and brotherhood right across nations and race before they leave Senior School. It is our last chance to turn out citizens. Upon this attitude, maybe, hangs the peace of the world.

SCIENCE

It is sad to hear reports that there are fewer young people taking an interest in this subject than expected or hoped for. There are such fascinating books now on such things as physics, which should stir interest. Also, if imaginative and play approaches have been made in the Junior department, it should help to fire enthusiasm. The improvement in the way science is taught now is quite wonderful. There is great encouragement for inventions too. Young people have invented some ingenious machines. Perhaps there could be more competitions in schools for practising and rewarding ingenuity. Associated with this and in conjunction with Art Department, there should be training in design.

Knowledge of chemistry is of the utmost importance. It is far removed from the elementary boiling and smells of earlier times. We desperately need to know about substances for improving health. We desperately need to know much more about side effects. We desperately need to know how not to ruin our Earth, so as to avoid all hair falling out and all animals and fish, and finally ourselves, dying of poison. They call it total toxic overload. We need to know more about nuclear power. Or is it already too late? Now that we have found out a bit about atoms (remembering that a little knowledge is dangerous) we need to know much more about Enduring Power; and how to force together all those things like deutrium and the others that begin with 'trit', so as to arrive at Fusion Power. Our young will have to find it, if we don't first – and how to really control all these things – lest the world in one last fatal foolishness, doth blow itself into that vast sea of dark material that lies waiting for us out there in space.

MUSIC

These teachers and their work have already been mentioned for their contribution to theatre shows. I hope many of them will be 'with me' in the importance I place on sound – in the whole of life. Some of us retain our interest in tune. But no doubt, young people ought to have experience of music without tune too. A musician friend of mine once said 'Oh, I wish I was a Modern. I spent so much time learning the old rules of harmony. These Modern chaps just press down all the notes at once and no one knows the difference.'

A young adult lady said to me recently 'Well, they sang my music at Christmas, so I thought perhaps I should learn harmony, because I just use my own. But a tutor in music said she didn't think I should change it. It might get spoilt.'

This is a bit like the Principal of a famous school of Art, who said to me one day, after I had asked questions about an exhibition, 'Well, you see, things and ideas have changed so much that I and the staff no longer think we know the criteria by which these creations should be judged.' In other words, keep an open mind. I remembered the time way back when I disliked Bach and Epstein, but by keeping an open mind eventually learned to love them both.

In glass, and probably other materials these days, the most wonderful instruments can be made. In one school, the whole floor of a class room was strewn (no, in careful equidistance placed) a family of guitars, beautifully shaped and inlaid and of all sizes. They had made them all.

The kind of music that has been so successful in recent years, particularly in shows, composed by talented teachers, is epitomised for me in the work of Colin Baines. The most wonderful experience was at the end of a visit to St David's, in Wales. Colin had composed the music for a particular play in the Summer Festival there.[1] There was a wonderful farewell song in it, which I loved. And, as I was leaving, they sang it again for me, just before my starting to ease off down the drive.

---

1   The Festival had been started by Jack Beckett, with his family, and for a time I was
     Vice-President.

Dance can be very useful for training people to listen in more detail. Some well known Music Schools have invited me, in the past, to outline the relationship between interpretation, gesture and musical phrase.

Pythagoras thought that music was part of mathematics.

MATHEMATICS

We are told sometimes that even after all the years of schooling, up to the age of fourteen, and sometimes more, that pupils leave school unable to count. Just as it may be found that some adolescents do not seem to have had their Dawn of Seriousness yet, nor got through the main cathartic years of the gang stage (normally seven to nine years old), it may even be useful to consider employing my *domino marching* (see maths section in suggestions for Junior School). This would be just in *case* it helps for their grasping a concept. Bit late, though, now. It may be found that active, cheerful people find difficulty over mathematics. Drama people very often do. They are more concerned with *personal play* rather than the *projected activity* with symbols. At least this is true enough for one of the considerations for starting the Drama Department at Manchester University being, I was told, to try and find people of ability to train for theatre management as well as artistic achievement. They are not easy to find. But for advanced students, no doubt they are informed about equations concerning space and other things. One section that may have been left out too much in the past is home economics. What it costs to run a home; how to mortgage a house; how to do income tax; save for a baby; estimating weekly shopping.

These are some of the things that can cause great problems in early, or young marriage – as can disagreement over drinks, clothes and cigarettes. Teachers here can suggest 'dropping' the last item! It would be healthier and much cheaper to do so. Warnings should be clearly given over priorities, the danger of credit cards, hire purchase agreements, and loan sharks. Some schools provide opportunity for book keeping. This might help in future setting up of one's own small business. Explanation of VAT would be useful.

In general, perhaps, as the economy improves, some encouragement might be given for going into industry. Also, the pros and cons of taking a job, even if you don't like the idea of it, rather than being on the dole. One report indicated that children, even older ones, left alone, or at a loose end for more than twelve hours were in danger of becoming involved with drink or drugs. Perhaps there are not enough business heroes to inspire us all.

ENGLISH

This subject should still be based on the love of sound, it is this that really lifts poetry and literature from what you 'ought' to like to that which can grow into real joy. Meaning, of course, has its place! A sudden idea, or way of putting things, can hit a young person and draw them to further discovery.

Once they are able to write fairly well, it is time for them to try and write plays, if they want to. As mentioned, in the Junior school first attempts are not really satisfactory. The labour and time it takes to write something is quite out of proportion to the speed with which it is acted. But now there should be less actual need for writing a story in preference and improvising on that. The writer now, one hopes, is more competent and must have learned a bit about life. Thus he or she has something to write about. One thing I do hope they will resist is writing, without thinking about how to get a person off-stage, '(Please), don't bother, I can see my own way out.' We hear it quite often, but can't they just *go*? I would rather have Columbo, who always keeps coming back. You can't get him out at all. At least, with him, you know there is a thought and a reason for his behaviour – intentionally irritating and putting the wind up a suspect.

This does not mean that one should not act out the story of a written piece. It can be wonderful. Efforts are just not so confined to that now, because of improving ability to create dialogue.

POETRY

Still do not overwork rhyme. We all can experience enjoyment from it. And at the end of a Shakespeare scene, the sudden sunrise of a rhyming couplet after a mass of blank verse, *lifts* the scene and the sense of excitement can be thrilling.

But the adolescent can be filled with bliss, or in dark vaults of fear, or depression. The poetry they write is sometimes mere prose but put in a funny shape. I have known teachers that were sometimes a bit too pleased with these attempts. On the other hand we sometimes come across occasional deep and thoughtful statements with, say, one word on a line, purposefully hanging there in time, because of its weight, stress, unexpectedness, number of syllables, which bring rhythm and flow in lovely proportion. Poetry, once found, is an important way for the bursting adolescent to spit, or pour, his/her anger or love into some satisfactory shape. As to the 'mere prose' type of poetry, readers may be aware of some of this by Moderns, who just cram in thoughts which shock and employ no music in the words whatever. This beguiles the young, who are easily deceived.

My Godfather, who was fairly well known in his day, used to say: 'Poetry should have a stone-like quality.' I think he meant chisel it down and down until you find the final form without frill. It is this stone-like quality which gives it dignity, power, sense and beauty.

GRAMMAR

With governmental advice that there should be more stress on grammar, may I plead for teaching about transitive and intransitive verbs. One hopes the difference is understood between what is a noun and a verb, because this affects the above. There is no harm in telling young people that a noun is a thing or a person. A verb is what you do, in the present, past or future. A transitive verb does something *with* something or someone. For example, I lay a cup on the table. But I lie down (intransitive) perfectly well without a cup.

The words lie and lay cause considerable confusion these days, it seems. 'There 'e was, laying down', one hears so often. Laying down what? The Law? It should be lying down (intransitive). *Most* unfortunately, the past tense of lie (intransitive) is lay. That really is unfair. But then here is the other verb to lie (tell an untruth) and a lie is what you tell. Things are made worse by the road signs of a Lay By. It ought to be Lie By, but that doesn't sound quite right in many ways. So they went for safety and sound effect, maybe.

I have mentioned earlier the horrors of 'was sat' and form*i*dable instead of formidable. But these days, when trying to be dramatic, tense of the past is switched to the present as well. So we arrive at 'So there I am, sat all amongst this glass and this man comes up and...' *What* man? You haven't referred to him yet. What the heck are you talking about? It might be another language. It is a pity that people seem to be so proud of speaking like this and we hear it every day on the media. No wonder our young haven't a clue about what is correct. Another common fault is the double negative. It is such a silly mistake. It does not add strength to the statement. It only needs a bit of thought about what one is really saying, for example 'I haven't got no money'. If you haven't got *no* money, you must have *some*. 'Didn't hardly do something' means you probably actually did! 'Didn't hardly know her' should be I hardly knew her. I don't believe that this cannot be pointed out, nor that it is wrong nor harmful to do so. Another thing we might teach about is comparisons: 'more happier' is incorrect. Happier or more happy is enough. There are also many words that sound as if they mean something else – for example 'enormity' is often used to mean something very big. It can only mean something very evil. (There is a feeling of 'enormous' in it, agreed.) The wrong use of phenomenon (singular) and phenomena (plural) has already been pointed out. Similarly criterion and criteria are often used the wrong way round. It is good to mention it early, but at this age it is our last chance to get it right perhaps, before any of our pupils go into parliament.

I mention again the new ugly stress on prim*a*rily and tempor*a*rily, volun*ta*rily. It probably comes from America. But in English the stress should be on the first syllable.

Then there is the section of words which are the same for the noun and the verb. The wrong stress is often put on these. For the noun the stress is on the first syllable, and for the verb on the second – particularly with two syllable words.

Thus:

> I will make a *survey*, but I will *survey* the place first.
>
> I will not only write and make a *protest*, but I will go out and *protest* in the street as well.
>
> And he/she who *protests* is a *protester* (protestor allowed) and *nothing else*.

In Theatre Schools, at one time, it was pointed out that the word clandestine should be pronounced as *clandestin*. There does not seem any very good reason for this, so I don't think there is much hope that it will last. Controversy suffers a lot. It should be *controversy*, but is generally *controversy* now. It changes the meaning a bit. *Controversy* sounds like a strong but gentlemanly discussion of a difficult problem. *Controversy* is a loud shouting argument, like in the House of Commons. All life is more violent now and no doubt *controversy* will win. It is more onomatopoeic of what happens and easier to say. The word 'like' is beginning to be used in a funny way: 'He came in like he was a thunderstorm?' Instead of 'as if he were' (colloquially 'was').

The use and meaning of words is, of course, bound to change with time. But I must admit that I found the enormously free rein of saying anything any way you like, after the War, was not only a pity but was in danger of being destructive of our beautiful language. New ways of puttings things and of inventive terms are another thing. Many of these are an enrichment. Many came from America. It is stress, apparent complete lack of care about grammar of any kind and use of swear and four letter words in such profusion that makes one wonder what we are coming to. In films and videos and plays these days there is such a chance for writers to use new inventive expletives, and adjectives that really enrich a noun. But all we get is a farmyard four letter word over and over again. It is so *boring*. Is it the only word they know? In the army the word is correctly used (sometimes) when getting something off your boot. But when a heavenly looking girl suddenly spouts it out as well, because she has knocked her knee, it gives one a bit of a shock. You were building up a real *thing* about her in this film. Now you wish she hadn't got a brother, or a boyfriend or an office to go to, from any of which she must have learned this silly unpleasant word. Certainly not on a farm. Again it is onomatopoeic and easy to say. As usual, the lazy way out.

All these things are not just my prejudice. They are what many people would call unfortunate facts and mistakes. Elementary training would put them right. We are not just thinking of accent here. True local dialects are a joy. What is less appealing is the mixture, which often happens in towns. In the South, you quite often hear people talking what is called accepted (?) English. Then in the middle of a sentence they would mention buttered wives (bit sexy) and buttered babies (nice for breakfast?). The convention is broken and you don't know where you are. In this sort of English, one expects the word battered and ought to get it. In the North (generalised) a number of words would be slightly different and, in a moment or two, you know where you are. In Yorkshire, no doubt, you know that battered is likely to be buttered and buttered would be bootered. It comes as no shock and sounds nice. In the South, or on radio how are we going to know whether they mean slam or slum? When it comes to theatre it is important. One can be fascinated by extremely good acting of a scene, say, in a middle class home in the 1920s or 1930s and suddenly we hear '…and Virginia, dear, don't slum the door when you go out. It causes such a controversy with yer father.' No one ever spoke like that in drawing rooms of that period. Slum the door? If not expecting it, one cannot help thinking (for a moment), does that mean behaving to the door as in a slum? Does it mean making it dirty? Oh – they mean slam! What a pity, that scene is dead.

In those days they may have had a barney, a shouting match, a quarrel, an argument, but an educated family would never have had a controversy. Too vulgar, my dear. Gentlemen might have been reduced to an unfortunate controversy. That is milder and better behaved. Sound is such a lovely and important thing. Both in Play *and* at Work it gives special impressions. It is a high form of civilised communication and although we all make mistakes, it is worth trying to get things right. (My own problems are with spelling and punctuation.)

Is this all to be considered pedantic or snobbish? I do hope not. I hope it is considered as a basic part of trying to keep a high standard. There are so many fine teachers of English that I have met and I have great sympathy for them in their difficult task. Perhaps we need a new Elise Fogerty[2] to keep us in order.

Other things that they will, no doubt, be aiding are – organising discussions and practising interviews for jobs. The Drama teacher ought to be involved with these too. They are both part of Social Drama. In discussions, do teach speakers not to interrupt each other. It is elementary civilised behaviour to wait for a person to finish their point. And it is so stupid for both to shout at each other at the same time, because no one can hear what is being said. This happens again and again on the media these days. The worst examples are when interviewers have a Minister or special personality being questioned. They interrupt all the time, forgetting that the person is their guest. As listeners we are totally uninterested in what the staff member thinks. We just want to hear what their guest has to say. Sometimes we are never allowed to. At the end, also,

---

2   Famous one time Principal of the Central School of Speech and Dramatic Art, then at the Albert Hall.

it is so rude to put things the wrong way round. 'Mr. or Lord So and So has been talking to Joe Blank.' He is jolly lucky if he has been allowed to. What they should say is 'Joe Blank (as a special favour) has been talking to Mr. or Lord So and So, or the name, then Minister for whatever. It is an honour for Mr. Blank to be allowed to ask questions, so he should be careful not to waste his guest's and the listeners' time. Hectoring repetition of some stupid point is a very bad example for viewers or listeners, particularly the young.[3] At time of writing, one stunning example of good behaviour is on BBC Radio 4 early on Sunday mornings. Questions, as one would hope, are put politely and carefully and there are no interruptions. It is like a different world.

A word more about pronunciation. This has to do with manners also. When thinking about the way foreigners feel, if we actually try to speak their language, we could try harder to find out how the names of places and people should really be said. Mentioned before was the South African word often pronounced 'Apartite', sometimes 'Apartate'. If we listen to people from that country, they seem to call it the latter. So why don't we hear constructively and do that too? The other word we never decided on was Maastricht. News readers probably have a better chance than anyone else of finding out from foreign sources what the sound should be and where the stress should lie. Yet we have heard differences every day; and from other sources: 'Maasricht', 'Maastricht', 'Mastrick', 'Meistricht' and 'Meistrit'.

Other words creeping in are 'reely' for 'really' and 'they' for 'there' and 'island' for 'Ireland'. Distinction is important for imparting a clear message. All good teachers, certainly of drama and English, will know that if you *listen* to noise, you can hear when it is getting quieter. And if you don't want to shout, you wait till it is your best time to speak. It is a pity that some interviewers don't appear to know this. In case any of our students end up on the media, let us teach them to listen to the sound. You can always tell when the end of a sentence from another speaker is going to come, if you try. Only if they never stop, should we break the rule and break in!

PLAYS

There is no doubt that teachers of English, with their love of literature, will want to produce plays. Often they do a good job and, no doubt, share the preparation of them with others, such as the drama teacher, someone good at lights. Please forgive, if this is recommended, for there are occasions when one has seen shows that they have tried all by themselves. On these rare occasions when the teacher did not know enough about theatre, apart from literature,

---

3   The same point has now been made by the Director General of the BBC at greater length and in more detail.

productions have been 'careful', and well costumed, but slow and dull. I once saw a *Hamlet* that felt as if it had taken five to six hours. We staggered out exhausted and were in danger of swearing never to see that play again.

Even drama teachers are sometimes hesitant to obtain help. It is understood that a production done entirely by them, if successful, may be a step up the ladder, professionally speaking. But although their show might be good, often, with a little extra help, it might have been 'electric'. Such little things count: light, as it hits a person at entrance; pause; eye work; moves and grouping; strength of a consonant at a strong moment; how to sit down in costume; being heard without effort; pace and attack depend on how well words are learnt. Keeping the scene up. This last is particularly important and just as a Primary school child may drag down and go flat when singing, so a producer appears sometimes not to notice when the scene is going down. If, by any chance, your area has a Drama Adviser, it would be a pity to be too proud to invite him or her to a rehearsal. The production could then become a team creation for the best for the children and all concerned, rather than an understandable bit of rather single glory for one person. They would get even more credit for the best *possible* show, for the audience might well think that teacher alone had done it. I am sure most teachers are well aware of the value of working in a team.

Surprising to say, but (for these and other as yet unexplained reasons), the best shows in fairly recent years often turned out to be those put on by science teachers (first interested in lights) and music teachers, who put on the most wonderful productions with their own music.

Theatre

Speech, pronunciation, behaviour, life situation and action bring us into theatre. For theatre is all of these and more.

One of the early things we learn about speech in the theatre is that by pronouncing consonants clearly, even banging them on occasions, we are more likely to attract and keep the attention of the audience. This is particularly true of consonants at the beginning of words and at the beginning of important syllables. It is part of what is called 'attack'. To be more sure of this, try muttering some sentences, using vowels as little as possible, or not at all. You will find that, on most occasions others will understand what is being said. Then try a bit without consonants, just vowels. As a rule, no-one will know what you are talking about.

For improving tone and carrying-quality in a simple way, try saying 'la' loudly and going low in pitch, then lower. After that, take big breaths and, if it is time for a bath, sing in it. Even declaim loudly, if you have anything to declaim about. I suggest the bathroom because your voice always sounds better in there. The bath acts like a TV dish. It is very encouraging. Sorry, household! It is important to understand that any speaking in public is different from ordinary conversation. You really do have to work harder and speak louder. This is particularly true of readers in church. Members of the laity (including children), unless they are aided, often speak too fast, not nearly loud enough, don't use consonants and drop their voice at the end of a sentence. They have no idea how to be heard clearly within a large area. It needs someone to be at the back of the church to say whether they can hear or not and to help the reader to *believe* they cannot be heard (just as in theatre production). The readers sometimes say they feel they are shouting. On rare occasions, which is very sad, they feel offended by any suggestion that they are not 'all right'. One must be as gentle and tactful as possible, for defence mechanisms come into play at once and people think you are criticising the *way* they speak. They do no always distinguish this from the manner in which they speak, that is, technically – and deserving of improvement.

All this can be said of young folk reading at assembly and, of course, in theatre on a stage. But we have not quite got there yet. In the natural shapes of Child Drama, there is first a move rather towards one end of a hall in adolescence, then to use the stage as a sort of locale (see diagrams of shapes in play, p.57). But they like to flow up onto it and off it too. For this reason I have always advocated rostra, or steps, in front of the stage in Senior schools. They then tend to form a long tongue shape, out from the mouth of the proscenium to the far end of the hall. Later this gets nearer the stage, in an extended half-circle, a sort of bulge. Finally, they may take to the stage and stay there. Yet later they may choose whatever suits a particular production. This is half-unconscious and half-conscious choice, not at all the same as any Juniors, who might want to rush up on to a stage too early; and then forming rings and turning backs, start to speak too quietly. (Again, don't make them shout, they shouldn't be there.) They will have no idea of the techniques of that form of theatre, unless trained by some adult, into some faulty semblance of it too early.

For the adolescent, we are nearing the end of unconscious dramatic play, though the qualities of the experience are going to enrich theatre tremendously in any attempt to create it from now on. Let us sum up what some of these qualities are and what effect they have on personality, if anything like what has been suggested in this book has been offered as part of Education.

By Child Drama

Love and hate can be worked off by use of treasures.

Sound can be slowly appreciated and finally loved.

Trial and adventure can become joyous.

Confidence is gained by practice.

Practice improves movement and speech.

Resourcefulness is developed.

A bond of friendship and trust is built with adults. This aids all learning, and civilisation needs this trust.

The gang finds a legal outlet; so do violent emotions.

Personal pace of development is provided for.

Obedience comes from lack of unnecessary frustration.

The natural process of in-flow after out-flow aids this too, and also adds to general scholastic attainment.

Memory is aided by trying things out and repeating them.

Sympathy is developed by personal experience, through acting, of other persons and conditions.

Spiritual experiences take place because of emotional training and aesthetic encounter.

Command of others and obedience to companions is learned.

Discovery may be made of who you really are.

A concern for economy in words, action, property and dress is engendered.

It is possible to develop taste, common sense and thrift.

Adequate use of imagination takes place.

Good manners are discovered.

A desire for dance is developed which provides further outlet for joy.

Many new and happy approaches to other subjects are found.

Grace and virility are nurtured.

At all ages the child takes over slowly the moral responsibility of good behaviour.

Pre-experience of possible later Life experience is encountered and dealt with.

This brings a steadfast wisdom and courage in adversity.

Sincerity is developed and aids concentration on values.

Creative writing is developed. Painting is aided.

'Depth experience' is more easily absorbed.

Let us add some dramatic values too:

The sincere form of playing helps the child to get into the skin of a part.

An enormous number of characters is experienced in a short time. Footwork, handwork body work are all learned, loved, and slowly mastered, instead of taught and not mastered.

Group, pattern and team work are studied.

Rhythm and timing become second nature.

Love of Drama is nurtured.

Unconscious absorption of the whole wisdom of historical theatre takes place.

The writing of plays is properly founded and encouraged at the right time – not forced.

Symphonic production is experienced early.

Imaginative interpretation of a part is expanded, as also presentation and production.

Good literature is slowly approached and more genuinely accepted.

Sincerity and Absorption become habits, bringing to acting a particular quality which is rare and arresting.

Spontaneity continues on into adult artistry.

Unbalanced, romantic, emotional young people discover other ways of life than that of cluttering up the professional stage.

A slow general approach to technique is evolved, *and craftmanship is attended to when artistry is certain to stand the strain.*

Every child has an *equal* chance, over a *long* period of regular work, of showing ability, so that genuine talent can be noticed and aided where thought fit.

USING TALENTS

As a 'smooth' into theatre, we can come one stage nearer to reality (as in Social Drama) by concentrating, to begin with, on things they know in life. We know what their talents are by now, so one can say:

SELF: 'Now, today we are going to do Telly advertisements. Spread out into little groups. Then straightaway, get on with making up an idea which you think would sell a product. Then we'll share each group's thought later. Give you – eight minutes.'

I wander amongst them to hear how they are getting on and give only very little advice, or a quick answer to a question if any one is stuck. But they should manage alone by now (you may have to sort out numbers to be a bit more even.)

SELF: *(After a time)*
          'Right, some of you have started to rehearse a little. Well done.

To others: Don't discuss too much more now. Just get up and start playing what you have thought about.'

(Leave a few minutes for 'trying out'.)

Self: 'Time's up. Yes, yes, sorry but we must begin. I think your group had finished first, then you and you and…yes, thank you – that group – Number one, you start.'

The idea has been practised for years, I hope, about sharing and not just showing off, so I do not repeat it here as an instruction. Depending on the amount of time available and purpose of the lesson, I would be going for imagination, snappy dialogue and slick finish. Or, for elementary criticism. Let us say we have time for the latter.

Self: *(After Group one)*
'Thank you. What was good about that?'

I always try to start like that, so as to implant the idea that criticism can be thoughful objective consideration and not only (unkind) destruction. If this is tried in Junior schools, you get some sweet irrelevant answers like 'His hat was too big.' 'She wouldn't have flowers' (She might!). 'He didn't kill him' (No need to). But here in Senior school, one expects good points. We can add some ourselves like: 'The man could get up quickly, come centre and make a quick showing of the package, couldn't he? That might make a snappier ending. You remember how we practised getting out of a chair last week at a hundred miles an hour, by having your foot in the right place, your leg as a prop and using the weight of your head?'

Boy: 'We did that in dance too.'

Self: 'Yes we *did*. When showing men's work as different from girls. But here, Man *or* the Girl could do it. I just feel we need to get this quick clean finish. Good – group number two, will you share yours?'

Thus one goes round the groups and we see as many as possible. If one group has not really finished, let them do as far as they have got and say how they intended to finish. Generally, we see some wonderful ideas now, and much happy laughter at sudden little bursts of wit and good dialogue.

According to the purpose of the lesson and your flexible outline plan for the term, one might say: *either*

'Did you think that one was good? Yes, so did I. I think we'll keep that one in mind, polish it a bit and use it in the Feature Programme we aim at doing at the end of Term.'

or

'There's one thing we've forgotten. I don't know if you realised, but several of your shows took four minutes or more. I know we are only just starting this, but on real TV that would be *very* expensive. So what we are going to do now (not 'I want you to do.' Firmly, 'we are going to do now', which has an indefinable effect on discipline) is to pare all the efforts sharply down. Let's try for not more than two minutes at the very most. Try for *one*, but don't spoil the idea you've got. Rehearse quickly. Get cracking – NOW.'

By relating their attempts to real life, one has half an eye on possible future, which is leading to adulthood. For sheer intellectual length, students at colleges of education generally win the prize. But they are so lovely when you face them with the horror of what it might cost on TV. Of course, in a one day school, they have only just begun to get used to making up a gang improvisation at all, so the TV advert would be treated in the same way, before actually thinking of it in real life. This is all part of experience and teaching them how to take the work. Also understanding their inexperience and possible lack of training.

FEATURE PROGRAMMES, OR THEME DRAMA

The idea of this is to feature some special idea. It is particularly useful for Drama clubs and/or for drawing groups of different ability together. Even in one class there might be different talents. Some people can improvise well, with fine *language flow* but cannot remember words; others can remember a script, but have poor *language flow*; some can't do either but they might move, march or dance. Someone can read well, so they can be a Narrator, whose task is to link and hold things together. There can be more than one Narrator if more convenient, if it suits the production, or offers more readers a chance.

In part of an Educational Drama Association pamphlet years ago, I was trying to clarify certain issues about these creations:

> '...*Documentaries and Feature Programmes*
>
> Although these merge into each other, there are distinctions, and to my mind perhaps, the word "documentary" is used far too loosely these days. Documentaries are concerned chiefly with facts. Feature Programmes are concerned more with a theme and with life situations. Too many facts over-burden some types of mind and make for dull theatre. Feature Programmes, on the other hand, may be stories or selected pieces of life situation, linked together by a narrator with a few facts popped in. If you really see the difference, you will be careful not to bore some simpler minded pupils stiff. At the same time the more intelligent ones need some meat to bite on. Future education including higher age groups is going to have to be even more discerning than at present. An intellect not stretched can become a dangerous thing anyway and a less able mind overburdened or uninterested, when forced to stay at school, may breed such savage hatred of the establishment that the disturbances of recent years will seem as nothing compared with them...'

Careful organisation and guidance by the teacher is essential in order to keep the different items moving. The final production should contain thoughtful contrasts, use space well, all speech should be clear, characterisations believable, lighting and sound should blend, and each scene flow easily into the next. The space used should be all about the hall including the stage, if there is one. In the final performance, the audience would be grouped round the walls. This gives the best possible use of journey for actors in the middle area. Simple Feature Programmes, to start with, can be built round a single word such as 'Horses', 'Kings', 'Happiness', 'Apples'.

To take the last ideas, some 'farmers' might come onto the floor of a hall and discuss the terrible low prices this year, a number of actors might 'shoot' apples off the heads of prisoners, miming bows and arrows (or guns) down the length of the hall. Something about apples might be taken from study of a three act play. Adam and Eve might come into it (improvisation) and try to find the old Beatles' Apple Centre. They can't find it, so record their story at another studio. Then they dance at the newer Apple Centre. Others dance too. A final line might be:

'Oh well, don't forget folks, an apple a day keeps the doctor away.'

The whole should be linked by a Narrator, or carefully devised scenes can flow straight into each other by intended contrasts.

Example –

NARRATOR: 'There was an ancient story about an apple. Do you remember?'
(*Enter Adam and Eve, who play out the above scene*)

Another Example – A Feature Programme, developed over four sessions, with a class of fifteen-year-olds, followed this outline:

Violence

(1) Five actors placed in different parts of hall. In turn each reads from a newspaper a report on some act of violence.

(2) Narrator in Centre Spot asks Why?
No answer.
He asks if we are safe in our homes or in our City streets.

(3) Improvised scene of violence in street.

(4) Result: (a) Scene of family – police arrive.
(b) Newspaper reporters.
(c) BBC News item.

(5) Narrator makes comment about violence between individuals, between groups, between countries – leads to

(6) Poem about War (written by boy).

(7) Parade of banners with group chanting slogans. (Banners made by children.)

(8) Scene – Nuclear War – mixture of script written by class, and dance – building to climax – explosion – all killed.

Silence, stillness, one spot held on scene of desolation.
Slow fade out.

Example: including rather more script study:

Understand – a plea and a statement

Script built from the book – *Strike the Father Dead* by John Wain, also passage from *Antigone* by Anouilh.

(1) Argument between father who loves classical music and son who is a very good player of Jazz (script built from dialogue in the book).

(2) Scene in a Club – Son enters, is welcomed, is happy. Plays with band – all others are dancing, dance expresses happiness, enjoyment, fulfilment – this builds to climax then music and lights fade down and dancers merge to edge of floor (all improvised).

(3) One spot left in Centre.
The Son walks from darkness into spot, pleads for understanding – has conversation with the 'voice' of his thoughts and conscience. (Polished improvisation.) Blackout.

(4) A family (improvisation). Girl and friends talking – adults do not understand their problems.
Cut to – Parents talking – children do not understand.

(5) Poem (read between three pupils).

(6) Music link as lights fade.

(7) Lights up – scene between Antigone and Creon (from play). (Scene began with the word 'Understand…')

(8) A final comment by Father and Son or by an 'outside' voice.

The following is an excerpt from one that I made up for a Religious Group entitled 'Memory'. It began with one line, or short line memories from many voices, such as 'There was a smell of may and sheep dung on Hampstead Heath';

'...my father, swash-buckling bully';...'Johnny and his punch below the belt';...'my first love affair'; 'I remember no love. No love ever'; '...another house like ours, back to back they was'...etc. Now we cut to the end part. This is the actual excerpt of 'Memory' (trying to include Literature they had studied).

VOICES: 'Lebensraum, Lebensraum.'

'It is mine...mine.'

STRONG VOICE: 'My patience is exhausted.'

'I issue my ultimatum.'

VOICE: *(shouting lines of Shakespeare 'Harry, St. George and England' speech).*

*(War Music **loud**...The Armies advance and fight in dance drama, one side is overcome, killed or taken off as slaves.)*

A VOICE: *(very quiet and old)*

'We should have remembered. It has happened before.'

VOICES: 'Yes, yes, it has happened before, all happened before.'

CAPTOR: 'Sing us a song, slaves.
You should have remembered.
You should have remembered someone has to lose.
It is the wage of war.
It has happened before.'

*(Psalm...captors required of us then a song... How **can** we sing a song in a strange land?)*

AN OLD VOICE: 'We should have remembered.'

VOICE 1: *(in megaphone)*

'Thou shalt not kill.'

VOICE 2: 'He who taketh the sword.'

ALL VOICES: 'Shall perish by the sword.'

VOICE 1: 'In the beginning was the Word, and the Word was God.'

A VERY SWEET VOICE: 'Remember now thy Creator in the days of thy Youth.'

(Violent change to rock 'n roll dance

Follow by extract: 'Yonder ye may see.
Youth is not stable
but ever more changeable
that his soul doth spill.'

NARRATOR: 'Soul doth spill.
Each man has so much libido and NO MORE.
Is that what it means?
Or is there something else,
some other thing,
we do not know of,

or half remembering
cannot be sure of.'

VOICE: *(slowly, wearily)*

'How many miles is it to Babylon?'

ANSWER: 'Six score miles and ten. If you hurry you may get there by candle-
light.'

A MAN: 'Wake up Mary. We must go.'

A GIRL: 'Yes Joseph. We must go.
The journey is at hand.
We must go,
And be refused
That the Scripture be fulfilled
And Man reach his promised land.'

(They journey to music. Joseph knocks. The door opens.)

JOSEPH: 'Have you lodging for the night?'

VOICE: 'No.'

(Goes to different 'house' in the arena)

JOSEPH: 'Have you lodging for the night?'

VOICE: 'No.'

JOSEPH: 'Please, please, it is urgent. We need lodging for the night.'

ANOTHER VOICE: 'No. No room. No room.'

(Others hurry in, knocking.)

THEY ASK: 'Have you...?'

ANSWER: 'No.'

(And it all comes to a sort of climax)

A BIG VOICE: *(off stage)*

'I have told you,
Told you before.
You will have to sleep in the stable.
There is no room.
no room in the inn.'

(They all begin to slink off.)

J. AND M: *(more dignified)*

'Come with us. We shall be always with you.'

(exit)

NARRATOR: *(slowly, taking his time)*

'See what I mean?
It's always happened before.
Boy meets girl.
You knock.

You bang a door.
Lebensraum.
No room at the Inn.
Struggle, sleep,
Love, deception, sin.'

(Boy crosses slowly to Girl again)

BOY: 'Do you remember an Inn Miranda?'

(He puts on Joseph's beard, perhaps.)

GIRL: *(very sweetly)*

'Yes, I remember an Inn.'

(She puts on Mary's cloak, perhaps)

VOICE 1:'I remember the good days.'

VOICE 2:'I remember my father...swashbuckling bully.'

VOICE 3:'I remember the downs, the air still with a cut in it in Spring.'

GIRL: 'That's better.'

VOICE 4: 'There was a smell of may and sheep's dung on Hampstead Heath too...and a horse-pond.'

(Girl nods approvingly)

NARRATOR: 'I remember, I remember the house where I was born. The little window where the sun came peeping in at dawn.'

(All turn to the girl and in urgent voices take lines from the prayer Memorare.)

GIRL: 'Remember now thy Creator in the days of thy Youth.'

VOICES: *(one line per voice)*

'In the beginning was the Word,
And the word was God.
Take not His name in vain.
For the Lord will not hold him guiltless,
That taketh His name in vain.'

VOICE: *(loud)*

'Open the Gate, O Watchman of the Night.'

(Building scene)

WATCHMAN: 'Whither go you? etc.

ALL IN STRONG CHORUS: 'We go to make the Golden Journey to Samarkand.'

(The music wells up as all march once round and lights fade and must blend perfectly with music)

EXIT

An observer concluded, for submission to magazines and newspapers:

> 'The value of this type of creation is that it includes script for those who can learn, it could have choral speech for those that do not move well, improvisation for those who cannot learn script, and dance, mime or movement for those who cannot speak well. Because many people can take part, such creations are best produced in arena form. They can dip into documentary detail, or be very short and simple. Examples of titles are "What is Monarchy?" devised by Peter Slade for production by the adult group at the Rea Street Drama Centre, his "Suez Crisis" at Birmingham University and "The World, the Flesh and the Devil" at a Summer School at Keele University. There has also been "From here to Paradise" devised by Michael Hall, on the same sort of model, at the Rea Street Centre. Manner of handling and production is at times very similar to that of polished improvisations but is a step nearer (for adolescents) conscious adult creations and is very close to modern professional theatre. But indeed, like many other things in education (through drama) we were doing it first.'

I remember the one at Keele. It included the King from *Henry IV part I* for being posh in the world, Falstaff was Flesh (Boar's head scene), some athletes did a wonderful Devil Dance and Faustus, after his final outburst in Marlowe's play, was dragged off to hell. Of the many we created, the one I shall always remember is 'Flight', devised largely by Sylvia Demmery, Andrew MacCallum and members of my last full time Teacher/Actor's Group for performance (partly as a model) to Senior schools. It was one of the most enjoyable shows I have ever seen and was filmed by Birmingham University. One that I made up as an example and used on One Day Schools at Colleges and Universities and other courses was 'Strike'. It started with someone in a corner trying to stir up a strike. Meantime, a 'band' came and played outside the Prime Minister's door to register 'Happy Birthday'. Strikers all marched round them and banged on the door of Number 10 Downing Street. A lot more went on that I do not remember, but 'We shall not be moved' stands out as being sung on the march. There was some reasoning included, for the pros and cons of striking. Finally the Prime Minister appeared and agreed that everyone should have more money, as long as they enjoyed inflation. So it all ended up in a 'happy dance' to 'I get around' by the Beach Boys. One of the points often made by teachers who had not quite understood that one can build up (or *not*) over a period to production was 'We wouldn't have time for this.' So we practised a bit and did the full show. And on one occasion I was able to mention 'I thought you said there wasn't time for this. In case you'd like to know we took twelve minutes to build up the show and you performed it in eight minutes flat. Well done.'

If you know what you are about, you don't waste time.

Approach to Literature, Example

This last division, Theatre, should be an extension of the work which has already gone on throughout imaginative and social drama. It should not be too formal, and as a beginning it is best to keep scripted pieces short. One can continue to help with the understanding and interpretation of dialogue, of situations between one person and another, by working on parallel themes using improvised dialogue, and as by now they will have become more thoughtful and will have a deeper understanding and interpretation of character and a wide area of experience on which to call, they will more readily cope with the art of full scripted Play Production – Theatre.

Before trying to push on to a fourteen- fifteen- or sixteen-year-old the great literary pieces of the world, think first 'Are they ready for it?' A simple play containing situations and language with which they can cope well will provide a good vehicle for early attempts. Consider various shapes for production and find the one best suited to the play and 'your' production. It may be that the young people cannot have artistry and technique at a high standard as understood by the theatre world, but by now they should make good use of space, feel rhythm, build believable characters, play with sincerity and absorption, be able to accept the discipline needed to achieve a polished performance; and we should experience the satisfaction of a final theatrical presentation which will have a special quality of its own. In a recent production of 'Oh What a Lovely War', by fifth and sixth formers at a comprehensive school, the quality of innocence which these young people brought to the play was tremendously touching; their timing was good, they could be still, and the difficulty of speaking a foreign language was overcome by using selected jabber-talk. Because of previous practice this was fluent, contained the right inflections and good timing, and was very successful. Some of the singing voices were not powerful but were clear, and by creating an atmosphere of quiet and stillness a charm and emotional sympathy were conveyed and caught.

EXAMPLE

For GCSE and 'A' level examinations a play by Shakespeare is often selected. One year it was *The Tempest*. The story and characters were talked about and the story summarised, then improvisations took place using situations and characters from the play. Next they improvised events which were referred to in the scene but which were not actually presented. Finally, passages from the text were selected, rehearsed and presented as a means of making the play a living piece of drama.

They were particularly pleased with their production of the opening of this play which began thus:

> Using the floor space in the hall, a dance sequence of Sea dashing against the ship (centre) opened the play; some lines from Act 1, Scene 1 were used and on 'we split, we split'…the humans were tossed into the waters and taken by Sea Urchins who gently cast them on to the shores of the island. This was a very good dance and scripted sequence. Into the now empty space came Prospero and Miranda, smoothly taking the action into Scene II. By these means an atmosphere was created and gave a setting within which the text could be lifted from the page and became a living, vital, meaningful piece of drama.

Thus Theatre with its added discipline and direction is reached, and, when text and improvisation are mixed, can be used as a vehicle for further study and understanding of a play or piece of literature. Sometimes the thought of examinations, GCSEs or anything else may make a group slow to react. If so, try some easy exercises to get them going, and warm them up, almost as you would for more simple minds, or those who are inexperienced. Very simple situations can be extremely telling as theatre, using a large flat space, not a stage.

Example: an improvised fight with imaginary weapons of air; everyone hurt. Spirits from another planet come and heal the pain; they go off slowly to music, then just at exit they turn slowly and lift their hand in farewell greeting. A spotlight strengthens on them, then fades as they turn and go. It is essential that the movements should be done together, or they lose their point; almost any large slow movement in a big group done exactly together, such as turning the same way, lifting an arm, dropping the head and so on can be beautiful, particularly if lit by one spotlight at an angle of 45 degrees. Just the light catching them creates something special. And the exact togetherness makes a discipline.

BRIDGE BETWEEN IMPROVISATION AND SCRIPT

Scripted plays are often attempted too early. With all ages it is important to have periods of improvisation which reveal where people really are in life. Apart from bringing freshness to creation, by the content of these pieces, one can judge the first types of play to try. But, even in an improvisation, some good remarks can be written down. We then have a part script. Ultimately a total script may be formed. This can go side by side with creative writing. But note, it is a script of 'our' making; a script written by someone outside that group is often another thing altogether, it is much more difficult to tackle. People often ask how to make a bridge between improvisation and script. This is one way of doing it.

Whilst we are talking about literature, perhaps I should just mention that some young people these days have a strong social conscience. We don't hear about them so often as those who cause trouble. But the ones I think of become keen on the psalms, when they are brought to their notice and then make up modern psalms of their own and either act them (the story within) or compose folk tunes about God. The gradual change from star performance to more of group message in theatre training, and the whole realm of sensitivity training in dance, is totally about concern for and duty towards your neighbour. It is possible to *experience* this reality, rather than merely mouthing old words and texts that, for young minds, may have lost some of their meaning.

USE OF MAKE-UP

There should be time for students to try this out for theatre work and instruction should be given for various characters. Also, increasingly important, different kinds of make up itself and how to guard against a hard edge on the neck, which often gives secrets away, about where the supposed person is and where reality really starts! Make up can be used simply as Art too. The face is then used almost as a flat plane and quite un-human colour, shapes, bars, flags are painted on it. Some startling and wonderful examples appeared before me in a holiday drama club session just lately, also in a One Day school for Youth Club leaders.

There is another use too, which perhaps we do not often think of, but which can be important to those who are likely to benefit from it. Knowledge of theatrical make-up might go side by side with beauty treatment and/or just skin care. It is not generally understood what agony some boys (let alone girls) go through when spots occur round about first shaving time. And this is not by any means only a question of diet, sometimes it is sheer local infection in enlarged pores. Lemon juice is very helpful here, though it stings. Other modern aids are advertised on TV from time to time.

In any case, half an hour or so of 'being another person' by stage make-up or wearing a mask can be a tremendous psychological release for those who are not too fond of an unhappy face of their own. But make-up must be cleaned off with a good cream and tissue, followed by a wash in good soap and final cold water. No towel should be allowed to get dirty before use, or be shared. Highly scented after-shave and talc often act as irritants and should be used with care, though a good clean talc very lightly used as a dry-up after theatrical make-up can be an armour against smoke irritant. For a tender or difficult skin, never use a coconut butter stick before make-up, but a cream base, then rub off gently and apply grease paint. One producer in charge of a stage production, using the same stick on many faces, may spread some infection unknowingly. Always rub off the end a little with clean tissue before re-using on another person and tear down the thin metal or paper case of the stick so as to be sure not to scratch. Masks are enormous fun,[4] and special head angles must be used to make them more effective. Study and creation of them may lead groups into further study of history or geography and add interest when visiting exhibitions. But they are hot to wear. For similar reasons of cleanliness as above, do not encourage exchanges. Half masks are cooler, as has been said, and may lead to a study of Commedia dell'Arte, the history of theatre and back to different types of improvisation, stock characters and established theatre roles in script.

With make up, thought should be given to how much is needed for the form of theatre used. In school productions, it is sometimes too heavy. Only large stages, highly lit, may need fairly heavy types. But character and good acting are better than a mess. In arena and intimate theatre, only light make-up is needed, enough to look clean or dirty.

Techniques

Arena or Space Theatre

Quite a lot has been said about acting in a space throughout the book. But there are particular points to watch, now that we have arrived at theatre.

FIRST IS SOUND

I am taking it that all teachers and those in charge know how to use a record player or tape machine. Never allow anyone who has not tested out and practised with the machine to take on a production. Machines are all slightly different and you must test the volume for *climaxes* and the volume control for scratch and whether it really fades right out smoothly for *de-climaxes*. Of course this is true to an extent for all the work described in this book. Teachers must be absolutely sure to turn the volume right down, so that there is no violent scratch noise, every time before you bring in music. You should have been building up an atmosphere. It can be destroyed in a second. Naturally this is all doubly true for the use of sound in theatre.

If it is quite clear what sound is to be used in theatre, pre-set tape recorded music can be used. It is less valuable in general education, as one often needs to go back on a phrase and pick it up immediately without fuss. In the sort of guidance I have been writing about you are watching all the time for the needs of the creation going on. You may have to go back, or even switch to another record. To try this quickly with tape is almost impossible, the noise of wind-back, slowness of arriving at the right place, make it almost certain that

---

4   Lately, splendid masks have been used by Geese Theatre in drama workshops in prison. Trainees and I used to visit Winson Green prison under Further Education in 1950 or so. Masks not allowed. Middle-aged men played as if fifteen years old, sometimes seven.

the atmosphere is lost. But in theatre, a cassette may be useful. What sound is needed is *known* and can be set beforehand.

SECOND, THE LIGHTING

You need a grid, or bars, for taking your spotlights, in theatre over a space; and light should shine down at no more than 45 degrees on the desired area. Often more direct downward is needed. There is a general mania amongst college students and some teachers for using moving spotlight beams (following spots) as limes in a pantomime. The great thing about the above form of theatre is that use can be made of dark patches. In a well planned production characters can move into a higher lit zone as intended; or a hitherto dark patch can be suddenly flooded with light, at change of scene, or a specially devised 'moment' of excitement.

It is an extreme enrichment, if actors know and understand about the basic shapes, or are guided into using them. Perhaps the young need not know of them at once (though they may have been using them unconsciously), but the producer certainly should, and can inform the actors of any moment when it seems advisable to make them conscious. I am talking of the basic shapes of all genuine Child Drama, as described in the early chapters. It is here that the child is teacher.

Don't forget the shapes are the circle, diagonal (half of the cross), the cross itself, S shape (half of the 8), eight itself, zigzag, triangle and spiral. All these are shown to us by the child and are absolutely necessary for purpose, shape and beauty in anything like arena theatre, otherwise blocking, masking, clumsy journeys and bad grouping are bound to occur. And, of course, if actors have not learned about Natural Dance, they can't walk properly or judge timing over a given distance (see Slade 1977).

In Theatre for Children productions (i.e. those acted by adults for children), I always set great importance over this, so that the first theatre children saw included the shapes they would use in their own play. This would be bound to have a strong unconscious link with what they were seeing or experiencing; would make them feel 'at home' with the experience, yet not quite know why; and would not drag them into thinking adult proscenium theatre was what they ought to copy – thus destroying belief in their own creations [see diagram 10]. The proscenium stage can be a very exciting thing, but it has its limitations. Psychologically it can become a drug, people can become addicted to the need for exhibition and other things. It has power, and is associated somewhere deep down inside us with King-of-the-Castle need. 'I am higher than you – audience!' Years back, when putting forward a recommendation for Theatre-in-the-round, a note was sent to me from Scotland, by way of encouragement, stating that all ancient Scottish theatre was in the round. Very interesting, if that is really so; but then many dances and mimes were performed everywhere

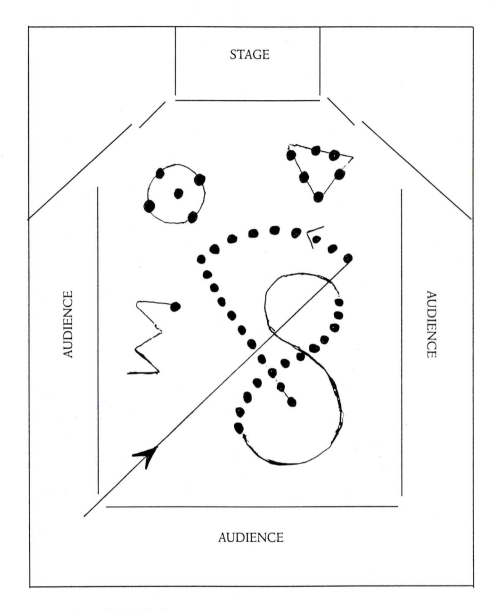

Diagonal is half of cross

S is half of eight. Face, back and sides are seen more than once by all audience members by use of the S shape. Actors do not stay in the shapes for long but should use them.

Diagram 10

in market places and so on (and still are) with an admiring crowd encircling them. The canny Scots perceived a need?

Acting-in-the-round is not the same as theatre-in-the-round. But you have to try and learn to act in the round to perform to the best of your ability in theatre-in-the-round. As said earlier, children do this naturally, we have to learn (or re-learn) it. To accomplish this is not very difficult, it is a question of thinking and giving. Thinking how your thought-action can come off the back of your ear and 'giving' intentionally to your audience still, even with your back when you exit, or move about the arena. When acting, it should not be done for your own sense of (or need for) power, but as *service* to those who are kind enough to bother to come and see you, even actually pay! The whole thing becomes easier, in this form of theatre, if you start really thinking of your utter self being the centre of you. Acting then from that centre outwards and all round the body. It is really an attitude of mind, an attitude to the work and a determination to have the highest possible knowledge and achievement that an artist should.

If these techniques are not attempted and employed, we shall continue to see occasions of somewhat artificial so-called theatre-in-the-round, I fear, which are really rather untidy. Four proscenium shapes outwards, at the unseen edges of an oblong or a square (see Way 1967).

Old actors used to know a lot about acting with their backs, at a period when in the normal proscenium playing, it was rather bad form (or very modern) to show such a thing, except at exit. Then, perhaps, they rather overplayed things. Dame Sybil Thorndike, without overplaying, was a master of this. Charlie Chaplin overplayed it on purpose, to evoke a sad-clown silhouette disappearing into…where? George Arliss always over-played it in films and one always waited for him to stop in a doorway, stick his hat on…one, two, three – tap. And off he went. The same techniques, as outlined for arena and in-the-round, would be needed for the best outside theatre too, if used as in a general space.

Theatre Outside School

Both dance and theatre are generally considered to be in-school activities, but 'happenings' and street drama could well be done by those who might benefit from being out of school. Occasionally productions might be linked with social work and performances given in hospitals or old people's homes. Also there are serious thought-programmes to create, about such things as pollution, anti-litter campaigns, training for survival. Environmental shock and future shock – plays to start you thinking, to start you talking, to discuss. Young people could often help Lord Mayors' projects in this way and feel they are making a real contribution to the good of the area in which they live. And why not also consider creating Theatre for Children plays, to perform to those younger than oneself? I always find that if you can instill the idea of *giving*, rowdy behaviour often calms down into a secret 'OK, proud to try.'

Whilst speaking of outside work, videos could be made of happenings, or outside arena plays, not only as a record but as example of any successful use of the above techniques for further training.

As 'telly' becomes used more often, in a technical age, this certainly should be investigated and learnt about also, for theatre, dance, teaching and establishing of body image. As to film, it is really extraordinary how some quite difficult types will take to this. Do not hammer away too much at tripod work and perfect focus, but have prowling expeditions, which seek out life itself and situations worth preserving; it develops habits of close observation, gets you outside yourself and makes life a richer experience. It may be necessary to start people off with simple ideas such as:

Collect situations that amuse you.

Film people who look sad.

Film people in a hurry.

Film animals and make up conversations as if they were talking.

Film nature and put noises or music on tape to go with the selected items.

Modern videos and cameras are now light and easy to handle.

LIGHT, ART AND DANCE

Still employing similar techniques for the action, sometimes it is a good thing to link subjects together. A short time before writing this, I was talking over, with a Director of Education, the creation of a flexible form of theatre, where large pieces of sculpture could be shown, as well as theatre itself. But as well as music being played whilst one looked at it – as suggested years ago by Epstein – it might be interesting to throw light on the exhibits in different ways, fading from one spotlight to another, changing colour and direction and blending with the phrases of the music. Stylised dance amongst, but in aestheic sympathy with, the sculpture might be tried out. My own feeling is that there is a possibility for deep training in harmony, discipline and taste, and many Art Schools say they are beginning to feel they can give no guidance. Some new thought is so way-out that it is no wonder Art teachers say they are out of their depth. Perhaps it is time to call a halt. Perhaps someone should state categorically that a lot of this creation is going down a side channel; it is decidedly trivial and in many instances is really infant work but it is just bigger and more expensive, that's all.

Other parts of general arena technique are: careful pause, knowing when light is on you, or off. Don't shuffle into it. *Get* into light – first time. Learn to enjoy the sound of footsteps and quiet use of profile. Use careful timing. The producer may use time-beat in rehearsal to outline shapes and grouping, but by time of performance it should have evolved into a rhythm of your own, in sympathy with the rest of the cast.[5]

Finally, learn to stand still and use silence. Don't drag it out, but a well built silence can be wonderful. It includes what all actors of all kinds of theatre, film and TV need to learn – REPOSE.

Theatre for Children

A word about this. If adults do it, then, of course, one would hope the above techniques and shapes would be used. Also adolescents, who can be wonderful in it.

For various groups, you have to develop great sensitivity about how loud to be and how close to be. Over cheerful Juniors, or Infants, may grab at you, if too close. Shy little birds, crouched in their seats, need much quieter performances and played much more centrally, so as not to be too close. Actors should learn to know immediately about this on entry. I cannot bear it when a show is shouted at the same tempo every time and actors are playing sometimes far too close, without any apparent *understanding* of the importance of what they are doing – probably harm.

People sometimes tease me about what actors, who work with me, call 'Slade's Golden Moments'. They try to get them, but don't always succeed. And those who seriously mock, if any, I would suspect have never had the experience and are not capable of achieving such a thing.

The sort of 'thing' I mean is: Knight comes in and has lost his sword. He meets a baby Dinosaur. Finally Dinosaur admits to having found something like that. He/she thought it was for toasting buns for tea. Only there wasn't any fire about lately. Knight is so pleased to get his sword back – yes, it is his – and because it is a magic sword too. So in gratitude, he decides to make fire and have tea with baby Di.

Now – you can't just say – 'OK, sword get on with it.' It needs to build up. So Knight, slowly, carefully raises the sword in his gloved hand by the sharp end. The metal handle looks like a cross. Then 'Oh, sword of might...and strength...and light, show us your power, now you have come back to me...show us – Fire!' At that moment a spotlight stabs the gloom and hits the metal cross in a red flash. There is complete silence for longer than you think possible.

---

5 A remarkable historic arena production was arranged for the opening of the Olympic Snow Games in Norway including people from under the earth, vast space, a huge egg that turned into the World, and out of it all appeared Doves of Peace plus fireworks.

Then Knight slowly lowers the hilt (still holding the blade) down to the floor. A red glow is narrowed and remains on the floor (from a spot-light making a narrow circle). No real fire? By magic of the child mind, there certainly *is* because Knight and baby Di sit down and have their tea by it. So everyone understands *that*. Sword is used for toasting the 'buns' and there follows a warm long moment of repose. Pin drop silence.

It is timing and light and experience that brings the moment; and daring to keep things slow. But belief and love of this kind of beauty, I suppose, is the real magic behind it all. For me it is a glory. I don't care what people say. These are moments of fine life, touched by something special. And I believe the little people with whom I share such moments find it *'speshull'* too.

Another example I often give is of a Princess who lost her voice. It was eventually found in a bottle in Paris. A suitor brought the bottle back and produced it for his Lady. In rehearsal, the usual thing happened. The stopper was pulled out any old how, the bottle could hardly be seen in the man's large mit. Someone slammed on the voice of Joan Hammond, on the record player and this touching, most important part of the story meant absolutely nothing.

So, first of all, I got the group to sit down and practise finding something in the 'grass'. 'It is very special. Pick it up slowly. If you give it enough affection, the whole world will wait for you. Dare be slow, just for this moment.' They got better.

In the final production, when the suitor brought in the bottle, I got him to lift the bottle slowly up – to make it special – then slowly, a spotlight opened up on it till the glass shone like a star. He took hold of the stopper and drew it slowly out. As he did so, that wonderful voice began very quietly to be blended in on the record, until it was in full volume. The Princess ran to him (in diagonal across hall). Record Music sharply out. She can speak. Her voice has been found.

I can only say, as one always has to, you ought to have been there to have experienced this. And it was the same every time it was played, yet now, something never to be felt again? Just the light on the bottle in itself was lovely. Something the child can wonder at and we, for cares of the world, forget what is simple, but rare, and lose our admiration.

Of course, there were modern situations too, but let no-one eschew the symbol of Prince and Princess. They are deep and important in the psyche. Somewhere in each of us, Man hopes to find in his wife, his love, a Princess to admire. And Woman secretly hopes, even through disappointments, that underneath the macho may lurk a gentle Prince. Other exercises for this kind of theatre would be two people, or small groups, to walk away from each other across space, then turn exactly at the same moment and catch each other's eye. It may have to be done in time-beat to start with, counting the sound of the footsteps (*group sensitivity*, through the senses). But after a time, they should make it their own and just do it (*group intuition*). Eye work across space is tremendously important. It can hold the scene. Sometimes it is fun for a minute or so to use audience participation and that is where it is easy to go wrong.

AUDIENCE PARTICIPATION

One used to see and hear some actors say things like:

'Now, I wonder if we have some very clever people here today. Do you think we have George?

G: 'Yes, I'm sure we have, Lindy. You only have to look around.'

L: 'Oh, I think you're right, George. Do you think we have clever people here today, children?'

CH: 'Ye-e-e -ss *(whether they do or not)*.

L: 'Right. Now what I want you to *(oh dear, already)* do is to help me fold this blanket.' *(She could perfectly well do it herself.)* 'Who would like to help me, I wonder?'

(Dozens of hands shoot up immediately and probably a little mob runs out on the floor. Often the poor Lindy then does not know what to do and either gets a bit angry and flustered or chooses two and sends the disappointed rest back to their seats.)

If you are going to do this, cut the cackle and go direct to one or more of the audience and say 'this canoe is too heavy to carry over there to the workshop, will you help me?' If someone doesn't want to, don't panic. Just go to the next child. It will not be long before you have your gang. Say quickly; 'You and you and you.' You have not promised anything. You have not let anybody down or disappointed them, or made them look a fool (nor you look one either). Then, when the task is done, just say 'thank you'. and perhaps add 'Couldn't have done it without your help.' They will just go back to their seats because of the logic. There was a task to do and now it is done.

In 'Experience of Spontaneity' I showed a picture of an Indian boy, playing wonderfully, the young Hunter who caught the early morning star, sitting on a cloud (a big bar). Some of the audience had to get up and become magnets to get him down. Again, the actors all knew what to do, so, the task over, everyone went back to their seats without any fuss. At various times, in many shows, between the years 1932 and 1977, I have never known it fail. There must be a *purpose*. One thing about the ending of a performance. Don't hang about saying 'g'bye...g'bye... children.' and wave hysterically, hoping the teacher will start them all clapping. This could be called bad taste. At the end of my shows, there was generally good reason for a march round, everyone still in their part. No cadging for farewells or applause. If a child actually said goodbye, no doubt someone would smile and bow as they went past. But nearly always the audience was too deeply in it. Music would well up and the players would be out and off *exactly* at the end of the sound. Lights would fade and if there was complete silence and no clapping heard till we were well down the corridor, or even in the nearby dressing room, we felt we had probably given a good show. Going back later to talk to the children was done if they asked for it.

Loud shouting from audiences, which some groups try to stimulate, is no sign of success at all. Obviously nothing has gone 'into' the audience, it is mostly Out-flow. True success in real Theatre for children may be judged not by noise, often by silence. Audience size should be about thirty to forty for the experience really to sink in.

Theatre in Education

These groups are perhaps an outcome of Theatre for children. Historically, there came a bit of a gap between professional Theatre for Children companies and amateur ones. Amateur ones were largely made up of teachers or students. Theatre in Education groups do a slightly different job. I understand there are some very good ones now. They are mostly professional. And because there has not been enough training for teachers, these splendid people are trying to do both jobs – that is, stir up an interest in drama as well as give opportunity for young folk to participate in forms of theatre, acting with them. It is not easy to do both.

I do not want to offend them in any way, for they have my admiration and hopes that they will be allowed to continue, under progressively difficult circumstances. But the ideal, to my mind, would always be for deep and proper training for teachers to carry out a progressive drama plan of significance in all schools and then (if they have no centre like Rea Street) to have visiting companies that would crown and enrich and know about how far work in a school 'had got'. There would then be less danger of any group playing too far in advance, but be a great help forward. Teachers could then do their full job of standing back, so as to guard, guide and inspire, as outlined, so children could grow in and through their own creation. Then a Theatre for Children Company could come in and purposefully offer an emotional and aesthetic experience of straight theatre, but totally in sympathy with true Child Drama – which is always what I tried to do.

Types of Theatre and Acting

This can be of improvisation. And let no one make a mistake about it, at its best this is of high art, apart from its uses educationally. There can be formal theatre in specially designed halls, though these should be flexible for different types of production. The highest forms of literature should be shown here. Intelligent scholars need stretching and will benefit from the riches of the past.

But, oh dear, do let us teach the elements of proscenium acting. If we use that form. Young adults at the top of our schools must not be allowed to slouch on to stages and spout frightful English, as if they were juniors improvising first attempts in the classroom. If teacher producers do not quite know what I mean, do forgive me, but go and attend an in-training course or ask for one – much formal production in schools is rather out of date. But the proscenium art is detailed, highly technical and fascinating and should be learnt by older pupils. I should have thought that selected students could be geared to full understanding and training in the difference between exterior acting and interior acting; in proscenium acting and theatre in the round; and in the realm of dance. All excellent material for A levels.

INTERIOR ACTING

This is more often associated with Stanislavski and the Method school. It sometimes goes to doubtful lengths and there was an amusing film about young students during their training period. One young man had been lying on a broad mantel shelf but eventually fell off. Asked what on earth he was doing, he answered. 'I was being an apple, but I fell off the tree.' The training of Stanislavski has one really fundamental point. It is the IF. 'If I were *really* that person in that situation what would I think, what would I do, what would I say?' This basic concept really makes you search and ponder. It is likely to help you to come up with an attitude which in portrayal aids believability. If pressed too far it might appear eccentric in behaviour of the part (or during its preparation!).

Some of its exercises suggest going to be with people you are going to portray and experiencing things which might be uncomfortable, dangerous, or extremely inconvenient. By its very label of 'interior acting' it can be realised that it breeds tremendous inner emotion. But unfortunately it can be so concerned with self that what a particular actor is on about cannot come across to others. In such case there is need for rather more exterior technique to 'put it over'. This would be particularly so on a proscenium stage, where one has to literally put a message over the footlights to a body of attenders-to. *Example:* of too much 'inner' and not enough 'outer' would be when an actor or actress is moved so much that they have to weep. If this were not over very soon, this person would have a restricted throat and would not be able to say the words properly, or be heard. Some tears in the eyes are a different matter. *Example:* In a film a very famous actor, who, it was said, was of the Method School, was trying to be extremely natural and behaving rather badly (on purpose for the part). So he was eating a banana whilst saying what he thought (nice touch). But, unfortunately, one could not hear a word he said. This comes under the heading of 'too clever by half'.

It is not possible to do justice to this extensive philosophy in a short description of this kind; in mentioning its pitfalls one can appear unfair. What is clear, though, is that whilst it should no be taken so far as to destroy its own aims, it has been responsible for bringing oceans more truth to a theatre which was beginning to become somewhat fixed in elegant but too artificial a style. Perhaps being used to this is the reason why productions at the Royal Court Theatre, after the war, came as a shock. For many reasons, further study of the Method philosophy is well worthwhile.

EXTERIOR ACTING

This obviously is the opposite from the above and is concerned with facial expression, careful gesture, how to come on and go off stage, rules about head angles, and posture on a sofa. It can become so sophisticated that it becomes metallic, you can almost hear it click. It is precision itself and its dexterity sometimes takes one's breath away. But you do not always *feel* anything. And occasionally, it is possible to miss part of the play whilst thinking: do doctors really do that? Does a young girl really behave like that? What is that ridiculous inflexion? I have to confess here that there is one way of asking a question, which is picked up at theatre schools, which no one would ever use as a normal inflexion in life. No-one ever really speaks like that.

I am sure this style of acting (Exterior) spawned the awful '...don't worry, I can see my own way out.' In this school it is rare to see a leading lady come into a room normally. They are apt to pose in the doorway and sometimes there is even applause, which holds up the play altogether, so she then comes quite out of character. For a moment or two she is the famous Miss, Mrs. Madame, Ms or Dame so and so. It takes a little time for traces of believability to reassert themselves. But her ability will soon bring that back if she really is a star.

Examples of formal style used to be seen in many a Repertory Theatre and I used to get extremely tired of a certain exit. You take about five steps towards the door, pause, swing round, lift the right arm, lift your chin, spurt your last line and plunge off.

I could not help being amused at a former actor of this kind, who asked me to discuss a certain project. At the end, I knew quite well that he didn't agree with me, but true to the last – five steps to the door, pause, turn, right hand up, chin all special, speak:...'and Peter (pause, just too long) *Good luck.*' He plunged off. We both knew quite well he didn't believe a word of it, but in the good old way, an excuse had been found and ritual had been accomplished.

> EXAMPLE: Du Maurier had precise rules about footsteps and was said never to cross the stage without fingering a chair, or something on a table, half way across. It made people say 'How natural.'

EXAMPLE: Sir Herbert Tree was said never to feel he had given a successful performance unless he could rattle the ash trays in the dress circle. Strange ambition. Myth or reality?

EXAMPLE: There is an actress on TV who is very popular and deals with crime. She always lifts her hand when a sudden thought strikes her and she has a wealth of wonderful facial expressions that never stop. It is occasionally a bit hard to concentrate on the story because of admiration at her inventiveness. Yet it is a little bit like a teacher who used to say to a class of Juniors. 'Show me anger...show me surprise.' Contortions follow. You can't show these really unless there is something to be surprised or angry *about*. It needs a situation to create a truth.

When Stanislavski visited a very famous theatre in France he said afterwards 'Very interesting, very clever. They twitch all the time like chickens. I remember some of what they did. But after it, I feel nothing. I have had no emotional experience and cannot even remember what the story was about.'

So, we see there are extremes and perhaps the best thing is to aim at something between the two. You need to be concerned with enough truth of feeling to make all action and attitude believable, but enough technique to put over satisfactorily the message you are trying to share. One of these things you can share is not eternal fuss, detail and turmoil but peace!

Proscenium Theatre

Because this has been an established shape for a long time, many people would associate it with *all* theatre. Indeed there is a muddle that still continues, between understanding drama as distinct from theatre. Drama can happen in life. Theatre is an artistic reflection of it. Drama-the-doing-of-life is what we ought to be carrying out in schools. Also, in recent years, because of other influences, theatre techniques on the proscenium stage have changed. There are now many.

In a short description I can only put forward a little of the training and philosophy that I suggested to all actors who joined my companies. And perhaps this is the time to mention that I treat anyone who cares to work with me in the same way. Whether they are amateur or professional I presume that they are artists and together we are going to create to the best of our ability. Therefore I can only say here what I would wish to share with them.

First, we need to understand fully that this is not a theatre of the round. Stand about mid-stage and put your weight on the up-stage foot (farthest from audience), swing your other leg in a part circle, casting an eye on the proscenium edge at the beginning and end of the swing (see diagram 11). You will have described a convex shape, part of a circle, and it is in this shape that one has to project out to the audience, through the large gap, one's personality and belief in the situation taking place on the stage. But it is not only to the front and

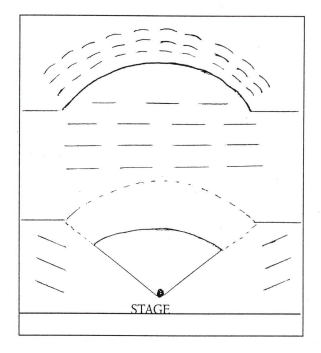

PROSCENIUM DIAGRAM

Diagram 11 Proscenium diagram

slightly at an angle to each side, but up and down too, because there are people in the stalls and the pit, the circle and the gallery with whom to try and make friends.

LIGHT

In all theatre forms it is important for actors to be aware of how light falls on them and to bear it in mind during training, but later one makes knowledge into a habit of ability and you can forget it enough to gain freedom from worrying about it.

On entry, one might remember that the audience is interested at first with the upper part of your body, so if you lift your chest very slightly, there is an indefinable extra light glow on you and this gains attention without anyone knowing why. If you try this, it will probably be too much and too obvious at first. So don't puff out like a pouter pidgeon. It should eventually be so small a movement as to be unnoticeable.

The same is true of the angle of your face as you turn in profile. You will be better lit and gain an unnoticed flash of light, for gallery and circle interest, if you tilt the head very slightly upstage. In school productions, unless you are going to perform in the Town Hall, or a theatre, you may hardly need this advice. But your head needs to be held up enough to interest people at the back of the hall. Sad to say, though, if there is a large audience on a flat floor, they will not see much any way. And if you have an old-fashioned very high stage, the producer, should test about chins, in full light from the back of the hall, as he/she should for voices. (Oh, or at back of expected last chairs.) For them, chins may seem too high.

Unfortunately, in modern, very large school halls, height is a problem as well as space; and it is very difficult for adolescents to try to throw their voice down them. It is really rather bad for them to try. This is particularly true for boys, who have only recently had a voice change – it is kinder, therefore, to have smaller audiences, nearer the stage.

Light falling upon a hand is important too, as any sharp movement in profile (as a sudden pointing of a revolver) will become more exciting if there is a flash of light on hand, arm and barrel, neatly parallel with the floor as a rule. It is all part of purpose, being sure of what you want to do, and how to express it. Often, too much front light is used. Side lighting makes things more interesting.

HANDS

These often seem to get in the way in early experiences of being on stage. You almost want to cut them off. Don't let both hands hang down like codfish. To the other extreme, don't make lots of unnecessary gestures. Perhaps, if desperate, carry something with one hand and let the other relax. It is almost true to say that one should not make any gesture that is not absolutely necessary. The leading actors will *not* thank you, if you scratch your nose, or head, or twitch, or feel obviously hot, during their best speech. But believe me the audience will notice one thing – YOU. It is probably the slight flash of light on your hand, apart from the incongruity of behaviour.

STANCE

Fortunately you are unlikely to have to put up with a raked stage at school. I advised strongly, with architects and the Ministry of Education and Department of Education and science against them (that is when the floor slopes upwards from front to back), whenever the question arose. They only add to difficulties for beginners and tend to throw you off balance.

I also strongly advocated that there should be no sharp edges of rough bricking left in the stage area walls. These are sometimes left without thought, simply because they are in areas not expected to be seen. It is precisely the 'not seen' attitude which makes them dangerous. In the dark, it is possible, whilst trying not to trip over cables, but still trying to remember your lines, to barge up against them and rough up or tear a costume. Indeed, if an inexperienced person gives you a shove, or if there is a swaying crowd it is quite possible to get hurt. In inspecting all stages and plans for them, I always insisted on smooth surfaces and the rounding off of all hostile edges.

The back wall could be made more useful in nearly all schools, not just partly panelled for 'speech day posh'. If they were all matt off white, *clear of radiators*, and exit doors far to each side, there would be a large central surface upon which to throw coloured light to enrich any scene and to add apparent depth to any stage. It would act as an artificial cyclorama.

But as to stance, it is wise to remember the first suggestion made and be sure that you have a 'main prop' well in mind, in case you need to move quickly. This is likely to be the weight slightly on the upstage foot. Or if sitting, the up-stage elbow. For instance, supposing you have been produced to go to the right side of the stage (your right when facing audience), right up to the proscenium and then have to turn suddenly back, it is certainly better to have weight on the upstage (right) foot. Then you can swing round, your left describing a neat part circle and your face is to the audience. Try this with your weight on the down stage leg and you will trip over your own left foot. The opposite leg(s) would be employed of course, if you were directed fully to your left side of stage.

ABOUT STANDING

The same can be said of this as for your hands. If in doubt, stay still. Don't move unless you have to. There is nothing more irritating than to see someone shuffling about when something important is going on or being said. Yet, every moment *ought* to be important and you can ruin it. Again, audience will notice everything they should not. So do not give them the chance. If you are really keen to be a good actor, continue times to work out your moves in exact number of steps (perhaps when everyone is chatting for ages before rehearsal begins, which happens too often). Don't be over strict about this, but get it more precise and see what bits of furniture to avoid. Remember equi-distance, and end up on an upstage foot, so you can turn neatly before returning, or going to another place on stage. This foot weight is good to remember even if you are going to sit down. You can get a neat swing round; and once sitting, could get up swiftly in the correct direction. It is a simple but most useful choreography and helps other actors, who will begin to recognise that you know exactly what you are doing, and they are less likely to bump into you. (If sitting or lounging, an upstage elbow gives you command of a difficult situation in swift change of position. You always need a prop for your weight. Decide.) In strong argument, amateurs often take a step backwards. This is a weak, and unnecessary move. Always turn and, after a step or so, turn back if necessary. The other move is like dropping a tea tray between you. I hate sloppy footwork.

WEIGHT OF HEAD

Is useful in a number of ways, but it is important to be aware of two things. One occurred to me whilst still at school, when I evolved something I called Drama-athletic-Movement. In the crouch start, we were taught in athletics, the weight of the head is useful in helping the first plunge forward into space. The head gradually comes up after arm pressure and the legs get fully going after spring-away. Well, head weight can be used for football and rugger too, for avoiding people at speed. I later began to use this in high speed athletic dance (in the zig-zag), head slightly to the left or right helps alter direction.

In theatre, it helps in getting out of a chair. Most people try to get out by pressing on the arms, so all gravitation is still pulling them back. Decide on your foot and leg prop, let your head swing forward and you will almost 'fall' out of the chair with ease. You know your prop, and the un-prop leg is free to take an immediate step forward or sideways if needed. Later, I used this in therapy, depending on health of the back.

The second main use of head-weight is for travelling across stage. If you are nervous, legs tremble a bit and feel they may not do their job. Let the head fall forward slightly. And if you *can* relax the rest of yourself, you will find you are starting to go forward too. But just as you must not show raising your chest at entry, you must only let your head drop a little at first, then straighten up as soon as you can. Just to get you going. The first time I saw what was then His Majesty's Theatre, the stage size filled me with panic. I wondered how I would ever get across it. It looked like a hundred yards. Then I remembered the crouch start and knew what to do. Conversely, in a swift rush across stage, letting your head fall back a bit (as well as using an upstage foot as a brake) is a help to stop you bursting through the scenery.

There are many ways of using Drama-Athletic-Movement, but no room for them here, except to say that coming over the back of a sofa can be neatly taken from hurdling. Not, of course, to fly it and land in the audience! You lift the front leg, pointing forward to go over the top. The following leg comes over knee first and you are there. The 'knee first' part of the second leg is what makes it neat. If you are supposed to be clumsy, though, *be* it. If you ought to be neat, be that.

EYES

A lot of people ask about what to do with these. To start with (unless the part directs the opposite) do look the person in the eye, at least part of the time. 'Part of the time', because you may be reading a book and show you don't want to be disturbed at first. But, ultimately you must make eye contact. Just as mentioned in Space theatre, eye contact can hold the scene. There are, however, moments when one needs to look front. It is concerned with time. Time present: You look at the person *on stage* (as described).

In time past or future, the audience will want to read this in your face. This is the legitimate time to relax and let your face go front. In sadness, your head will probably be down a bit and eyes about the fourth row of audience. The next is for memory, or prophesy. Head goes up a bit, to be 'read' better; eyes nearer the back rows (or pit, in a theatre). As memory goes further back, or prophesy goes forward in time, the head goes higher and eyes would be roughly where the dress circle is; but not looking at an individual member of the audience, because if you are doing your job, you are looking at the past, or future, in your own mind (but not enough to forget your lines!). So you would be seeming to do so, to some sincere degree. For the truth about all theatre is that if you create truth, or as near it as possible, in a particular place, the audience will come with you and believe in it too. If you don't, why should they? Well they won't.

Now, all this is for straight theatre. In period theatre there are 'asides' and clowning and moments of direct audience contact. But the Director or Producer will have to arrange that, then click back to the rule of on-stage eye contact. What you must *not* do in straight theatre is to look out front when talking to someone on stage, in a manner of really sharing too much with audience, rather than with the person you are talking to; and cadging for personal applause, so to speak. It was a curious part of past training and began to creep into musicals as well. It is Music Hall stuff. Then, thank goodness, the Americans began to swamp us with wonderful musicals. In large parts of these, people actually looked at each other and tried to sound sincere. We improved. In straight theatre (even in quite a lot of comedy and farce) you must look at the person to give meaning to what you say. It is no good a man saying 'Oh darling, I do love you' and looking at the audience. The ladies in the first rows will wonder who on earth he is talking to. Anyway, it is extremely bad manners and he had better not try it in real life either.

LEARNING WORDS

This is always a grind and all actors seem to have their own way of doing it. Some of them like to have script in hand and it comes to them by repetition. Others like to part learn it and 'accept' the rest through repetition. Others again like to just sit down with a ruler or book and swot it up, line by line. Many actors see a sort of shape in their minds of the actual printed page. One thing they often miss out, apparently, is to focus a bit on other people's lines, because very often there is a question, or a statement, which needs answering. This helps a lot in logic and consequence of what you yourself are going to say. Occasionally, actors like to learn a few moves and pencil them in on their script, visualising furniture and props as part of the link with words, thus helping memory – rather like the point about other people's lines. There is a related and extra memory jog. Learning has to be agreed to some extent with the producer, or director. But, whatever their attitude, there comes a time when words *must* be known, or the whole process of preparation and polishing during rehearsal is thrown out of gear. One late learner can inconvenience everybody.

Sir Noel Coward always wanted his cast to learn words before coming to rehearsal, because he explained 'There is so much else to learn at rehearsal. Let's get words out of the way.' Certainly it is a marvellous feeling, as producer, if words *are* learned early, as then the whole creative energy of blending and polishing can take place without hindrance. Advertisements in *The Stage* newspaper sometimes added such things as 'Fast learner', 'Good memory'. But, for comfort to all those who find learning hard, some (generally older) actors used to have little notes placed about the stage to help them along. And finally, when trying to learn some unaccustomed wording, even Lord Olivier was once said to have been found leaning over the prompt copy, past the moment when he should have been 'on'. Turning to the actor telling him it was his cue he said, 'This is no profession for an adult'. He then, no doubt, went on and gave a brilliant performance.

LOVE-MAKING

This is naturally something which causes hoots in school rehearsals. In single sexed schools, there may be girls taking men's parts and boys taking women's. Get over this as soon as possible. In mixed schools there may be genuine embarrassment of an extra kind. There may be an opportunity for the producer for putting in their own points about reasons for good behaviour.

But here is some technique to help over embarrassment at all ages. General advice is – don't funk it. It shows. Say, two people are going to come together central stage and are to hug and kiss. For both sexes general advice may have been given for knees to be kept together. But on this occasion, if in profile, it is helpful if the girl keeps her feet and legs a little apart (men's feet are bigger than theirs). The man can then sandwich his feet in between hers. This enables him to bring his hips and tummy right up close to her with no gap. This is essential. No one can believe you love someone, if there is a large gap between both of you. His bottom sticks out and the man looks like the cartoon of a washerwoman bending over a tub, not a man loving his girl. Moonlight could be seen between them. The hips must be close.

There are other points which help with control. It is now almost like a dance. Sorry girls – man should lead. The girl can stay normally upright and the man can take control of the upstage prop, with weight on his upstage foot. This gives one unexpected advantage. Their noses do not clash! He is upstage of her's and there is no dodging about, like coming round a corner and two people apologise and do just that, before one gets by. Noses out of the way, without wondering, the two on stage can go straight to the kiss.

Extra to this is that with the man leaning slightly upstage, he has an upper and lower grip on the girl, say behind her shoulder and at her waist. Because his hands are out of her way, she can have the same hold on him, an upper and lower grip. Thus they can truly hug. And if they are nervous, this gives tremendous confidence. They feel safe. One or two people may laugh or snigger, but not for long. It looks right and it *is* right. Those in small parts, vaguely hanging on to someone should keep attention on the scene, not leer out at friends.

Forgive a little lecture. But I feel this sincerely. Questions and discussions may arise out of all this and it is an opportunity for training in relationships. It can be a bit of fun explaining the technique, but finally we should not fear to point out that showing affection, or love, on stage is a symbol of the finest of human feeling. It is an honour to do it and we should therefore show it as competently and neatly and sincerely as we possibly can. At least the producer should bear this in mind.

THE ATTITUDE OF THE ACTOR

I am always sad if actors young or old, amateur or professional, have a sort of contempt for audience. After all, the audiences keep the 'pros' alive. I would hope that all actors would have a deep respect for their craft. In schools there is very little time to get a show ship shape. There should be moments of fun, but there is no time for larking about.

I would expect all actors to develop further what they should have been doing all their school life. That is, having great absorption in the task and great sincerity about doing it. For this reason, it is not clever to be talking, or joking; or teasing someone, just before going on stage. It is best to learn early about feeling yourself in your part, before going on. At one specialised theatre in London, very small and where the dressing rooms were very close to the stage, everyone was expected to keep absolutely quiet and think themselves into their part before appearing on stage. Young actors should be taught at once to be quiet in the wings. No whispering, or talking, or nervous laughter. And do not trip over cables.

Sometimes young folk who do not want to act, or are not chosen, become keen on lights and their use. They are also prepared to scene shift. These must not be allowed to form a separate gang of their own and laugh and talk. Every single person should consider themselves as part of the show and be alert at all times. Indeed, I am for a feeling of team altogether. For in a tense scene is is sometimes the entry and exit of a small part player, executing perfect timing, which *makes* that particular scene, not the leading characters.

For this reason I originated a Team Award for a certain Youth Festival Group. I feel so strongly that this needs encouraging.

As to the use of all technique for sports, music, theatre or dance, one should learn it, make it your own, then forget it; so pass through to a new world and just PLAY.

PSYCHOLOGY OF ACTING

Most of us recognise in ourselves, from time to time, moments when we wish we were someone else – or at least slightly different from what we are. This desire manifests itself in many ways and can be a powerful motive for good or evil. Related to it are envy and ambition, but also the desire to be better in character. It can be a desire consciously connected with inner or outer achievement.

The desire is recognisably fulfilled in the realms of theatre, as we know it and understand it, and make-up and masks both play their part in the realms of outer achievement. They form rather the materialistic outer skin of the character portrayed. They can make things easier, in some ways, both for actor and audience, in the process of believing in a changed character, but such is the intricate balance between outer and inner self that they do not always make things easier. For instance, an actor may come to rely too much on clothes, make-up and scenery, and become lazy about the work of inner creation. The audience may then, to some extent, be gulled into accepting an outer vision of something, but they receive less emotional message. It is therefore more difficult to believe in and understand the character in the play, not unnaturally, because less of it exists. Sometimes the actor does hardly any work on inner creation, particularly when concerned with showing off. At these moments very little, if anything, is created. There exists, in fact, no character. We cannot share what does not exist, and the audience leaves the theatre emotionally unmoved, except perhaps for the pleasure of the spectacle. The intelligent theatre critic feels cheated.

In the best theatre work of the usual type, we would hope to find the make-up or mask used as a blended part of creation. The inner creation is the core of it all, then comes technical achievement, the make-up or mask being added to it and becoming thereby a crowning of the achievement.

It is important to understand this process.

Intimate Theatre

This evolved into something special for me, for two reasons. Before my final full-time professional acting team, working with a splendid amateur group of the Educational Drama Association, I had a feeling that, if they did Theatre for Children all the time (and after watching some other groups), there was a danger of their becoming a bit twee and that they needed hard work at their own adult level. The second reason was that when having lunch in a canteen, I realised that most of the conversation was no longer about football, bureaucracy, horses or salary, but fierce discussion about enacted story. That was, what had been seen on TV last night. It seemed to me this was a new type of audience, who might never go to an ordinary theatre. But if they did go to one, they would want something more intimate, closer to them, more like what they enjoyed on TV; and someone ought to do something about it. I accordingly gathered a keen selection of players and explained that my plan was to throw, so to speak, theatre up against a wall, a window, a door or a platform in the small hall at our centre, with the audience (only about forty) being in a different position for each production.

It began. This was where I was able to carry out more of what was in my mind about symphonic production. At close quarters, this works very well. It is the conscious and intended use of every single sound, sigh, breath-take, footstep, word, silence, into a planned rhythm (acting technique never overplayed, lifelike and very sincere). The consequence is that theatre is not treated here as a social event, with rests and drinks in between acts, but as a total aesthetic and emotional experience. There are no time divisions between acts, which would break the spell. Everything goes on smoothly, every incident doubly calculated, with scenes changed by dimming of light, sometimes to music, then straight on again, but action taking place in a slightly different area [see diagrams in Chapter VIII]. The result, with actors so close, is an electric atmosphere, often pin-drop silence from the audience and an experience, I have to admit, that I have never had in any other place. Audience would only be by invitation or by request. So a keen group from a Senior school, either because of keenness (or on rare occasions because their producer might not agree with the idea yet), Councillors etc. would come. The chief Education Officer came to every production and urged others to come. Members of the Drama Panel of the Ministry of Education always came. One result was that a drawing of the place was shown in an Exhibition at the Institute of Architecture, in London, with a description of what was done, in order to show what could be achieved with very little space and hardly any money. Of course, we were lucky, because the hall was provided and we did not have to make things pay. Thus an audience of about forty could have a unique experience. It affected some schools quite a bit and one of the best school performances I have ever seen was on a curved staircase for twenty minutes in the lunch hour.

Attitude of Producer or Director

There are, no doubt, by now many forms of direction. Some shows give the impression that they have not been directed at all. These certainly are not produced with pride in standards of presentation. But the main two forms might be considered as Highly Planned and the other as Wait and See.

Highly Planned

This is where the Producer plans as far as it is possible before rehearsal. Scenes, ideas, by-play, high points, ways of speaking, moves, characterisation effects, are all built up, with some anxiety, into a dream of what might happen in the final show. Models of the sets and designs for costume are included in this. The last two items might be necessary for many shows, particularly for big ones. But in school productions, beware of overplanning. For this life is never perfect and the final effect can fall far short of the original dream, or at least, in unexpected ways, be different from it.

If you feel that John is the right person to come downstage a bit and then yell at Nellie, and Nellie yell back, you might find that John could not let go and yell properly; and anyway his walk was awful and he had better stay farther upstage. This upsets the whole plan, and the producer then has to spend more anxious nights revising the choreography for that scene, or desperately thinking of whom he could get instead of John. But John is dark and big. The only other person available is Andrew who is thin and blonde. It means a totally different type of character and will inevitably cause a complete change in the way the scene is played. Meanwhile, Nellie is getting edgy and may get ill with nerves. The mistake which is now often made, is that High Planners will try and force the thin Andrew into what was hoped of the way John would play the part. Ten to one it will not work. High Planner may then get angry, or at least be depressed, or even wonder why he ever started on this nightmare.

Wait and See

The more children came into my life, the more I changed from a fairly careful planner, into the Wait and See type. It is really a question of flexibility. It is also more courteous really, because it means that you respect the ability of the actor or actors to bring something to the part. With young people who have not had much drama training, this may be very little. Sometimes they burst out with repressed talent in the wrong way and they need to be calmed and guided.

Others get opinionated. But those who have had some training often have a lot to offer. It is well worthwhile to let them enter the scene in their own way and to see what happens before you gently guide something.

You might have been expecting (as in the scene above) a straight walk down and John to yell. But what eventually happened was that John lumbered down, paused, thought, then spoke fairly loudly. It would give us the chance to say 'Oh, John, I liked the way you paused for thought *very* much. And as you spoke there was just a hint of sarcasm in your voice. I think we will keep that. Let's try you being even a bit more sarcastic. And as you are not going to storm down in a rage, you could perch on that wooden chair half way down. The sight lines will still be all right. After your fairly quiet sarcastic lines, Nellie can still yell back – perhaps she will enjoy a moment of female domination!' (Sounds of yeeeah.) By this handling you have not had to say anything unkind about John's walk. Far from being disappointed in it, you have used it. So also with his voice that was less violent than you expected (or than the stage directions suggested). But everything now has been a little enriched. It is less *my* show, it is becoming *ours*. If John had even come in at an unexpected entrance, as long as it had been far enough from Nellie to make strong cross stage atmosphere, it might have been worth considering as a possible keep-in. But if part of the *purpose* of the lesson was to help the young people to obey rules, then directions should be obeyed. But suppose one character came on too early, they would overhear the quarrel between John and Nellie. It might enrich the whole plot. If so, decide whether to keep it in.

In dealing with theatre in Youth Clubs and in Senior schools, I soon found, years ago, that one should never be surprised at what happens. Often you can use something unexpected, if you don't get put out, or panic.

Example: Three difficult boys were messing up a production I was doing of Obey's *Noah* at Newcastle under Lyme. At last I found they were interested in scene effects and put them in charge of a crane. This was to lift a cabin clear from in front of the stage (which would have blocked next view) so that Noah could go smoothly up on deck (the stage) and be seen again without a break, for that marvellous (literally) golden moment, when the sun comes out after the flood.

Also, some younger boys were being a bit of a nuisance playing football in the hall underneath ours during rehearsal. So I persuaded them to become animals and arranged for them to run round in the lower hall in their big boots at a sign from 'scouts' on the stairs. This gave the whole building the feeling of being the ark. It must have been; because at the right moments we could hear the animals 'getting restless' (and how!) down below. Newcastle shook.

Sometimes actors, for keeping confidence, try to stick too closely to the stage directions in the book. They say things like, 'but it says here, 'she goes to the window.'' Possible answer: 'Yes, you are quite right, but I liked the way you just pushed the table a bit, as you went up stage. This time, do it as if you meant to, not because it was really in your way, then turn slowly from there and complete the sentence to Brian. You need not go to the window. By the way, everyone, don't take too much notice of the directions. They were for a different show, with different people, at a different time. This is *our* show and this is Us. Do what comes into your mind and I will tell you if anything needs changing or polishing.'

As to polishing. Beware of too much of this. With young people you must judge carefully. Too much insistence or repetition will kill 'life'. You can always tell when a show has been over-produced. But, in all shows be sure of climaxes, moments of peace, certain consonants, speed of playing; improve bits you can't put up with and 'keep the scene up.' You *might* just judge that: 'with this lot' it is the best you can do. But the result may well be better than you think. Probably the wisest approach is half way between Highly Planned and Wait and See method of production. But I think the more experienced you become, the better you are at perceiving how something or somebody can contribute. As politicians would say – it is events you have to watch out for.

General points about Senior Education

Single Sex Schools

The question often arises as to whether it is better for girls and boys to be educated separately. Girls undoubtedly do better from the academic point of view, if in a separate school. They are not continually interrupted by male interest in them. There is some indication that they give way to these more bold, or even brash companions and do not ask questions, allowing boys to get ahead. Girls' schools always give at least outward signs of being very civilised too, though their pupils (without male companionship) suffer somewhat from a late true self-identity.

Boys suffer more from single sex schools, for the female presence does act as a civilising influence. They do not mature quite so fast as girls. But these days, where a mixed school premises is too large for proper supervision, harassment, or worse, can take place. But with a reasonable crowd of lads, they do have some chance of learning how to treat young women, particularly if Social Drama is taught properly, and thus to a better preparation for marriage. No doubt there is separation sometimes, but I often wonder whether it would be best to have a twin set-up so that each sex could be apart, but come together for thought-out occasions.

The Minister has recently suggested that schools should fly the National Flag. If they do so, let us hope it is flown the right way up. It is quite often upside down these days, occasionally even in Service Units. When the flag is taken as if it were a clock face, the wider white stripe should be above the red stripe which stands at ten minutes to the hour. Once you get the pattern into your head, it comes as a shock to see it the other way flown.

This, except for a special chapter on Dance, ends the outline of ways in which the child normally develops psychologically through Play. Less usual circumstances follow.

Suggestions have been made for a constructive, progressive, programme from babyhood to the young adult. We have arrived at the age of sixteen in some places and eighteen in others. The next period of mental and physical well being is dependant in part on further vocational training and whether employment is achieved. Those going to University, or colleges, will have feelings of starting all over again, mixed with well deserved triumph over success. Young people who have been to boarding schools may well be happier than those who have not, because they are used to being away from home. People who have never been away from home can become seriously distressed. Members of staff at colleges and Universities, where there are students in these straits, often recommend that they should talk to *them* about their difficulties and not go home in their first term – that means for any half-term break. It is better to try and stick it out, as return to college, after being at home again, is even more tough. If they hear about distress, parents will probably not know what to do.

There may be an occasional chance of being away from home before going 'up'. It is worth trying for practice at this, because I have known instances of people who went to the desired place, but have returned home like a bullet, because they had no idea how to fend for themselves, were ill with homesickness, and found the circumstances of life, as it really *is* out there, more than they bargained for. Great encouragement and support is generally necessary in this situation either to try again, or for help in any way possible to regain confidence after a considerable loss of self-esteem; also for probable consideration about another way in life, or energy to try to obtain a job, even of a kind which is likely to be considered poorly paid and/or beneath one's dignity. They should be urged to take this, nevertheless, if they are not going to try again for their original (or like) goal. A job will help in facing life, and with luck, bring back confidence a bit. It may give other ideas for the future and discovery of new companions, and anyway will bring in a little money, which builds, for all of us a bit of a feeling of security. Parents may be financially relieved too.

In this situation and because of our laws over state funding, there may be a temptation just to go on the dole because it is easy, or offers more. This is not wise, considering the psychological state. Unless determined effort is intended for 'having another try', whilst on DSS funding it is too easy to sink back into a forlorn state of lost hope. Be careful, this can blight one's life. Yet, at their age, is the very dawn of adult opportunity. Let us salute and wish all school leavers 'Good Luck'. They face a difficult period of history in discovering how to keep our world clean, avoiding wars, dealing with crime, subduing unemployment. In their lifetime, they will, no doubt, have to find a non-vindictive less centralised socialism, or some form of humane capitalism in a kind of mixed economy, in which we in our generation, have not been altogether successful. Otherwise, worse may come. They will also have to tame nuclear power by inventing something else, and probably avoid so much growth that too many things are made for people to use or buy. They may face world anarchy.

As a reminder of the stages we have been through, here is a set of diagrams of the shapes seen in Dramatic Play from babyhood to top seniors. These shapes only become fully apparent if enough thoughtful guidance and proper opportunity has been given for this important human behaviour we call Play, to flourish and enrich our lives.

THE SHAPES WHICH CONSTANTLY OCCUR IN CHILD DRAMA.

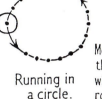

•
Self

Area round self explored.

The Area widens is slowly dominated.

Running in a circle.

Meeting companions three 'selfs' each with an area round

The three run in a circle equi-distance is achieved.

INFANT SCHOOL

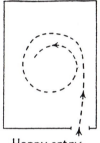 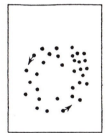 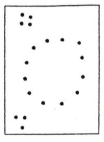

Happy entry.
The spiral.

After spiral,
the ragged circle.

Typical big circle of infants, some smaller ones beginning.

JUNIOR SCHOOL

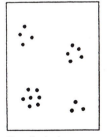  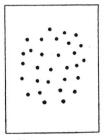

Small circles appear more frequently
(7 yrs.on)

Medium circle and S-shape, which is half of figure eight common in running play.

Very common
Good filled-in circle with equi-distance
Age 9-11. Here whole class feels group entity.

SECONDARY

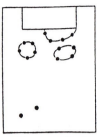

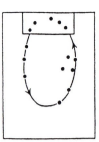

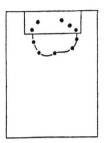

c. 12 years – 13 plus
Circles appear but
nearer stage.

c. 13 plus. Stage is
used sometimes, but
there is strong flow
on or off   This is
the Tongue Shape.

c. 14 years
Proscenium stage
influencing more .
Less flow. We see
the Bulge in front
of stage.

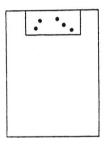

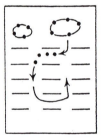

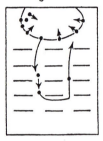

Where proscenium
is finally chosen lines
become straighter.

Where· work has to be done in cramped
classrooms, we still see small circles and
the bulge. Some movements between desks.

Dance

'Man, catch that poetry, see how he g-l-i-d-e-s.' (American dancer)

The word 'dance' conjures up various images. To some it will mean steps used for folk and country dancing or for ballroom dancing, others will think of ice-skating or of ballet, and others use the word dance for the performance of technical skills or the highly developed form of physical and technical accomplishment achieved by the Olympic gymnastic star.

A strong urge for dance started at my last school where a group of us stole away occasionally, and took part in violent athletic dance to blow off steam and improvisations about the 'death' of masters we disliked. We all became happier and even started to pass exams. Before leaving school I had finished developing my own system of what I called Drama-Athletic-Movement. In later years, after using it in Germany, I made it basic for training actors who joined my companies. But one evening, on my way home, I saw a small girl crooning away and dancing on and off the pavement as she circled, with her arm round the slender waist of a misty lamp post. Then, with a sudden shriek at a companion's call, she fled away into the fog. I realised there was a whole world that most of us had not considered. From then on my methods changed and became more concerned with starting with imagination and evolving towards technique. Most other methods (as mine had) start with technique, some of which can make the full use of imagination more difficult. Dance is mentioned quite a lot in this book, but it is of the child's making, which we can eventually develop into something nearer our own. For it soon became clear that there is something which belongs to the adult world, which is somewhat akin – it is Natural Dance (see Slade 1977). The subject is worthy of a chapter of its own, so as to make more clear what is the content and what the method advocated.

Dance which is linked with drama needs to be concerned with imagination and to contain emotional involvement. An objective report[1] of this method ran as follows:

---

1 Report by a visitor from abroad.

'In the Child Drama approach to dance, each child dances to the best of its ability; movements are not copied, beauty and style are learned naturally by giving an aim, a purpose for the movement. By giving guidance through imaginative stimuli the child is helped to know *what* to do, but is not told *how* to do it. The ideas stimulate the child's imagination and give it confidence to move. It becomes involved in what it is doing and this brings absorption and sincerity. The "not telling how" provides the opportunity for the unique personal style of moving and responding to develop. Other approaches to dance give a movement vocabulary first. One method uses words like "strong" movement, "light" movement, a "flicking" movement. But for drama and dance the guide needs to think – What *idea* can I give that will lead the person to *use* a "strong" movement? If I want a "light" movement what *kind* of "light" movement? The gentle touch of a finger smoothing the petal of a flower without bruising it?

The emotional feeling of giving affection by the quality of a movement? The careful step from one star to another, or the "light" bodily feeling of turning ourselves into a swirling, travelling cloud, moving with wind across the sky?

If training in some form of technique is given too early, this personal style can be destroyed, or not develop properly.

Each person needs to be given time to experience dancing on their own in response to many varied ideas and suggestions, and accompanied or supported by all kinds of sounds and music. Next, to work in pairs, then in threes, and finally groups, building sensitive relationships, moulding to and sensing the needs of other dancers. Now one tests their ability to take directions from the "dance guide" – the name given by Peter Slade to the person taking the dance session, for she/he guides the pupils through the various stages of development rather than directing and demonstrating.'

Although dance is and should be included naturally as a part of the drama session there will be some within the age range of thirteen to eighteen years who will wish to develop dance further. For this a separate weekly session would be an advantage. If one cannot be fitted into the normal school programme then perhaps a time after school could be considered. Having provided an opportunity for further dance what should be our aims and our approach? Just as time is needed to cover the necessary stages of development before a scripted play can be successfully tackled, so are there stages of development in dance. These should be considered carefully. One too often hears of a teacher who is interested in developing the dance work in a school being asked to produce a

Dance Drama; sometimes the teacher himself or herself sees dance only in terms of a Dance Drama production. May I plead that such a production is not approached too early. Let them learn first *how* to dance. The results will repay you and them.

Just as we convey a message and communicate with words, so can meaning and emotional feeling be conveyed through the body. Throughout the primary school years (and into the middle school) or secondary age range, the spoken word, movement and dance, develop side by side; all are included within the drama session, and there should be a flexible link between active involvement *(personal play)* and the more passive occupation of reading, writing, painting *(projected play)*. If movement has been introduced and developed through imaginative ideas, and the child allowed to develop his or her own personal style and not led to copy or become over-concerned with technical accomplishment during early trials, if he or she has then been led gradually to become less clumsy, more graceful, agile, inventive, controlled and responsive to a musical sound, he or she will, by thirteen, be ready for the more advanced dance which includes technical accomplishment.

Throughout these stages imaginative ideas are offered which will test mental involvement and the dancer's ability to cover space, to balance, to listen to a musical sound and to respond to it, to hear a time-beat and to work to it precisely and accurately, to use hands, arms, head, legs, feet with agility and grace, to become involved with absorption and sincerity, and be unashamed of expressing emotion within the dance creation.

As personal style becomes established the dancer becomes less concerned with self and is able to make a relationship with another without losing absorption. After a time the dance guide will need to help the dancer extend 'vocabulary'. Lazy and unimaginative movement is corrected early by further suggestions, but never by example or rule. Now as we approach much more advanced work the dancer is asked to consider angles of limbs, the relation of and the space between one limb and another, the angle of the head, use of eyes and so on. Having made these possibilities conscious the dancer is given time to test the ideas, to feel the different way muscles, weight and balance are used and build them gradually into his or her vocabulary. Imaginative ideas are such as asking the dancers to become swirling fog (to electronic music) or changing cloud shapes drifting across the sky, or a balloon blown by the wind (to music by Delius or Elgar). For contrast to this, overcoming an enemy, hewing coal, cutting logs with an axe (to Holst's *The Planets*). Then back again to 'slow motion film' of winning tennis at Wimbledon. Then, 'Dance any way you like'. This gives one the chance to observe any improvements – new, or more imaginative ways, more purposeful ways of deeper quality and dexterity and precision in expressing to the sound.

As a beginning, here are some general ways of promoting action and simple situation, so that the dancer has the confidence of knowing what that action is *for* (reason, purpose). It is a list proposed by Sylvia Demmery of the kind of ideas, which could be offered at various stages of development. Some I have suggested, others she has invented herself, using them in her own imaginitive way for developing this method. Each teacher, or guide, develops their own ideas and way of conducting sessions.

Find a space and kneel or stand. As soon as you hear the music:

Paint a design on a large canvas. *(Music is quickly 'faded' in.)*

Experiment with painting to a group of notes, musical phrase, or musical sentence. *(Fade music out.)*

Your feet are covered with paint – make patterns with your feet all over the floor to this rhythm. *(Tap out rhythm on the tambour.)*

Hit a huge gong on this time beat – *(accompany on tambour)*.

Chop a path through thick undergrowth to this rhythm *(again give these beats and rhythms on a tambour)*.

Walk on these rhythmic beats as well as chop.

To musical sound you are walking across marshy land by stepping from one tuft of grass to another. *(Music will need to have an obvious beat to it.)*

Use beat in music for springing from one tuft to another – travel across the marsh in this way.

A tuft of grass turns into a spring-board, use it and spring higher and higher.

Now spring from one board to another.

You have a rope, skip to the beat. Try double jumps. Now try in pairs, one behind the other, but only using one rope. *(Fade out music.)*

Sit down, prick soap bubbles with a long pin on the beat. *(Fade in music which has a different beat.)*

Drop dewdrops into bluebell heads. *(Fade music to quiet to give new quality.)*

Do anything you like. *(Either keep music at same level or bring it up or fade into a new musical sound.)*

You have six darts. The dart boards are in different positions all round the hall. Aim for a bull's eye on each dartboard, throwing your darts on sound.

There are stepping stones over the hall, travel from one stone to the next, using each beat that you hear *(the beats need to be given in quick progression;*

this tests their listening and physical accuracy). There are bushes made of spikes – step over one carefully, lifting one leg over the top – now lift the back leg over it. Step over another. Now try one more but this bush is taller.[2]

(As this is for balance it helps if the action is accompanied by a sound such as the shaking of a tambourine for it will lead them to sustain the action and make it more precise.)

Barrels have been left all over the floor – lifting both feet off the ground together, run and jump over four or five to this rhythm of sound *(tap out a rhythm).*

Now run and leap over as many as you can – see how fast you can go, but also see how clever you can be about changing direction if necessary so that you do not bump into anyone else *(this to music).*

There is a beach ball at your feet, scoop it onto the palm of your hand, balance it there and walk with it until you find a space. Keeping it balanced, lift it high above your head, now slowly kneel on one knee – keep lowering yourself and gently roll on one side, then lie flat on your back. Push the ball up into the air and quickly lift your legs so that you can catch the ball on the soles of your feet. Spin the ball with your toes – now push the ball up into the air with your legs, quickly rise and catch it on the palm of your hand before it reaches the ground. Throw the ball – run fast but at the same time try not to bump into anybody else *(repeat this three or four times).*

Having tried out these various ideas link one to another, adding any further ideas of your own, but keep the movements flowing; travel and work to a background of music.

Change to a period of calm and part rest.

All kneel or sit comfortably.

It is raining – gently lift your face so that the rain falls on to it. *(Fade music in as a quiet background.)*

Close your eyes – now lift your arms and let the water sprinkle down onto them and your hands…turn your hands so that the rain is felt on the backs and the palms.

Open your eyes – cup your hands and let the water collect in them. *(Fade out music.)*

---

2   Comes from Drama-Athletic-Movement. Hurdling.

Look at the water – is it dull or does light shine through – open your fingers and let the water drip through.

Shake your hands dry – vigorously *(this to shake of tambourine)*.

You are sitting by a river or stream, watch small fish darting in and out of weed – notice the way the fronds of the weed sway, curve, move with the water…slowly curl yourself up and become the weed. *(Bring in music.)*

Let your arms uncurl and move with the currents of water…now unfold and kneel and let your body, head and arms move with the water.

(Bring music up a little.)

Grow and become a larger mass of weed and, as if you suddenly become detached from your roots, move with the faster moving currents of the river or stream. *(Music up.)*… Enjoy the freedom, and using your frond-like arms and limbs, travel swiftly through the water…then you reach a quiet stretch of the river *(fade music down)*, find a calm place, fold yourself up and rest.

*(This kind of development was used to create a dance of sea urchins who tipped and split the ship at the beginning of **The Tempest**.)*

Lie on your back, lift a leg and with a toe draw a design in the air – draw with both feet in the air. Sign your name, writing with your toes. Lower your legs slowly to the ground. Roll over onto your tummy, keeping absolute control so that the whole movement is flowing – slowly fold your legs and rise into a crouch or kneeling position, making this a flowing continuous movement, pause in this position, keeping control – there are long ropes of cobwebs hanging from the ceiling, catch hold of one with both hands and pull yourself up until you are standing.

There are lots of huge cobwebs hanging around you, sweep them away with your arms and hands. *(For boys you would slightly change the imaginative suggestion perhaps to 'pick up a great sword and cut the thick ropes of cobwebs away'.) (Music for this.)*

When all cobwebs are cleared, dance in the space you have provided in any way you like. *(Music up.)*

Note the Dance Guide has fully understood the importance of providing periods for dancing in their own way to observe any change, but also to allow the group freedom to express and perhaps to enjoy any new movements they have thought of, after these exercises, to add to their vocabulary.

The importance has been noted, also for difference, between men's work and girls'. Nevertheless it is interesting to see very often that tough men make gentle movements too. That is a general outline of the work. It will be seen that in each exercise there is a job to do, some task to fulfil. Suggestions are made so as to improve, test or elaborate the action without needing to criticise.

Some Ways of Starting

Let them imagine they have a large balloon in their hands. It escapes slowly. Dancers rise up and try to catch it as it floats about the hall (girls). The balloon escapes more quickly. Leap up and dash after it (men). No one to bump into each other.

As mentioned earlier, suggest finding the sound and feel of things in the room, for example stroke curtains, first at will, then in time to music. Shut eyes and come away from the objects. Stroke curtains again in own imagination. (Nearly always, movement appears more graceful and 'wider', when imagining with eyes shut, than in reality.) Open eyes. Find other 'curtains' about the hall. Move to music from one place to another.

For Difficult Lads

Pick up an imagined battle axe from the floor. They are made of air, so no actual touching anyone. Imagine an enemy near you and give him a good swipe to each drum beat, but stamp sideways, or round about, on each swipe. (Music brought in.) Swipe to each loud beat. Throw axes away and stamp around any way you like. Now leap from one place to another precisely on time beat. Show how clever you are by moving fast about the hall; any way you like to the music.

They are now virtually dancing without the word 'dance' being mentioned. This could be followed by using the 'axes' with real partners, if judged ready for it. Again, throw away axes and see how clever you are at moving any way you like to this sound (fast jazz). Swift change to boxing unseen opponent nearby – then all over the hall. The same sort of 'stamp' can be done with real chairs. Using the weight of a lifted chair and stamping each time you thrust it sideways. Chairs down. Move in own way to music. Leap up and snatch at apples high on a tree. Exhausted young men are easier to deal with.

For Any Groups (Old or Young)

Pick up plates, coloured balls or clubs and start juggling. Move about as you do it. Juggle with partners. Throw all away and dance as you like. (Guide observes and sees what to suggest next.) Most groups show some indecision when 'props' are thrown away. They dance vaguely on one spot. One often has to remind them to travel ('journeys' again).

Dancers who have not had much experience often concentrate on one part of the body, say, legs, or footwork. Arms and hands become weak. I would suggest something like 'You are in a space machine, still dancing slow and weightless, but there are knobs and buttons to press above and all round your head, otherwise you won't get to the next planet.' This ensures they do something in their own way, probably beginning to use fingers for the first time, rather than relying on some standard repeated gesture, which becomes a habit.

There *are* repeated gestures, for nearly all people share some actions and shapes to start with, but as personal style develops, it is wonderful to espy movements one has never seen before. Some people develop an almost magical ability to invent a wide vocabulary.

More Advanced

Fingers are mentioned in the exercise above. Most people do not use them much at first. But in first class dance of this kind, and the sensitivity it brings with it, it will be discovered that each finger has a separate personality and a 'voice' of its own. It has different strength too, which can be used for different purposes. *Example:* The middle finger is strong and can pull. If you are pulling someone out of a chair fast (by *their* fingers), the first two fingers together give you very adequate strength. But if you want something very gentle, for coaxing a lady out of a chair to dance, by using the fourth finger (that next to the little one), an appearance of gentleness flows all through the body and is apparent also in the effect it has on the partner.

Music

Different types should be used so as to offer different opportunity of every kind and as dancers become more experienced more detail should be expected in precision and use of parts of the body, which show that beat, pause, runs, climax, and so on, have been heard and appreciated. At first dancers often plod round on the alternative beat; later, this is *not* all right. One expects every beat to be used in some way. Choose music which will offer variations of pace, mood and rhythm, contrast between loud and quiet sounds, tone and stress, climax and de-climax for the dancer to interpret.

Some Ways of Finishing

Care should be taken to do something special to the last note and phrase; and I train people to learn slowly how to use their every finger tip to show appreciation of a last musical 'remark' (it would be good training for an ice skating dancer), then to stay in that position for a time at the end, until the dance guide quietly 'lets them off'.

For a change though, once they have mastered this, suggest a running finish. To a long drawn out note, this makes a special picture as the dancer speeds through light – and gives them a new experience too. It helps the dancer to break free also from danger of repetition-habit – that is, getting lazy, once you are clever.

Sensitivities

'Mirror' work can come early or late. If early, it may be treated as a bit of a joke. Train people out of this. The idea is that one person does an action. A partner facing them copies their action as if in a mirror. It can be shaving, doing your hair – anything. But, as it develops high and low should be used, not just static and at own level of the head.

Palm to palm work comes under this heading. One dancer raises a hand, the partner puts their hand about an inch or so from the other and, although travelling about space of the hall, the inch should be kept. Don't let arm or wrist get stiff or you will get in a muddle. Later, try with one hand above the partner's. Now you can swivel the hands, as if there were a bar through the palms and it makes travelling easier.

'Filling of Space'

Is where two or more dancers make a shape with each other, then dance away. Their pattern should look like a statue.

Shadow Dancing

Is where one dancer dances behind another (about three feet away) and guesses accurately and in detail exactly what the first dancer is going to do. After years of practice, you know exactly what is likely to happen. Don't suggest this early in training, for beginners are likely to trip each other up. Shadow dancing is best left until the upper end of training. It is of sensitive nature when done properly and must not be allowed to become a gimmick. If done too early it develops merely into an amusing game and much of the purpose is lost. It is another form of mirror work in a way. There are also forms of awareness about other people moving at speed; and use of the weight of the head will help in swift change of direction (sometimes the zig-zag shape too!)

Contrast

Sometimes we forget that dance is not all activity. Sometimes the best moments are when a person stops moving, just as some wonderful moments in theatre are on silence rather than speech. The change from tremendous action to complete repose can be extremely effective but can also be used by an advanced dancer as a moment for rest, so you don't wear yourself out by over-enthusiasm.

Light

Use of light can be developed, so that dancers learn how to feel the warmth of a spotlight on their skin and know how they are lit. A very small movement of the head or the eye when done perfectly in time to music is dancing with the mind. Use of hair for a girl and chin angle for a man are particularly important here.

Different Tasks

Some people can dance the bass and some the treble. Often the main air is particularly suitable for girls and the harmonies or the main beat by men – either in jazz (or its derivative of pop) or classical. After this the more difficult task of dancing a fugue might be attempted. Bach seems best for this.

It is particularly important for young men to learn how to use muscles in the upper part of their body as well as their legs, by swinging chairs round their head, also, using the weight and balance in passing a chair to another dancer; stylised marching whilst throwing the weight of a chair slightly to one side and then the other (arms in front and parallel with the floor), although tightly clutching it still. Any fit young man should be able to jump a chair, or six feet off a stage and land precisely on time beat, when he has had practice in learning what can be done.

Precision

Total intellectual appreciation is now revealed in footwork and hand work. In early stages dancers nearly always take the easy way out, of plodding to the alternative beat. Now stretch them by getting them to move on each beat. French songs are helpful here – having to move a step to each syllable. Finger and wrist work, too, need developing at the top end, so as to fit with detail of phrasing. This should also come into the journey of the dance plus some difficult swings and balances for a long chord. In many good jazz pieces, there is a part in the middle where development of the theme becomes exciting. Make sure your dancers recognise this and react accordingly.

Mood

One of the crowning parts of artistry in dance is appreciation of tone and mood in the music. It is not slavery to the sound when you learn how to sympathise with what is being played so that brass and strings show differently, swift drumming and the elongated note of an oboe are shown to be loved. This is beginning to be mastery.

There is an unconscious Dream Stage that sometimes takes place. Dancers (more often adults), stop still and appear to dream they are dancing when they are not. Do not disturb them. More of this in the section on therapy. It is rather like the coma-acting that one occasionally sees during drama in the Junior School.

This can only be an outline of what happens, and what can happen, in human 'exertion' during this type of *personal play*. Teachers taking the work in schools should try to make sure that there has been plenty of practice and to watch for, at least, some consciousness, arriving out of the unconscious state of Child Dance. Then one can give more direction without causing resentment, or just irritation at being interrupted. Each dance guide has to judge this carefully.

For young students – and for any of us adults who dance also – it is probably true to say that some music offers stimulus for dramatic ideas, for story theme which can be expressed through dance. Sometimes the dancers should be asked to work without a background of sounds or music so they rely on their own inner creation. As this and the above stages are reached, more and more direction can be given by the Dance Guide without destroying the *personal* style which by now may have become established, but always offer periods of time when the dancer can be released from direction, and interpret in his or her own way without interruption. When these stages have been offered and fulfilled then the dancer is emotionally, technically and artistically ready to take the full direction needed to create a Dance Drama.

When the unconscious image of what you imagine you are doing matches up with what you can actually do and when dancers can use detail, precision, mood, emotion and control them, and when they can do action which is really difficult, but make it look easy, and still impart a moving message to the beholder during graceful but highly athletic movement, they are beginning to be artists. The resulting sense of achievement is necessary for young people at the top end of schools, if they are still keen, and if their interest is to be kept. But take each step little by little, for too much pressure will kill the lot.

After School

This is almost as far as one can go, in this particular book, about the general development of dance and it will be seen that much, or little, is suggested for in-school work, particularly at the top end, according to the judgement of the Dance Guide. It will be seen that practice and opportunity help to decide how far a young person is successful in evolving from Child Dance to adult Natural Dance. But the last and most important influence is, of course, the knowledge, perception, experience, sensitivity and artistry of the Guide.

One of these was John Hudson, who at one time brought a group of Senior girls that he had been training on this method to a small hall in London's Bayswater,[3] almost every Saturday afternoon. I used to take sessions with them

---

3 Improvement to the floor of this place was largely due to the generosity of Audrey G

and also with other groups of doctors, nurses, teachers and those undergoing therapy. But this is where we pass on from that particular talented group of John's young people, one of whom later came top of the class at a quite formal professional dance school. They were amazed that she danced so well. 'How and where had she learned such grace and ability?' Perhaps more people could achieve this, if technique and imposed vocabulary are not presented to them too early.

When Further Education and YWCA asked me to undertake something of this dance training, because they had seen remarkable results of it in schools, I outlined a whole method for Personality Training in Industry and the Retail Trades. Our watchword, I insisted, must be 'Welcome'. That is what customers need. Dance came into it quite a lot. Here is a short example:

SELF TO GIRLS: 'Dance in your own way. Now, two groups go through each other. Don't touch. Four groups go through each other. Faster. Don't bang or touch, think how maddening it is when people push you in the sales and queues. *You* try not to. Faster. Two groups and two other groups dance through each other from four corners of the room. Somebody touched. Start again…Oh, this time, well done. Sit for a bit.'

I then walked round being rude to each in turn about dresses, hair, make-up or expression. They were expected to give clear, crisp, polite quick replies and not get rattled. When the tension was almost unbearable I would change and give a compliment (laughter). This was done often on the courses, to establish 'the customer is always right' attitude.

As relief and de-climax, I let them dance again. Smootchy slow music this time, to relax them. This might be followed by dancing up onto the stage and down the stairs. 'See if you can do it without looking down. Walk the stairs if you are not sure yet, then resume dance'. (It always amazes me when fabulously well paid personalities on TV often do not appear able to do this.)

After a little practice. 'Now dance your way into groups, then break off when I clap and quickly form a shop window with dummies exhibiting the seasons. It can be a tennis window, skating, sports, swimming – anything you like, NOW.' They rush in to separate areas, muddle a bit, then stay still.

SELF: 'Not bad at all. Well done. Now we will talk about your windows and we can discuss colour, space, mass, line of bodies, gear and what might attract passers by. This might become an important part of your work, so we will build this up seriously and give time to it, not only in dance. But the ability suddenly to form an interesting tableau shape, after rushing about, is a good exercise for imagination and control of limbs. After that we will talk about office relationships, what your boss might reasonably expect and loyalty to the firm.'

There was also practice for each student to take command of the whole group and the room, from the stage, as the beginnings of elementary management in industry.

Older Boys after School

Towards the end of a late dance session I had been asked to undertake, at our Educational Drama Association Summer School at Keele University, some lads respectfully filtered in. They were apprentices in the Electrical Industry on a course of their own. One of them said, 'Can we have a go?' I sighed inwardly a bit, as it was midnight already: 'Yes, all right.'

> 'We've been here before and joined in, another year. We're interested.'
>
> 'Oh good.'
>
> 'It's sort of free expression isn't it? We want to know how to do it 'cos we've all been invited later in the week.'

'All?' I said slightly appalled, for it was a very big course. There must have been some. chat in the bar.

> 'Yeah.'

Then they crowded round, about ten or fifteen perhaps, asking questions: 'Do you do what you like?' 'It's free expression, ain't it?' 'I don't know what to do. How d'you know what ter do, like?'

> SELF: 'Well no. It's not quite free expression. There is a way of going about it. There is a technique, but you build it up slowly. It is based on the individual style of movement. Everyone has a style of their own. It is this that we build on. I may suggest *what* to do, this helps when you are unsure at the beginning, but I hardly ever show *how* to do it. That is left to you (except in certain exercises); that is your chance for individual style. During actual dance itself, you will have longish periods of doing things entirely by yourself discovering how your body works and using your imagination.'

They began to undress a bit, coats came off, shoes came off, ties were thrown aside. It reminded me rather of preparing to enter a swimming bath and, for them I suppose it was something like it. I noticed two members of BBC Staff enter the gallery. They may remember better than I exactly what happened, but I think it was something like this:

> SELF: 'Now, we'll just make this a short burst, as it's pretty late and I shall go rather faster than usual. That is, I shall take the progress in quicker stages than one would normally. We shall do what might be covered in a much longer period, in a short burst, rather like a potted course.'
>
> *(They laughed a bit and one or two nudged each other.)*

SELF: 'Righto – now come on out onto the floor. Spread out.'

(They dived into the swimming bath. No, they lowered themselves carefully into the water.)

SELF: 'Now, the first thing I want you to notice is the difference between men's work and girls. You have seen the girls work and how they can become smooth and graceful and flowing. Don't copy that. To start with, think of yourselves as men. Try not to do any meaningless, wet sort of movements. Think of your muscles up from the tummy, over your chest and neck and along your arms and make them work. Just to get this right, pick up a chair.' *(I picked up one myself.)* 'You will notice, I am showing you his, because it is an elementary exercise and we are not beginning to create yet.'

(I raised the chair with my arms parallel to the ground and spread my feet wider.)

'Now, you do that. Now, take steps forward and throw the chair from side to side a bit to the extent of your arm, but still holding on with both hands. Good. Do you feel the pull all up the front of you and on the biceps and spine? *(One or two slight gasps.)* Notice also how you are using the muscles above the knee. Right. Now the next step – walk forward like that, stamping a bit as you go. The upper muscles of the leg must take quite a lot of the strain.' *(I showed them.)* 'Now, I'm going to stop showing you. You do it by yourselves and try and find a group agreement in the stamping sound. Yes. Now, try moving about the room more. Don't all go round in a circle with your hearts to the centre, nearly everyone does that at first, carve a journey out for yourself and go there.'

After a short rest, I asked them to do the same again to the sound of my hand beating on a chair, a straight, slow bang in measured time beat. After this I began to turn it into a proper drumming rhythm and they began to move about in quite an interesting way. After a second or two – 'good, now use the chairs in any way you like.' I complicated the rhythm further and made it louder. The building of the climax, of course, induced more exciting action.

'Splendid. Well done. All right still? Sure? Don't strain yourself at the beginning. You don't want to do this for too long. All right, one more short burst. You've done this to stamping and knocking, now to music.'

(I put a fast version of jazz on the record player and they fairly threw themselves about.)

SELF: 'There, see? You are dancing already. Fine, now get rid of your chairs, but don't just put them away. Dance them away; start to be neat about all action, involve it with the sound of the music. Ow! Horrible noise. Pick up the chairs again and this time, put them down quietly, dead on the beat of the music.' *(They did it well.)* 'Dance on without them.' *(The record ended.)*

'Imagine there are apples on a high tree. You have to jump and get them off the topmost branches.' *(I made a bang on a chair seat for each jump.)* 'So far you have moved to my sounds. Now, you do it in your own time and I will try to accompany you. The feeling and process is different. Notice it.'

We went on then to the use of various weapons. We fought with imagined axes, and lances. As said, it is useful, with lads, to have 'weapons of air', then they can't hurt each other so easily. But they *can* be energetic. Finally, we did sword play (two of them had heard of the Three Musketeers). This was to Count Basie music. Now I wanted to work backwards to see 'Where they were in life'.

SELF: 'Do you enjoy Christmas parties?'

ANSWER: 'Yes; sometimes;' 'Yeah, on the whole;' 'Well, you know.'

SELF: 'Well, you've got funny noses on. March about the place with them on. *(The Golden Bullet – Count Basie.)* You've got tall hats on; large tummies; you're skating; you're carrying hampers on your heads; you're juggling, like on telly. You're very clever jugglers, you can dance about too. Don't just stay in one spot. Now, throw clubs up and across the floor to a partner on the other side of the room.' *(The record ended.)* 'Now a bit of balancing. I'll put on slow music to move around; then you lift up a leg in a difficult posiion and hold it there, pass a leg over the top of a chair but go on dancing as if it *isn't* difficult. Master yourselves.' *(This to A Closed Walk* – Pete Fountain.)

After this, we went on to some exercises that are 'old friends' that one has used down the years – exploring under the sea to, say, *Daphnis and Chloe* by Ravel, also a slow motion film of overcoming a sea monster; meeting other monsters on other planets; coming more up to date by walking in atomic treacle. Pressing buttons that are difficult in space craft. Then pressing buttons quickly (jazz again). Pressing buttons everywhere, all round you and above your head. Must get the spacecraft away somehow and back to earth. 'Quick, the monsters are coming.' (Time was then left for them to think out and feel the action.)

SELF: 'Well done. Now a slow piece. *(Stranger on the Shore* – Acker Bilk). Try to get the feeling of it. You are carrying something. Not just keeping it for yourself. You are going to *give* it to someone you like.'

I think this symbol is very important to suggest to young people in these days of affluent materialism and, with delinquents, I go on to press home the idea of ultimately giving a beloved object to someone they *don't* like, or even hate. For they hate nearly everyone, not knowing that it is their own image.

We also had a nightmare, rose up gracefully from being tied in a knot, explored the moon rather quickly (as it was nearly one in the morning) to *Electronic Movements* by Dissevelt and Balton; then finally:

SELF: 'Well, by now, you should have some ideas about what you might do and where to put the various bits of yourselves. Dance in any way you like.

Use some of these ideas that we have tried or some of your own. Do anything you like.' (*Say it with Music*, Les Brown version.) I stopped them once to make them aware that their wrists were a bit stiff. 'We all tend to be like hams from the elbow down, to start with. Try to use your wrists more. Make them more flexible. Fine. Now, the last bit, *Anything* you like to this, but really *work*.' And they really did, to *Honeysuckle Rose* (Joe Turner and Albert Nicholas quartet). It is often interesting to use the same music again at the end, it gives an even clearer indication of any development or improvement that might have taken place during the session. 'Phew, Sir, I'm about dead.' 'Thank you very much, Sir.' 'That was terrific.'

Then one lad said very seriously and formally after some whispering: 'Sir, me and my mates want to thank you very much. It was fabulous. Absolutely fab.' I said 'Oh good. It would be better if only a small number came again, but, if the whole course does finally come, at least you people will have some idea of what you might like to do! You won't be fumbling for ideas. I hope you won't feel shy any more, anyway. And don't forget, use your muscles. To dance well is very hard work. It's not a bit wet.'

One boy said: 'What I want to know is, why wasn't we taught this at school?' Another said: 'Yeah. It's, well, you know – it's geometric really, I mean.'

If that was their standard of what is good, what makes purpose for them, so be it. What was so exciting was that they had wanted to do it and had worked so well. If one can only find a way to show apparent purpose in the discovery or rediscovery of fun or of things beautiful, I believe there is a lot of hidden longing for it in people of every kind. Let no one think that any one kind of person is necessarily outside the pale.

For those interested in movement work, this description might be of value to those in further education, day release and technical colleges, but also to teachers in secondary and comprehensive schools.

Vienna and the Hungry Musician

Example: Dance drama, Adult Group, Rea Street Drama Centre, Birmingham, 1954.

SELF: 'You remember what we have been saying about the love of sound in words during the earlier part of the evening, and I related the drawn out sounds and the short sharp percussion sounds that we do in Infant Schools to the vowels and consonants, and you saw how this widening of the imaginative orchestration brought a new quality to our reading. Now, do the same in our dance tonight. As we progress, try and pick out more carefully the soft and hard-sharp sounds. By taking more care we learn to love them more. They need a different sympathy, different interpretation.'

'You remember in the past you were all doing the same sort of mimsy
dreamy self-sentimental movements that are common when first personal release is established in free improvised dance. Now, what everyone else does is not good enough for work in this centre. We have
worked long enough together for me to share any thought with you. If
I'm outspoken, you know now that I'm not being unkind – that is a
great release for me, because I don't have to be on guard. We are building a wisdom together. Anyway, improvised dance is so personal a thing
at first that you don't know how you look until a sympathetic person
tells you. We can easily fall into habits of expression too. That's why I
continue to tell you. *(One probably wouldn't with beginners.)* Out of that telling has come the progress you have established. Right – now for it.

'Men, last week you were mimsy too, in some of your movements. You
went on too long with the softer expression. Be careful not to "catch"
too much from the women. Don't be afraid to be different. Women's
minds are very different from our own, as we know to our cost and
pleasure. I shall do more exercises for virility later. Men's work is going
to be strong in this place or bust. You know now about Running Play
in Child Drama, well think in terms of a further run at adult level. Jump
onto things sometimes and jump off again, but mind you keep on the
time beat *just the same as before*. Use bigger contrasts between relaxation
and tension. But, all of you, girls too, relate the earlier part of the evening to the present. To start with, then, strength for the men; great attention to the sound; distinguish in your mind between soft and sharp
sound; bear in mind the difference we have discussed beween time beat
and the magic life, which is rhythm. Ready to begin? Now – Sorry,
there is one person moving, quite quiet please. Now – Someone moved
a hand. – Now.'

When there had been complete stillness for several moments, I faded in a record of
Mexican music.

> SELF: 'Not good enough. Five people started late. Now you have heard the open-
> ing bars try and begin all at once.'

We began again.

> SELF: 'No. Two people still not quite on beat. Look, in proscenium theatre a lot
> of people chatter, whisper or mess about in the wings before their cue,
> and scramble onstage when they hear it. That is not good enough. You
> should be thinking, and in your part *before* you go on, then you are
> more likely to keep the scene alive. Art has responsibilities. Now, be
> thinking and ready and more sensitive for your dance, too. Be quicker
> in your reaction. One of the differences beween "any old dance group"
> and a good one is that you all start at once in the good one.'

We began again. Everyone was in time. I left them without further interruption
because they were now keyed to the necessary pitch of discipline without loss
of their original urge to create. One must judge carefully about this. Sometimes

it is better to let them smooth into dance straight away and suggest (if necessary) later. But this group is advanced so I do not allow any slackness.

I wandered amongst them (they are trained not to bump into me). I began to half dance in sympathy with one person so as to keep up with them and pass a message.

SELF: *(quietly)*

'Make your footfall firmer. Listen for the end of a sentence in the music.'

(Later to another)

'Try and relax your hands. They are stiff at the wrists. Loosen them first, then use your fingers more.'

(To another)

'Good; hands *much* better, now try bringing your message right off the fingertips more. Decide which one should do the last job as the music ends.'

During a sad piece in the middle of the music, I stopped by one person: 'I see you have begun to suffer; good. Be careful though. Suffering brings sympathy. But remember there is another step after that. Don't become top heavy or sentimental, there is a *mastery*, even of the suffering. That brings the final control and adds an indefinable sort of dignity to your art. You are going to be a professional. Your work is good now, so you will understand what I mean. Most of the dance one sees hasn't got the final quality. Work for it, and ask me questions *whenever you don't understand*. Don't let a single uncertainty stay in your mind, and don't allow any second rate movement to slip through. *Master* it. This is the difference between the "wet" dancer and an artist. You'll get your chance to learn in this place as nowhere else perhaps. Don't waste it.'

SELF: *(to everyone)*

'Not quite satisfied with that ending. There wasn't a proper group agreement about the moment of finish. Therefore we didn't get the sort of electric moment of the thing well "said". In a way – though you will understand that I don't mean it entirely in a literary sense – dance can be like writing. It needs purpose of idea and punctuation. Pause and clarity. Now, your dance has got to the stage when you have punctuation, logic and purpose in the message. But your paragraphs in sympathy with the musical phrase are not concise enough. At the end of that piece your movement showed no obvious paragraph and some of you forgot the full stop at the end. I think you can improve on that finish. Let's try again.'

We tried and this time it came off very well. They stayed in their positions without any wobble (one of their exercises). So I left them for a beat of 26 seconds on complete silence after the music had stopped. Then judging that the atmosphere would hold no more, said quietly, 'right', and they relaxed.

SELF: *(after leaving them to chat quietly and judging the moment carefully)*

'Now, we'll try something where you are not just creating your own dream. We pass on to the greater discipline in improvised dance – of keeping your own creation fresh whilst beginning to accept a producer's dream. We won't discuss it and make it a group creation this time. There'll be a simple story and you'll be produced a bit. Just relax, close your eyes and listen.'

I put on a record and let it play for a bit.

SELF: *(quietly)*

'Right, now, you've just heard enough to get something of the mood. This is our story – At the beginning, where the sad part is, we are in Vienna. The sun climbs slowly up to slit the throat of clouds and break in day. A musician is asleep in a little top room, he lies for all the world like that famous picture of a dead poet, something grey and faintly moon-blue about the room – till the sun catches it. As the warmth moves in, stealthily, through a broken window pane, mothering him with kindness, he becomes aware, and wakes to a new hope. – Have any of you ever had any of this in your life? If you have, remember it *hard*, enjoy it again. Bring it alive. Be grateful. Repeat it. Act your thanks…'

'The musician gets up slowly. He is weary and ill. He is starving. When you haven't eaten much for a long time, you come to a sort of new life of the half-dream. He has come to that. He gets off the bed and goes to his violin. The violin he thought he'd never play again. But music is with him, in his mind; or is it that the sun sings? Who can tell and who can care, for the music is *there*. So he plays it as his own. As he plays, visions of his old life come before him again. A girl moves towards him. He remembers his love in a flooding flash of pain. He passes forward, out of the window, over the roof tops, through a drifting of space as of damp clouds slowly wheeling, and approaches her. He looks his love, but she becomes embarrassed. He follows, but she avoids him. He becomes frantic, searching everywhere. But life crowds in on him. He is in the streets now. Vienna comes alive. Many people throng at him, all busy with their business. There are many smiles and laugher, but not for him. Every man has his girl but not he his. Occasionally he sees his love in the crowd but always she is unobtainable, like some of our own deepest hopes, there is always some wall in the way, so he tries to forget her.'

'Later in the record you will hear the main theme change, and more instruments come in. Here he decides to devote himself to his work again as in the years before, but instead of his failure, the crowd parts in two mountain waves, diagonal in un-dilemma, and motions him welcome with a great waving of oncoming hands, like Milton's hosts "horrid in arms", but in this case in wide open-palmed salute, at once both Fascist and face-saving, and he enters like a King into the great hall where the vast orchestra is playing, and the conductor waves him to the throne where leading players may sit between rehearsals. He starts to play, and such playing has never been heard. But as he plays he looks up and behold the conductor has changed. Instead of the bearded man, his girl-love is there conducting with accusing stabs. He cannot advance to her for he *must play*. As he plays, the other players rise up and get bigger; he crouches down, but they leer up larger than ever, till in a fleeting moment he sees his love's face once again. Now it is kind at last. But as so often in this life – it is too late. His heart breaks, and Music, symbolised by the efficient grotesque orchestra of time-beat mechanical giants, stands over him as he dies. Mechanical music has again killed art and the true artist – '

(Forgive me for this elaborate jabbering. You know what I'm like once I get into Language Flow. So let's get down to detail.)

'Now, I'm sorry, the actual music breaks off rather suddenly there, on the record, so you will have to make it very rigid and purposeful to carry it off. But we'll add a happy ending later. Let's use the stage for part of this, plus some rostrum blocks. Orchestra, Vienna and Girl on the whole stretch of the hall floor, and the tiny stage can be the musician's garret. He "passes forward" out of the proscenium arch onto the rostrum blocks to meet his love on the floor of the hall. We'll have Pippa for the poet – I mean the musician, because she'll do it so well. Nita, you be the girl, and Tom – will you be the Conductor, please. Jane, you deal with the dimmer board.'

'Right now – orchestra, come to the centre – who shall we have? And doing what?' A good short discussion ensued on the personalities of members of the group and the instruments they should play. When this was over we were nearly ready to start.'

SELF: 'Musician – on the stage, please, on his bed. Let's start from darkness, then fade the light up just on the stage. A cold light, then gradually warm it. Take care to blend things so that music and light fade up as one. Pick up on spot bar No. 1 as the musician moves forward, then use a flood and one spot for the centre of the arena, fading out at the end, leaving one spot on centre: Ready? Quite quiet –'

The music was slowly faded in and the light blended up with it, as if it were part of the sound. The warmth of the sun moved in, 'stealthily through a broken window pane –'. The dance had begun.

SELF: *(later)*

'Good. Now, you know what a wonderful sight it is when the strings of a large orchestra move all their arms together. On the occasions when the light strikes their forearms in unison it gives me almost more joy than the sound they make. But together the two things are sort of intoxicating – do you know what I mean? Well, let's have our orchestra like that. Overstress it a bit too. Our orchestra would be more grotesque that way. It'll need practice.'

We practised the same short piece some fifteen times.

SELF: 'Nearly got it. You know I never show you a movement if I can help it, but prefer you to find your own. You tend to get out of time because of the beginning bar of your phrase here. May I suggest you start like this. *(I did show them this time.)* The short sharp moves will get you strongly into the lilt. Get over that bit and the next is easy.'

When that had been improved, we played through the whole story without interruption.

SELF: *(later)*

'Good. Some beautiful moments. Now, just so we won't be too depressed by the poor man, let's say what happened after – this is what happened – when he died he found himself on a cloud and he felt full of good food. The sound of music came to him, music of the sun, his own music, the music of the grotesque orchestra, but grotesque no more. It was charged now with golden comfort and the breath of a holy wind. And there, coming towards him, and smiling true, was his girl-love. She came to him slowly and raised him up. And he, taking her calm hand in his, walked off with her, slowly, across the clouds in a garden of bright light to some far safe place of their dreams, we know not where.'

(This was played out to the last half of **The Walk to Paradise Garden** (Delius)).

SELF: *(to end)*

'Some of our work has been much better tonight. I feel we could really go on to more difficult stuff and more polished. It was a lovely fade of light and sound at the end of the lovers' walk. Now, just remember, if you can, what we've been exploring this evening. More conscious pleasure in "vowel" and "consonant". Less fear of joy in simple beautiful things. How to let go and yet not be sentimental. Repose and its relation to sincerity; mental association of long and short sound to vowel and consonant; punctuation in dance. There are a lot of other things too, like precision of movement with music. But the most important is that I would like you to remember the experience – which most of you clearly have had – of bringing polished improvisation to the point of conscious prepared dance drama. And lastly you will have felt the deep experience of moments of atmosphere which can only be described as "Good Theatre". You created that this evening, and I am very grateful to you. Good night.'

Comment

The first paragraph refers to a more imaginative approach to speech, also to the techniques of diction and what is called 'attack' in the theatre. Making the best of vowel sounds too, rather than shortening them.

'I began to half dance in sympathy' – this is a technique I use with adults in order to get the feel of how things are going. It helps me to decide on what are their needs. I often shadow dance behind them for short moments too, for a good dancer, without knowing it, throws off personality, message, energy all round his body. It is similar to the process of acting-in-the-round as mentioned before. When not fully 'lit' by the fire of expression, this thrown-off message is weak in dance. Shadow dancing (dancing behind) also helps me to know whether a dancer is still in the personal dream stage, when much of the work is somewhat private and withdrawn and the courageous and vivid description by the mind and body in harmony is not yet fully established.

But anyway, if there is a question of self-consciousness because, as Dance Guide, you suddenly dance in front and face to face, it is kinder to dance behind. This would, of course, apply more to the inexperienced than to this group.

At one time I used to take groups in dance, after taking sessions of drama, the night before, for people with various handicaps at my London Studio. I travelled up at the invitation of the late Lord Cheshire (of Cheshire Homes), as part of an investigation and report.

Example – (a Saturday Group, Hampstead. Notes by an observer):

PETER SLADE:

(1) 'Start by doing your own dance.'

(2) 'Some people not using their hands very much, so bounce clouds about on your hands.'

(3) P.S. I'm going to finish this off again, and will repeat music ending. Try to make it your own (not just doing what 'teacher' says) – think what happens to your clouds when you finish. Don't be mentally lazy, really create in your own mind.

(4) P.S.: Children wait to be told what to do. Then there is the moment when they should feel free to do as they feel. For us, there is a breath of fresh air. Sink to the floor, feel relaxed, at peace. When the sound comes, come to life and do anything you like. Decide for yourselves the moment when you want to move. *(Drum music.)*

(5) P.S. Questioned how many had had enough before the music faded. You feel tired? Yes? Well – Think of a PE lesson. A teacher will sometimes expect children to keep moving for forty minutes. Now – from your own experience, remember what it feels like. Best work can only be given for a short time.

(6) *Change of sound. (Only three moved at all.)*
P.S. Begin by moving with your arms and hands. Make a statement which is answered by another part of your body.

(7) Dance in pairs. Do not be afraid of dancing apart – you have not been forsaken by your partner, even if right across the floor.

(8) P.S. To be able to keep your 'two' although at a distance, strengthens one's sensitivity, perhaps makes one more aware of another person's happiness or sadness. Their need. Anyway: makes one more aware of another person. Part of kindness, which is the basis of all our work as teachers and therapists.

(9) *Change of sound – rather slow, with some marked phrasing. They did own dance for a time; then*
P.S. – some of you are trying balancing to this music. All try some of this, see if you can pick a leg up high. Bend a knee sometimes too. Do not always go stiff legged when you lift your leg. Don't be proud that you have done it all! Do it gracefully and make it look easy.

(10) Now include some more journey, and your own dance as well.

(11) In life, people are often trying to grab things all the time. Sometimes it is good to *give*. Try this feeling of 'giving' in your dance. Have a reason. Do not make it an academic exercise. Perhaps finish a phrase with giving *(MUSIC)*.
Don't think about it – *do* it. Don't go all thoughtful on me and stop. Keep dancing and then – GIVE – in mime, if you like (but know what you give) or give in your tummy and your mind. *True* giving.

(12) Sudden change. Queen of the Sun. She sends her messenger to wake the Souls of persons left about. *(He says this because they are now relaxed and 'flat out' on the floor.)* Then – they come and offer the Queen of the Sun a gift. Queen – 'Give me your blessing.' She then leads them to a better land. It is *your* land. Make it real for you. I shall know. *(He has led them from an exercise to a simple drama story.)*

(13) One of the difficulties with older people can be to get them off the floor quickly. *(He tried reaction to jazzy music.)*

(14) You are only using every other beat. This is really the lazy way. With your footfall, try to hit every beat. Most improvisers do not do this, so *you* try.
Our group ought to do this. It's got to be better than any other group ever was. After all, its *us* isn't it?

(15) P.S. mentioned ghosts in *Blithe Spirit* walking across a hall. All tried this, walking naturally in diagonal journey of a straight line – separately.

(16) He adds – you are carrrying a cloud cloak draped from your shoulders. Lovely… Now do anything else you feel you would like to.

(17) *Quick change of music*
P.S. See how quickly you can pick this up.

(18) (i) See if you can make a running finish, excitement – freshness to the *last.*

(ii) Keep dancing when I fade music out. Try that. Not always 'down tools' at end of music. *(Music in again to find if they have kept time-beat.)*

(19) (i) If you are tired, sit *down* and 'juggle with balls'. Perhaps juggle with someone across the room.

(ii) The brass buttons on your new reefer jacket need cleaning. Polish them.

(iii) The floor round you is dirty – clean that up a bit.

(20) (i) Tie yourself into a difficult knot on the floor and come out of it gracefully. *(This is a useful exercise to do quite often.)* The more you try the more graceful you become.

(ii) *Music suddenly changed.*
P.S. Something happens to you – what? *(They invent in dance the 'What?')*

(21) P.S. With chairs. Touch them. Balance. Now swing chairs up and still balance. Now walk forward with them flung wide. No crashes please. Now swap chairs with someone near you. Make it look *easy* during dance.

(22) I expect you are tired, but now dance and do not show it. Find your moments to rest by looking at something, picking up something, but when you do dance again, make it dynamic.

Really fine. Please rest.

P.S. *(Summing up a bit)* Sometimes – as a group – you become over careful, which stops you moving freely. Think and judge yourself. Do you think you are doing the same movements over and over again? Do you make journeys? If not, is it because you are deeply in your own dream, or is it merely because you do not use the floor space well enough? You know what I mean about the Personal Dream stage, when you are so involved that in fact you do not travel over the floor space. Is it that? Or something else?

Never mind *(he laughs)*. Think about it.

Perhaps that's enough for today. Notice, in handling this work, how I bully you gently and arrange moments of great quiet. I only gear you up gently, little by little until you wouldn't *know* how good you are. But, you have done some beautiful things today. At those moments you give to me. Thank you so much. Good-bye. *(P.S. would always finish very quietly; and suddenly: 'Goodbye'.)*

Towards the end of my time at Rea Street I thought something ought to be done to show appreciation of the time and enthusiasm that some dancers had given. For those able to teach the method and dance particularly well themselves, the Peter Slade Dance Award was established. It consisted of an undertaking to receive some extra training, or to be selected from past knowledge of ability (as, for instance, one or two people in Australia) and to those few who passed, a badge would be given. It was a bit like a specialised club to which only a few people gained the privilege of belonging. So, if you ever saw that badge on anyone, you would know they were 'good'. And other people might ask what it signified and become interested.

One Summer, Sylvia Demmery and I had been invited to visit a community down at St. David's, in Wales, of young people who put on the Summer Fesival of Theatre there and of which I was still Vice-President. I had taken one or two sessions of dance with them at their request. Another unexpected invitation came, for a morning drink at a little place on the edge of the sea. It was from one of our dancers (now an experienced lady HMI). The sun was shining, the sea was beautiful, so was everything around. It was then I saw that our hostess, all in white sports gear, was wearing the Dance Badge.

The question is sometimes asked 'What is this dance for?' I hope by now some answers will be apparent. But to answer in more precise terms, it makes people happy and is, in its early stages, simple to do and beautiful to behold. That would be enough. But there are other things, too.

(1) It makes for fuller development of the individual.

(2) It provides training of the emotions.

(3) It helps people to express themselves.

(4) It builds up self-confidence.

(5) It helps in development of social awareness, sensitivity and perceiving the needs of other people.

(6) It develops the poet's eye through regeneration of interest in simple every day things that tend to be forgotten in life's rush.

(7) It makes one less ashamed of beauty, less uncomfortable in its presence.

(8) It is a training in aesthetic good taste.

(9) It helps people to be more graceful, to know their own bodies better and to be master of them.

(10) It gears up and combines aesthetics with athletic prowess to some
     practical purpose. It also helps to keep you slim.

(11) It leads, in fact, to an *ability* to dance, not for a few talented
     individuals, but for the many. This dance may be individual; as part
     of a group; for dance drama (either as enactment of a ritual, or for
     sharing with an audience); or for no audience at all.

(12) At its best it can be a form of prayer.

Since this was written a medical report has stated that children in our schools
do not get enough exercise. In any case they need *personal play* to balance
psychologically against their *projected* three R work. For both these reasons
dance would be of value.

Figure 20 Example of 'filling space'

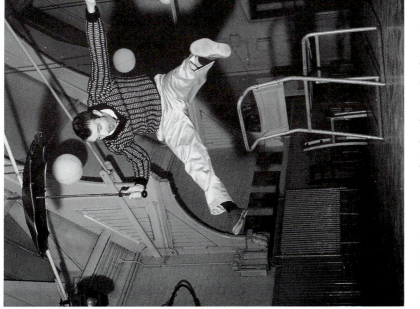

Figure 19 Springing over a chair (good example of energy)

Figure 22 Author showing example of exercise. Chair taken from sitting position and returned to same place while still reading book. (use of thigh muscles)

Figure 21 Filling space (personal style developing well)

Rea[1] Street Centre

A Short History

The street gang and Pete's Kitchen experience, as mentioned in Chapter 3, had strengthened my determination to obtain a proper centre. The Education Committee had asked me what I needed for my work. My answer was a place where children could come; and where teachers could learn how to guide and handle children in drama; and use of a hall for rehearsing adults prepared to perform Theatre for Children. The Educational Drama Association (EDA) already had Committee meetings downstairs in an old school, in a room that smelled partly of toast but mostly of gas. After the Bonnington Conference, when the EDA had invited me to be their Director, it seemed sensible to use the upper hall, once the bomb damage had been mended. The main building then became a Junior School and I was allowed use of one Committee room and (by kindness of Charles Adams, the keen Headmaster) occasional evening use of the upper hall. Thus started the thirty years in which I endeavoured to be Drama Adviser (later Inspector) and slowly in charge of Education of the Emotions, to the City of Birmingham. Then as the EDA grew, it became not only national instead of local (overnight after Bonnington), but its ideas and ideals permeated other countries and, at out Summer Schools, we trained leaders from all over the world and lecturers represented me in various places abroad. It was all rather humble and there was very little money. After a number of years I think we rose (one year) to a grant of £750 *once*, which gave us enough to publish magazines and pamphlets, the first of which contained a letter from Bernard Shaw.

There were iron bars across the old hall and to these we eventually attached spotlights. The local authority allowed me the first rostrum blocks which I insisted must be strong enough for adults to jump on (as well as children), so that during training they could use the higher and lower level exactly as children

---

1 Pronounced 'ray'.

do and thus share (or re-learn) the pleasure and fun of it. In making the blocks very solid, they had a sort of wooden cross bar underneath, and in part of this, if the block were placed on its side, a small child could nestle into the upper part of the cross. Disturbed children often did this and made a little nest.

My first task seemed to be for training, not only for the teachers' voluntary group of Theatre for Children players, which already existed, but for the general use of Child Drama in Education. I tried running the first course under the Education Authority and we got about eight applications. So I tried it under the Educational Drama Association. This attracted some four hundred applications and we took the lot. After that came course after course and conference after conference. In the meantime we opened the place for a children's evening after the staff had had a swift tea. But one day I came down to the centre and found some very young children sitting huddled together and shivering on a door step nearby – like cold little birds in a nest. I said

> 'Poor you, it *is* cold. Ought you not to be at home having tea before you come down here?'
>
> 'Can't.'
>
> 'Why?'
>
> 'Locked out.'
>
> *(They were brought in out of the cold.)*

Diagram 12 Disturbed children. . . often made a little nest

I said to the staff: 'We shall have to open directly after school and work in shifts, to allow you each to have time for tea.' So someone took the tinies, then the older and so on. Large classrooms off the hall acted as 'containers' for new arrivals until the group before them had finished. Later we were allowed other evenings in the hall, until it seemed that we were there almost every night. This allowed for Theatre for Children rehearsals, children's evenings, adult learning sessions and dance. Then, of course, performance. For the Theatre performances we charged at first a penny per child. But after a time, I felt that the children that came often had nothing. So from then on we charged nothing and it grew into a proper contribution to the educational service and teachers would bring groups of children from school.

After the Educational Drama Association Group had been trained to use the shapes that children use in play, in an open-space style of presentation (with audience round), we used to try to produce two shows a year. One, if it went well, but we would be rehearsing for another.

In the thirty years of 'residence' perhaps it worked out at about forty-five to fifty different story-performances altogether. There were some reservations amongst the local Inspectorate about working with voluntary organisations. But the Educational Drama Association had come into being after a course by Esme Church, sponsored by Sir Barry Jackson, founder of the Birmingham Repertory Theatre, before my arrival. So I felt it wrong for a local authority to suppress or ignore such enthusiasm. And in view of what had happened over my first course, when the local education authority one had had to be abandoned, there was less that could be said about where and how the interest would be kept going. Anyway, it was democratic to allow EDA's voice. Thus these wonderful people were at least allowed to exist. And the Education Office would occasionally allude to them slightly sarcastically, but not really unkindly, as 'Your private army.' (Once, they admitted they were grateful not to have to try to do the work.) I took the joke and thanked Heaven for that army. Perhaps it would be right to put on record here that in all the work these teachers did and all those who staffed the Summer Schools all over the country for thirty-two years, no one ever received (or expected) any overtime pay, nor a penny in fees.

As time progressed, we became more established at Rea Street and some different types of children used to come for 'their' evenings. Often they would be distressed, so these evenings for their own play moved more to therapy sessions. In 1954 my book *Child Drama* was published and received a good press. It led to more and more invitations to speak at Colleges of Education and to sign copies till my wrist complained. This in turn led to inquiries from the Home Office and hospitals. For many years I spoke at all courses for social workers in the area, visited clinics and took courses in hospitals, explaining that certain patients, before or after treatment, were much like children and had the same needs. Therefore it would be valuable for staff to understand the processes of Child Drama and the stages of development which it revealed. In this way they could learn exactly where each person *'was in life'* and to treat them accordingly. This would bring so much more understanding of real need and avoid many moments of possible *mis*understanding.

There was what was then called a Special School inside the grounds of Moneyhull hospital and a lot of my work was done there, under the supervision of Dr R.J. Stanley (and later at Mayfield hospital) for both children and the older people. At Rea Street things moved again and people started sending us young folk they could not deal with. So slowly, one evening in the week moved towards children in trouble and we then specialised in delinquents for thirteen years. My own form of Dramatherapy was used and it proved very successful, leading to further courses for Home Office staff in different parts of the country. During this time Rea Street Centre did pass through a brief period of minor fame. But it is sad to say that I do not remember that a single Councillor or member of the Education Office staff ever came to see the work for delinquents, although psychologists, some police, priests and educationists were visiting from a number of other countries. When I was allowed to speak of it to a group of MPs at Westminster, I have to confess that it was a little embarrassing when they asked what my Education Office thought about it. I felt I had to be loyal but I can't remember *how* I got out of it. My answer may have been a bit limp. Perhaps that is partly why absolutely nothing was done and I was asked to specialise and help in something else for a time – it might have been Adventure Playgrounds. Every now and again, though, much later, some very odd groups would be wished on us for short periods.

Meanwhile the adult dance evenings were making strong progress and I had been learning down the years more and more about handling the development of it and the drawing out of each dancer's personal style; also learning how far one could add technique for some who had only come there because they were fed up with other technical training. and were delighted at actually being allowed to *dance;* for the others too, who were not yet very accomplished. In a mixed group one needed much wisdom. Later it became possible to take advanced groups separately by calling them A or B to avoid any distress.

Quite early on, I came to the conclusion that it might not be right for talented actors and actresses to remain only in Theatre for Children shows. It would be better for their whole development to be in tough adult theatre too. After inquiry it seemed they would like this. So (including the reasons given for doing something about 'theatre like TV') that is how the Intimate Theatre productions began.

I had opened the Centre with an arena production of the *Midsummer Night's Dream*, at which the audience described themselves as slightly amazed. I was told by most of them that it was the first arena production they had ever seen and certainly the first of that play.

Soon after this we were allowed occasional use of a small hall that the school hardly ever needed. It was useful for conducting auditions for those applying for grant aid to enter theatre schools. In it I produced *Cheapside* by Parish, then a mediaeval play in the big hall, then a play about a murderess in prison (small hall). Then 'St Patrick' that I had adapted from my radio play just before the War, broadcast from London. After this came the Intimate Theatre proper and plays (one per year) included:

The Old Ladies	Ackland	(adapted from Walpole novel)
Strange Orchestra	Ackland	
This way to the Tomb (Act 1)	Duncan	
After October	Ackland	
Separate Tables	Rattigan	
The Chalk Garden	Bagnold	
Private Lives	Coward	
Blithe Spirit	Coward	
Billy Liar	Waterhouse & Hall	
The Living Room	Greene	
Rattle of a Simple Man	Dyer	
Look Back in Anger	Osborne	
They Came to a City	Priestley	
Ring round the Moon (modern dress)	Anouilh	

I had been in *Strange Orchestra* in London in the early 1930s and produced it in an ammunition factory during the War.

This was a red and white production at Rea Street and it was an outstanding experience, as was the *Old Ladies*. There were other plays too, but I don't remember all of them. But in *Private Lives*, part of the fun was to see gramophone records and vases flying about the room, all carefully and well aimed, so the audience would never really have been hit, though they certainly thought they would be. After seeing the *Old Ladies*, the Chief Education Officer went round all Senior Administrators in the office and more or less ordered them to come and see it, as 'one of the experiences of their lives'. After *Strange Orchestra* a high lady official, who always looked stern and hatchet faced, cried into her coffee. I didn't want her coffee to be spoiled, but I did want her to be *moved*. She was.

In one of the plays (I think, *The Living Room*) a man had to leave his mistress and was going back to his wife. I wanted to create the feeling of real parting and loss (for the girl), so he was directed to open the door and go actually down some stone steps. We then heard the bang of a door at the bottom of the stairs and his footsteps walking away across the yard. It always held until the footsteps had died away. The spell was created by the timing of all the sounds in a sort of music, blended with the pace of the last sentence of speech, which symphonic production brings, and it was probably the dance training which helped over the precision of the foot sounds, the bang of the door; like good radio, only this was live.

It should be remembered that there were no breaks between acts in these Intimate Productions. The performances went straight on from start to finish so as to link each sound and movement, without unnecessary pause to break the atmosphere and symphony.

After *Look Back in Anger* my first full time assistant, Michael Hall, became ill and, sadly, subsequently died.

Now a new phase seemed to dawn, somehow all a part of Rea Street. London clinics started to ask me to give talks about the symbol of Prince and Princess and the anima 'which no one would talk about'. They had also heard from a Jungian society that Dr Kitchen had said that I was the person, she felt, who would show what Jung meant by 'active imagination' (they were not quite sure what he meant). Some results had come also, perhaps, from the publication of my *Dramatherapy as an Aid to Becoming a Person* (Slade 1959).

It was about now that I met Leonard Cheshire and Sue Ryder. After a number of discussions Leonard asked me to investigate the use of drama for people with various handicaps and to provide a report for him to study. There was no place to start it in, as a serious investigation, so I bought a studio in Hampstead and that for a number of years became the Peter Slade Centre in London. Wonderful Rotary Club members used to pick up people all over the place (from Potters Bar to White City) and drive them to this studio. After 'killing' sessions of work in Birmingham, my wife and I would drive up to London on a Friday evening and find folk already on the doorstep. We would start sessions almost at once. Then next morning I would take a few patients referred to me by clinics or doctors and, in the afternoon, dance sessions, either in Bayswater or Hampstead.

The studio provided a place of complete break at holiday times, generally at Whitsun and I was able to write the book *Natural Dance* there . Visitors from abroad who had not time to dash to Birmingham could meet me there. And HMI would occasionally come in and talk things over quietly – what we had all discussed at the Working Party and what should we do next. The final agreement and decision for the Drama Diploma Course which I had been ploughing for, at the University of Newcastle-on-Tyne was made there. I could not get a full Child Drama Course yet. But the original idea was that each Diploma course from Newcastle should visit Rea Street, hear lectures and have practical work; and thus, as Professor Stanley extremely kindly said 'Everyone will then know that you are our patron'. (I am sure this was not so.) Details of the working up to this point and diary dates of meetings appeared in *Experience of Spontaneity*. A good link with Manchester University was also made, but unfortunately I was unable to accept their kind offer of close co-operation at the time which has always been a matter of regret.

The Personality Courses for Industry and Retail Traders took place in the 1960s. A diary date in the above book tells me that the Ministry of Education had been impressed to the extent of asking me for an appointment at the Hampstead studio for a little conference on the 21st-22nd of April 1964 to discuss the possibility of using the method in Day Release throughout the Country. As there was only one of me and one of Sylvia Demmery, my assistant, this could hardly be done unless we set up a proper training course under the Ministry (or industry) and showed, and shared with other people, what we did. One thing we found during these courses was the tremendous lack of social training received by these students during school hours.

In 1967, during a conference at the Questors Theatre where I was on a panel with, I think, George Devine, Saint-Denis, Glen Byam Shaw and Dame Sybil Thorndike, I heard that it had been arranged for me to buy St David's House and the old Junior Church of England School behind it, at Moreton-in-Marsh, in the Cotswolds. This subsequently became the North Cotswolds Arts Association and a Centre for College of Education students to come to me for courses, notably from Oxfordshire, Gloucester, Worcestershire and Hereford. I now realised that in order to carry out the work I was asked to do, I had six different offices and, not being at all efficient, it often meant having at least five or six copies of notes and often different diaries as well. The first Seminar for a meeting of methods for drama as therapy with the Sesame Group was held at the Moreton Centre.

On February 26th 1967 the Society for Educational Drama was founded in Denmark, based on my work, as a result of visits to Rea Street and EDA Summer Courses. The Child and Youth Drama Association in Canada had been founded before that, under the direction of Don Wetmore after publication of *Child Drama* (recommended to Canada by Lord Beaverbrook).

Now a near miracle happened. A Headmaster who had been fighting me for years suddenly saw what Child Drama had done for his children and for a particular teacher at his school. He approached the Education Committee and demanded to know why they had not honoured 'their eminent Drama Adviser with a special course for his outstanding work'. I was what they call gob smacked. But bless him, it worked. On July 3rd 1967 the Birmingham Education Committee decided to start a Certificate Course under my direction with two assistants. It lasted for about eighteen years and some wonderful people came on it. Sylvia Demmery carried on direction for a number of years after my retirement. It was based at Rea Street where more and more rooms became available and were 'allowed' for Drama. Finally the Junior School gave up and we had the whole of the top floor.

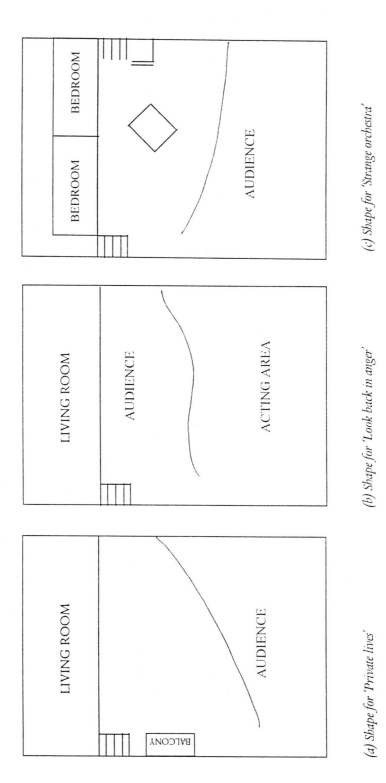

(a) Shape for 'Private lives'

(b) Shape for 'Look back in anger'

(c) Shape for 'Strange orchestra'

Diagram 13

Near the end of my time, partly through the success of the course and partly from the work of the EDA Players, another near miracle happened. I was granted my own full time Theatre for Children Group of Teacher/Actors, salaries paid by the local authority. Sylvia Demmery came back from Oxfordshire, where she had been County Drama Adviser to become my Chief Assistant.

The joyful work of my last years at Birmingham began. All members of the acting team had to pass through the Child Drama Certificate, so they would know how to take Child Drama in schools and we could take out plays *to* the schools as a crowning enrichment for children's play. And they could come to *us* for special performances, particularly of Feature Programmes for seniors. It was the ideal set-up. All the actors were trained teachers – professionals in their own world, all chosen through audition for their talent, and all prepared to be rigorously trained in theatre. For one short period, I was allowed the whole Rea Street building, which provided for rehearsals or active work by EDA on the lower floor and the Teacher/Actors upstairs, or the Child Drama Certificate Course and the Teacher/Actors below. But that did not last long. L.E.A. storage was required. We *could* manage without the lower floor, but used that hall sometimes. We probably just had a passing silly pleasure over unexpected pride of possession.

Some of those actors did very well; one became a Drama Adviser near Birmingham, another became a TV producer, all of them obtained posts of some responsibility. One who visited from the Newcastle Diploma Course at Rea Street for Child Drama instruction also became a well known County Drama Adviser. Really it was out of the dedicated work of the EDA players that the Teacher/Actors grew.

I have many happy memories of the Rea Street Centre, although there were terrible anxieties too. But I can still see some of the faces and movements of those in the Theatre for Children productions and the beauty of dancers swinging and flashing by. The only Drama Adventure Playground, with special objects built, is rubble now. And Rea Street Centre is no more. But let us not forget that this amazing place was in a Digbeth back street; and Digbeth means 'breath of a Dragon'. Perhaps the ghosts of many actors, dancers and of children that were made a little happier, may rejoice in the warmth of that dragon's breath we never knew about when we were there. We made our own warm breath. But ideas and action do not come from places. They come through people. So I hope there are old friends now in many places ploughing, perhaps, a lonely furrow wherever they may be, but exhaling as they can *their* warm breath of knowledge and understanding to all those in need.

Figure 23 Learning to 'welcome a new member to Rea Street'

Figure 24 Juniors at Rea Street Drama Centre: rhythmic head chopping (good absorption and believable situation)

Figure 25 Rea Street: passing a chair as smoothly as possible by swinging its weight during dance

Figure 26 Only use audience participation when there is a job to do, like very carefully dusting crumbs off the prince's chair

Figure 27 Theatre for children (good strong entrance almost too close to audience)

Figure 28 Theatre for children 'Chinese play'. 'I bow' and everyone started to do it too. No grand scenery or props – only the acting counts

Figure 29 Intimate theare: 'The old ladies.' Relaxed silence as lights go up almost at once for the next act

Figure 30 'The old ladies.' Using shadow to add to excitement

Figure 31 Adult intimate theatre: 'Private Lives' balcony scene

Figure 32 Adult intimate theatre: 'Private Lives' balcony scene

Figure 33 Adult intimate theatre: 'Private Lives' studio scene

Dramatherapy

'The handicapped are with us to teach compassion.' – Leonard Cheshire

It might be considered that there are three main divisions in the sort of therapy we are concerned with here:

Constructive education

Prevention

Conscious and intended therapy

I have already written at some length about what I believe to be constructive education, in the early chapters about parents, out-of-school play, in the years of school life. In schools, a wide and wise system is meant, including not only the three Rs, but also time and opportunity for aesthetic discovery, with training of the emotions and development of a balanced personality.

Prevention often arises out of all this. It is largely concerned with the way parents deal with their children and their success with relationships; also, of course, the wise and knowledgeable guidance received at school. If the arts have been used in anything like the ways suggested, a lot of natural therapy will have taken place. By prevention is also meant the elimination of unnecessary suffering by more thoughtful and knowledgeable behaviour on the part of parents to children, teachers to children, children to children and adults to each other. By conscious and intended therapy is meant all forms of carefully applied drama, such as psychodrama, and what I have called dramatherapy. It is needed when constructive education and prevention have not been entirely successful, sufficient, or have indeed been lacking. Drama has an important place in all these divisions as an aid to confidence, hope, feeling of security, discovery of sympathy and to concentration, for work and study.

In America, comes Solution Therapy. It sounds rather like mine. It is built up on behaviour and its changes, some quite small. It is brief, not long drawn out like psychotherapy. It concentrates on the good things, 'the good hours', not the bad ones. It shares with mine the hopeful attitude 'I must win despite all that is happening, or has happened'. By win is meant, not vanquishing competition over others but over hard circumstances experienced. In my therapy, I employ some spitting out of the present and past, but employ hope in a practical, sure way, to embed a firm confidence with which to face the future.

Depth psychology aims to deal with causes and reasons for behaviour and suffering. Dramatherapy, as I have called it and used it, deals *directly* with behaviour (whatever the cause), because this concerns the immediate unhappiness of the patient and behaviour that may not be acceptable by society. It should be dealt with as soon as possible. It is here that dramatherapy can make a considerable contribution, for if the situation is not yet dealt with, both the patient and everyone else may suffer further consequences, even though depth therapy may also be needed. They can go in parallel.

In any writing or speaking about method, I always point out that we should beware of treating the *apparent* problem for immediate acting out. The example I often give is of some very structured work, which was started by a doctor in a Special School. It was not going well and they asked me in. I obtained leave to stop all that was going on and to use pure Child Drama. The psychiatric social worker had not been happy about the child's home, nor about the father, who drank. Thus the apparent problem was used in the drama, based on these views, and scenes were suggested where a not very nice drunken father, always appeared as a main symbol. The child became more unhappy and at times violent.

I decided not to take overmuch notice of the psychiatric social report and started giving opportunities for quite unstructured Child Drama to take place – either with me alone, or with a small group of other children. An unpleasant father never appeared. It may be remembered that in an early chapter I recommended that all testing should be done in both realms of *personal* and *projected* play. So after what I guessed was taking place as seen in the *personal* realm, I used the box test (*projected* play) as well. For those who are not familiar with it, this consists of simple squares on a paper, like boxes. (It may have been invented by a Mr Box, I don't know.) So then I would say: 'This morning we are going to play at story making. This is a house and the squares are rooms. It is a nice happy house. Which room do you think you would like to be in? (The child would make a mark in a square.) Good, where is your sister's room?...And your mother's... And father's?'

I did not do this once, as a hurried therapist might have to do, but quite often, over several weeks, being careful to keep things 'live' by developing a story about the family from either the child's suggestion or my own. With a clean chart each time I might ask: 'Is the little girl's room in the same place?' I put it deliberately like this, as the nearer we came to a 'confession', the more I offered the little person defences. This way the child might not be agitated at admitting too soon that she and the little girl were one. We had moved away from indication that we were only talking about the child herself.

In almost every session the girl's room was chosen as the same ('Looking out on a nice view'). Once or twice she chose her sister's room, which I guessed to be a way of not letting *her* come on top. But that was not immediately what I was seeking, though of course it had to be considered. I was trying, in general, to find what had gone wrong. The mother's room was fairly near, but the father's room was always put next to the little girl's.

In active improvised drama father always appeared as a kind, acceptable, loving person, once the structured drunken character had been banished. After careful observation and when I was sure, by particular questioning, which was aimed at seeing whether Kind Father was a smoke screen, a hope figure, a dream of unreachable happiness, I felt sure of the situation. Then I was able to say: 'You were treating this child all wrong. Although he sometimes gets drunk, the father is the only person this child really loves and you were keeping him away, both in the dream world of play and in reality.'

Treatment continued on my lines only, after I had left. Something was done about the home situation. The child improved considerably, became happier, started to learn lessons and ceased bed wetting.

Defences

It is important to have a regard for these, I always feel. There are moments when a therapist may need to be stern, but it is not kind to use a position of power to strip a person emotionally bare and then leave no avenue, nor room, for confidence to build, or rebuild, so as to go forward again after what becomes a crisis. Crises may be large or small, but all are important. It is better if some never happen. Some need not.

DEFENCE EXAMPLE

A child was learning to swim. He was a bit afraid of water, but facing it bravely. A shout came 'Look, look, I can swim!' I noticed that after every second stroke a toe touched the bottom, for the 'swimmer' had carefully chosen a journey across the bath, rather near the shallow end.

'Well done', I shouted back, 'it is a fine sight. Next time, I look forward to seeing you swim even farther – even down the length of the bath.'

The little boy would not quite know whether I knew or not what was going on. It would be enough for him to be bearing the fact of knowing he could not yet swim. He was trying; and I knew with this particular person that more failure (of which he had much) could shatter him. Everyone is a particular person. Everyone has to be treated in a particular way. So I let him have his defence. The opposite would have been. 'Don't lie to me. I can see your toe touching the bottom. I shan't come again till you can *really* swim. Why add criticism and disgust to his predicament?

ANOTHER EXAMPLE

I often use the 'constructive lie' as a halfway stage to improvement or ultimate success, in physical handicap and particularly for reading difficulties. The latter may be mentioned again. But roughly it is that one has to learn to read a book that isn't there. After practice in improvisation, language begins to flow and a child can 'read' a story from quite a 'big heavy book'. Down the years I still see before me little tear-filled eyes, but excited faces, suddenly turned up towards me and hear the joyous cry 'I can read, can't I?' My answer, tearing at the heart, would always be 'Yes, yes, darling you can! What a lovely story and how *well* you read it from that book.' Both the child and I would know that if I tried to read 'that book', they could say 'No, no that's all wrong. It doesn't say that at all.' Perhaps the words from that book are important, because we have not dealt with any other kind of book yet. But the defences have not been stripped away. There has been some pleasure associated with the music of the word 'book' as such; and I have been intentionally building up what I call the Hope Process. With blind people I have always been so touched when they say things like, 'Do come again, it has been lovely to see you.' In a way that is a constructive lie too. But yet it isn't. Perhaps they see you in their mind's eye, if they have not always been blind, or are imagining you if they have been. It serves a brave purpose of acceptance anyway, and a living hope of normality. With physically handicapped children and grown-ups, there are times when people in a wheel chair will say – during or after drama – 'I ran that race fast, didn't I?' or 'We were jolly fast jogging round the block.' Dear, brave people. Yes, yes, I showed you how to do it. If not in reality, in your dreams. And in your dream lies Hope – and courage.

Long ago I began to realise this business of the psychic Bank Balance: When you have too many failures, you get an overdraft. When you have enough successes, you are in funds again. It really can be seen and be made conscious in these bleak, straight words. One of the most important tasks of dramatherapy is to provide a means whereby Success and Hope can be achieved. For I found that successes *even in the world of dreams* (i.e. imaginative drama) could bolster hope to such a degree that the overdraft could be reduced – and sometimes even overcome, to find a few brave pennies in the Bank. That is the start for a slow climb up, or back, to normality, getting slowly richer with new pennies of happiness, until they turn to pounds.

From Now On Events are in Chronological Order

Perhaps all this started for me as a personal experience, for at school, for a time, I and a few companions had lost all hope. But after regular outpourings of improvised drama and violent athletic dance, we magically revived, began to pass our exams and even started to want to live. (None of this was known to our teachers.) So I felt there must be something in this stuff and so have based my therapy on Hope ever since, because I know what it is like for anyone to be without it. I also learned how powerful drama could be as an antidote to failure. Here is part of a report asked for on the subject.

'Our tale ended with about forty minutes of strenuous improvised dance by the "inmates" and their "keepers", during which many detested masters were caught by the keepers and added to those who were best put firmly out of harm's way.

After such a session as this, we would be greatly refreshed, and more ready to face again the horrors of everyday school life and the dark cloud that descends every Sunday night on all those unfortunate enough not to get through their prep.

On other occasions, the themes were more sedate: I remember one very serious ballet about five fine men (us), who were brilliant at cricket, and who had been left out of all tests by sheer oversight. (This had in fact happened to three of us.) But were they disgruntled? Never. They set to work like fine men should, and perfected their athletics by practice. When they ran on the playing fields, they were obviously so fast that they all got into relay teams and won their colours. After becoming Varsity Blues, they were all decorated by the King, except one who became a missionary. (One of us did, but not that one.) This story included much ballet built upon the athletic movements of jumping, putting the shot, throwing golden javelins dipped in poison, pole vaulting and hurdling bushes. Thus we perfected the style taught us by our school Olympic coach.

We also practised that day, and thereafter, the changing of the baton in relay racing, hour after hour. The perfect change is as exquisite a piece of art as the perfect flying of a hurdle, and to this day is for me one of the most exciting examples of technical drama. Determination, mastery, excitement, production, footwork, dexterity, thought for others and "good theatre" are all present in this wonderful moment of time.

Other things we danced were the stories and myths of ancient Greece. We placed great stress on sincere sadness, and always had forfeits for lack of agility or virility. Sometimes we spoke, but mostly we had no breath for it. The form of work was in itself a strenuous form of training, and at the same time a remarkable opportunity for acting out deeply, not only our own griefs, but the griefs and joys of the gods themselves in the great stories of the world. I look back upon that dancing as something which instilled into me once and for all the deep knowledge of the standards of effort and beauty, which have been my yardstick, since, in the judging of professional and amateur work of every kind. Such dance as this was, many years later, to form the basic training for the Pear Tree Players, and other professional companies that have asked my aid, or that I have started.'

I only mention this in more detail, because so many people ask me how and why I started the work I have tried to do. I also considered that I had perfected my Drama-Athletic-Movement before leaving school, largely inspired by this dance.

After returning here from the university town of Bonn, where I studied German, Economics and Psychology, I started what I am told were the first full time (adult) professional companies, in this country, playing specialised Theatre for Children (about 1932). My Parable Players for taking mediaeval plays round Churches were formed in 1936. Apart from many forms of theatre, commercial and otherwise and starting my own Theatre School, I had become the youngest 'Uncle' in BBC Children's Hour; then started an Arts Centre.

In my first Arts Centre, Worcestershire (1937–8), people heard of my efforts and slowly came together, shopkeepers, printers, tyre sellers, hospital staff and daughters of clergymen. And if they didn't come themselves, they began to send their children. One or two of these were backward or disturbed. After a time a considerable number went through my hands and I began to find myself in classrooms too. It was the exciting results of these experiments that finally took me nearer London again. For in nearly all the children who came to me, their state seemed to be totally unnecessary and I determined to try to bring the results of my work to the notice of the medical profession; I also took an inner oath that I would one day somehow get similar but simpler work than my therapy into *general* education as a form of prevention. I went to a church in Ludlow and prayed about it.

Here is an account of one trickle before the flood of unhappy young; some of the first to come:

SELF: *(to children)* 'Have a sweet.' *(I offer them round. John remains over in a corner alone, staring at wallpaper. I go over to him.)* 'Nice pattern.' *(This is said in a low voice, and my approach to the child is from behind so as not to distract his attention sharply, but rather to attempt to join him and speak as with his mind.)*

JOHN: 'It's go a 'orse's 'ead.'

SELF: 'Yes, it has.'

JOHN: 'It's a bad 'orse – like my teacher.'

SELF: 'Some teachers are good.'

JOHN: 'Mine isn't. She 'its me.'

SELF: 'Does she?' *(The boy looks round at me then, saliva coming a bit at his mouth. Perhaps he is interested that I take all for granted, no surprise, no anger. Now is my chance.)* 'Have a sweet.'

(Long pause.)

SELF: *(as if I had not spoken)*

'Have a sweet.'

(Long pause.)

SELF: *(in exactly the same tone)*

'Have a sweet.'

JOHN: *(coming to)*

'Yuss.'

SELF: 'They're over by the fire.'

(I had left them there on purpose. John follows me, and is thus induced to join the group without any commands being given, which might remind him of other experiences I don't want him to think of whilst he is here.)

SELF: 'Let's squeeze in near the fire. How is Janet? Do you want to read to us today?'

JANET: 'No.'

*(I am secretly rather relieved. Perhaps everyone is. Janet can't read, which is partly the reason for her nervous condition. She **looks** at an open book sometimes when she comes to us, and either takes five minutes per half word or makes up a story, pretending to read. By letting her do this without reprimand, she is beginning to get confidence to **try** to read again. Her mother cuffs her, for not being able to read, which makes my task twice as hard.)*

SELF: 'Let's have some ideas then, John. Have you got one for us?'

JOHN: 'No.'

SELF: 'Anne?'

ANNE: 'No.'

SELF: 'What, no ideas. Well I never did. How did you come here tonight, Anne?'

ANNE: 'Walked.'

SELF: 'Did you notice anything on your way?'

ANNE: 'No.'

SELF: 'No houses, no people, no trees – no buns – no monkeys with hats on?'
        (A few little giggles begin.)

ANNE: 'Fat dog.'

Self: 'Good. That's a *lovely* idea. Anne has given us a fat dog.' *(The little group is warming up now.)* 'Bill?'

BILL: 'Warm fire.'

SELF: 'Yes. Now, just one more. Let's have one more – Janet, have you got one for us now?' *(Janet shakes her head. There is a permanent drip at the end of her nose.)* 'Oo, I don't believe it, I'm sure you have.' *(Then, taking a dangerous chance:)* 'Tell us something you've read about lately.'

JANET: 'Sugar bun.' *(It's not very imaginative, and hardly her idea, but I accept everything.)*

SELF: 'Grand. Now we've got Fat Dog; Warm Fire; and Sugar Bun. Once upon a time there was a *sugar bun*. He was a beautiful bun, King of all the buns in Bunland, and he lived in a wonderful biscuity palace surrounded by copper taps. Where shall we have the palace? Oh, over there I think, under the table – and his crown was a lovely blob of sugary spice, and he was fat – my he was fat! *(Giggles)*. One morning the guards, those copper tap chaps, turned on their swishing noise to wake up the King, and he rolled over on his golden dish bed, and opened his curranty eyes. Then those currants nearly popped out of his head: 'I must buy a dog,' he cried: 'a nice fat dog, that's wot's the trouble with me. I've got no dog.' 'Very dangerous, your Majesty,' said a copper tap chap, 'nasty treacherous things dogs.' *(Janet's nose drip wobbles and I bend over to her and whisper hastily 'not really'. After receiving a pale grin, I continue.)* But the King wouldn't believe it and jumped out of bed, jumped into some frilly paper trousers, like you have on cakes, and jumped through the door – What did he do?'

JOHN: 'Jumped out of bed...'

JANET: 'Jumped into some... *(bursting into giggles)*...'

BILL: '...frilly paper trousers...'

EVERYBODY 'Y '...jumped through the door...'

Then we all said this all over again about the jumping, until it developed into a sort of chant repeated several times. When it had been a satisfying group experience, I tried to get on.

SELF: '...and then he rushed down the road, but he couldn't remember the shop, so he walked round and round for a bit – in the middle of the floor there – just to get his mind settled. When he felt giddy he stopped and there straight in front of him was the pet shop. In he went and bought a big fat gentle yellow dog. Now when he got outside the gentle dog didn't look gentle any more, suddenly, and with a slobber noise he swallowed the King all in a gulp. Was that King cross!? But the dog didn't know what he had swallowed. You see you've got to be jolly careful what you swallow whole in this life. And two things suddenly started to happen. The King sent out electric currant messages for help, inside the dog, and from all the streets there came a marching sound – big buns, little buns, pancakes, rolls, roly-poly puddings, Swiss buns and doughnuts. Every brand of bun you can think of marched against the dog. And when the King heard the marching sound he got boiling hot with excitement, and as he got hotter and hotter the dog got hotter and hotter.too, till all at once he burst into flames. "Hah", said the host of buns – that's all the buns outside, you know – "silly old dog. Silly old dog. My what a wonderful *warm fire* he makes!" And they melted their sugar at him a bit. "Call the guards", someone said. So the copper taps

> were called. They turned themselves on and put out the dog. Then one
> of them got very cold, and made an icicle ladder and stuck it in the
> dog's mouth. So out climbed the King. But his crown was just a sticky
> mess. "Don't think I do like dogs much", he said. The fat dog said.
> "Sorry your Majesty, I didn't really mean it, I didn't really know", and
> he crept back into the pet shop. But the King soon felt better, and bor-
> rowing some sugar from two Swiss buns he quickly made a new crown.
> "All is forgiven", he cried and they all marched back to the palace and
> sang songs of sticky thanksgiving for the rescue of their King.'

When we had settled who should be what, the children wanted me to be
something too, so I agreed to be the golden dish and was promptly sat on hard
by John. My feigned discomfort started things off well. We imagined the
hundreds of buns marching, and made knocking and stamping noises for their
feet coming. We all 'swished' hard for the 'copper tap chaps' and to make
everything happy at the end of the session, we finished up with the dance of
the Electric Currants (twenty minutes violent improvisation to the tune 'Top
Hat, White Tie and Tails').

It is essential that there should be no confusion between electric currents
and electric currants. The latter are vastly superior.

(This report has been pieced together from various jottings taken at the
time.)

COMMENT

This is an example of putting what has been learned to the benefit of other
people. We are back at children again but for a particular reason, to help another
group of adults, those many teachers, specialists and psychologists who have
asked me how I would adapt Child Drama to the needs of backward or
disturbed children. (The description has been used and discussed at a number
of psychological conferences.) Perhaps it might help parents too because, as
well as their child, they can be desperately unhappy over a situation and often
they are so hastily judged.

Lies so often begin because of misery or fear rather than sin. One can give
great courage sometimes to children by asking them to read a book that is not
there. They can read *that* book but you couldn't. It wouldn't be the same if they
handed it to you, they would tell you you were making it up! You do not let
them get away with this for ever; one day, during treatment, you will help them
to know the difference between dream and reality and thereby truth.

I felt it necessary to state where the palace was. With less disturbed children
I should have asked *them* to tell me. The chant which was encouraged was a
way of helping them to share and communicate; it was to bring collective
happiness from which the unhappy isolate is normally debarred. It is sometimes

well worth pausing even in the middle of a creation to serve out a little happiness.

'...he walked round and round for a bit – in the middle of the floor –' It is a direction, it establishes the geography for backward children so as to give them confidence but as it is wrapped up in the story the purpose for their action is clear (as mentioned before) and it does not sound like a command that these particular children might not obey. Try to avoid a command, arrange a *fait accompli* whenever you can, in early stages with this type of child: '...as he got hotter and hotter, the dog got hotter and hotter too' – intentional building of climax, all this part, in the rhythm of a drum beat to excite them into action, for I knew by now that children divide sound into time beat, rhythm and climax. I learned this from the streets. For withdrawn children, climax is especially necessary, for the hyper-active de climax and peace.

Direct speech of a character is given occasionally but here it only heightened the story, I knew these little moles wouldn't even attempt my version of actual words. In case anyone is worried that I was sat on – this was an out of school group! In any case there was a sort of logic in it for I *was* the dish and it all had the atmosphere of games at home. Only these children didn't get games at home.

Moving swiftly on, after this: I had returned to near London, and then to London (after being Hon. Drama Advisor to Worcestershire) to try and obtain the interest of doctors in the use of drama as therapy. The results with such a lot of cases at the Arts Centre had been so successful, I thought it essential to try to get the ideas and method better known.

Doctors, at this time, were very wary of drama, particularly of imagination. They all tended to say that many of their patients had too much of it and they were always trying to damp it down. It was hard work trying to get them to use their patients' imagination and to see that one must start with people where they *are*, not where we would like them to be. It was a triumph, therefore, to be allowed to be the first person to speak on what I stated was Dramatherapy at the British Medical Association before the war. As said, though, both Dr Kraemer and I were made Foundation Members of a Jungian Society. But it was to be twenty or more years later that, to my amazement, I received a standing ovation from – of all things – a London Freudian Society.

Once in London again I was still doing a little BBC work, but teamed up with William Kraemer once more. Now that he was a full blown doctor, we started something called the Contact Club, for people who were lonely and wanted to meet others. Somehow, out of this – and partly by recommendation – came some of the first patients to this particular place, near Chalk Farm. Dr Kraemer was correctly sceptical of my ideas at first, but was won round by proof.

To start with, he would take patients in Jungian psychotherapy in one room and later they would pass on to me, I having received a little information about them. I would then suggest something to begin action (being careful not to structure a supposed problem to any degree. And generally, of course, not at all). The moment that Kraemer really began to *believe* was when, in my drama action work a patient 'broke a dream'. He suddenly remembered something considered to be of extreme importance. He then returned to Kraemer and a whole chunk of an obstacle to progress had been removed.

My own first patients seemed to be, for some reason, mostly High-ups in industry. One particular case comes to mind:

Example: He was a self-made genuinely important person, but was rather short. His problem was that he felt he spoke badly and nearly all the people under him had been to universities and 'spoke posh'. He was at a loss when he had to check them off and he felt inferior. So we embarked on a lot of scenes whereby I became progressively ruder to him (as an underling), gently inventing ways to screw up his courage. This strengthened his resolve as he got used to it. Then one day he burst in shouting, 'I've done it. I've done it.' 'Done what?' I said. 'Well, yer know all that 'orrible stuff you did on me; then one day you said 'think you are tall and stretch your 'ead to heaven and look down on the cheeky so and so's'. Well I did just that. I felt – oo, ever so tall. And I looked down on 'im (me!) and I tore 'im orf *proper*. He slunk out like a frightened puppy.'

He gave me a small fee and wanted to give me more; I never saw him again.

Conversation about this time.

LADY PATIENT: 'Oh dear, I do feel ill.'

SELF: 'Oh, I am sorry. Is it bad?'

LADY: 'Oh yes, it is, I really feel terrible.'

SELF: 'Do you want to tell me about it?'

LADY: '*Well*, you would never believe it, but my doctor says I'm not ill at all… Shall we do drama?… Your tie does look nice.'

SELF: 'You are the Queen *(fait accompli)*. Have you any orders?'

LADY: 'Yes I have. Will you please kill my doctor?'

SELF: 'All right. How?'

LADY: *(coming out of character)*

'Oo, you naughty thing!… Oh, I say, your tie does look nice… Do some more.'

SELF: *(rather firmly)*

'Your Majesty, would you please give your orders for the day?'

(She gave some and I acted as her Chamberlain. The drama was quite deep for a time and I noted carefully what commands she chose to give. Then, as often happens with neurotics, she broke back to reality again, not easily able to concentrate on one thing for long.)

LADY: 'I say, that was a help. You see, I'm never allowed to give orders at home. My husband gives them all.'

SELF: 'Well you can look upon this place as your Happy-Order-Giving-Centre, can't you?'

LADY: '*Yes...* I *can*, can't I?... No, but seriously, do you think I am ill? My doctor says I'm not. But I know I am.'

SELF: 'It doesn't matter.'

LADY: 'What *do* you mean?'

SELF: 'Well, you think you are ill and he doesn't. But if you think you are ill and you are not, you are ill anyway.'

There was a long atmospheric pause.

LADY: *(very serious, with tears in her eyes)*

'My God, you are kind. Do you know, I think that is the most lovely thing anyone has ever said to me.'

MAN PATIENT AT CONTACT CLUB: 'I don't want to *criticise*, and you know how calm I keep, but when I see Matthew and his *(getting louder)* big white hands *(louder still)* and his preaching and preaching, – if he really doesn't stop I could KILL HIM.'

KRAEMER: 'Do you feel calm now?'

MAN: 'No. Sorry, sorry, sorry. Didn't mean to *criticise*.'

SELF: 'Would you care to go further with this? Care to tell me more about it?'

MAN: 'What about it doc? Think so?'

KRAEMER: 'Yes, certainly. You might find it very helpful.'

(Man and I went into another room.)

MAN: 'Sorry about that. Sorry.'

SELF: 'That's quite all right. We all need to say things at times. If we don't speak, we pop!'

MAN: 'Oh *yes*. That's right.'

SELF: 'So what about this 'Matthew' business? Do you think it is the white hands; the fact that he talks too much and you can't; or just the name?'

MAN: *(after pause)*

'All three.'

SELF: 'Want to tell me which is the worst?'

MAN: 'I think – the white hands.'

SELF: 'Ever seen any like that before?'

MAN: 'No, never.'

We then went into exercises where I suggested he should shout as loud as he liked. He shouted the name 'Matthew' a lot. 'Hate' a lot and finally 'White Hands'. I shouted a bit and held up my hands and moved them about like Matthew. Suddenly the man stopped. 'Gosh', he said, 'I've remembered something. And I suddenly feel much better.' 'Good', I said quietly. (De-climax after the shouting.)

MAN: 'But listen, I remember coming into a greenhouse somewhere and a large man came in later. He was wearing white gloves – well creamish – and was carrying a riding crop. He thought I was going to steal plants and he beat me with the riding crop. He came at me with his whitish yellow hands to catch me. They seemed very big. I felt frightened and furious at the injustice, but didn't feel I could tell anyone about it.'

SELF: 'Well you told *me*. That's wonderful. Do you still feel better?'

MAN: 'Yes, I do. I feel much calmer.'

SELF: 'Fine. It's good to blow off steam like this. Not everyone gets the chance.'

MAN: 'No, I suppose they don't.'

SELF: 'I think you should see Dr Kraemer again for a few minutes now, before you go.'

This is the sort of thing which would happen after drama sessions. It was so helpful for any patient to be able to go between one or other of us, for I see psychotherapy, with all its symbols and sedentary situation as nearer *projected* activity, whereas my work was obviously guided *personal* play. The opportunity of receiving both – just when needed – at the same place would offer a balance of the two realms of activity and may have had something to do with our apparent rate of success.

It is interesting to note the almost text book situation of hate being transferred from a hidden and buried memory, in this case, onto the luckless Matthew (though he may have deserved some of it!).

No doubt Dr Kraemer helped to open things further and to discover whether any true annoyance attached to the name of Matthew, or whether that was incidental. My own guess would be that the annoyance at not getting a word in edgeways, when Matt was talking so much, was connected somewhat with 'I couldn't tell anyone about it' that is, being unable to talk. That must have been a pretty strong feeling when the original huge man was ranting and giving punishment without allowing the victim to put his point of view. Oh – incidentally – Matthew was large too.

Example.

LADY PATIENT: 'Oh, I am tired.'

SELF: 'Do you often feel tired?'

LADY: 'Yes, nearly all the time.'

SELF: 'Any idea why?'

LADY: 'Of course not. Why the hell should I? I wouldn't be here if I knew, would I?'

SELF: 'But you told us you didn't come for treatment, just for company with the Contact Club group.'

LADY: 'I don't remember saying that.'

SELF: 'Never mind. Do you want to talk about being tired?'

LADY: 'Oh, all right. Well, I just feel tired that's all.'

SELF: 'Have you seen a doctor about it?'

LADY: 'Yes, he's given me some pills but they don't do any good.'

SELF: 'So, you don't think it's a lack of some chemical?'

LADY: 'No, not really.'

(Pause)

SELF: 'Are you tired of anything that goes on in life?... Or fed up with a person, anybody in particular?'

LADY: 'Yes, I certainly am. What made you ask?'

SELF: 'Just wondered.'

LADY: 'Well, I'm fed up with the daily round. Fed up with going to the office. Fed up with life...and there's a man who looks at me in a way I don't like, every day, and I feel I have always got to be on guard.'

SELF: 'That must be very tiring anyway.'

LADY: 'Yes, it is.'

(Pause)

SELF: 'Well, would you like to have a little rest?'

LADY: 'Yes.'

SELF: 'All right, lie down over there, then, and close your eyes.'

She did so and I moved about, farther from her (so she would not be anxious) and put on some very quiet music. Suddenly she sat up.

'Sorry, I can't do this. I can't keep my eyes shut if there's a man in the room.'

SELF: 'Oh, I quite understand. Please don't worry. Only stay if you want to talk.'

She decided not to stay that day. It was my mistake in asking her to close her eyes. It was too soon. I should have come to it more slowly, more gently. But by what seems like (or actually is) a mistake, one can learn. In this case it showed me that there was something more deep seated than I had thought. If you don't panic, you can often obtain information about a situation. I am often telling teachers – 'If something you try doesn't work, don't immediately think you have failed. You have offered something and it has not been accepted, that's all. It tells you your class is probably not ready for that yet. Very useful information.'

This patient came back; and after many gentle steps forward and tests of courage to help her to shut eyes, first with me going out of the room, then me in the room, then longer, then with me and Dr Kraemer both in the room, she got braver. After acting a number of scenes about office life, it slowly came out that she had been what she called 'fumbled' (about with) more than once in earlier life. The way the man at the office looked at her would cause her suspicion, but I did once suggest that it might be just appreciation. That cheered her a little, I think.

> SELF: 'Do you think that part of why you feel tired all the time is because you are continually in a state of anxiety because of the past…and you cannot get rid of it and it makes you suspect everything and everyone and puts you permanently on guard? That would be extremely exhausting.'

> PATIENT: 'Yes…I think you are probably right.'

> SELF: 'Well, see how it goes. And remember that you can always come back here and either see Dr Kraemer or do some more drama, or both. If you get better, you will feel you need to be energetic, even dance. Think of that (my Hope process)!'

> LADY PATIENT: *(smiling)*
>
> 'All right. Thank you very much. I will remember.'

As people became less worried, reports began to change somewhat. Here are some parts of quite a long one, of one of my talks to a Medical Association.

> 'The adolescent may become aware of situations, which have caused his problem, but sees that the situation cannot be changed. He does not then receive strength by merely acting out scenes about his broken home, but much more so by being helped to discover through the almost dream-process of imaginative creative drama, some home which is not broken, i.e. his own possible *future*, not his past. This is what ultimately brings hope. Without this process of offering pictures of the future, or other circumstances, much psychodrama that only deals with the present troubles or past disappointments and fears is sterile. When you come to grown-ups it is much easier to apply conscious situations for acting out problems, but there is still a vast realm that would still be untouched by this. There is the evolving of what I have described elsewhere as "group sensitivity" and "group intuition", by which a person slowly becomes more concerned with the needs of other people and his relationship to society, also with the personal creation of imaginative beauty and one's personal style of dance. All these things are important to the personality and without some training in them an individual may lose much in life.

But common to all age-groups a constant danger in psychodrama is a pedantic application of symbols in dramatic form. I am more and more sure that symbols cannot always be easily and helpfully applied in this open way. They are used, certainly, in an unconscious manner, in drama of a therapeutic nature, and characters and situations can be seen to be linked with symbols. But it has not yet been fully recognised that imaginative acting is like the dream. Symbols are thrown up, but there are many parallels, which may be as it were symbols of these symbols, and through which the truth behind the original symbols is equally stumbled upon. The apparently haphazard or casually related train of events may represent a stark reality. So, it is not necessary to be too careful about including symbols in suggested scenes. Adults, and particularly children, will often include them as their state leads them to do so.

So, with all age groups we should beware of treating as of paramount importance the apparently obvious problem to be acted out. It is of importance but is not the only thing. Apart from what I have already inferred, there is no doubt a considerable realm, which will be discovered in the future connected with the "living myth". I have occasionally touched upon some outline of imaginary story, which brought a bright response from a person, and in sorting it out have perceived that the explanation of a sudden interest or unexpected re-vitalisation could have been due to a coming near what was a truly living myth for them – deep down inside. There may be important ground to be covered here between drama and Jungian Psychotherapy.'

I, of course, mentioned a lot about movement, action, balance of *personal* and *projected* play in the life style for health and the value of natural therapy through Child Drama and other Arts. But particularly (as this was an Association for Mental Care) the importance of realising how Child Drama can be used directly with mental patients to indicate 'where they are' in life, that is, at what stage of development even adults are revealed by play to be. For this of course, one must be fully aware of the stages of development which are the norm in childhood. One's frustration here is the apparent appalling ignorance of the subject, which could so easily reveal so much that we desperately need to know for the good of mental treatment. Practitioners still tend to feel that anything to do with the word 'Child' is unconnected with adulthood, however frail that grown-upness may be.

I tried to show how education, good behaviour, parental control and therapy were all linked as 'allies' and part of the same nurturing process. The Arts should be accepted and integrated for healthy inner development. The report continued:

'The arts must be integrated with the rest of education or they can become a "nuisance". But, if integrated, they bring a renewed strength unto themselves also, because the house in not divided against itself.

Mr Slade then mentioned that there was increasing interest, particularly in London, in his views on the value of drama in the process of transference. The basis of them was that by gaining personal confidence through acting, the patient either put less reliance on the psychotherapist, placed reliance for a shorter period, or helped himself to emerge from the situation with greater strength. Psychotherapists had also suggested that they saw in his method a useful and constructive way of patients making their ideas conscious between visits for treatment.

Here is another case which belongs to the pre war period, but should not be discarded merely as unimportant history. It was a pre-runner of hundreds of other cases, 'small' or 'big', which followed; and probably many unknown, where people could have been helped.

Example: This patent suffered from a stutter and had been passed on from a speech therapist, who appeared unable to help any further. I had just started a discussion and a few questions, when it became clear that an important contact had been made. The patient became rather excited, then said: 'I suddenly remember something else.' He then told a story about having had to pass a house each day on his way to school. Each day a fierce dog rushed out at him and each day he suffered agonies of fear and anxiety about this dog. The daily experience went on for a considerable period, and some time after this the stutter had started. Here was no imposed problem. This was real. We started at once, and acted at going past the gate. At first there was a considerable re-living of the situation, and some signs of genuine anxiety. But we went on and on over several weekly visits until finally came the moment for me to say: 'Now you see, you can pass the gate, can't you? The dog doesn't hurt you any more.' The stutter began to improve.

Now it would be very easy to make big claims here. At the moment I am not claiming anything. It might have been the psychotherapy that opened the door. It might have been the drama. It might have been both. I just say what happened. I do not know if there was a final cure. The patient left off coming and I did not see the end of the matter. All I know is that before the patient left I followed up these experiences with what I have called the 'Hope' situation. We acted some scenes about passing exactly the same gate in the same way. But this time there was no dog. Finally we acted a different gate, the gate of his own new home, and the patient left me in a much more calm and confident state, and the stutter was better. In this treatment, did I strike a 'living myth' early on?

After this, Dr Kraemer and I helped to start a hospital in the West Country at the beginning of the war; soon after that I was in the army.

Example: A backward squad in the war. Men who had been kicked around for not fitting in easily with army life, some not of very high intelligence, some with perhaps too much intelligence. Almost all were individualists by accident or on purpose! Their greatest and most obvious difficulty was drill. They could not keep in time. I applied two principles. First: the training in sound that I now use in Infant Schools, and second: training in 'group sensitivity' that I had formerly used with my professional actors. The first was built up by walking about separately and making 'tunes' out of individual footfalls and noises. Then, when listening ability had improved, group tunes would be created. This helped them to join together, and finally the 'tune' of the drill movement was learnt. In the group sensitivity exercises they would be asked to shut their eyes and, when in line, listen to their neighbours moving an arm up and down. Then taking a leader from either end all would try to do the same move, guessing how high the arm had been raised by listening to the sound of clothing and jingling of equipment. In time they became quite good at arriving at the same gesture together. Then they were allowed to open their eyes, and finally, by the 'tune' of their feet and their bodies, they achieved some passable drill. Our special squad was a special squad no longer. What is more, they had gathered to themselves a strong social feeling as of one group. This unity was probably as valuable for them as their individual success.

I have written elsewhere about training for dispatch riders. Part of it is relevant here. 'What the hell are you going to make 'em do, Sir?' asked my Sergeant. The answer follows. As a sort of therapy, it might help those going overseas to be happy, or at least have fun, for some moments of time before they have to go. I wanted to reduce tension.

SELF: 'Right, now we're not going to have a formal parade. You've worked hard in the last few days and I know what you feel like, hanging around this place when the job seems done. So we're going to do something which I hope you'll quite enjoy, but at the same time you will be tested fairly strenuously. So take it seriously or someone may get hurt. We are going to do a story, like in a pageant, and I want some high-class driving as well, and some of it at speed. What's the name of the hero of our Western story?' *(Laughter and some applause.)*

We finally settled for Jakes Heslop. And the hero-ine (they would pronounce it as rhyming with 'wine') was Legs Amour. After some men had been sent to bring some motor cycles, I started one fair-sized group rather like one would in an Infant school – not by casting immediately, but by letting everyone play each part.

SELF: 'Jakes Heslop leaps onto his steed.' *(Each man leapt onto his motor cycle.)*
'He wants to get onto that hill-top there, to see if any Injuns are about.
He digs in his spurs and off flies Brown Bess.'

(All cycles except one started up and wobbled away at different speeds to the top
of a mound. Several knocked into each other slightly on purpose.)

'Flaming ruddy _____ !' said my Sergeant, 'you'll have a _____ massacre in a
minute, Sir.'

'Maybe,' I answered, 'but not the way you mean.' Then to the men (through a
megaphone): 'Right, come back, you lot.' They returned, slightly sheepishly.

SELF: 'Off the bikes! Next lot, you have a try, and don't bash into each other or
   . the Indians may see you. Worse still, *I* might see you. You know our
rule here. You'll be scalped pretty quick if I see any of that again.'

This went down quite well; the second lot saw we were serious beneath the fun and
made a passable get-away to the top of the mound.

SELF: 'Jakes Heslop looks round. He can't see anything at first, but suddenly he
catches sight of a thin cord of smoke rising to the sky. He watches carefully and sees a skulking figure coming towards him – that's you lot.'

(I indicated some of the others who were not yet in the story. Most of them took to
it quite well, a couple sniggered a bit and held onto each other for brotherly mar-
tial support, but a few threw themselves to the ground and alternately wormed or
stalked their way closer to the conglomeration of noise and smoke that passed for
Brown Bess.)

'You two'll get a _____ poison dart in your backsides, if you don't stop sniggering
and get fell in,' interjected the Sergeant helpfully, and just to show he was conversant.

SELF: 'Jakes takes a quick shot at the Indian.'

(Several different noises were made here, one or two the same as children make.)

'The Indian falls, but Jakes, realising he's short of ammunition thinks
it's time to scarper. So he revs up Brown Bess, aims for the thin piece of
rock there – that plank will do, over the ditch – and makes for base as
fast as possible.'

All those being Jakes started off well, sorted themselves out very creditably and
flew in single file, with only one skid, over the plank, down the farther mound
and back to me. As the dust and smoke of these modern khaki Besses rose from
the semi-circle in front of me, I felt the old thrill of the theatre and had to
restrain myself from cocking my hat on one side and flashing my badge like a
sheriff, confronted by his posse. I noticed two Injuns still dying in agony under
the withering watchfulness of Sgt B.

On these sort of lines we worked for about forty minutes, changing the
groups, changing character, making the tests more difficult until remarkable
absorption set in. The men really tested themselves too, and seemed to attain a
certain extra dash and courage by flinging themselves into the simple story. By

this time I judged that they had, what, in an Infant school, I would nowadays call, 'reached their dawn of seriousness', and were ready for casting. I sat them all down, chose my cast and discussed the story and situation with them. They suggested some very remarkable tests. Out of what they suggested I built my final story:

> 'Some old campaigners, who have been set upon by Injuns already, enter slowly from the left there. They no longer have horses. Almost at once they are spotted by another band of Injuns (on bikes) who swoop down from the mountains (mounds) and start to circle round the old campaigners, shooting as they go. Luckily, Heslop is riding through the ranges at the right moment, whistling as he goes. He sees what is happening and starts a stampede of wild horses – that's you men, all of you who are not in it yet. I want you to charge as if you'd met Jerry in the village – between mounds one and two. Sorry we haven't enough bikes to go round. You scatter the Injuns, who leap off their steeds and hide behind rocks. As soon as the stampede has passed through, Heslop leads an attack by the campaigners on the dismounted Injuns. They overcome them – now, no bashing up of anybody; just shoot 'em with an imaginary gun, or stick 'em through with a spear that isn't there – and seize their horses. Then, with much jubilation, they make for the nearest small town and its saloon.'

We invented quite a floor show in the saloon and the story was somewhat held up whilst one soldier sang, in a rich Irish tenor, one of our favourite songs. 'But the real reason why Jakes Heslop had come to town, you remember, was to see Legs Amour', I interjected hastily before another encore threatened. We were able to leave the saloon then. The singer was chosen for the Amour woman, and I shall never forget the way his bike was managed. He sort of put it on like a pair of high-heeled shoes and veritably minced out of the saloon on it in a most voluptuous manner, by judiciously turning his steering wheel from one side to the other in a gentle sway. It was terrific. Jakes and Amour 'embraced' by driving slowly towards each other and stopping dead in the right place, side by side, so that an outstretched arm from each passed across the battledress breast of the other. A mixture between a traffic cop signal and a spaceman's salute. It was stylised, balletic, fascinating. 'Finally they agree to marry and the sheriff holds a party and all the township dance.'

Here I stopped things a minute.

> SELF: 'I'm not sure of this bit, I just want to try something out. What I really want is for you all to drive over the top of that line of air raid shelters, up down, up down, up down, then come back here to the centre.'

I borrowed a bike and tried it myself. It was just as I hoped. One *could* get up onto the roof mound at one end of the line, drive along the top, drop down the far side, and by cutting the throttle back hard and applying a gentle brake for a yard or so, then letting it free, could float up again almost to 'fall' on the momentum of the machine to the top of the next mound in a rhythmic gliding dance, like children running over roads and pavements in the heart of big cities, or rather, like their dream of what they are doing when they do it.

So that, after a fashion, is what we all finally did. We, who had bikes, went rhythmically over the roofs of the shelters, and then we danced on the flat ground by swaying our machines in a sort of waltz, driving across and between each other, whilst some men without bikes did a sort of jiving knees up in the middle. All the others sang the Blue Danube to a ghastly raucous wailing 'dah' and beat on their mess tins for drums. The sound, the concentration, the sweating men, the excitement and dexterity all seemed to ascend to Heaven in an incense of powdered blue exhaust, which billowed its way up to the stars and Him who watched, climbing a pale Jacob's ladder of light from the evening sun.

'Christ, Sir,' broke in my Sergeant, 'I should never have believed it. Did you see little Candy Tuft *(a pale carrot-headed Scot)* take that bridge? 'E's never dared do it like that before. Did you see it?' I did and had. 'Oh well, Sir, I always did say "try anything once". Whatever we do in this crummy joint and 'owever much we _____ up Kings Regulations, we always 'ave the shine on your belt.'

I never quite see the logic of this remark when I have thought of it since, particularly as I was in battle dress. But it seemed entirely appropriate at the time. Perhaps it was a sort of symbol, a kind of poetry by mistake, for it held for both of us a deeper meaning than the words themselves convey.

This is one of so many examples of – when a story situation is there, daring increases. I have seen it so often. Thus Candy Tuft suddenly became a motorbike hero. Let us wish Godspeed to all who have to train in a very short time for this brave and dangerous work of dispatch rider, whatever method is used.

Something similar happened when I was taking patients in a hospital later; with leg and arm injuries they were likely to suffer pain during convalescence and were often being urged by the staff to exercise the limb. During the spontaneous work I started with them it was noticeable that once really absorbed in the drama, the situation, they would forget the pain, running a step or two, catching a cannon ball (tennis ball) and throwing a javelin (walking stick), such is the way we are made. The physical pain, without the drama, can sometimes be cruel.

Battle Stress, shell shock, experience-horror, whatever you like to call it is very real. To get over it, the mind distances itself from reality. Unreality is a womb to climb into. But as a person gets better there comes a sort of mixture – rather like in childhood. I think the following piece shows hope that reality is being found again and possibly welcomed.

Example: An officer undergoing treatment, used to come for dramatherapy. One day he said: 'The escape is tomorrow. Will you see that the boat is there? I can cross the river and get away from this place.'

'But the boat is there *now*,' I answered, 'over there, look. Why don't you take it?' He went over to the far side of the room, and, looking at me very suspiciously, climbed into the boat that was not there. I got in too and we paddled and rowed until we were exhausted. This went on and on at each of our times together. Finally he said to me one day with a slow apologetic grin: 'There isn't really any boat is there?' 'No', I answered, 'there's no boat except in your hope and in your wishes.' 'No boat', he repeated. Then very brightly: 'Christ, but I feel better. I wouldn't have missed that rowing together for anything.'

The build-up after treatment is so important but quite often it seems that nobody has much time for it. Perhaps none at all.

Example: This is concerned with preparation for life outside hospital again. After physical treatment – such as electric shock therapy, insulin or drugs – the patient often appears to be better, but in a way has been brought down to par. He is simple, rather childlike and lacking in confidence. (The same might almost be said of some cases after psychotherapy.) It always seems to me of paramount importance that confidence should be restored. The job is not finished until it has been! A person may be able to remember how to make a journey again, but still be afraid to get on a bus in case of not counting money properly. A person may be able to stand up and walk again, but may not have the courage to buy a lipstick, or razor blades. This last occurs sometimes with men patients who have at one time had their razors taken away from them whilst in hospital. They would probably take care not to admit it. My method here is almost exactly the same as I would use under the heading of Social Drama in Secondary and Grammar Schools (or those now outside LEAs). It is a question of practising the events of life and becoming master of them, sometimes before they happen. With young people at school, one gets them to answer telephones, take messages, go through the business of an interview with their boss, give polite and efficient service in shops, enter a cafe and order tea. With patients, after treatment, one can help to build up confidence about life in exactly the same way. A Major who had walked about in his uniform for weeks and who never seemed to speak to anyone, came to see me twice and never said a word. Later he came again and did a little drama, but not co-operating very well. Then one day he said: 'Can I tell you something? I feel I can tell you somehow, I couldn't tell the doctors.' 'Of course,' I answered, expecting some fearful revelation. 'Well, it sounds silly really,' went on the Major, 'but I have been walking about, now I'm allowed out, with a box of cigarettes in my pocket, but I can't use 'em because I daren't go and buy a box of matches. And I've got so wound up with it now that I can't ask anybody for one.' 'Is that all?' I said, 'ask me.' Finally he did and I gave him his match. We then started a little drama about entering a shop. I would be every kind of shop-keeper, cheerful, kindly, off-hand and finally tough. The Major triumphed. He went on and on until he was quite sure that he could go in and buy a box for himself in the fearful outside world. Just before he left hospital, he said to me: 'You know I shall always think you did more to get me well than all those b_____ doctors. I don't think I should ever have got out of this place but for you.' This is the sort of moment when the lay therapist is tempted to give way to pride and joy of quite the wrong kind. It must be resisted at all costs. 'No, no,' I answered, 'you mustn't think that, we've all helped to get you well. But for the doctors you wouldn't have been well enough to come to me, and in the end it was you yourself who had the courage to face life again.'

I do profoundly hope that this preparation, for life after hospital, will one day be accepted as a regular form of treatment. I believe this part of dramatherapy to be not only a necessary part of helping to ensure the hoped-for cure, but a matter of human kindness. It is not just, to allow people to suffer the final humiliation of anxiety over such trivial matters on the threshold of freedom, when a little imaginative treatment could help them. I wish there were more centres to train people in this work. It is not difficult and it is extremely interesting. The layman has his uses, if he works hand in hand with the specialist, and it is greatly to be hoped that the future will bring further opportunities of extending the use of that art, which is drama the doing of life, and by which man assumes various roles until he finally discovers who and what he really is.

As said, in this chapter, the examples of patients' reports and descriptions of method are now placed in chronological order. So now we are back at children.

Art in Make-Up

This is arrived at rather by considering the face as a flat plane, and when a make-up is rushed through in order to start rapidly on *personal* play, often the front of the face only is coloured and half the sides are left bare. Only a flat frontal view, easy to see in the glass or through a companion's eyes, has been considered. This is far from confined to children though; one has seen many adult actors who have forgotten that we must not see the mechanics of their art, leaving a hard edge of make-up at the side of their face or neck.

Children help each other with make-up, and paint their companion's faces just like a canvas. They may use all sorts of things – burnt cork is an old trick, but generally adult imposed – boot polish, pencils, wall paint – anything may be seized upon. These are examples of making the best of a bad job; they may go on often without our knowing it, and be the cause of perplexing skin troubles. Perhaps we should provide more materials.

An adult making-up a child generally does it in a quite different way, often for somewhat different reasons. The mental attitude is not the same, particularly the mental 'Art attitude'. The make-up is generally devised for productions on a stage, whereas Child make-up, whether pertaining to *personal* or *projected* play, is intended to be seen at close range in a Land where drama is all about you. Too early an impact of adult stage make-up (as opposed to street make-up) will shatter the child's own attempts, and we may never see the occasional wonders of pattern, which rock our grown-up self-satisfaction by their overwhelming dignity of association with things fundamental; most of our make-up is merely trivial and representational. The type of make-up used in ballet would seem to resemble most nearly the best older Child work. But then this is nearer the Children's Land, in many respects, and is the most fresh of our adult arts.

Typical of the pictorial approach to make-up (with a rather unhappy child) is the following: I was sitting at a table opposite a little girl of seven and a half who had been drawing. I said: 'You've got a lovely mark just under your nose.'

CHILD: 'Oh, have I? Let's see.'

She rushed to a mirror, made a face and rubbed off the mark. Then she stared at herself, and with her blue pencil drew a line just where she had rubbed out the original line. She turned to me to see what I would say.

SELF: 'That's smart. Do you like that line?'

CHILD: 'Yes.'

She pulled a face to fit in with the line, then started on a small piece of acting. The line just happened to fit in with a natural shadow, so perhaps suggested realism and *personal* play. But the fascination of this new thing was too much – the child returned to the mirror. She stared for some time, then slowly drew, with ordinary pencil, a flag with a cross on it on her forehead and another on one cheek. On the other cheek she drew a blue line. She drew a red stripe on her nose, then a cross, then a blue line under her lower lip, and finally a circle on her chin. She then laughed delightedly. I shared the delight. Then she rubbed off the marks on her nose and the two flags (note: All the clear 'pattern' marks). What was left were the simple swift lines in natural places. She stared again, then rubbed off the circle on her chin. This left only the blue shadows. *Personal* play started at once. The child walked fiercely round the room. Then suddenly: 'Oh, dear, I suppose I'd better wash.'

SELF: 'Yes, I think you'd better. Did you enjoy that?'

CHILD: 'Yes. It was the wonderfullest thing of *all* day today.'

If make-up is discovered late it is nearly always bad at first, as we would expect, as years of missed practice, discovery and judgement have to be caught up with.

By then the child is well on with *personal* play and acting things out. This may go far into adolescence, although we often hear the older child ask pathetically, 'Is that all right?' of a wash which is very bad indeed. But such a child has missed the Summer of Child Art, perhaps, and may not have been aware of make-up by seven years or so, which might have been an added happy experience.

Puppets and Marionettes

So many people ask about these that a short section on the subject is included. Puppets can be of immense interest, and become an absorbing part of Child creation. There are, however, certain difficulties about them. But let us take the things in favour first.

In Favour

Puppets encourage concentration. Long periods of constructive play can take place with them.

Their very toy-likeness makes them beloved. There are many trials of behaviour to be obtained by play with them.

They provide a valuable incentive for playing out violent themes, difficult themes, themes that pertain to personal fears.

Older Children can find out a great deal about stage performance by them, also stage production.

They teach about colour, design and organisation. There is an obvious connection with crafts of many kinds.

Puppets can take the place of companions, brother or sister.

They teach patience. They can aid speech.

They stimulate imagination and become thereby a source of inventiveness.

They can be useful for aiding shy children, who will only begin to 'live' through puppets or speak through puppets, or speak and live when hidden behind puppets or puppet stages.

They can aid us with 'difficult' children, as well as aid these children themselves. Periods of release and temporary co-operation either with other children, with adults, or both, may become apparent during Play.

Puppets can become life-like in one sense, but are seldom actually 'photographic' to look at, and so are nearer Child Art.

They are often genuine products of Child Art.

They are the living essence of *projected* play and can be, therefore, very valuable treasures for the best adventures into life experiences, in the sense that all these terms have been used and described in this book.

They can be used as a half-living visual aid to many educational subjects. In recent times we have had the delights of 'Sesame Street' and the 'Muppets', who brought us messages about numbers and letters on TV in the most loveable way.

Against

They are often too ready-made; in a way, often too glamorous. This implication will be understood if the earlier suggestions about the clear relationship between happiness and creation, arising out of the child's ascetic sense, have been understood. Apart from this, most of the drawbacks are connected with the lack of understanding on the part of the adult.

Puppets often become a sort of fetish. If this happens, it is quite possible for children to become arrested in the doll stage.

The adventures of *personal* play are renounced; in shy children quietly avoided. The children spend far too much time in *projected* play and can become quiet, wide-eyed and odd, instead of healthily using their whole bodies, speaking out as themselves, or courageously and personally being different people (*personal* play). And, although shy children can obtain cover enough for release and build up confidence with puppets, too much use of them brings the habit of seeking cover, which is the very opposite of this.

In addition, we often find continual concentration on one body position, which causes round shoulders and drooping head. The other position, as from underneath, is better, but the whole body is cramped.

The workers of puppets can never be quite sure whether audience reaction is the result of success or failure in achievements. Both can be entertaining in a puppet show. This can lead to a slapdash attitude.

There is (by reason of adult handling, suggestion and imposition) too much stress on audience and show. This is foreign to the best in Child Drama, and, by overdoses of the wrong kind of puppetry, the delights of Child Drama, even the attitude necessary for it, are pushed farther away. We have seen earlier how one of the beauties of Child Drama is the immense concentration on immediate creation and the desire to participate, which often makes audience redundant. Despite concentration on the puppet and his part, there comes an over consciousness of audience too often and too early, where too much puppetry is done.

Using Puppets

As well as too much feeling of 'show', the adult often unthinkingly introduces the proscenium form and conceptions of theatre, as differentiated from dramatic play, far too soon.

The proscenium puppet theatre will *really* be more correct for thirteen years upwards and even the script play.

From the earliest employment of puppets, full consideration should be given to the child's ability to make things. Puppets are often more loved if made by children, and the organic development of Art and of Crafts is not so upset as when ready-made puppets are given out.

With older children we should expect the dolls to be really well made, and shoddy workmanship should be challenged. Work of thirteen years upwards is more like adult standard. But do not be harsh, and do not hurry anything. Encourage. Differentiate between the swiftly made toy and an important piece of craftsmanship at this age.

Teach history – particularly costume, setting and manners – by puppets and marionettes, with older children.

Watch for any disinclination, though. Strings may not be used for dangling, they may be wound round. There may be a desire to pick up and fondle the doll. Allow this. It is important affection, and may anyway be a smoothing over from concentration on the doll as actor, to use of doll as mere treasure in wider Drama. The doll's master may now be going to become the actual actor (*personal* play). This is healthy and, probably more important.

Any frustration of *personal* play, as just described, starts the arresting of the child in the doll stage, and localising of dramatic play. Either in glove puppets or dangled dolls, any set habit of this kind is very difficult to eradicate.

If you come upon a group of children bound in a habit of puppets and experiencing no other drama, forms of liberation may be discovered by finding space *somewhere*. Spread children out, suggest picking up of dolls, stimulate drama by story, singing, sounds, music or mere running. Dolls will become treasures, or will even be discarded. For 'bad cases' of permanent glove puppetry, try a puppet on one or both hands. Find space if you can and start simple dance or play with children spread out. I have known children dance happily about with a puppet on each hand, but slowly discard one, then the other, and finally, with bursts of energy, enter with happy liberation into the free *personal* play of full Child Drama and normality.

With older children, when judged ready for manipulation, more strings can be used with dolls. They can walk about the floor just like other people, and chat. Do not always send the puppets to prison in a rotten little theatre box. Immense and wonderful crowd scenes all about the room can take place, either with forests of glove puppets held high, or with manipulated 'people' (marionettes). Look out for interesting examples of the circle and equi-distance in this crowd work. We have a mixture here of *personal* play and the patterns of carefully placed objects found always in *projected* play.

So, in conclusion – do not let your own mind be cramped by puppets and marionettes, or your own vision of Drama as a whole be limited, either by them or by one sort of theatre connected with them.

Puppets can be of value, but their value is limited. They can be done without, though they can be a pleasant enrichment of experience if used with discretion. They are not as important as the child itself acting. It will often use dolls during play, and in fact thereby use puppets according to the natural laws of its own Drama. Dolls are discarded in time and are not used all the time. That is as it should be. Avoid becoming sentimental about puppets, saying, without due thought of children, 'But they love them so'. Children love anything that gives them joy. So they love puppets, but they love Child Drama more; and, not altogether unimportant – it is better for them, both physically and mentally. It offers more opportunities.

The success of the Muppets came about, not only because of their wonderful invented characters, in different situations, but because of their *precision* in linking words, 'thought' and movement in such an exact way. This is what gives these extraordinary 'people' such reality. We had never seen such high perfection in these things before, and it is what we should put to our children as criteria to aim for. Too many puppets (particularly glove type), even on TV, still jig and shake about in a mad unthoughtful way. It is lazy thinking. Do not allow this. It does not do much to keep the very young child's attention, it only teaches bad habits.

Child Talk

Words of a disturbed child who suffered from headaches. On her seventh birthday:

> 'My face was covered with water and you couldn't see it and they opened me up and took *everything* away and then put seven years inside and closed me up again and a block on my head. And when it was lifted it was all *new*. Isn't it lovely? But I am still me.'

CHILD: *(age six years)*
> 'Oh, I'm unhappy. I've got a very hot ear.'

ADULT: 'Oh that means a friend is thinking well of you. Which of your friends do you think it is?'

CHILD: 'Well, you are my friend.'

ADULT: 'Oh yes. I was thinking well of you.'

CHILD: 'Well, do stop.'

Wonderful selfish bluntness of a distressed child *in* distress.

When something unexpected happens and a child is shocked, they often cannot say anything at first or speak about it. I have sometimes found, though, that those who have had practice in drama and developed *language flow* find it easier. They are unplugged.

Example:

> CHILD (7): *(in a very difficult state)*
>> 'Did you know _____ was a naughty man?'
>
> MOTHER: 'No, what did he do?'
>
> CHILD: 'He hit a woman.'
>
> MOTHER: 'Oh, he must have been drunk. But very few men are like that.'
>
> CHILD: 'It broke my heart. Down the lane it was, near the Church, so I thought of God.'
>
> MOTHER: 'Yes, darling.'
>
> CHILD: 'Why didn't you know he was naughty? Miss _____ knows. I went into her house and she took me across the fields to the post office and I lay on the sofa.'
>
> MOTHER: 'Did you cry?'
>
> CHILD: 'No, but I wished I was with you. Why did you leave me? I am never going to leave you again.'

The unfortunate thing was that this child had made great friends with the man, and he assaulted a woman in front of her. It broke down her confidence in human beings and made her frightened and obstinate at the least command or suggestion. The following was, perhaps, a sort of continued bravery, and kind of bravado. She met the man in the post office later and said. 'I'm not afraid of you.' She is none-the-less afraid of everything and everyone now, but covers it up when she can. At least her habit of *language flow* helped her to pour out the first part of the problem. She had quite forgotten (in 'why did you leave me?') that she was the one who always disobediently ran down the drive away from her mother. After telling her story, the child wept and seemed to be better for it.

Treatment (to try), would be a lot of Child Drama, in case there was anything further to come out, plus painting pictures. *Not* many questions. This is a common mistake. Ultimately the hope process would be gradual, occasional suggestion that we should play with nice people today. 'There *are* some.' Building then to a man friend who could be trusted, though the dream-trust built up through play would be but a beginning; the reality-trust would take much longer. But if play is *not* used, the scar will not heal. If the scar does heal, the memory of the event may still be there. But our objective would be that it should no longer hurt. This is what *can* happen and time and again does. At the very least, constructive, well guided play would bring relief.

CHILD(6.5): *(declaiming)*

> 'I am the wickedest one. I whip all the people in pink *(noticing her baby sister, and then hurriedly)* – except babies. *(Self defence coming in)*: I am wearing pink and red, but that is a uniform.' *(So **obviously** that is different.)*
>
> *(She was wearing her mother's dressing gown.)*

ADULT: *(bringing child's attention to breakfast)*

> 'Will you have some royal treacle on your porridge?'

CHILD: *(not yet wanting to stop acting because of being fairly well in the part)*

> 'That is not royal treacle.'

ADULT: *(far too wary to be caught in **this** argument, in which she would undoubtedly be outwitted, tries another tack. There is something green behind the treacle and this shows through it, as it is poured from the spoon, changing its colour)*

> 'It's green treacle.'

CHILD: *(not going to give in just yet, but beginning to smile)*

> 'No, it is shamrock colour. It comes from a speshull island, the island is called...*(remembering)* Doblin.'

That is the only word in her mind related to that particular adult. Having, as she thought, proved her point, the child felt more confident. She then sat down at once and ate up her porridge quite happily.

It may be wondered why this child was not told to sit down straight away. But this little girl was a particular case, and the adult knew by now (and understood) the importance of *near-finish*. The child had had certain experiences whilst away from home, which were very unfortunate, and these, together with too much scolding and a slight backwardness in simple school work, had tended to make her lose confidence in herself. By allowing her full advantage of play and opportunities for *language-flow*, she is becoming happy and balanced again. Obedience is slowly returning, by avoiding wherever possible a direct command, which might arouse a defensive opposition.

The actual words used, though interesting in themselves, often reveal a great deal about general background. If we never encourage *language-flow*, there is much that we shall never know about children. We will not be able to unplug many of their deepest feelings. In the realms of education, this lack makes the friendly bond between child and teacher very difficult to build. Without this bond there is much that can never be accomplished, and, on the even more practical side, it makes the control of large classes very much more difficult. Of course, we know that children who find learning difficult and who disrupt class teaching, make more difficulties for *themselves* (as well as others) in the general learning process.

In the whole of life, the ability to express, at least to some degree, what is boiling away inside us – or just bubbling – is of extreme importance. In marriage failure, a main cause is often simply that the habit of open-ness is not there and the couple end up by finding it impossible to speak to one another about what is the matter. The wall has grown up and they are in a prison of growing hate.

A recent survey indicates that young children who watch too much TV become stultified in their ability to speak and have even been believed deaf. They hear other people, or 'creatures' do it, but don't bother to do it themselves. Their vocabulary remains, no doubt, very limited and their 'flow' does not exist. Verbal communication should be encouraged from the beginning, together with training about moments to keep silent.

With modern discoveries about fluoride and other things (and despite the charge on visits to the dentist at the moment), one hopes that the state of children's teeth is improving. But there may still be some fear about visiting for treatment. There certainly used to be. I had a recording of an improvisation about it, by Junior children, which went to many parts of the World. It showed fear, glee, but also compassion. Remarks in it still remain in my mind. Overplay of an adult voice being patronising: 'It wont 'urt you, dear, just sit there and be calm. It will soon be over.'

Once the patient had been 'put under'.

NURSE: *(to Dentist, with a certain amount of glee)*

    'Now's your chance to pull them out!' *(When the patient wakes up we hear)* 'Did it hurt?'

CHILD: *(firmly)* 'Yes.'

NURSE: *(as complacent adult, uninterested really in the child's words)*

    'That's only your dream, dear. That's only your d-r-e-a-m.'

The record ends with a little conversation with me saying something like:

SELF: *(quietly)*

    'Is it really like this?'

CHILDREN: *(also quietly and with great sincerity)* 'Ye-es.'

The recording was a valuable example of the way in which children play out fears and what upsets them in our adult attitude. They also use drama to spit out what has shocked, upset them or led them to violent and evil thoughts and behaviour. I wish many more people would realise how valuable, important and helpful this is. It might be worthy of note that when this record was played at courses, adults nearly always laughed. (We often look down on children, as either a nuisance, or fun.) I used to play part of the record again and get them to listen in a different way. Will we never learn?

I think the recording is probably in the Archive Department of the University of Manchester. Despite being a touching and outstanding example of the way Juniors find release, I could have exemplified many other such scenes about dentists, doctors and hospitals. Rather more violent scenes mostly, from boys-only groups. One I remember.

SELF: 'I hope they didn't really knock you out with a cricket bat.'

And to another group *(with a smile)*:

'Did they really cut your leg off with an axe? It looks all right now. They put it back rather well.'

BOY: 'No. But that is what it felt like, it 'urt so. And they wouldn't believe me.'

Constructive Forgetting

School for the Unhappy

Unhappy only because of home background, inability to learn fast, or physical complications. Otherwise, at A.E. Tansley's school, happiness was a main objective. He had been concerned with visual image, tracking, space relationships too. Reason: Some patients understand about movement, but their bodies will not carry out their mental intentions, whilst others have quite capable bodies but their minds cannot give the command.

A number of tests were made, therefore, on balance and overcoming simple obstacles. One child had improved to the extent of being able to balance on an upturned bench and walk along it. But it was still rather cautious. I was asked in to comment. My suggestion was to invent *reasons* for doing these things. By giving purpose to exercises, delight was increased and speed of achievement also. Walking faster along the bench to get a magic bun at the end was quite different from walking cautiously along it as a dead exercise. Others then wanted to try. A child who could hardly lift an arm was put in charge of the 'buns'. On several occasions he was able to raise an arm and dole them out. One child, who had never been seen to run, ran half way across a room to 'catch an ice cream van' and avoided two obstacles on the way (see Slade in Schattner and Courtney 1981).

It had been years earlier that I suggested, when speaking to a physical education conference, that nervous children would climb faster and higher if in a cop chase, or as a Sheriff catching outlaws. It is so much more interesting to have a reason and a purpose. Once involved, we can overcome some of the things that usually impede. This unexpected sense of victory must eventually go into the unconscious as a hope-habit. I would put the process under the label of Constructive Forgetting.

Forgetting Unhappiness

A forlorn little group at a clinic was introduced to me. All five of these had pretty awful home conditions and they all rubbed their eyes a lot.

I have noticed this in disturbed children quite often. In fact, the eyes can tell us a considerable amount about the depth of child disturbance. The skin under the eye changes and a sort of owl's skin comes over the main eye, as if a candle behind it has gone out. I always watch the skin under the eye for first signs of improvement.

SELF: 'Anyone want to say anything?'

I lay down on my back and looked at the ceiling, so they wouldn't have to look at me. I guessed they would not speak otherwise. They didn't yet anyway.

(Silence)

SELF: 'Mmmm, I agree.'

There was a teddy bear nearby. A thought began to come to me.

(Silence)

SELF: (suddenly)

'My goodness, did you hear what that bear said to me?' I sat up. I looked at one small boy. He shook his head a little.

SELF: 'Anyone else hear?...No?...(in a very quiet voice) Well, all of you come round close to me and I'll tell you.'

(They crept round)

SELF: 'He said – you've got a pink nose and we don't like people like that here. Big ears, yes. Pink noses, no.'

A LITTLE BOY SAID: 'Mary's got a pink nose (true).'

MARY: 'So've you.'

Well, they all had pink noses come to that and I don't think I had. (It was only Teddy who thought so.) I breathed a sigh, the ice had been broken.

After that things began to go a bit and we went to the sea side. Only one knew what that meant. We built castles and knocked them down. (Important for anger and I noticed the particular type of noise.) We paddled. We came off the beach and ate ice creams. We roller skated to get them moving (they had seen that in the streets). Then we went into an arcade with funny mirrors that made us look peculiar. Things were picking up now. Invention was pretty fair.

SELF: 'One mirror is very special. You are looking into it, when suddenly the funny shape beckons to you.'

(Two children now lifted an arm and beckoned, as if to be sure that their mirror image was doing the right thing.)

'The mirror person beckons you right through into another LAND.'

(I was longing for music, but today there wasn't any.)

'In this land is wonderful sunshine, there are the most wonderful trees and flowers and animals. Just move about as long as you like, enjoying this different place.'

They did so slowly and for quite a time. Only the sound of an occasional sniff and the heavy breathing of young children when involved in anything important.

SELF: 'Pick a flower or a piece of fruit, if you like it a lot. *(Near finish beginning to be arranged.)* Now you feel you are being d-r-a-w-n back to where the mirror was. Yes, oh, you have to squeeze back through it, oh…and there you are all "peculiar" again. Sit quietly down *(de-climax)* and rest. You look down; and those of you who picked a special flower or fruit, see it is still there. So it *is* true. There *is* a special Land better than this one. Don't forget that.'

One little girl put her hand into mine. I looked round. All was that wonderful silence I love so much.

'Darlings', I whispered. 'I will come again and we will go to that Land again…and again. But don't forget we have to be very brave and come back through the mirror. But we get warmer (getting louder) and stronger each time we come back. Now just before I go – take a paint brush and a big pot of paint and paint your name all across the clouds – NOW! That's right, move all down the room. Your name needs to be big because *you* are important. We all are. Did you know that?… Well done. What interesting clouds! All those lovely important names.'

Then, 'Oh, do you know the name of that land?' *(They look a bit puzzled. I waited for an answer. Speech may take some time to flow.)* 'It is the Land of Hope.'

A different story. My turn to wonder. I went to an Infant School and was asked if I would take a try with a certain class. After I had said yes, the Head kindly added. 'They are completely out of hand. We don't know what to do with them. See what you can do.' Encouraging.

They came in and the noise was enormous. They didn't actually hit each other, but their behaviour was extraordinary. 'Not human. Hyperactive mad monkeys' were the first words that came into my head.

Next came: 'Slade, they are out of hand, aren't they?'

SLADE: 'Yes.'

'Know what to do?'

'No.'

'So what are you *going* to do?'

'Haven't the faintest idea. Probably nothing.'

Then a near miracle happened. I continued to sit absolutely still. One or two children noticed me and very slowly the noise subsided until almost quiet, then quiet – except for the breathing.

I can only imagine that they were so unused to being in a room where an adult did not shout at them automatically that they came round, first in curiosity, then perhaps with amazement. For that is what happened. After a few moments,

I was surrounded by a flock of quiet little birds (no longer mad monkeys) wondering what I was going to do or say.

I don't remember what I said or what we did. I only remember the experience. And I record it in case it is of any encouragement to those who teach, or practice play therapy. We can all be at a loss at times. We learn very slowly what we really ought to do. One way, though, of dealing with this sort of situation, I have learnt, is to make one very big bang. It must be louder than all their noise. In the one surprised moment of silence that (I have always been lucky enough to find) follows – YOU SPEAK!

Must Win

Example: Worse than the above, sometimes the therapist, in a one-to-one situation, may suddenly realise they are going to be attacked, even by a Junior Child. The only thing one can sometimes manage is to let them come, catch them and hug them. This hug must be strong and may seem like hours. You have got to hang on and you have to win. If you believe in prayer, pray. Because you are locked in a moment of evil intent and it *must not happen.*

If you let go, you could be seriously hurt and also, once having 'won', the child will try it again. Hang on for dear life and, with luck, the little person will suddenly go limp, try to slip away, probably on to the floor. There may then be a bit of screaming, but more likely some sobbing. A secret may then be imparted about why it happened.

Junior Girl at Rea Street Centre

We had been taking in numerous children one night per week and letting them play out anything they liked. Some of the stories were rather upsetting. One dear little creature played out a terrible tale, then went to sit on a rostrum block somewhat exhausted. I felt she needed comfort, so I quietly sat on the same block next to her. We both looked front, down the hall, into distance. I was careful not to look at her yet. Then came the moment that I have often mentioned. Very quietly, I said, 'Is this your life?'

GIRL: 'Yus, this is me life, this is me dark dream.'

After a little further near-whispered talk, in the semi-darkness, I offered her the opportunity to come to the centre and play out her dark dream whenever she liked and hoped that one day we could move to a dream that would be a happy one.

We always had low lighting for these evenings at Rea Street. Lighting is very important and the setting of it has to be just right for the successful promotion of fullest confidence.

Of course there is a whole world of coloured light to be more deeply investigated. The effect of colour on different individuals is fascinating, as is the eating of cheese and/or chocolate on boisterous behaviour. Even hyperactivity on a windy day.

A Hazardous Adventure

Morning, at a centre for those hard to educate, Birmingham, undated.

A SMILING HOSTESS: 'Well, here we are, Mr Slade. What are you going to do? I don't know what you will be *able* to do with us, but here we are.'

She took me round and told some young people I was a visitor. Some able to take a little notice, some not at all, some too much.

One lad (fair sized) very affectionate, followed hostess round — like a pony. Sometimes she turned and gave an affectionate, gentle tug at his tuft of hair. He loved this and gurgled with laughter. After inspection and careful 'take-in', with every kind of group, always start: 'Where are these people in life?' Make your mental note.

SELF: *(suddenly)* 'Can they cross a road?'

ANSWER: 'Sometimes, not always.'

SELF: 'Well, let's practice, then.'

With help of staff, all lined up.

From now on, I can write things up more fully from the notes, for the experience is strongly in my memory.

Patiently, we got them all in a row and then patiently, all holding hands. This was to stop some of them turning round the wrong way. I and the staff were dispersed along the row. I extricated myself and joined two other hands together beside me.

SELF: 'This is a road.'

'This — from here *(pause for slow walk)* to here — is a road.'

'A road.'

'This is a pavement. Pavement. *(I walked along the row smiling.)* Pavement.'

'You are on the pavement'

(I showed a crack on the edge of a floor board for the kerb).

'We will cross the road'

(some hunched their shoulders, excited).

'Look right — that way. All — that way.'

(It took a bit of time. The staff were very helpful.)

'Now — that way'

(the other, it also took time).

'Now — that way again — that way'

(gently again).

'That way. That way. That way. Good.'

'Now we will cross. I clap and we cross.'

(I clapped)

'We cross.'

A slow surge forward with staff and everybody. One or two members of the centre were lame, so we went slowly, partly for them.

We did this several times. Then we came back. Then we tried a few people doing it alone, in a row still, but not all with hands clasped, though some still were. We did it several times. By now people began to chant on the footsteps. One counted, singing out loud. Discussing quickly with staff, I judged some had had enough and they went back to other tasks, but the others had not. In fact they didn't want to stop. So we went on and on over the same few boards, from 'pavement' to 'pavement', very sincere, very absorbed at times, occasionally laughing at our own mistakes, but able now not to hold hands, any of us, although occasionally we forgot and turned left or right instead of facing over the road. Then finally, the climax I had been working up to – one of the staff became a bus – **a bus** – and drove slowly and gently along the road. We had to judge when to go across the road. We had to let it pass first, then go.

SELF: 'It goes first. Then we go.'

'It goes. We go.'

'Look, there it goes. Slowly past. It goes'.

'Now. We go. We go – now.'

(We surged over – triumphant.)

Just one or two finally did it all. They waited for the bus, let it pass and 'went over the road', without me and without clasping hands. Once the bus honked and one or two people echoed it. Then everyone honked, it seemed. The whole room shook with joyous honking. My smiling hostess calmed them down.

One tall girl looked at me a long time and came forward. The lad mentioned before came over.

THE GIRL SAID: 'I crossed the *road.*'

'Yes,' I said, terribly moved, 'you crossed the road.'

In my mind a famous last line kept paraphrasing itself – 'and the crossing shall never be done'. So ended our great adventure. For some of us a small thing is a great thing. Achievement is a question of degree.

It was time for lunch, I looked at my watch. We had taken the whole morning.

The reader may guess that this group was actually labelled ineducable. Yet they did actually progress, although there is no means of knowing whether they retained the ability they had won. However, it made me change their description to 'hard to educate', rather than the final label. At a totally different and more advanced level, it is worth noting that the various stages of development are built up slowly and gradually so that in personality development in day release or in general therapy work, for instance, one would make the exercises a little tougher each time so as to stretch the ability to face shy-making situations and thus strengthen the inner person. Here we are attempting very elementary acts in a simple situation, but the method is the same. First we hold hands and do things all together, then some try alone, we all turn round together, then some alone. Finally we wait for a bus *then* go over the road. Note the triumph of the girl who said 'I crossed the road'. Yes, in her mind she did, not just a yard or two of the room.

Many years ago now, I conceived a deep compassion for those who cannot do the ordinary things of life. Oh, all you who live everyday life with such ease, catching buses, writing letters, buying things in shops, washing yourself, counting your money and able to make decisions, how lucky you are! There are many living who can do only some of these things and some none. They desperately need help and hope. But hope only comes by help, though triumphs may be of the simplest kind.

More Adventure

It had long become clear that in developing adventure for children, who hang by the wall because of uncertainty, there was need for extra struts of confidence. So I generally let them face the wall in first group exercises, then face the hall, then make journeys (first with help, then with less, then trials for none). But it seemed valuable to have a place of security to which to return. So a mat or chalk circle is useful as a home base. It can be an encouragement.

Example at Tansley's School

SELF: 'Everyone, come away from the kind wall and move towards me...slowly coming...anyone need help?... No... Well done!'

'Now, see this mat? That is home. That is home. So when we walk out into the hall – yes, we are going to do that. Isn't it exciting! – We all come back to this mat because – why?'

'Yes, well done, because it's *home.*'

We then merged in a progress rather like the description just above, but a little more advanced.

SELF: 'Lovely. Everyone, join hands in a row. Off we go to build a snow man.'

Clutch and un-clutch happened quicker here and some fairly independent work took place.

SELF: 'Let's throw snow balls and Snowman can see who is best... Ow! That was a good shot...*(after a while)* My word, it's time for bed.'

We all managed to turn round alone, all came home, all touched the mat for safety, all sat down together, (on or near the mat) warm and safe. We cleaned teeth and went to bed. Similar adventures were established as a regular exercise and the staff took over the work once their confidence had been established.

I have to tell against myself, though, that this was the school where one staff member used climax drum beats with a hyperactive child. It was so 'successful' that the boy was fully excited, jumped out of the window and absconded for most of the day. I had to explain all over again that you use DE-CLIMAX for the hyperactive and *climax* sounds for those who are withdrawn. To balance the mistake, though, it was here that with one little girl, I was taking one-to-one work and trying to calm her with a very slow music *de-climax*, when a gang of visiting nurses and three doctors came in. It took much longer, but I eventually got a severely brain-damaged child quiet. The doctor in charge suddenly said 'That is the first time I have ever known her be calm.'

Visit to an Institute for the Blind (adults)

At tea they taught me about adapting to home life; what they felt like when with other people; their gratitude for aid but not liking to be patronised; and the importance of not having too much sympathy. Some of them were very frank and one in particular described the self-centred person she used to be. After that meal I was no longer nervous but inspired – by their courage, patience and hope and by their sound common sense.

Now was the time for our drama. They spread out round the hall, but rather in little groups and there was a lot of chatter. I touched a gong and on silence we began.

> SELF: 'First of all everyone, find or touch something near you. Move your fingers over it and tap or scratch it quietly.'

This was a loosening up process. At first everything was very cheerful and they were a bit apt to get hold of a neighbour's ear or nose and one man started to scratch his companion's head. But this did not go on for long, and by saying that all the sounds were so far a bit too muffled, I got them to search a bit more carefully for more appropriate objects. It suddenly became more serious then and I put a record on a record-player, quiet but with a pronounced time beat, and everyone tapped in time with it. One person gently jangled some keys. Next we progressed to a polonaise by Chopin (popularly known as 'have a banana', I believe), rather more difficult and with a less steady beat. Then having secured some serious interest and effort, I asked them to make their sounds without any music and then to tell me what they reminded them of. These were the answers: typewriter tapping; church bells; a mouse; a bicycle. Out of these I built the story.

MY STORY

Over here is a house where an unknown genius lives (laughter and some applause, which faded out as I walked over to the place I meant and as they needed to listen for my whereabouts). He lives all alone and has very little to eat. He has no friends. His only companion is the *typewriter tapping*. But one day he felt he must go out and hear real human conversation, so he went into the market place over here (I moved again, then said to the people near me: 'You remember that this is the market place, won't you?'). He heard conversation all right, but it was nearly all about things he couldn't buy, particularly clothes and food. He stood looking at the food for a long time but in the end he had to go away. Finally he came to a pet stall and on it was *a mouse*. The mouse caught at his heart. It nibbled so and had a white blob over one eye. When the stall keeper saw him staring, he asked if he wanted to buy the mouse, but the genius replied that he couldn't afford it. But he went on staring and in the end the stall keeper became embarrassed and said he would give him the mouse if only he'd go away! So he accepted the mouse with surprise and walked off with it.

When he had gone back to the food stalls a man stopped him. 'What a nice mouse,' he said, 'would you sell it to me for my little boy?' The genius was sorely tempted by the smell of the food, but when he looked at the mouse he couldn't allow himself to give him away. He went home instead and naming the mouse – what shall we call him? (someone answered 'Charles') – all right, Charles – he sat down to type. So, for the first evening for years he had a companion. He slept well, for him, that night but dreamt of mountains of food. Next day he was awakened by a tapping on the door. He got up and went downstairs. A small boy was in the street, with a *bicycle*. 'Won't you sell that mouse?' said the boy. 'No, I can't do that,' said the genius. 'My father told me about it. He says it's a nice one.' 'It is.' 'Well, could I come up and see it?' The genius agreed to that and he and the boy went upstairs. When they looked at the mouse, they saw that an extraordinary thing had happened – there were several baby mice in the same cage as Charles. 'Well, you don't want all those, surely,' said the boy. 'I haven't any money but I'll swap you my bicycle for all the babies.' The genius was worried about this at first but finally gave in. The father at first was furious, but finally, seeing the funny side of it, he bought the bicycle back for his second son, so the genius at last had some money. He spent it nearly all on food and was therefore so full of energy that he finished his first great work quite soon. The publisher, whose firm was over here, was delighted with it and offered him a large advance on royalties. This was the first of a number of great successes and the genius became famous, as all geniuses should.

Now in time the boy with the mice grew up and became mayor of the town, but there was an awful fuss about who should succeed him, and, sad to say, some bad miscounts on the vote. So everyone agreed they would ask the well-known genius to be mayor. The boy, who had grown up, led them to the author's house and they all carried him away in triumph. There was general rejoicing in the public square and a pealing of *church bells*. The genius looked round him with somewhat ancient and watery eyes. 'Is this really the place where I looked at the food on the stalls,' he thought, 'and couldn't buy it? All came well because I was true to my friend the mouse and wouldn't sell it. Everything began then.'

And though the genius has been dead for many a year now, his work lives after him. But there's one more thing (I moved one last time), here in the museum is a special glass case. And in it, eating, sits a large mouse with a white blob over its eye. Underneath is an inscription which reads: 'This mouse died at the ripe old age of twenty-one years. Its name is Charlesia.'

There was rather a lot of joyful noise and it took us a bit of time to get sorted out. The pet stall was a great success and somehow an elephant and an octopus came into it, but we decided that they couldn't stand *on* the stall, they would have to sit by it. They finally had to be moved, because both of them kept nibbling at passers-by or entwining them. But after that the genius managed to get near enough to 'see' the mouse. Church bells were largely tea cups clattered by spoons plus singing. One final remark stands out in my mind. One of the Aldermen said: '…and now Mr Mayor, you'll be feeling tired perhaps?' 'Tired,' replied the genius, 'I'm never tired. That is the secret of my success. I'll only be tired when I'm in me box.' Well, it never does to tempt providence, for in our story he died soon afterwards. I always feel that descriptions may be helpful, if analysed and thought about, because the specialist will see into it, see further and probably adapt and develop.

My own eyes were gradually getting better, at the period this account was written about, but I still had a particular sympathy for those worse off than myself. In the third line of this report, for 'office chairs', of course, read 'wheel chairs.'

The Ideas Game is arising out of noises, just as in an Infant school, yet this is with adults. Blind people enjoy sound and will often make a noise unexpectedly and with gusto. In the part ' – and naming the mouse – what shall we call him?' we have an example of the test questioning again, to keep the group on its toes to test whether they are with you and to help them feel the creation is a joint one, that we are all doing it and it is a community creation.

It is important to get the geography straight, with all groups, but with the blind even more so; that is why I moved round the room to get areas identified, as in 'You will remember that this is the market place, won't you?' so that, if necessary, they could call later to their companions. 'This is the market place – over here – we are the market' and so on. If done with glee, so much the better, it lightens proceedings. To give confidence and happiness is partly what we do this work for. I want them to have experience of spontaneity too. Sometimes people come up and say things like 'Of course you couldn't do this sort of thing with the blind (or some other group), could you?' almost as if they didn't want you to, that it mustn't succeed. I always feel sorry for them, only rarely furious, because I think they must be rather unhappy somewhere in themselves.

Unusual Happenings at a Sclerosis Club, London (Whilst Helping Leonard Cheshire)

We started with shopping scenes, buying and selling. One woman said 'Cor, she wanted to buy the clothes off me back, good thing she didn't want to buy *me* wasn't it?' (This is the sort of brave joke people sometimes make about a hopeless condition.)

Ideas: A fishing rod; A cigarette lighter; Roller skates

'A man at, say, table one (if you imagine the tables to have been placed in almost a domino pattern of six) was living in his house *there* and the different tables are different houses in the village. Everybody watched this man because he used to come out into the village square and play cards with some rowdy companions, and he smoked a lot. (There was a lot of laughter here because one man had been smoking a pipe all the evening.) And to light up his dreadful cigars and pipe (I smiled at him during this to show it was only fun and he beamed back) he used a huge cigarette lighter that had a large hooked handle. The people, who looked out of the other houses, were always gossiping about this and objecting to the noise, and a man living in *that* house (we had invited volunteers for this and I pointed to them) – that would be table two on the same side of the aisle – tried to get the cigarette lighter by casting a line on a fishing rod, as if he were pretending to do trout fishing, in the hope that he would be able to get the hook under the large handle of the cigarette lighter.' (At this point that particular man did some wonderful fly-throwing across the room, and I then went swiftly over to another table – which would be table five, the middle of the other three and the other side of the aisle) – and somebody there had a big walking-stick to help them.' And I suggested that he pretend to be using a long pole, which was leaning against a wall to help open the top windows with. (They seemed to like this geographical touch.) He turned the crook of his handle up so that it looked like a hook on the end of this pole, and, from the window in his house, encouraged by his family, he tried also to hook the large cigarette lighter. His family, just next door to 'the card players' – that would be table six in the pattern – were, I think, 'washing clothes' or 'mending' and jabbering about the card players, but at table four was an ingenious family who talked about how to be sure of getting the lighter, and they decided to send two members on electric roller skates, dashing at ninety miles an hour, and all that family would make the noise of the roller skates going fast. This was splendid imagination for a first try at this sort of creative doing!

Two people in wheelchairs were helped to get their feet comfortably settled up on the rest for this, and then (partly by my help and partly by another person's aid) we whizzed them fairly gently across the floor while they smiled and burred hard as if they were on roller skates, supported by the others who had decided to make this noise. They rushed up to table one, pretended to snatch the lighter and made off round the room. They told me they wanted to go much faster than that. 'We can stand it.' 'Oh fine, ' I said and we did. I think I then finished by suggesting that 'the card players broke up because the leader refused to do any more without his lighter, because nobody had any matches and so he couldn't smoke. Therefore there was general rejoicing in the village.' And I think we put on a record for that, for terrific 'rejoicing', which started up, though I can't quite remember. Anyway it finished in joyous uproar and a spontaneous burst of clapping.

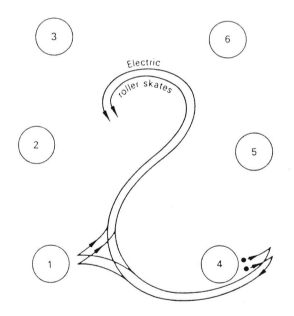

Diagram 14 The tables and journey

One member suggested that, for the first time, people had moved from table to table and not stayed dumped with one lot. Though liking their 'lot' it had proved wonderful to meet others. (This is not unlike the tyranny of the gang with Junior children, mentioned earlier.) 'What very useful information,' said the club secretary, 'another good thing coming out of your evening with us!'

The last thing is that in every club visit there has been a pathetic gratitude that anyone should bother to come and do this work with them, and in every case there has been an invitation to come again, and whether it was enjoyment of the actual drama or not is of little importance. The point is that in this work, everybody can join in; that all feel part of the party; and we try to ensure that for one short space of time, *all* have forgotten their problems, have had sincere moments, but have laughed and built real joy between us. One person told me later that the joy had lasted her all one week – 'Me, what thought I'd never know what happiness was again.'

Part of Notes (for a Letter) About Drama with the Deaf

...The exercise actually turned into Shakespeare's Tempest eventually. I asked the group to count seven from a given moment then SCREAM. The moment when the lookout man raises his arm to shield his eyes from spray and lightning was also a time to start the screaming. Music and drums were also used, for those who could hear somewhat and for those others (and also any possible audience) who, as helpers, might hear perfectly well.

Mime, of course, is a useful thing too, though many can speak in small bursts. If you have understood my main message so well, you will find and invent other ways of your own of helping, I am sure. Mime sometimes needs a leader, and more copying might be needed in adapting the work than would be advocated for children without handicap. (Mime stories can be made by a narrator who tells the story in words *and* signs. The actors act it.) Sign language can be used in its own right. I used to elaborate it – as it were 'over-sign' – and you get movement which is wide and poetic and almost dance. Then there is part of dance – such as my idea of finger conversation, face-pulling, filling of space with partner or group, imagined mirror work in twos. Then finally dance itself.

You might find other information in my *Experience of Spontaneity* book (unfortunately out of print now) if you can find a copy. But a 'must' might be my *Natural Dance* book.

I do hope some of these thoughts might be of use. My very best wishes for all you try and do, dear x. Thank you so much for your interest.

Yours sincerely – Peter Slade

Self Conscious and Shy

In the Personality Training courses for those who had left school, we found many who had no idea about general manners, no idea how to treat a customer and were tied up within themselves. Most of them were very nice people, but they had no *language-flow* and were shy about many things. All this could have been taught about through Social Drama in schools.

In speech it was found that they could not say things across a circle at first. So, to cut down the space which they feared, they were asked to mutter first into a 'telephone' (body all crunched up) then 'ring up' a partner, back to back; then both facing front; then face to face; then the person one along the circle from their partner. Finally they were able to speak across the circle, over space. It is always interesting to invent ways of helping people to screw up their courage. And for successful therapy of the kind described in this book, it is not only kind but essential.

Another Shyness: A lady patient used to come to me every Saturday morning, referred by a clinic. We had played out many scenes and I had taken note of their content. But one symbol was always missing.

Suddenly she said, 'Have you ever wondered why I don't include my father in any of our drama?'

SELF: 'I noticed it.'

LADY: 'Well, I think I *could* tell you. You see, well you see, when I was young he used to make love to me. I felt it was wrong and it was all my fault'

    (quite a usual feeling in such cases).

SELF: 'Why your fault?'

LADY: 'I don't know. It was all so strange. I felt it must be... But I loved him and still do. And I think he loved me. He was ever so gentle. Oh dear, I don't know why he did it. Do you think it was my fault?'

SELF: 'No. I think you should get that right out of your mind... You say he loved you.'

LADY: 'Yes.'

    (Pause)

SELF: 'Did you ever consider that he loved you too much – so much that he didn't know what to do about it?'

    (Long pause)

LADY: 'Oh, that's wonderful...it's wonderful. Oh, I feel much lighter. Thank you so much. That makes me feel, for the first time in my life that it wasn't all my fault! I felt so shy, so shy, I couldn't talk about it and didn't know what to do. I feel a great cloud has lifted.'

Practice in language-flow had helped her to become much more open and less shy. Perhaps this eased the way to opening up the one great shyness of her life. My remark of course would not be appropriate in every case. It just happened to be right for this one.

With Physical Handicap

I often used to take stories from the newspaper, let people improvise and tape what they had done. If anyone's voice was getting weaker, the mike (without their knowing) could be moved nearer to them. Then, when the play-back came, their voice sounded just as strong as everyone else's. In one particular case a patient would only take the part of a parrot until hearing 'that voice' back. It was so strong that it gave courage to tackle other parts for over a year, until the final illness prevented it.

Dream Stage

Only a short mention to do with therapy, as we have dealt with the subject of dance at some length. The unconscious Dream Stage is important. One sometimes notices a dancer become still, in the midst of a group. They stay on one spot and their head drops down. They appear to be deep in thought. They may, of course, be just thinking of how to move next! But the condition I describe is not the same. I think, in this, they are deep in their dream. They can't always tell you what is happening afterwards. But it seems that they are really still dancing hard in their mind, although their body is not. I do not think they should be disturbed. Signs that they are coming out of it are quite clear. The head slowly comes up and they begin to recognise things three-dimensionally again. They appear to recognise others dancing past, slowly join in and perhaps act as a partner to them. They are back with us. I knew one person who danced regularly. They often went into a short dream stage. It was two years before they came fully out of it and were conscious all the time. They had had other treatment and had been recommended to come to the sessions for build-up and release.

One other group met regularly with me on Saturday afternoons in Bayswater, London. This particular group was very mixed in ability and there was always some tension. One lady always wore gloves. She was very frightened of one other person. That person was contemptuous of her. One man was contemptuous of everybody.

As in an Infant school, I thought one day it was time to try something – with these to dare! I suggested they take a partner. That went well, I then suggested many changes to a different partner. At the end of the session, the contemptuous lady said, 'I had to dance with so-and-so. It wasn't too bad. She isn't *too* awful after all.' The anxious lady said, 'Did you see? I danced with HER. She was quite nice really. I quite enjoyed it. I don't think I am going to be afraid of her any more. Once you've danced with a person it's never the same, is it?' I noticed she had taken off her gloves.

Near the end of my time at Rea Street, children said to be difficult would be occasionally sent. But also, local authority inspectors would send teachers who appeared obviously good material for Headships, but through shyness or inability to express, failed their interview. I would build up slow tests for these last – in the room, close; explaining their views a few feet off; up on a stage; into a room full of people. Screwing up courage as explained.

Almost on my last day came some 'difficults'. They all read newspapers. So I walked round behind them and saw what they were reading – football! So that is what we did. We did a football dance and mime. And I put two toughs in charge of training the teams. The exercises they gave them were a great deal more rigorous than I would have dared suggest! As usual we all knew where the ball was, even though there wasn't one.

To cut things short, but to fill a few holes, here are some remarks, either statements, or in answer to questions people often ask:

Sometimes a young disturbed child will only obey through your use of a doll or teddy bear. They will obey the doll's voice but not yours. Be not abashed, but rejoice in the day when they say 'Why do you always talk to me in that silly voice? Why don't you just tell me what to do?' They are either getting better – or just growing up.

A child often thinks that if a mother leaves home, they can't be worthy or able to be loved. They think it is their fault.

Oh yes, but don't jump to conclusions, don't judge too quickly. There's always a reason for human behaviour; the therapist tries to find it.

Men are often tied up, in a way. They have been taught to keep a stiff upper lip. They sometimes get ill purely because they are afraid to show tender emotions. It is not always a bad thing for the anima to be allowed to show.

With unhappy children, it is not always that something bad has happened, but there has been a Nothing, no relationship with parents at all.

If you are empty inside, you try to grab something to fill the gap. You eat biscuits and grow fat. You eat chocolate. You eat too little to look like your idol. Food, romance, money, drugs. They may all be replacements to fill the gap.

Too many people want to *have*. Overcoming is good, but not always of people – but of ourselves. The danger is instant gratification. I want that – Wham! That is where civilisation goes out of the window. We can't always have what we want and should not take it.

Children catch ideas from many places, which become a disease. We have got to think out entirely new ways of saving them from what they see and hear. Sometimes they are too young to judge or to resist.

Abused children often implode. They turn in on themselves and are filled with undeserved guilt. Our task is to help them ex-plode under guidance and spit out what has given them such indigestion.

Oh, there is absolutely no doubt at all that violent films, TV and videos cause copied violent behaviour. Those who really deal with the subject know it well. Children tell you so anyway.

The young offender often thinks 'Well, if they are going to treat me as an outlaw, I'll jolly well be one.'

What I say is only to show a way to mental health. Through considering the inner as well as the outer need, I am guarding Childhood.

It is said that the next generation gives us another chance. Are we giving them the right chance? Genuine Drama is a thing of the emotions, the adult is needed to guide or make one remark at the right moment. This does not mean interfering with what is going on, but children often do like a grown-up to be present, and do invite them to make the occasional suggestion. Our presence has value. As a teacher, or therapist, one needs to judge when to be a presence and when to guide more obviously towards a considered aim.

I believe that in each handicapped or seemingly abnormal person there is a level of functioning to be discovered or a candle of normality to be lit. It is up to us to find it.

Oh, after all this, don't think there is anything wrong with you if you were happy as a child. That is allowed – really. It's called Normal!

Oh my goodness, in healing, some of us fail quite often or make mistakes. But we have to have a go. You are a church group, so perhaps you will understand if I say – I don't think God always expects us to succeed, He only asks us to *try*.

Oh yes, 'Community Care' is a nightmare. How anyone could shut down hospitals before proper alternative arrangements were made is beyond understanding.

Just as I finished writing this, a report has come out on radio that surgeons in Leeds are using imagined situations as practice for emergency operations. Providing experience before the real life event – first class Social Drama.

This section can best be ended by a remark I shall always treasure, made by a girl who came to one of the Personality Training Courses. She had been very tied-up inside herself. In saying good-bye she added, 'to be frank, when I first came I thought all this was daft. But then I was in a knot and now I'm not.'

Some Ways of Avoiding Delinquency

Lo, Masters, here ye may see beforne
That the weed overgroweth the corn;
Now may ye see all in this tide,
How vice is taken and virtue set aside.
Yonder ye may see Youth is not stable
But evermore changeable;
And the nature of man is frail,
That he wotteth not what may avail
Virtue for to make.

(Interlude of Youth, Medieval, Anon.)

I would not have it thought that only unhappy children came to the Rea Street Centre. Hundreds of them, most of them, were happy (or were after it) we believe. But some of them came to share their sadness, others came because they were sent, or somehow found us. The nature of these last ones was often 'frail' and they certainly 'wotteth not what may avail virtue for to make', and didn't really care.

So our first problem was to find whether our new unusual guests were sad, bad, or mad. For, some awkward young need kindness and understanding, some sternness, others punishment. There will have to be sterner treatment for younger and younger offenders, I expect, but there should not be mere vengeance. Let us hope the Government's plans for various types of centre will be a success. But, of course it depends on what is done in them.

At ours, we did not know what our visitors had done; who they were; and often, why they had come. So for all these considerations, and because we had no facts, I pronounced that our motto must be 'Non-Judgement'. I then explained to the voluntary staff that we must consider this place to be our Ark, I was Noah, they would be my dear family and sailors on a rough sea and that some very funny animals would seek entrance here. They did. That started our thirteen years out of thirty, when we had some very special experience of dealing with delinquents, or as I preferred to call them, children in trouble.

Roughly, my plan was based (by now) on a firm optimistic conviction that a lot of acting out of worries, anger, sorrows, bad experiences, and sins would have a constructive effect. How right I was. And this coined for me the words 'Experience without Sin'. That is experience of an emotional nature, under lawful and careful guidance, leading to a spitting out of evil that was either already there, or that we and our adult world had put into their minds. We often feed evil to the young, with little knowledge or care and then wonder at the result.

This leads us to why people, as we say, 'go wrong'.

Causes

These are so numerous and so particular to each case that it is impossible to be accurate about every one person. I have already mentioned various points in the early chapters, which perhaps might not have been considered hitherto, about small things in bringing up, which can turn into large. They contribute. But causes which are common are: home environment; poor, or unwise upbringing; lack of any form of firm religious training; lack of good role models; absent (or often so) fathers; leading to tired mums; school influence; large senior schools; marriage breakdown, resulting in shock and change of conditions; physical and mental abuse; gang influence; fashion; alcohol, glue, drugs; neuro-chemistry; unemployment; poverty; boredom; computer games, films, TV and videos of violence or pornography; lack by society in general, of any wide plan for avoidance.

High on the list I would have to put tired mums (not necessarily their fault, no offence, just a fact) in the very early years; (not on the list: Ignorance about the Dawn of Seriousness in the Infant School); large senior schools; drugs, for which you have to commit crime to obtain the cost; violence seen on every kind of media all the time until the senses are completely dulled and you copy without thought. You also learn tricks; and car chases lead to 'nicking' and crashes in reality.

As to the effect of violence, one could quote the case of a young girl who stabbed another child and slit her from throat to belly and was disgusted by the amount of blood. 'There wasn't any blood on the TV cartoon I saw', she said. Fortunately, most children have not yet felt much pain, but this leads to many of them having little or no idea of what they are inflicting when they copy what they have seen.

About role models, I could wish that the police were portrayed as rather different. Not necessarily as Dixon of Dock Green, but couldn't they sometimes be a bit more pleasant? I have met many who are nice. It is understood that authors want to make them seem tough, but there are not many police on TV dramas that I would want to meet, and God knows what the young think of them.

In our centre we were not concerned with punishment, though we certainly had rules. As few as possible. I went for education and containment and above all it was *one place for blowing off steam*. We tried to individualise them and split up any gangs. A bad gang gives you shelter from guilt and allows you to do things in herd instinct, that you would *like* to do, but otherwise would not dare.

I realised all this and that delinquency starts in very small things, very small ways, and very silly lack of guidance. It can start with dropping litter. This appears to be endemic. It is an outward visible sign of 'I don't care about you and your grass (or pavement) I just drop what I want (symbolically) on you'. It is one of the first big outward signs of total disregard for other people. This is a basis for evil. I do not jest. It is this attitude which is at the base of all crime. Utter selfishness.

It is often said that crime is the result of low self-esteem. It may be, but in those cases it is still selfishness and greed which tries to compensate for it. (I am not speaking of mental disturbance.)

I said above that we had few rules. But those we had were kept. If you did that, *this* would happen – automatically and always. Nothing personal, just a natural result. This helped people to know how far they could go. But, of course, there were many tiring and dangerous try-outs which were all part of the learning process, before they reached a hitherto unknown security, which better understanding brings.

In Child Drama, fighting is a symbol of overcoming. It is not necessarily a sign of delinquency and indeed in many instances, if you get enough of it in play, you get sick of it and do not want to do it any more – either in dream or reality. On this line, backed by long observation and conviction born of experience, we based our method. So dream-like violence, energy, expressing anger came first, then calmer themes later. It was a bit like a water fall. A huge explosion first, then confusion of bubbles often roaring down, finally the new found peace (deep down) as the calm stream meandered away as if in a different World.

Bullying

This took place at times and we had to be eternally on the watch for it. Fortunately the place was not too large for regular patrols to keep on the march near likely places. In large schools the task is extremely difficult, but it ought to be dealt with. One method mentioned lately is the establishment of Children's Courts. If young folk are well instructed for this, they could work well, if not, of course, it would merely legalise the bullying as in the case of prefects at some earlier private (and 'public') schools.

An even more constructive scheme is that of the training of young counsellors. They do not try to stop a fight in progress, but call a Staff member. After that they go in and mediate. It appears to be very successful. Perhaps we need both schemes.

Parents must not be afraid to contact Heads about bullying. Heads may not know about it and schools are there to protect their pupils enough to teach them and not allow anyone to fail in lessons through anxiety. And for those who do the bullying, it can become a habit, if not stopped, and will undoubtedly affect society as a whole.

Activity in general and *interest* is what helps. Chess clubs are good, adventure clubs are good, painting clubs are good, car and maintenance centres are good. Bradford is running a car driving centre for young offenders. How often I recommended Specialist Youth Clubs, in cities, rather than so many general interest clubs, where people slouched around a ping-pong table and not a lot went on. It would be a red letter day when an outside person brought in a special interest – but that would not interest everyone anyway.

One Clergyman I knew started a Motorbike Club in a very difficult area. Members were taught mechanics, maintenance, road sense and sensible driving. (Not like the terrifying gangs one sees in films.) Of course it was a tremendous success.

I have noticed that in well run Pony Clubs, girls seem to live *with* their mount over jumps, boys tend to try and master it over. This is particularly true of 'Special' Pony Clubs (not the usual ones), where one notices that nearly all disturbed children treat their pony badly, not necessarily in a cruel way, but without thought. Unless watched, they don't handle it and manner their animal, they seize opportunities to gallop it like mad.

But the horse is also an archetype – a sort of demon affair, that which plagues. The gallop of the horse of the night (nightmare) bears the sleeper away in an onrush so terrific that it cannot be resisted. The dream-horse represents an instinct that is dynamic. Shakespeare refers to 'the Lubbar fiend', this loob plays the fool with us, for it leads us away to do foolish things. Thus it is unwise to give way to primitive instinct; it leads to regret. Those who treat their pony badly, treat it like a motor bike. And the modern, unruly ton-up boys are riding their Lubbar fiends, which often lead them to do foolish and unpleasant things.

Our centre was a Drama Centre. We accepted everyone who came. One lot started to arrive in a lorry, driven by a lady in a fur coat, I was told. They would just be deposited on the steps and later on there would be a loud whistle and off they all rushed. Lady in the coat would drive them furiously away and I never really discovered who she was or where they all came from. But they were no dream! They often made reality felt.

What They Did

Not the lorry lot, on the whole, but what we had to deal with in general. They would beat each other unless stopped. They would try to do the opposite of any constructive suggestion. They would bring in blood-curdling weapons. They would sometimes put a knife to the throat of female staff and they would try to burn the place down. Two or three boys would tend to hold pretty girls down, 'fondle' them, then burn their face with cigarettes – be it noted, in domino patterns.

General behaviour, of less violent sort, would be to rush to the wall (for safety?). At any suggestion made twice, they were apt to fall on the floor and make animal noises and curl up in a foetal position (mostly when closely surrounded by adults, of which more later). There was often a rush to the movable dimmer board, a wonderful old arrangement on wheels (almost like a dinner wagon), which I had ordered, so that command of lights and sight angles could be made for both open space or proscenium-type drama. We found that those too shy yet, unreleased yet, to act; or those who just did not want to would often stand or sit apart, but take great interest in the lights, particularly for 'lightening'. But it was a bit boring to have a sudden thunderstorm in the middle of a quiet scene, together with guffaws of mirth by the perpetrators.

One visiting HMI remarked: 'I suppose you would say that those on the lights, and organising them, were rather more concerned with *projected* activity than *personal play*, I think I see what you mean.' Well I had not said so, but, yes, I would.

A quite generally shared action was to duck, any time an adult came anywhere near them, as if they were always expecting to be hit. I found that sad. They never were at our place, though it looked as if they were used to it elsewhere.

What We Did

First of all we would try and induce action. I would put some fast jazz on the record player. With luck, a few people would get up and 'muck around'. Sometimes they did not. Nobody moved. So I would quietly walk out of the hall for a moment or two, leaving the music on, but listening hard for any sounds of murder, then almost immediately stroll back. Nearly always some had by then started. And once a few had begun, others often joined in. We knew this by trials of going out of the room even if a few were dancing or rushing about. On return, others would have joined in.

Once a reasonable bunch was in action we offered them 'dares'. I suggested this to the staff, because I knew that peer approval was a strong influence with these sort of blokes and blokesses. There had recently been occasions reported in the papers of children being dared to run across the road like a chicken in front of speeding cars, resulting in fearful accidents. (In America lately, young-sters have come to grief by trying to jump across a wide space from one roof to another, for approval, and have dived to their death.) Approval, approval. Did they never get it, from parents, teachers or anyone? They had to do idiotic things to try to gain it from cruel gang leaders or idiotic friends.

Our dares (milder ones) above mentioned, would be high leaps, then jumping from rostrum block to rostrum block (still to fast jazz) until they were almost exhausted. Once they were exhausted, we felt we could deal with them. Everyone would stagger back to their seats by the wall, too tired to fight for 'their' chair if challenged. Then the main events of the evening would start.

Here, I think I must give praise to those who helped me. First came the Hon. Sec. and sort of mother of the family, Miss Phyl Lutley. Also Jack Beckett, who was absolutely brilliant – and brave – in some of his handling. Other helpers came and went, then a final core stayed.

Jack would go up to a belligerent looking oaf with a chair sticking out in front of him. Sensible, in case of being attacked. The young man would be encouraged to grab hold of it. He might do so with an embarrassed grin to avoid Jack's gentle prodding with the chair. He would then find himself swung into space and beginning to dance. Much applause and jeers from those around, who would then be encouraged to join in.

My own method would often be to get things going through the stamping business, as with the apprentices at Keele University. It might get rid of some anger. Short situations would be suggested (like swishing heads off with an axe). Longer situations after this. Some feat they would like to do: A lot of hard boxing, of unseen enemies to drum beats; and without drum beats if they became involved; a lot of sword play (swords made of air); a lot of shooting. All this led up to the longer playing out of violence that they had seen on films.

One of the techniques I suggested was that of 'fielding', rather like in cricket. As so many of our clients would try to rush to the wall, if anything was suggested about it taking place in the centre of the hall, I felt it important to find ways of making them obey. Thus, if a ring of people were around, they might stop them, or at least put them off, from getting to their objective. Shooting off to the boundary, so to speak, to 'not be' where they had been asked to be.

One night Jack Beckett had been making suggestions with one large chap. As usual he fell on the floor and made animal noises. Jack helped him up and this very tough customer came like a cricket ball towards me. We fielders closed in a bit. I remembered all they say about lions and looked him full in the eye, wondering *who* would win. Suddenly he wavered and turned back to the centre. Now, this was a very important moment for him. He had tried to disobey by refusing to take the faint suggestion of staying in the middle of the room. He wanted to reach the wall of the room, but in failing to do so, what did he do? He obeyed by mistake, and so, not to lose face, just like a cat, he pretended he was going to stay in the middle of the room all the time. I think at that moment he knew he had to co-operate and possibly found it wasn't so bad after all, for to my mind, he began to get better from that night on.

There were three lads, who had a peculiar relationship. One poor little one, often being set upon by two older ones. He would ingratiate himself often, but the strain of his fear was written all over his face. He was like a gangster's 'moll', sometimes treated with affection.

One night, the three of them had been playing about very roughly, but settled down, more or less, to a simple piece of drama. Even so I got tired of their behaviour and felt intuitively it was time to win. I very seldom raise my voice, so it is a sudden shock, if I suddenly do it and this is reserved intentionally for very rare occasions. I roared out: '*Sit down*, Claude, and play it properly.' He sat down on some rostrum blocks and was busy 'murdering' the younger boy. He clutched at the smaller one's hair, forgot the play and tugged hard. I went forward at speed and caught Claude's wrist.

CLAUDE: 'Sir, wotcher doin' that for? I wasn't doin' nuffin'.'

SELF: 'You're pulling his hair out.'

CLAUDE: 'That's what it's for.'

SELF: 'Well I think he looks better with his hair *in*.'

CLAUDE: 'Looks_____ silly to me anyway.'

SELF: 'Never mind what you think. We'll play the scene this way, if you don't mind.

CLAUDE: ''Ark at 'im – if you don't mind.'

SELF: *(shouting again on purpose)*

'Claude, shut up and get *on* with it.' This very close to his face.

Now an extraordinary thing happened. He suddenly went quiet and played through the whole scene with me holding his wrist all the time, so the younger boy didn't get hurt. I give this example, because it shows part of my method. I think, for the first time then, he discovered how to play a situation through emotionally without actually using physical violence. This is the process I call 'experience without sin'. It is one thing that the drama can offer, in a way that few other things can.

There were many different human species that 'found' us. Some for whom one could only feel distressed, others one was sorely tempted to bash. But, going on the line of 'non-judgement' we managed not to.

There was the mild one, who was dressed all in yellow – not a bad lad, I judged. Wanting to make him feel at home, I wondered what on earth to say. Suddenly it came to me. I walked past this canary and whispered 'What a *remarkable suit.*' His face lit up, it was sheer luck – just the right thing to say. He never made any fuss, just generally looked lost and wistful. He probably had to try and feel he belonged to some group.

There were girls on probation and one lad who hated grown-ups so much that he intended to tear the guts out of all of them, so, for practice, in the meantime, he was tearing the guts out of horses in a knacker's yard. But this was the one, who much later came back 'to give sweets to the kids'. I didn't like to ask where he had got them from, but the point is he had at last thought of someone other than *himself*. I bring this idea into play therapy from time to time, as it is an attitude that must burst through into consciousness. But, fortunately for humankind the giving of sweets in play is anyway a recurring symbol in that realm. I treat it as a sign of recovery. This lad had brought it to actuality.

One thing one would like to bring more into the light, after our years of investigation. It is the burden that some young people live with, being of actual age so-and-so, but when induced to act spontaneously, show the play patterns normally associated with a much younger child. This one expects, to some extent. But I have known numbers of fourteen- and fifteen-year-olds – even eighteen-year-olds – liberated successfully enough to play as eight- and nine-year-olds. Going back to the 'cathartic years'? Going back to the last time they were allowed to play? Going back to safety or the last time they were happy? In any case, for a fifteen-year-old to play like an eight-year-old is a great unbalance. In the *personal play* realm, their emotional maturity, so to speak, is halfway behind actual age. For them it is an unbalance of half a life time. Do we realise what a strain that must be to live with?

I seriously wish many more people did this work. It is desperately needed. People need training and there should be many such places where the young can blow off steam, so they don't need to actually 'do the deed' in real life. They have to be helped to see the difference between dream and reality. Even punishment might be more justly assessed, if something like these methods were used; for a fifteen-year-old, seen to play consistently in, say, the pattern of a fourteen-year-old (and if this is compared with other tests) probably needs a smart smack in the pants, but a fourteen-year-old consistently playing as an eight-year-old needs treatment. We may fear that, as things are, the wrong child gets the wrong sentence, for their behaviour is not properly tested, one suspects, before sentence. Younger children are often let off too lightly. I have talked with a previous Home Secretary about this and got as far as speaking to selected MPs in the House of Commons, for it appears to me to be a matter of great importance and of human justice.

Superficial investigation of these points might end in the notion that group therapy is superseding attempts at using spontaneous drama, for some drama methods are considered only as a form of structured grouping. But this is a very inaccurate calculation if applied to proper dramatherapy, and entirely leaves out the actual nature of young people, their power of using constructive (and destructive) imagination, the manner in which they can be guided through personal dream play to conscious expression, from selfish personal expression to work in pairs and then the group, watching continually for ways in which to offer them opportunities of working off aggression, until harmony and co-operation are established. But even then, catharsis is not enough and this, one suspects, is where most methods fail; there must be an added hope process. I have written about this in *Dramatherapy as an Aid to Becoming a Person* (Slade 1959).

One of the things we all became quite good at: If anyone had picked up a real weapon and was going to use it, we would whip up and pluck it from them. Quite often the drama would be played on, quite satisfactorily, without the real thing being used. The staff used to practice this whenever we got the chance. The swifter the snatch, the more likely was the scene to remain uninterrupted. Perhaps we learned this from Claude, or perhaps it was common sense, or just fear of what might happen otherwise. Whatever it was, it worked. This gave us deeper insight into what might be done and was further proof about my point over the importance of 'absorption in the task'. For those young people, particularly, the more absorbed and involved was the play they experienced, the better.

I used to arrange 'King of the Castle' situations quite often, because of the need we all feel to be King of our own domain, as mentioned earlier. As most of our folk suffered from low self-esteem as well as extreme selfishness, it was important for them to build up the one and work off the other! I believe in America this is called 'King of the Hill'. If this is so, I do so prefer it. 'Castle' has inner meaning, but is a place of static defence (obstinate somehow) and there are not so many of them about. There are many more hills and high places to defend *actively*. And because of the delight children have in finding the highest place and, for once, looking down on other people, it is particularly important at times for the outlaw to be boss – 'monarch of all he surveys'. This implies height.

One evening, a great glowering creature was sitting opposite me. He had not joined in anything for three weeks. Suddenly he got up and lurched over to me. I thought 'Now what?' A half smile came to his face and he asked "Ow are yer...(he sat heavily next to me)...mate?' By that last word I thought I had really 'arrived'!

Example of Rules Kept

Another time I heard some scuffling going on behind the stage and heard a match strike. Someone was going to set fire to the curtains. I called out, 'If you don't come out of there in two minutes you can never come here again.' Two miscreants shuffled out, then made a run for the exit door, crouching in fear I was going to hit them. I stepped in their way.

SELF: 'Where are you off to?'

LAD: 'Well, you said we couldn't never come 'ere again.'

SELF: 'No. I said if you didn't come out of there in *two minutes*, you couldn't come again. But you did come out under two minutes, so you can stay.'

LADS: 'Oh.'

SELF: 'Do you want to?'

LADS: 'Yeah.'

SELF: 'Well for God's sake stop behaving like stupid little kids. You look like sensible young men. *Be* that. Now come along and *get* in the other room where everyone else is – and behave yourselves!'

As our customers learned a bit of control, stories became longer; and some of them, carefully selected, were allowed to go into the small hall and make up stories of their own. A few 'lighting lovers' would go too.

Example:

SELF: 'What are you going to do?'

BOY: 'Like to use lights fust.'

SELF: 'All right.'

They shone red, blue and yellow and decided that red was for blood, yellow for daylight and blue for sky at night. But they then got a bit stuck. So:

SELF: 'I see you have built up a lot of blocks. Why not use that wonderful archway in the wall and use that as an entrance for somebody *(intimate theatre)*?'

BOY: 'Yeah...for a ghost or a murderer.'

GIRL: 'Oh, ghost, yeah. I'd like to play that. Frighten all the boys to death.'

MALE CHORUS: 'Ye – ou!'

When I came back they had made their story. A man bashed his wife about until she was fed up and left him. She went to live with another man. The first one came to 'get' him (possibly to get her back again, but this was not at first clear). Finally, after some splendid oath-words, some of which I did not know, he killed them both. Lighting for all the first part was straw. As the murdering went on it was mixed with red. After both deaths, the bodies lay together in a small circle of bright red. There was a slow change to all blue (red out suddenly at end). Only fairly effective. Two policemen came in and took off the murderer to a cell in a far part of the room. Then from the archway, slowly down, came the ghost of another man who had been murdered (in green light). The first girl and man rose up as ghosts and all moved greenly to the cell. They throttled the murderer. Lights all went to red again, though there was no blood. Suddenly the house lights flashed on. All the players rose up beaming. 'That's all, Sir.'

When I said above, 'only fairly effective', it was no criticism of the production, there was a reason. We only had four spotlights in that hall and a small dimmer board for them, to which young folk progressed, after using one separate dimmer only, in the large hall. Afterwards they went on to the movable board of twelve. In our years of treating delinquents, this arrangement proved invaluable.

Much can be done also in associating light with mood and tone of voice. I have helped some people to stop shouting all the time by work in dimmed down light.

Go ahead and make experiments, they may prove of interest and value. English teachers particularly should work on tone of voice with light, and for poetic values. Parallel with work at any centre should go work in schools and other places.

Boys Remand Home

We had tried a bit of the *Tempest*, because people seem to be so fond of storms and shipwreck. 'We split. We split' is always popular. Extra remarks were: 'I'll split 'is bloody 'ead, if he don't give me that spar to 'ang on to.' 'Farewell Uncle, Aunt, Cousins. Farewell Mr Gougalo – Mr Anthony – well, whatever your name is, farewell.'

Other remarks were, perhaps, too explicit to repeat here. But we ended up with a wonderful 'swimming match' along all the length of the hall.

Perhaps this is where the short description of a visit to a girl's Remand Home should come, though it happened later. Miss Demmery, my Assistant, was looking all blonde, with white dress, bag, shoes and parasol, all white (I must say she looked stunning). On entering the hall there was a gasp and we used the occasion.

'Ooh Miss, what a lovely bag.'

SYLVIA DEMMERY: 'I am glad you like it. Would you like one the same?'

I *think* the answers indicated something like yes (certainly), but it wouldn't suit their boy friends or their style of life. I can't quite remember. But such first wide-eyed reactions were not uncommon, though this was an unusually strong one.

Sylvia Demmery was on particularly good form that day and guided the conversation swiftly round to why wouldn't it suit their friends? Could they not strike out for a different style of life and other friends? This was always something we aimed to put to young ladies in an awkward situation, and it nearly always appeared to be something that had never occurred to them and about which they had doubts and anxieties.

The importance for many young, is to catch a *glimpse* of another way of life. They are often so enslaved, imprisoned by their environment, mores and cronies that they give way to carefully low-esteem dress, in order to pronounce loudly: we are an under class, we intend to look dirty. But isn't the world cruel to us? Not always, no. Did it ever occur to you that if you spent less on drink and cigarettes, you could save up for a bag like that?

I always feel it valuable to try and open windows, give a wider perspective. The seriousness and success of this discussion stands out because of the type of girl. For, these sometimes alarming ladies were usually incapable of walking slowly down a hall without hitting anyone.

I always thought it important in special sorts of situation and visit (as with the Personality Training Courses), that we would provide both a Father and a Mother figure whenever we could. They could relate then to whichever their unconscious needed at any particular time. It certainly worked. At other times it was better to be alone.

I am sure Sylvia Demmery took some exercises with them. But the whole atmosphere had greatly improved after the discussion and because of the white bag. So, on this red letter day a special memory is that I finally managed to get them to walk slowly down the hall, winding between pillars. No sound of punch or smack (how dull!), only the strains of *Walk to Paradise Garden*.

At one school, I hear, the police came in lately and turned some children into 'police'. They were sworn in and did real jobs, as on call. Results – a better view of police. We could do with more of this. Also, in the therapeutic Children's Unit of a Young Offender's Institution they have a graffiti wall, to work things off.

After doing all we could to offer opportunities for playing out violence at the centre and getting rid of it we would follow up with Social Drama which should have been done in schools.

Social Drama

Civilised society demands that the child, the young person, should meet certain basic requirements if he wants to share in the life of the group. Society demands a standard. Today the growing adolescent (and younger child) is often not given the help and example he needs and seeks.

Thought, imagination, language, movement, dance are all part of drama. Through the development and use of these the person develops and matures. He/she can be helped to listen, to become absorbed, to look at things with greater awareness, to develop vocabulary, to gain greater confidence in themselves, and be more at ease in an ever wider selection of situations.

Social drama is concerned with preparing the growing person for Life. Practice is given in carrying out daily tasks with greater efficiency and confidence, exercises are offered which develop the power of communicating personality by its projection through speech, movement and appearance. This helps to diminish the feeling of awkwardness and self-consciousness when he/she is asked to meet visitors at a club or in the home, look after a guest, welcome the Mayor, or Councillor, or the speaker who has come to the school speech day, or cope efficiently with telephone messages and enquiries, and because of practice and help offered during a drama period of this kind, he/she feels less inhibited, more confident in putting forward points of view, and in asking questions at a meeting or during an interview.

Because of developing self-knowledge through personal experience, the young person becomes more thoughtful, better able to cope with the sudden new experiences which life offers and they will more readily accept a challenge, make use of an opportunity which earlier they would have felt too shy, too inexperienced, too inadequate to tackle.

To save space, here are some answers to questions that came again and again from visitors to the centre, or have been raised at summer and other courses:

I think some – perhaps many – people do unwise or even terrible things because of loneliness.

Boys are not supposed to show their feelings. They are supposed to compete all the time and 'be a man'. This may be good to some degree, but if pressed too far it is bad for the man and also for society. If you are nice you are considered weak. It even affects the colour of your watch strap. Dirty brown is manly.

I think evil comes in drip by drip, step by step, influence by influence, or whatever. It was the Archbishop of York, who said lately 'Wants become needs, needs become rights, rights become law'. So the delinquent thinks 'my law is to take'.

No, I don't mind you asking a lot of questions, it is wonderful that we have this chance of being together; and your interest is a great kindness. Asking questions is not only useful for making one think, but the best way of getting an answer!

Some fathers who have to work long hours, or manage large enterprises become outlaws in their own home. Their wives make new friends, their children drift emotionally away. Their whole family have different interests. It is very sad for them and they compensate by having an affair.

Oh, fear is a terrible thing. It affects people in so many ways. Apart from violent phobias, you can alter behaviour by being afraid of not being liked, you become delinquent from fear of not being admired. Fear can make you take to drink or drugs, or it makes you eat (for comfort) and you become

fat. I suppose it is there for self-protection, helping us not to fall off cliffs
and so on. It makes you afraid, if you look, so you don't. And unless under
pressure, you don't jump over either.

Well, after trauma may come dissociation. Suppressed feelings can lead to
fantasy and violent or extraordinary behaviour follow.

Oh yes, there is absolutely no doubt that violence, seen on TV and everywhere,
causes violent behaviour. I have been saying so for over forty years. A
violent youngster, recently asked where he got such thoughts from
answered 'Well, you see it on TV and that gives you ideas'.

Abuse leads to abuse in many cases. You hear young people say things like 'I
tried abuse of other people when I had been abused. It was at first a sort of
experiment, later I enjoyed it and it became a habit'. It is quite common for
young, quite young, children to carry on a chain reaction after being
abused themselves.

If you push unhappiness down too far and it cannot escape, your conscience
begins to get smaller: 'If I am unhappy, you should be too'. That is why we
offer many opportunities for helping unhappiness to be played out here, to
avoid these young ones from violating other people's rights.

Parents who have had a bad up-bringing don't know how to discipline their
children. Too much discipline is wrong. Too little discipline is wrong. Try
not to despair, parents must certainly think very hard about what they do.
They should attend courses, if need be. They *must* care, but in the end they
can only do their best. But it should *be* their best.

Oh, school leavers today! The thought of them goes to my heart. They need
hope. We must plan for a decent way of living, as a community. Too many
of them who cannot get a job feel they are not legitimate members of
society, so they develop a different attitude to right and wrong. We are
back to 'Well, if they treat me like an outlaw, I'll_____well, be one'.

It is the most extraordinary situation we have got ourselves into. Everyone
needs a hug sometimes. Today you dare not give it. You might be had up.

Yes, it is easy to become too soft, it is also easy to become too hard. We must
not stoop to mere vengeance. That is to become exactly what we deprecate
in others. The more you delve into human weakness and behaviour you
abhor, you may find there is always a reason for what is happening. It may
be genes. We should not jump to conclusions and judge too swiftly. In
every human being there is a candle to be lit. It is up to us to find it.

A year or so ago I was on an Advisory Board for a school for lads in trouble. I
had managed to get an 'any questions' session arranged and agreed upon.
After it, one boy said quietly 'Why should anyone like you be interested in

us and what we think?' I felt able to answer, 'Because everyone is important. So, of course, I am interested. It matters to me what happens to you'. He looked amazed.

At the End and After

After the end of our time for trying to help children in trouble, on an 'ordinary' evening, I was told someone was asking for 'that man'. I took it that might be me. In the doorway stood a figure I knew — two of them.

SELF: 'Claude, how wonderful to see you.'

CLAUDE: ''Ere, I brought some sweets for the kids.'

SELF: 'Oh Claude, thank you. What are you doing now?'

CLAUDE: 'Oh, me and me mate (you remember *'im*), we're lorry drivers now and we 'aven't driv over no one on purpose...yet!'

Dear Claude, he brought sweets 'for the kids'. Kids he didn't even know. Certainly my sign of hope.

After our thirteen years, we became quite convinced that watching bad behaviour on the media *leads* to bad behaviour. Of course it does. We just know it. I knew it years before. But what is more important is the fact that it is perfectly possible to get rid of, and spit out, the evil we put into young minds. What else are they going to do with it except copy it and use it? Media criminals become role models.

What we need are many centres for this work. This is what I strongly urged to MPs in the House of Commons thirty years ago. I warned what could happen if nothing was done — let us not be bashful about an attitude over 'I told you so', the situation is too serious. I did say so, and much could have been avoided.

I am not pretending that this form of dramatherapy alone could stop all delinquency now. It is too late and it probably never could have. There are new temptations anyway now. But thirty to forty years ago it would have made a *considerable* difference, particularly allied with proper education of the emotions in schools.

To cut out Drama as a subject in the syllabus (except for Shakespeare) would be the height of folly. Even now quite a lot could be saved. Dramatherapy of the kind I have described could still make a good contribution to improving behaviour which, in a general sense, is now nearly out of hand. It should be used in schools, correction centres, therapy units, cottage homes, prisons and so on. Also, for all those at risk or on the brink of bad doing. It could still help. There is need for education and containment as well as punishment.

For those who even now have difficulty in believing what has been said, I would quote the sort of remark that came again and again and again from both sexes 'Thank you very much for 'avin us 'ere. If we 'adn't this place to spit out what we seen, we'd be doin' it on the street.'

With the methods I have described, it was considered by us – and by many others – that we had eighty per cent success. It was nearly always, if any member thought they were being 'judged' that we lost them. We tried prevention and containment. A recent survey informs us that nine billion pounds is spent on correction, only seven million on prevention.

At the end of our time for the 'difficults', I sat watching a group of girls. I realised that those now before me, in the half dark, were once what seemed like sullen, dirty, deranged damsels, now dancing like angels. Their last dance here. When the music stopped they bashed up nothing. They hugged.

From some 'strond afar', not too remote, I as Noah loved them too. They had triumphed. No longer animals now – PEOPLE.

Adult Training

Some Ideas: Mostly for Teachers and Therapists

Perhaps the most important thing here is the ability to find, or re-find, the child inside oneself. This is particularly true of teachers and therapists but is true for parents and social workers also, if they are to come closer to understanding their children and avoiding many misunderstandings. There is a natural feeling that dignity has to be preserved and that, once grown up, one puts away childish things altogether. It is hard enough to become grown up anyway. Certainly one can never be the same as a child, and ought not to try to be. Each adult has to discover how much dignity to preserve in order to maintain discipline amongst the young – or ourselves. But often, it is quite possible to appear sensible and firm on the outside, whilst smiling, even chuckling to oneself on the inside. To 'know the child', both ways (i.e. in ourselves and in the child), is a great advantage in perceiving why certain behaviour takes place, but even more so if any judgement has to be made. It is then much more likely to be correct and also fair. The effect of unfair judgement can be devastating and may suck away a person's energy from the rest of their life, even after the first shock has apparently worn off. This does not mean that every time a child cries 'But that's not fair', it *is* in fact unfair; for they do it quite often. So we should not get in a panic because of what they have said. The point is to get nearer in understanding the stages of early development, allow our sense of humour to widen and our imagination to expand. If we can understand and recognise the importance of the two child qualities of *absorption* and *sincerity* and have expanded our inner self in confidence and without fear, we are doing pretty well. Even so, there may be some occasions when you know children will not understand, but you are being bravely firm all the same. They cannot, because the circumstance may be beyond their experience. We are then almost at the stage of 'this is an unfair world and the sooner you learn it the better', as mentioned in the chapter on Senior Schools. But wiser, is to help them to see this is something you know they will not understand and will they please do it this time 'because I say so', but with assurances that it is for their own good, tough as it may seem. Dr. Sue Jennings in her book *Play Therapy with Children* (1993) speaks of 'facing the child within us'. This is an important point. Because of insecurity, some people are afraid to face the child within them (as to many other things, perhaps). Examples of this would be shame at:

Being caught dancing alone.

Talking to oneself in a mirror.

Just talking to oneself.

Talking to a doll and playing with it.

Even leaving a doll or dolls about the place.

Talking baby talk to an animal.

Playing with 'young' toys.

'Being' an animal.

Dressing up in childish ways and 'being people'.

I do not mean to the extent of fantasy nor transvestism (though that may be part of it, being 'stuck' in part of childhood).

Deeper things may be concerned with unacceptable behaviour, which a therapist brings to the surface – to do with the child within, which cannot be recognised without help, or is recognised but not improved upon. Here, though, we are in the realm of over concern at being caught in the act. In mild cases of shame, this is over concern. In fantasy behaviour, fear of being caught is more understandable and is very genuine. The over concern at being thought merely childish is a pity, particularly when it is really being Child-like.

Dr. Jennings may have meant other things as well, but for me these points are important. Fine distinctions again – in other words, discovering, re-finding or admitting of the child within; or on the other hand refusing to admit it, imprisoning it, smothering it over, or letting the child out of prison on rare occasions and hoping to God you will not be caught. That is not facing the child within. Then, of course, some people find, or know about, the child within but cannot face it, because they do not like what they see.

Perhaps we should be very conscious at this point, all over again, of the difference between being child*ish* and child*like*. By the first we generally mean such things as angry, selfish, spiteful or cruel action, even violence without due cause; doing unwise things; also unexpected offence taken; jumping to conclusions and lying for self protection. Of these we should be ashamed and try to grow out of them. By the second we mean such things as a certain innocence, even naivety; an affectionate and trusting nature, unashamed of simple imaginative behaviour and creation. A certain commodity of these things can only enrich any wisdom or experience that an adult may have. A balance of them *with* prudence produces a civilised being.

For Parents

Please consider the points in Chapter II again, also Chapter I on Play itself. Do consider the importance of the sounds 'Yes' and 'No'. Try to be sure of understanding the difference between *personal* and *projected* play, the child's need for active play, but also the intelligent use of *near-finish* in the early years. Play with your children if you can bear it, follow the suggestions written in the chapters for the child's development during school years – and possibly encourage such things to take place if they don't. It is vital for your child's later happiness that their inner development still takes place, despite the necessary tightening up of outer, obvious competence. It will be a sad day if we make the mistake of creating hard and clever zombies, when the world needs kind, compassionate, imaginative and wise minds to face the considerable problems of the future. There is a danger that, in panic, Play may be squeezed out of the school curriculum. Guard it if you can.

For Teachers

Obviously you will have to concentrate somewhat on the age of children in your charge. Please try to understand the importance of *personal* and *projected* play and the value of time-beat, rhythm and climax. And above all de-climax for discipline. For the early years, there may be some new thoughts in what I have written about suggestions for Infant and Junior Schools. Only do what you can, but remember that on your success may hang a large part of the inner emotional training of the adults to be. Certain things become either blocked in the personality, or constructively implanted in it at a very early age. The seeds of delinquency start right down in the very young. I have merely tried to outline some ways of avoiding it and of presenting certain forms of Play as a constructive need.

For Teachers in Senior Schools

An important part of the work is in understanding the shock that some young people have in coming to a big new school. The acceptance of the divisions Imaginative, Social and Theatre are really crucial in the Drama Section, and I cannot overstress the value of a wide use of Social Drama at this age. If you *can* do it, allow it, fit it in, please do. You cannot know how important it is. The almost total lack of it was so terribly clear during my years of experience in running the courses for Personality Training in Industry and the Retail Trades in various parts of the country. It was almost pathetic, what the students had missed. Do forgive me for saying so much about Theatre. If it is your love, you will either be annoyed or pleased. But bear with me if you will. I started my first professional adult companies of Theatre for Children in about 1932. I have seen an awful lot of school work and plays since then. It is a fair stretch of time to have worked with young people, those both happy and sad. I would just like all school plays to be as well presented as possible. And why should young actors not 'know their stuff' and evolve early into the patterns of technical ability which will enhance their personal style and achievement? Allies in Drama, you might manage to get a lot of it under the heading of Vocational Training, apart from exams. But an important part, as you will know, is a training for Life.

Practice in Imagination

For teachers, nurses, social workers and therapists. This is a shortened outline of what can be suggested in a One Day School, which is a potted version of a longer course. I always prefer to go through the theory of Child Drama and Art from, say, the Infant to top Senior School in the morning, It is tough, but it is so important that we know what we are doing and what is the *purpose* of it all the time. Then we do practical in the afternoon, not pretending to be children, going through exercises which belong to child behaviour but at our own level, with plenty of reference back to the needs and application of what we are doing in the professional situation.

Ways of starting have been mentioned, so let us start with one of them.

SELF: 'At your feet are some coloured balls and lovely clubs with spangles on them. Bend down, pick them up and start juggling with them.'

(Music – make sure that volume is right down before you bring it up.)

They stay in one spot, so I now get them moving:

'Good. Now you are very clever, you can dance about as well as juggle.'

(They only cover a little ground.)

'You can dance even more about the place… Juggle with a partner too, but both of you keep dancing.'

Watch to observe for a moment, time it and then…'Throw everything away and dance anyhow you like.' At this, the movement is nearly always rather indecisive. We have been going through exactly what one might offer to children of any age from about six years upwards but at our own level – *as people* – in order to stimulate imagination and to learn what it feels like to play about in space and in three dimensions. But this is now instruction for instruction, so I add extra remarks to make things conscious that they may have been doing half-consciously, or unconsciously.

(Music faded out. So they stay still.)

SELF: 'Notice that you felt a little lost, didn't you when I asked you to throw
        everything away? You see how important it is that action should have a
        purpose. Here, that was the juggling. To create, nevertheless, just to the
        sound is more difficult at first. But it is a different purpose. Also, note
        that I did not say anything like 'Werr! you're not dancing at all, you're
        just flopping about', when you had to dance in your own way. But I
        would now say 'See if you can cover more space and move your arms a
        bit – in your own way. That is more encouraging, more constructive and
        does not sound like criticism. You behaved just as young people would
        do, so you know now what it feels like.'

        (Music up)

SELF: 'So, off you go again, dancing in your own way.'

        *(They try. I leave them at it for a bit and then fade music slowly out again. All is
        still.)*

SELF: *(in quite a quiet voice)*

        'See how quiet everything is? I created a De-climax and as the music
        faded out, you obeyed the sound, and then obeyed the nothingness. So
        you did nothing. Your children will do just the same.'

        (Music slowly up)

SELF: 'Now for some quick other ideas. You are painting a large picture... Now
        paint someone near you, a partner, on face and all over. Yes, paint back!
        (laughter and a bit of a struggle). Throw your paintbrushes away and dis-
        cover you have the largest nose in the world, what are you going to do
        with it?'

        (They march round)

        'Oh, all right, put magic powder on it and shrink it... Oh! gosh, your
        shoes have springs on them, they are making you jump. Throw away
        your shoes and find you are a frog.'

They may jump a bit harder. Don't keep them at it for more than a few seconds,
particularly if any are elderly. Even judge not to do that exercise.

        (Music out. Perhaps some laughter.)

SELF: 'Lovely. Do sit down a minute and rest. Now, in the exercise of painting
        each other. Perhaps don't try it if you don't know your class or group
        yet. Youngsters might get a bit boisterous and you won't know what to
        do. Don't forget they must have paint brushes of air and not actually
        touch. Did you notice that you all went round the room anti-clockwise?
        Your children will do the same. I always tell people that if a group goes
        the other way, a leader is probably left footed, highly intelligent, or just
        anti-social and you soon learn which.'

At that point I might judge that they should continue and would give them
other imaginative ideas. They have had a rest, so get on with it. Keep control.
Keep things going. Don't waste time. Never seem uncertain. I might try asking

them to jump up and down on the rostrum blocks and feel the fun of higher and lower level. Perhaps play King of the Castle.

> SELF: 'When the music comes again, you are walking about in a very posh hat, looking posh too.' *(Remember we 'did' hats with children.)*
>
> *(Music up)*

To save space, and because it will probably be apparent by now how one would make kindly suggestions without criticism, here is a list of other suggestions for developing imagination, any of which might be used at this point:

> Be a naughty snake and bite an unseen person.
>
> On roller skates. If too slow, 'escape from enemy.'
>
> Boxing match. Fight unseen opponent to music or drum.
>
> Fire at an unseen enemy – as gangster or police.
>
> Shoot arrow as Robin Hood.
>
> Overcome serpent as St. George.
>
> Be a horse with a gammy leg.
>
> Be a Dinosaur playing truant and feel lost.
>
> A Dinosaur winning a beauty competition.
>
> Be a racing car.
>
> Be an aeroplane (watch for an S or 8 shape).
>
> Be a balloon (calmer action).
>
> Be a train engine. Modern, or old fashioned puffer.
>
> Be an angry bus, all red with rage. 'He needs a kind *(unseen)* conductor and is put gently to bed. Don't forget he must clean his teeth *(invent a nice noise. Rattly?)* before he lies down'. *(Declimax. Silence.)*

Apart from the last suggestion, one could stop after any of the others. I would then, perhaps, suddenly suggest they talked to someone near them and tell them all about the barmy things this man had asked them to do. As a rule, there is generally an outburst of laughter and loud talk at such a moment. There may have been laughter at some of the other suggestions too. I wait for sound to die a bit, giving some time for communication between them to take place.

> SELF: 'Right, I think perhaps you've had time to tell each other a little of what you think of me by now. Do you remember that you laughed at one or two points and held up the action? Your children will do the same. You won't be angry with them, will you *(said as a statement not a question)*.'

This is the way to help adults to know, or to remember, what is natural human behaviour. Whether we realise it or not, we all, young and older, share more than we are aware of.

This could be followed by the exercise of picking up a musical instrument and to march round playing it. Then an instrument unknown, so far, to anyone.

PAIRS: Moving now to relationships with others.

        Swap known instruments. Tell how to play.

        Swap unknown instruments. Tell how to play.

        (Watch for and enjoy wonderful invention.)

        Winning at tennis at Wimbledon. Slow motion film.

        The same. Normal motion film.

        Slow motion with partner, not near, across room.

        Throw javelins, slow or fast. Feel difference.

        (Fast is more like drama. Slow like dance.)

        Golf fast or slow *(partner shows how to 'do it better').*

        Cricket *(one bowls, other bats).*

        Football, all the group.

        (Rest, and allow talk).

SELF: 'You note that at this stage I judge and give you plenty of time to talk. It is important to allow this, we want to encourage language-flow. Music will be a background again in a minute, but first of all, in pairs, one be looking into a mirror, the other be a reflection. With children, one of them often goes too fast and the other can't really 'reflect', or they may do it on purpose to catch their partner out. Don't allow it.'

(They try and it is not too bad)

SELF: 'Good. Now to music. Here it comes, nice and slow. Use high moves and low, if you have got past hair-do's and shaving.'

After this we progress to something a little more complicated where they are not copying each other but filling space.

SELF: 'Fine. Now *(to near person)* Would you just make an interesting shape, please? Yes, that's great. Left arm a little higher perhaps and bend the elbow. Right. Looking at her, you see one arm is high and the other low. If you were making a picture or a sculpture, two spaces are empty and need to be filled. So I put one of my arms in a space under her high arm and my other above her low arm. Thus together we fill space. Slowly we change and make another shape. *(To girl)* Thank you. Now everyone, *you* try.'

After this, I might see if they could enrich the shapes by putting a foot and leg over the top of another person slowly, keeping balance and bringing it down without mishap (it is important, as success or failure is information about the group); then doing it in time to music for further control.

The filling of space exercise is valuable for all those with learning difficulties, because it is one simple step away from copying and gives an indication of elementary personal responsibility.

SPEECH: *(sitting in own place about the hall)*

> Ring up someone 'over there' about ordering groceries.
>
> Ring up a plumber. Fearful trouble.
>
> Ring up to borrow money, plus reasons.
>
> Ring up laundry about lost item.
>
> Interpol re big theft.
>
> Find partner (on feet now). Shopping. Customer and shopowner.
>
> Change round. Then hear one or two?

Explain to them that it is all right to walk amongst the class as Guide to the lesson. When, where and why to do it.

> At home resting. Suddenly a Teddy Bear rings up in a panic and asks what to do because his fur is all coming off. What would you advise?

Once you feel the group is becoming released from shyness, imagination is growing and language beginning to flow, you may judge it time to start story making. Form a circle and start something yourself.

SELF: 'I am going to start a story and then point to someone to carry on. Go round the circle to start with. Later on we can dot about and point to anyone you like, to carry on. Here we are then – a happy cat is walking up a ladder... *(with smile) You*, what happens next?'

They carry on. Nearly always, though, someone (even a clever person) gets stuck and they repeat. This is one of the rare occasions when I would interrupt.

SELF: 'Hey, just a moment. Cat has been going up the ladder and down again and finds another ladder and you keep saying "he climbs up and up." We know that now, but so *what?* Nothing has happened yet. Make something happen! I do understand, you are stuck, but you are just filling in. A story must move.'

So we get better and perhaps go into smaller groups, approximating a few friends, then Junior School gang size. If any stories are acted, take care to stress sharing the story, not acting *at*. If there is time and if Infant teachers are present, I would hope to explain at least about the importance of the Dawn of Seriousness and let them try out and 'be' a Family Casting, Group Casting and make a Conglomerate aeroplane or dragon. If time permits, this would be followed by more serious gang play stories, as in Junior School. These would be imaginative at first. Cricket ball, bulldog, exploding bicycle; blue spider, pink motor and an artful wasp and so on. After this try some playing out of violence.

Express hope and show how to lead out of the cathartic gang stage into more peaceful even fairy-like realms in the golden years seven to eleven plus. Work for more serious absorption and sincerity now. Real believability.

As to Senior Schools

Explain about environmental shock at change of school and make clear the need for being patient over the first year. Then point out the evolution through Imaginative, Social Drama and Theatre.

There might be time for some trials of Social Drama and explanation of Feature Programmes. Depending on who is on the course, one could plan time for more Secondary than Junior examples and perhaps try a feature Programme on such themes as:

> Strike (as before mentioned).
>
> Power.
>
> Fear.
>
> Employment.
>
> Drugs or no drugs
>
> To smoke, or not.
>
> No smoke without fire.
>
> What price environment?
>
> What is a Common Market? (Too vulgar, my dear.)
>
> Team Spirit (wot, ghosts or whisky?)
>
> Is 'good business' cheating?
>
> What is competition?
>
> Honesty always pays.
>
> No pride without a fall.

Any of these to be very short but to include improvised dialogue, possibly poetry, short play excerpts and dance (all easier on larger courses). Give an exercise, if necessary, to strengthen sincerity, like the one following about a baby dragon or dinosaur.

> SELF: 'There is a baby dragon with a bad cold near you. Now really think, summon up some compassion and really *give* from your heart. what are you going to do for him/her? Does *he* need disprin. Will you get scorched if *she* sneezes? Imagine you are presenting part of a play for children. You must be utterly engrossed and believable. Or, if you prefer, just create for yourself a lovely moment, to the deepest of your ability and 'freeze' this moment in kindness – so we all feel it all over the hall.'

Also for Seniors, try living newspaper i.e.acting stories out of a paper and discussing the situation. Try a short one.

Try TV adverts. Most attempts at first will be too long, though some of them will be, no doubt, amusing. A long time is taken in preparation and students on the course generally sort themselves into little gangs of about half a dozen, just like children. And, as said earlier, quite often one person becomes a sort of boss and tries to organise the whole thing, just like children. The 'democratic' groups without a strong leader, generally, do not get very far and have to be helped to finish, just like children. After first attempts they should all be helped to understand the importance of the adverts being shorter, just like children. Cost of *their* length in real life would be prohibitive.

In the part above, about the baby dragon, I take a known risk. If you judge that any particular group is not ready for it, suggest a more every day theme like a road accident to a friend. But a large part of the purpose of training in this way is to stimulate imagination near a child's thinking and if you do not take a risk over attaining the highest quality of work, you are wasting both time and opportunity. You may never meet this group again.

Jabber-Talk

There might be time to try this in a short course. Certainly it should be included in a long one. It will be clear by now that there are several ways and reasons for using it, but one that we have not yet mentioned is for adult theatre training. Into plain jabber, we can learn to put real feeling and expression. The use of long vowels gives us great opportunity for expressing sadness or love. A lot of consonants can sound like anger, excitement or cheerfulness. (Shakespeare knew this well.) Try splitting the group into pairs and suggesting one person asks a question and the other answers. After this can come 'telling a story' or 'reading a little from a book.' I have known people become so proficient in jabber-talk that they could almost know what the other person said.

In therapy it can be valuable as a form of spitting out. I have suggested it for patients who have so much anger that there are no words left in their own language to express their feelings. After a little practice they found they could rant in jabber-talk and not break up the house. For sadness too, sometimes people found they could tell 'sad stories of the death of Kings', so to speak, and dreadful secrets – I suggested out of the window, so they wouldn't have to look at me. They always looked relieved when they turned back.

Domino Marching (As Described in Junior School Section)

I would only use this on longer courses. It *might* help some children. It is a question of recognising a concept. There is some pleasure in 'being' the dotted shapes in *personal play*, marching about, that is, to be three and four; two or six; and nine makes a jolly crowd with one special chap or chapess in the middle of one of the fours.

At the time earlier mentioned, when I happened to be dealing in addition and subtraction with groups of four and five, a professor of mathematics entered quietly. After it, he sort of exploded, 'My God, this is marvellous, it is almost a break-through. Do you know what you are doing?'

I answered, 'Just making children a little happier, I hope, and more able to understand.' Professor: 'Oh no, it is *much* more than that, you are teaching them the fivishness of five!' It is always useful to know what you are doing.

The domino marchers might talk to each other in jabber-talk after 'addition' and they met – if they came from different 'worlds'. But it is not always wise to try and do too many different things at once, so perhaps experiencing utter Five is more important to begin with. But in repetition, other things might be added. It depends, as usual on the purpose of the lesson.

Simple Exercise. Pairs:

> 'You are in your office, just looking through a dictionary to remind you of words you have learned in a course about space-jabber language under Further Education. A Spaceman comes in and asks for a job and when you are not sure if he has the right qualifications, he demands to "see your Leader". It is awkward, as the Prime Minister happens to be out of the Country. But at least you are proud to be able to converse with the Spaceman. Off you go – now!'

I have made it easier for them by suggesting a complete outline, but more difficult by complexity of the situation. So I might add a remark before starting, or later if they seem to flounder.

SELF: 'I have given you a situation which is a bit complicated. If you are worried, do just part of it'.

(I wander round, listening to the wonderful vowels and consonants as they wing their vibrations through space.)

On a longer course, one might try jabbering the *sound* of various languages – French, Italian, German and so on. And finally, improvised Jabber-Opera.

By the way – if any members of the group seem a bit shy at first, I turn them all into statues and select one willing Wizard Person to dance around and touch one, then another and so on. At his/ her magic touch each statue comes to life and dances too. If necessary, to avoid anyone being embarrassed at the end of this, Wizard can turn them back again. I might ask them to sit down and talk about, or explain the work. (It is interesting that they will come to life for a member of the group.)

For relationships there could be a Prince, or Princess, with a magic touch. A lot of potential brides or suitors could be brought to life, but only one chosen.

The others go back to being statues, whilst the happy pair drift away in a slow walk, to music of *The Paradise Garden* (Delius). This is beginning to be preparation for polished improvisation or for Theatre for Children.

Example: Course for intending foster parents in Cottage Homes, Birmingham.
Men only

> Ideas given: Singing   Cricket   Cry   Wet
>
> My story: A selfish young man would play *cricket*. He didn't like it really, but wanted to be Captain and go in first. He went in and was bowled first ball. He was very angry and retired to the pavilion and started to eat ice cream. While the others were still playing, he ate up all the ice cream. Then it suddenly started to rain. It came down like the outpouring from giants' buckets and of course the players and pitch got very *wet* indeed. It was clear there would be no more play that day.
>
> The players ran to the pavilion. When they got there they remembered the ices. But when they looked for them they found that the selfish young man had eaten them all up. At this a great annoyance fastened itself upon them, and they remembered all of one accord that there was one thing the young man couldn't abide. He hated *singing*. So just to punish him for being so selfish they made a ring round him and began to sing louder and louder and louder.
>
> At this, the young man became very angry indeed and got hotter and hotter. His blood boiled, and jets of steam shot off from the ends of his hair, till the whole place was in a cloud. His feet got hotter and hotter too, till they became red hot like electric irons left on too long. Then two little streams of smoke began to appear and his feet burnt right through the floor boards.
>
> Suddenly there was a fearful *cry* that froze the singers to silence. The floor opened up, and the young man disappeared and was never seen again. So that, you might say, was the end of him. And you know you'd really be quite right.
>
> NOTE: *The play took six and a half minutes: and they sang D'ye Ken John Peel. It was splendidly intolerable.*

As the men and women were a little shy of working together at first, I began with them separately.
Women only

> SELF: 'You walk round the room thinking "Will I do this or will I do that?" When you have walked once round you are influenced by evil. These three here are the evil ones.'
>
> 'They get up and follow you but you give them a withering glance and they fall back, in these stylised steps *(I show them. I should not have done so unless stylised)*. Will everyone make percussion noises to accompany their feet please! You, the Woman, pass on, but of course you are not strong

enough to stand up to Evil all alone. But you pass into the sphere of influence of Truth and Justice *(two nuns took these parts sitting in chairs)*.

'As you pass them we see you bear yourself more strongly. You are fortified. Yet even now you are not safe, though you pass the evil ones this time without being tempted, so the spirits of goodness come to your aid. As you pass them, they take flaming torches of righteousness from brackets in the walls of the Palace where they live and follow after you in solemn procession, step by step to the end of your journey.'

'And will everyone else please accompany the solemn procession by making noises!'

(Several of the students pulled out pipes from their music work, and we ended on a fine sort of dirge.)

We also had an improvisation about gangsters (men and women) and acted out a story in a newspaper.

They were now prepared to work together.

Comment

There were to be many courses down the years for the Home Office and for intending parents in cottage homes. Not all of them would be able to take this sort of activity, but there is a desperate need for personal expression through Child Drama in children's homes. Ordinary and more fortunate children have their games at home, and parental love, but the children in cottage homes, and orphanages, have virtually nothing. However much we try, we can never quite make up for what they have lost. Nevertheless, I was trying to give these good folk an experience of being young again and of experiencing acting in the round as a preliminary to rediscovering what it is like to be young – a process I would strongly advocate for Colleges of Education – for we forget so quickly what it is like to be a child. Indeed, why should we not? It is very hard to break from unconscious childhood to conscious adulthood. The very process tends to let down a curtain behind us and we fumble to find the opening back, full knowing that even if successful we cannot stay, but must return again with wisdom to reality.

Nevertheless a number of staff in homes and schools of various kinds, for unhappy or deprived children, *have* succeeded in rediscovery and have since done splendid work in bringing some happiness and spontaneous outburst to those almost without hope.

In the section on 'Ladies only' in this report, the two nuns were turned into Truth and Justice because they were hesitant to take part. I know it will be forgiven if I say that nuns seem to be divided into two distinct kinds in their approach to this work, they either wish quite understandably not to take full part – and then one can nearly always include them as something 'abstract' – or they tuck up their skirts and become more active than anybody else and dash us practically off the floor with their gusto. Other people, though, and any children, even bombastic ones, can sometimes be helped by being turned into an inanimate object like a lamp post. Regarding the note on stylised work, this may involve repeated and somewhat 'unreal' movements in which the pattern in your own mind *has* to be shown in order to be re-enacted at all. Unfortunately, some teachers demonstrate every movement, as being the easiest way to obtain results but, of course, children only copy them, become lazy over imaginative work and less confident in their own creation.

I have spoken about the Ideas Game. In case it helps, here is a short list out of hundreds of other ideas which were used, old notes tell me, with various groups to help them to be young in heart and to develop their imagination. The different groups selected show one can do this work almost anywhere with anyone.

House   Mother   Umbrella   Sun
(Teachers Course, North Staffordshire)

Blue hat   Food   Walking stick
(Early E.D.A. General Teachers' Course)

Imagination   No tea   Dancing in the theatre   Cattle
(Adult Theatre Group)

Blue Glasses   Milk Churns   Record Player
(Special Schools Teachers' Course)

Pistol   Hate   Table
(Group in Prison)

Cat   Wall   Orange Peel   Garden
(Junior School Teachers)

Piano playing   Open window   Brown Bag
(Central Council of Physical Recreation)

Yellow bag   Big Feet   Shut up   Cold Feet
(Townswomen's Guild, Worcestershire)

Putting Mike together again   Bomb
(Day Continuation College)

Codfish   shop   Chicken in striped Pyjamas
(N.U.T. Refresher Course, Somerset)

Interpol   Fishing Rod   Electric roller Skates
(unusual happenings at a London sclerosis Club)

Two Dolphins   Caliban   Whale
(Tempest in a Remand Home)

Knife   Full Moon   Good bit of Blood
(Professional Theatre Group, London)

So, almost any ideas from a group of any kind, can be used to make up a story. JPs in training and High-ups in Industry could have been added to the list, also Service Units and police.Included here, as Adult Training, is an outline of one of the Educational Drama Association (EDA) Summer Schools, showing the sort of thing we used to do.

Educational Drama Association: Thirty-First Annual Summer School
Drama, Communication and Relationships

Director of Course: Peter Slade, F.C.P., F.I.A.L., F.R.S.A., President of the Educational Drama Association; formerly Drama Adviser to the City of Birmingham Education Committee; B.B.C. producer and announcer; member of Children's Hour Staff; author of 'Child Drama' which Dame Sybil Thorndike describes as 'one of the really important books of our time', 'Experience of Spontaneity' and 'Natural Dance'.

Each day will begin with a talk by Peter Slade, outlining the whole development of Child Drama.

Main Courses: Child Drama in the Primary and Middle School

This course is designed as a basis for the understanding and development of Child Drama for those particularly interested in the age range of five to fourteen years.

There will be practical work at adult level with reference back to various age groups of children.

The syllabus will include:

'How to begin', with careful consideration of handling and discipline. Use of sounds and music in the development of Speech and Dance, and as an aid to Drama Development of Language-flow and communication. How to make stories for playing.

Group play-making and polished improvisations based on the great stories of literature.

Contribution of Drama to other subjects and how it can help the individual towards maturity.

Tutor: Sylvia E. Demmery, L.R.A.M., L.G.S.M. Inspector for Drama to the City of Birmingham Education Committee; Director for the Child Drama Certificate Course; formerly Oxfordshire County Drama Adviser; Senior Lecturer in Drama, Loughborough College of Education.

Assistant Tutor: Patricia Young, teacher in charge of Drama, St. John's C.E. Junior/ Infant School, Birmingham; formerly Head of the Infant Department. Holder of the Peter Slade Dance Award.

Secondary Course

This is intended for those who have a basic knowledge of Child Drama. This course will provide practical experience in

Improvisation Work

Social Drama Preparation for Feature Programme and Production.

Tutors: Sue Pomroy; Teacher in Charge of Drama, Selly Park Girls School. Member of the West Midlands Examination Board Drama Panel. Holder of the Child Drama Certificate.

Malcolm Pomroy: Teacher in Charge of Drama, Brandwood School. External Assessor C.S.E. English. Both Tutors are members of the E.D.A. Children's Theatre Group. *With assistance from Peter Slade.*

Drama with Handicapped Children

The course is intended for those who, having had some experience of Child Drama, wish to explore its relevance to the education of handicapped children in special schools, special classes and 'ordinary' schools. Special attention will be given to the problems presented by slow learning and emotionally disturbed children.

A practical approach will be followed throughout the course but there will be opportunity to discuss the needs of these children and the interests and problems of members of the course.

Tutor: Gordon Pidgeon, M.Ed., D.C.P. Head of Language Development Centre, Sandwell; formerly Advisory Teacher, Sandwell Schools Psychological Service. Holder of the Peter Slade Dance Award.

Evening Course: Peter Slade Method of Dance

The dance will be based on individual style of the personality. The course begins with the early processes before going to the more advanced stages so as to give a general view of the method. Much of the work will be concerned with the development of the individual rather than with group work, and will be at adult level for personal experience, but will refer to the needs of children in Junior and Secondary Schools.

Tutor: Sylvia E. Demmery, L.R.A.M., L.G.S.M. Tutor in dance and holder of the Peter Slade Dance Award.

I am sorry, the above may all look a bit like 'jobs for the boys' – and girls, but all the training was entirely voluntary. Nobody on the staff ever received a penny for their work. We all believed deeply in what we were doing and wanted to share the message with people who came from everywhere to hear and find it. And I would only use tutors who really knew their stuff, were properly qualified and who had proved to be outstanding, so that the best explanation could be given to those who kindly came. It will be noticed how many of the tutors had special qualification in what might be seen as the realms of both *personal* and *projected* activity. As seen, by this time, Sylvia Demmery had taken over direction of the Child Drama Certificate Course after my retirement, but I still undertook direction of the EDA Summer Course.

Lastly, here are details of the Child Drama Certificate Course.

Certificate in Child Drama

The Education Committee has been conscious for some time of the need to fill a gap in the training of teachers of Child Drama. The Child Drama Certificate Course is intended to meet this need.

Mr. Peter Slade, the City of Birmingham Education Authority's Drama Adviser, who is recognised as a pioneer in this field, is the course director. The venue will for the time being be the Drama Centre, which is part of the building at Reaside School, Rea Street South, Deritend, Birmingham, 5. It is hoped that an advisory service on Child Drama will be set up in association with the scheme.

Eligibility

The course is primarily intended for teachers in Birmingham who have completed their probationary year of service. Consideration will also be given to applicants who are in other professions, for example Social Work, or who are not employed by the City of Birmingham Education Committee, or who are from overseas.

Period of Training

The course work will be spread over a full year. Each of the three terms will be of twelve weeks' duration, students attending on one half-day every week. This timetable will allow participants to continue with their work in schools and to make use of their course experience in the classroom.

Staffing

Mr. Slade, as director of the course, will be responsible for tuition and partly for follow-up work. He will be assisted by an experienced head teacher seconded for the work, by a peripatetic teacher of Child Drama and, on occasions, by outside lecturers and an outside assessor.

The Award of a Certificate

The Award of a Certificate will depend on the satisfactory completion of the course and on the result of a final examination, both practical and written work being involved. The Awarding Body will be the City of Birmingham Education Committee.

Outline of the Course

The first term of each year will be devoted to an introductory course to be followed by all students, but for the the remaining two terms they will specialise in either primary or secondary drama.

First Term: General Course

The course will begin with an introduction to the whole subject of Child Drama and discussions on the history of Creative Drama in England and on the nature of Child Drama.

Practical work will be at adult level, but with frequent reference to the needs of children in similar situations of their own making, and will include improvisation, an approach to social drama and basic elements of theatre, particularly children's theatre. Dance and movement will be based on the personal style of the individual.

The general course will include practical advice on starting Child Drama at any age and on the manner of obtaining discipline and personal development with different types of child. Ways of helping immigrant children through Child Drama will be discussed and suggestions made on its relationship to other subjects, for example, mathematics, English reading, creative writing, religious instruction and foreign languages.

Apart from some detailed study, the main task of the general course is to stimulate the imagination, so as to enable students both to see more clearly the needs of the child and to develop their own talents.

Second and Third Terms: Specialisation in Primary Drama

1. How to take general Child Drama with infants.

Development of personal expression in speech and movement; relationship of oneself with the community.

Ear training; learning about child's reaction to sound; how to use it.

Emotional control.

Selection of Leaders.

2. As above but at a deeper level, as appropriate for juniors. Also training in groups suitable for children seven to nine years. Training for elementary therapeutic work, cathartic play and avoidance of aggression.

For children nine to eleven years, training for polished improvisations based on great stories of the world as an approach to theatre.

The beginning of facial make-up and its association with child art. How to make and use simple costume, what music to select and how to use it in simple productions.

How Child Drama can aid children who are backward by bringing a sense of happiness and success.

Relationship between Child Drama and reading.

Aiding the backward reader.

Child Drama and creative poetry and writing in general.

Child Drama and creative music.

Use of rostrum blocks.

Child Drama as an aid to learning French and numbers; as an aid to social studies, history and religious knowledge.

How to obtain and keep discipline.

How to know more about children, so as to be able to inspire them to create, without fear of losing control.

How to start and to develop dance based on the individual personality; how to develop work from broadcast music and movement programmes. General Personal developments through drama and practice in communication.

Second and Third Terms: Specialisation in Secondary Drama

1. Thorough investigation of the three main divisions of

(a) Imaginative Drama

(b) Social Drama

(c) Theatre

2. How to deal with first year. How to link improvised speech with group play making (part script) achieving final link with script.

3. Imaginative Drama. Considerable practice in improvised situations of an imaginative kind at adult level for helping the student to remember how a younger mind works and with frequent reference to children's needs.

4. Social Drama. Training in manners, relationships, preparing for real situations in real life before they actually arise; how to help children in relationships with parents and teachers; how to face interviews, answer telephones, take messages, speak in public, serve politely in shops. Dealing with self-consciousness in adolescents, which may block their energy and enthusiasm both for the arts and other lessons.

5. Theatre. Thorough consideration of different styles of acting and different forms of presentation. Study of Theatre for Children a particularly important item.

Consideration of living newspaper; how to create feature programmes; how to select suitable plays.

6. How to use Drama as an aid to backward groups, particularly in reading but in general by promoting happiness and hope, which later normally leads to a will to try again.

7. How to use Drama as an aid to language learning, social studies, mathematics, written and oral English, and general practice in communications; also boy and girl relationships in mixed schools.

8. Special preparation for improvisation section of examinations.

9. Development of Dance Drama.

The whole course will be concerned with the development of personality and the actual experience of life so that students should know how to help every young person to make the best of himself/herself and be able to communicate and express their ideas. The course is so designed as to enable attention to be given to the particular needs of individual students.

In this chapter I have deliberately used some of the exercises suggested for children and tried to outline not only a few discoveries about ourselves, but, after preparing ourselves, to learn some detail of how to take work with those who are younger.

Through drama our aims have included helping children to see and listen with greater awareness, to develop their vocabulary, to become absorbed. Absorption needs to be tempered with the needs of other people, so sensitivity needs to be there too. Sensitivity is to do with values and believability. When you are enacting something and are serious about it, it becomes absorbed and sincere. The tone of voice is important too. Through movement and dance we become more graceful and agile, through guided personal experiences we become more thoughtful because of a developing knowledge and understanding.

Many more people 'take' drama now. Let us hope it does not get squeezed out. Not all appear to know the pattern of development or to consider the aims and progression of their drama session. We all know drama can take place as part of any lesson; it can help the teacher see children as individuals with a point of view as 'legal' as one's own; the teacher can help the growing person to create the right balance between liberty and licence, and with thought and knowledge offer guidance which will enrich the personality physically, emotionally and spiritually. Some teachers of Senior children feel a number of these sort of exercises are all 'a bit young'. They do not realise that many of their students are still in psychological need of such things – and they themselves?

Early in the book I rejoiced that student teachers might be going into schools more, under new regulations, rather than write so many pieces on theory and comparisons (though they must know their subject(s)). They would really see conditions and meet children and have more time to consider actualities. They might even bring new ideas and equipment to the school. The danger will be to swamp schools with visitors and make it more difficult for children to pay attention and teachers to teach. Some clever way will have to be found perhaps for assimilating small groups of visitors at a time and for these to gain by observation, rather than teachers ceasing to teach children in order to teach *them*.

A few answers to statements or questions that always arise:

Oh, yes, do try to understand the differences between personal and projected play. It will enrich your life.

Don't pretend to be children. In these exercises, just be yourselves. You may be (or have been) surprised at what happens.

Yes, always think hard about not seeming critical or rude when dealing with your class or group. Remark on what is *good* about what has happened, or is seen and shared, unthoughtful criticism (even if jolly) can be destructive.

Well, suggestions for the happiness of children have taken up so much of my time that people began to believe I had no interest in theatre. Creating it has been my chief love and it is little known how much it has been part of my life. But there is a clear progress from Child Drama, as I have shown, towards theatre. Little actors, having experienced their own art form of drama, become much better actors in *our* form of theatre later on.

To understand children better and not jump too swiftly to judgement of behaviour, remember the great IF. If you were *really* that child in that situation, what would you think, what would *you* do and what would you say?

We all have to guide or teach in our own way. If you can understand and agree with me to any extent, find a way that suits you and *your* group, but keep to the main principles.

My own preference would be for teachers to take (and learn how to take) creative arts education in schools and a good company to come in and present straight theatre (appropriate for age), as an emotional and aesthetic experience to crown their other experience. The two should be separate to some extent, but allies and components of the whole.

It is surprising how people change, after experience of training in Child Drama and for Theatre for children (i.e. as adult players). The reality-feeling of sincerity in imaginative situations brings about newer forms of humour and release of inner self. You see, there is a continual (often unrecognised) strain in having to be adult all the time in a hard competitive world. Once learn how to admit and discover the child within and you can take joy in simple things and sights, which offer you moments of relief from the hard facts of life. Of course it helps you understand children better too!

How and why did I get into all this? I am often asked; and I suppose the short answer is that I was so unhappy at my Senior school that I was determined that no child that ever came near me should ever be as unhappy as I had been. It made me less swift to judgement and more objectively concerned with the needs of my neighbour. After all, isn't that what many parts of education and all therapy are about?

In therapy, always try to find ways of screwing up a patient's courage to face reality, or what they fear, step by gentle step. And don't forget to include some process or avenue of hope for a better future.

In every one, there is a candle waiting to be lit. In education, therapy or life, it is up to us to find it and strike the match.

For all those of you for whom this chapter is intended, not only teachers, I have to repeat, it will be found easier to work and guide with sympathy and at genuine depth, if we first re-find without fear, or too much hesitation, the child within.

Whatever childhood you yourself had, it is never too late to have a *happy* childhood. If in doubt, start now.

Few Last Words

This book is an attempt to outline some parts of human nature and the importance of play, based on over 60 years of knowledge, experience and loving observation. That is in addition to my own discoveries during youth and childhood.

Some people are surprised that I have given so much time to it. Against some challenge, I am not sentimental about children. They do sometimes annoy us. They can be irritating, worrying, perplexing and sometimes they enrage us. Occasionally, these days, they even frighten us. Yet I think they often have a tough time, maybe because it has been difficult for many people to burst through the clouds into adulthood, and we find it hard to go back. So we forget about what children are like. But children provide us also with fascinating behaviour, penetrating remarks and beauty. If we are not too proud we can learn from them; so for all this I would champion their cause. Their voice is not always heard.

There is, at the time of writing, a strong swing away from what is called child-centred education, with some reason. I am pleading for *child-concerned* education, which is different. Because of a deep interest in behaviour, this takes into consideration violence against teachers, parents, old people and other children as well.

I never outline any item of observation, until it has been seen many times. I saw one movement (as mentioned in a previous book) up and down the country, employed by thirty-four thousand children before I wrote a word about it.

In all our guiding, as parents, teachers, guardians and therapists, we have to employ forgiveness. It all becomes easier if we develop a non-sentimental objective love of humankind.

The world is in a strange state. Perhaps we need a new attitude in our society. I have tried to indicate some ways of inducing that from the beginning of a child's life. I am aware that, under present circumstances in education, teachers will find it difficult to carry out some of what has been suggested, even if they agree, but I have written of what I think we *ought* to do – and why.

It will be a tragedy if all inner education is forsaken on account of outer apparent efficiency. Yet, if so, the pendulum will swing back when the loss becomes clear. Then people might want to know about the kind of things of which I write, all over again, for they may have forgotten what to do.

After long years of careful study, it is easy to begin to think one has a little knowledge, or is at moments even wise. But delving into the truths of human nature is always a mysterious task. God has created us as such complex beings. For this reason it is wise to be wise about being wise. We may at times think we know a little. Then the humbling truth doth dawn – the more you know, the less you *know* you know.

Peter Slade

References

Jennings, S. (1993) *Play Therapy with Children*. Oxford: Blackwell.

Schattner, G. and Courtney, R. (eds) (1981) *Drama in Therapy*. New York: Drama Book Specialists.

Slade, P. (1954) *Child Drama*. London: University of London Press.

Slade, P. (1958) *Introduction to Child Drama*. London: University of London Press.

Slade, P. (1959) *Dramatherapy as an Aid to Becoming a Person*. London: Guild of Pastoral Psychology.

Slade, P. (1968) *Experience of Spontaneity*. London: Longman.

Slade, P. (1977) *Natural Dance*. London: Hodder and Stoughton.

Slade, P. (1993) 'Afterword.' In S. Jennings *Play Therapy with Children*. Oxford: Blackwell.

Way, B. (1967) *Development Through Drama*. London: Longman.

Index